Library of Congress Cataloging-in-Publication Data

CIP data for this book can be found on the Library of Congress website:
http://www.loc.gov/index.html

Paperback: 978-1-68123-509-7
Hardcover: 978-1-68123-510-3
E-Book: 978-1-68123-511-0

Printed in the United States of America

Beyond the Online Course

Leadership Perspectives on e-Learning

A Volume in
Perspectives in Instructional Technology and Distance Learning

Series Editors:
Charles Schlosser and Michael Simonson,
Nova Southeastern University

Beyond the Online Cou

Leadership Perspectives on e-Learnin

Edited by

Anthony A. Piña
Sullivan University System

and

Jason B. Huett
University of West Georgia

Information Age Publishing, Inc.
Charlotte, North Carolina • www.infoagepub.com

CONTENTS

PART II:
LEADING COURSE AND PROGRAM DESIGN

PART III:
LEADING THE DEVELOPMENT
AND SUPPORT OF ONLINE STUDENTS

PART IV:
LEADING THE DEVELOPMENT
AND SUPPORT OF ONLINE FACULTY AND STAFF

PART V:
LEGAL AND ACCREDITATION ISSUES

FOREWORD

Melanie N. Clay

Even as online learning has become one of the most rapidly growing and competitive industries, I have noticed that there is a certain comradery and sharing of would-be trade secrets among those who lead online learning programs. Rather than a guarding of strategies and best practices, there is nearly an unprecedented zeal to help one another. I personally witness these phenomena weekly (if not daily) through phone calls, meetings, journal articles—and now this book. I believe that this sharing of information is an outcome of distance learning administration being a field unto itself, quite distinct from other leadership roles in higher education or in business.

Distance learning administration shares many of the same activities as other types of education administration, including student support, faculty support, curriculum development, training, budgeting and marketing (though we tend to wear more of these hats simultaneously than do most of our peers). Principles of change management and transformational leadership are also applicable as distance learning administrators must carefully navigate a clear path through rough and unpredictable waters.

Yet, there is a bit of an X-factor that distinguishes this field, and makes it both easier and more challenging than others. This X-factor, in my view, is a combination of the relative ease of attracting the primary consumer (students) combined with a vast array of competing pressures that move and change at a pace many times faster than do other disruptions. Many of us have enjoyed great success in our online programs—if only

Beyond the Online Course: Leadership Perspectives on e-Learning
pp. ix–xi

measured by sheer enrollments of students. We have also made remarkable strides in quality, and years of efforts have paid off resulting in a wealth of online courses that meet or exceed the learning experience in the traditional environment. If we measure success in terms of accessibility, we have collectively approached a gold standard here as well. I can count myself as among those who would not have a PhD had it not been available online. At the time I started my PhD from the University of Nebraska, I had a demanding job (in distance learning administration), a teenage daughter, and two children under the age of 3. Even if I had pursued the degree in my home state of Georgia, it would have required a 2-hour commute, and frankly, it would have never happened.

So, there is a certain meaningfulness in distance learning administration—a satisfaction that comes from having the opportunity to personally help so many students. I have yet to experience a day in which a life-or-death situation occurred, but still come home believing that we may have helped to indirectly save lives by providing and supporting opportunities for a positive life path for thousands of students.

But on to those competing pressures and the paradox: distance learning administration is a political art, and one in which tomorrow's agenda is going to be quite different from today's. The more successful we are in serving online students, the more of a threat that we are perceived by some. The more revenue we generate for our institutions, the larger the question looms of our effect on our long and rightfully proud traditions of higher education in America.

I have been a distance learning administrator since 1996, I and was only in my first week at work when a top-level administrator told me to go ahead and look for another job because "distance learning is going to be a fad." Since then, the dialogue has become more complex, but the message is sometimes still eerily similar—"maybe we want distance learning to just go away." Clearly, it is not leaving anytime soon, but the biggest imperative is that we, as distance education leaders, not be reactive, complacent, or prideful in these conversations.

Rather, I see our role not so much as an advocate for online learning, per se, but rather as calm advocates for balance. This ideal balance is not hesitant about moving forward, but does so deliberately, and in a way that protects the core values of higher education. The best administrator will frequently find herself a target, right smack in the middle of what may feel like a battlefield. So, it is not a career for the timid, or those who take great discomfort in being misunderstood.

Yet, we are traveling every day into new territories. In the late 1990s, it was online. More recently, MOOCs have come and faded, but left questions so deep that we will never go back to the way things were before. In the mid-2000s, we saw the financial crises, decreased state funding, and rising tuitions. Now, there are concerns about the very survival of many of the institutions that we hold so dear. While wisdom and visions and strategies abound from other administrators and well-meaning politicians, it is often the fellow distance learning administrator who can provide the best support and understanding of issues where such a lacuna of valid research exists. It is for this reason that we share without hesitation.

I am excited about the work in this book, and I am proud to know both editors. Dr. Tony Piña is a fellow dean and a respected leader in the field of distance education who once keynoted our distance learning administration conference. He is a kind soul, a wicked guitar player, and a champion of learners of all ages and circumstances. I am a close colleague of Dr. Jason Huett. When Dr. Huett first arrived at the University of West Georgia 8 years ago, his department chair told me that he would become a top leader in the field of distance learning. Today, he is relentless in his pursuit of better and more affordable models and is extraordinarily articulate and savvy in his approach. He is a wonderful balance to my pragmatism and dog-headedness, and the world of distance learning administration is surely a much better place because of him.

Enjoy your journey beyond the online course and toward new perspectives in distance leadership.

Melanie N. Clay, PhD
Dean of eCore, University System of Georgia
Director of Extended Learning, University of West Georgia
Founder and Editor-in-Chief,
Online Journal of Distance Learning Administration

PREFACE

Beyond the Online Course

Jason B. Huett and Anthony A. Piña

In 2009, *The Perfect Online Course: Best Practices for Designing and Teaching*, edited by Anymir Orellana, Terry L. Hudgins, and Michael Simonson, was published by Information Age Publishing (Orellana, Hudgins, & Simonson, 2009). This book brought together 30 articles on instructional design, teaching methods and engagement strategies that had been published in the *Quarterly Review of Distance Education* (QRDE), a leading peer-reviewed scholarly journal and *Distance Learning*, a leading practitioner journal. *The Perfect Online Course* has become a comprehensive reference for those interested in scholarly and practical ideas for online design, teaching, and learning.

Michael Simonson and Charles Schlosser are the editors for both the QRDE and the Perspectives of Instructional Technology and Distance Education Series for Information Age Publishing. *The Perfect Online Course* was part of this series, as was *Real Life Distance Education: Case Studies in Practice*, a book recently edited by Tony (Piña & Mizell, 2014). We both happen to be on the editorial board of the QRDE and so we expressed our desire to Mike and Charlie to do a project similar to *The Perfect Online Course*, but with a focus on program, administrative and institutional issues. We gave our idea the name *Beyond the Online Course*.

For the past decade, online educational enrollments have constituted the fastest growing area of higher education, with an estimated one in

Beyond the Online Course: Leadership Perspectives on e-Learning
pp. xiii–xviii
Copyright © 2016 by Information Age Publishing

three students taking online courses. Researchers looking into market trends in online education have noted that the number of institutions offering online courses and programs has also increased markedly in the past 5 years (Allen & Seaman, 2014; Clinefelter & Aslanian, 2014). However, the available literature has not kept up with the growth in the number of distance education programs and is especially lacking in direction for those called to lead e-learning programs. Very few books are available on administration and leadership perspectives of distance education and articles dealing with the topic are scarce and scattered.

The dearth of resources available to distance learning leaders is understandable, given the fact that the vast majority of those who write academic books are faculty, whose concerns lie primarily with online course design, online teaching methods, interactions with students, learning communities, and other course-based issues and topics. Faculty tend to be less directly involved with institutional and administrative issues, so they tend not to write much about them. For those actively leading distance learning programs, there often is not time to "put pen to paper" to write about and share what they are learning on the job. When you couple all of this with an educational marketplace that is rapidly evolving, a student demographic that is quickly shifting, and a political and regulatory landscape that is as confusing as it is contradictory, a clear need emerges for books like this one dealing with e-learning leadership.

Part one of *Beyond the Online Course: Leadership Perspectives on e-Learning* is about leading innovation and change. Coeditor Anthony Piña starts us off with a discussion that centers around 30 factors that should be considered when institutionalizing distance programs. Jason Neben drives this point home from a different angle with an examination of faculty perception of online education and the institutional, technological, financial, and pedagogical barriers to successful implementation of distance learning. Baiyun Chen and Dana Gutman deepen the discussion with an indepth look at the impact of distance learning program costs as well as faculty resistance to and concerns about online teaching and learning. Leah Wickersham and Julie A. McElhany bring the discussion full circle with a detailed examination of administrators' concerns related to online teaching and learning and offer recommendations for bridging the gap between faculty expectations and administrative vision.

Leading course and program design is the focus of the second part of our book. Marcia Ashbaugh begins this section by identifying the critical instructional design competencies needed to produce effective designs for modern learning. She asks a cadre of expert instructional design professionals: What is needed to improve quality in online courses? What characteristics of instructional design are lacking to meet global socioeducational demands? What competencies may be critical for designing effective pedagogies for a changing student body with diverse needs? Atsusi "2c" Hirumi is up next with a very interesting and updated framework for designing and sequencing e-learning interactions. Jomon Aliyas Paul and Justin Daniel Cochran continue to stress the importance of interaction by presenting a conceptual framework highlighting how key interactions are foundational in the development of successful online educational programs. Arthur J. Borgemenke takes the instructional design theme in a different direction with a look at why institutions may want to advocate for the adoption of universal course shell templates. For those interested in cohort approaches to online learning, Mary E. Engstrom, Susan A. Santo, and Rosanne M. Yost provide practical recommendations for making the most of online cohorts. Finally, Ontiretse S. Tau closes out the second part with a fascinating look at the lessons learned when the University of Botswana transformed itself from a conventional university to a dual mode institution with substantial distance education offerings.

The third part of our book shifts focus to, arguably, the most important player in this discussion: the online student. Coeditor Jason Huett and his colleagues explore the ARCS model for online environments and how small communication adjustments in online courses can have significant impact on student performance and motivation. C. Eugene Walker and Erika Kelly tackle questions about student satisfaction with online instruction, while Aries Cobb writes about the power and potential of assistive technologies when working with special needs learners. Kaye B. Dotson and Hui Bian discuss online facilitated internship programs and the evolving needs and expectations for site supervisors.

Shahinshah Babar Khan and Saeed-ul-Hasan Chishti begin the fourth part of our book, "Leading the Development and Support of Online Faculty and Staff," with a study that examines the impact of training and professional development on faculty who teach in online mediums. Jane Waweru reminds readers that effective online teaching and learning is not just about the classroom when she explores the role that human resources professionals play in successful e-learning initiatives. Barbara Stewart and her colleagues examine the challenges faced by off-site faculty teaching for online programs, while Newell Chiesl provides some pragmatic methods for reducing cheating in online courses. Coeditor Anthony Piña and Larry Bohn explore how to assess online instructor actions and engagement apart from the quality of the online course design. This section comes to a close when Steven Schmidt and his colleagues take a look back at how university faculty members developed their online teaching skills and offer suggestions for cultivating the next generation of online instructors.

The fifth and final section of our book delves into the legal and accreditation issues surrounding distance learning. Soonhwa Seok starts us off with an overview of distance education standards, guidelines and benchmarks as well accreditation considerations. Douglas A. Kranch and Loggie et al. tackle the sticky issue intellectual property and online courses while Kevin L. Crow helps us make sense of accessibility requirements with an overview of five pieces of U.S. legislation and the practical implications of these laws as they relate to accessible online education.

We hope that you enjoy the book. We believe the time has come for a more well-researched and systemic approach to preparing the next generation of e-learning leaders. We have both had the privilege (and the challenge) of working in distance education leadership positions for years. Over the past decade, the online teaching and learning landscape has evolved so rapidly that we can attest to the fact that we have often felt like we were building the plane while flying it. We could have used a book like this, and we suspect many people in e-learning leadership positions can relate. We hope that this book will provide guidance to those already in leadership positions, those recently recruited into service, and those new to the field.

Sincerely,
Jason Huett and Tony Piña

ACKNOWLEDGMENTS

We express gratitude to Mr. George Johnson, publisher and president of Information Age Publishing and to Michael Simonson and Charles Schlosser, series editors for Perspectives on Instructional Technology and Distance Education, for their support and encouragement for this project. We also wish to give thanks to each of the authors who were willing to contribute articles that ventured beyond the online course and made this book possible.

REFERENCES

Allen, I. E., & Seaman, J. (2014). *Grade change: Tracking online education in the United States.* Babson Park, MA: Babson Survey Research Group.

Clinefelter, D. L., & Aslanian, C. B. (2014). *Online college students 2014: Comprehensive data on demands and preferences.* Louisville, KY: Learning House.

Orellana, A., Hudgens, T. L., & Simonson, M. (Eds.). (2009). *The perfect online course: Best practices for designing and teaching*. Charlotte, NC: Information Age.

Piña, A. A., & Mizell, A. P. (Eds.). (2014). *Real-life distance education: Case studies in practice*. Charlotte, NC: Information Age.

PART I

LEADING INNOVATION AND CHANGE

CHAPTER 1

INSTITUTIONALIZATION OF DISTANCE EDUCATION IN HIGHER EDUCATION

Anthony A. Piña
Sullivan University System

The purpose of this study was to determine actions that colleges and universities can take to institutionalize their distance education programs. Thirty factors found to influence the institutionalization of innovations were identified from the literature. These were rated by distance education faculty and leaders as to their importance for influencing the institutionalization of distance education. Data were analyzed according to institutional role, institutional academic level, and institutional locale. All 30 factors were validated as indicators of institutionalization of distance education. Distance education faculty and leaders demonstrated a high level of agreement as to the importance of the various institutionalization factors.

Less than 2 decades ago, the authors of an influential text had this to say about the state of distance education in the United States: "Distance education, although a popular and effective concept in other countries, is still something of an unknown quantity in the United States and, with the possible exception of correspondence courses and telecourses, has until now had little impact here" (Verduin & Clark, 1991, p. 9). This sentiment was also echoed in the educational technology journals of the time. Clark

Beyond the Online Course: Leadership Perspectives on e-Learning
pp. 3–20
Copyright © 2016 by Information Age Publishing

3

(1989), for example, acknowledged that colleges and universities in the United States were "not leading practitioners of distance education at the adult learning level" (p. 7).

As the first decade of the new millennium draws to a close, it appears obvious that this situation has changed considerably. The advent of the public Internet has facilitated a meteoric rise of online instruction (Simonson, Smaldino, Albright, & Zvacek, 2006). According to research conducted by the Sloan Consortium, 83% of colleges and universities now offer courses at a distance (Allen & Seaman, 2007). However, far fewer of these have established institutionwide distance education programs that include centralized coordination and complete degree or certificate programs available at a distance (Bear & Nixon, 2006; Boyd-Barrett, 2000).

FROM ONLINE COURSES TO ONLINE PROGRAMS

Individuals and groups critical of online and distance learning have often characterized it as a scheme foisted upon faculty by money conscious administrators (e.g. Carnevale, 2000; Noble, 2003). Although some higher education institutions engage in systematic planning by administration prior to offering online courses (Gersten & Evans, 2004), it is common for distance learning programs to evolve from an initial group of online courses developed independently by faculty—"the result of random acts of innovation initiated by risk-taking individual academics" (Taylor, 2001, p. 7).

Once a college or university begins to increase its online course offerings, it can either remain in the mode of decentralized course delivery or it may take the journey from online courses to the establishment of an institution-wide distance education program (Hunt & Piña, 2004). This "tipping point" can be brought about by a number of factors, including declining student enrollment (Oakley, 2004), pressure from students or faculty, or competition from competing institutions (Olson, 2002; Picciano, 2001). Unfortunately, many higher education institutions take a reactive, rather than a proactive stance toward distance education. In a study commissioned by the nation's largest teachers' union and a large online learning management system provider, Phipps and Merisotis (2000) found that many institutions were struggling to come to grips with the demand for distance education:

> Because of increasing student interest in Internet-based distance education at some of the institutions in the case study, administrators revealed that policies are being developed to catch up with practice. One administrator said simply that the institution is moving ahead without all of the answers.

While some institutions were farther ahead in their planning than others, some institutions that are struggling to keep up with the demand for Internet-based courses have made a conscious decision to serve students immediately and plan later. (p. 7)

ADOPTION VERSUS INSTITUTIONALIZATION

The situation described above tends to occur when the institutional focus is upon the adoption or implementation of an innovation, rather than its institutionalization (Curry, 1992). When an organization institutionalizes a program or procedure, it becomes an integral and permanent part of the organization (Fullan & Stiegelbauer, 1991). Kanter (1983) describes an innovation as being institutionalized when it becomes "part of legitimate and ongoing practice, infused with value and supported by other aspects of the system" (p. 299). Surrey and Ely (2002), point out that once an innovation becomes institutionalized, it is no longer considered to be an innovation—it is now looked upon as a normal and vital part of the organization.

Models of organizational change, though systemic in nature, tend to identify adoption as the final step in the change process (e.g., Kotter, 1996; Rogers, 2003). The problem, as Surry and Brennan (1998) observe, is that the research based on these models tends to demonstrate "a deterministic bias—it assumes that once an innovation has been adopted, it will continue to be used" (p. 2).

INSTITUTIONALIZATION OF A DISTANCE EDUCATION PROGRAM

It is common in the literature to find descriptions of distance education as a "normal," "integral," or even "essential" part of higher education (e.g., Gunawardena & McIsaac, 2004; Jones, 2002). Such language gives the impression that the institutionalization of distance education programs at colleges and universities is commonplace. However, findings from several researchers (e.g., Levy, 2003; Taylor, 2001) report that planning, development, and implementation of distance education is often haphazard and nonsystematic. According to Boyd-Barrett (2000), "Decisions about distance education are made too often without adequately considering the broader institutional context" (p. 1). Interviews conducted with online faculty as part of this study revealed that several felt that pessimistic about the current and future state of distance education at their institutions. The following is representative: "The campus as a whole has developed a dozen courses for on-line delivery as part of some grant money that was made available a couple of years ago. Now that this money has dried up, the on-line courses are starting to dry up as well. There is no one to push it and no funding to keep it going."

Perhaps the principal challenge in determining the institutionalization of distance education and other innovations is that "the successful transition from implementation to institutionalization is rarely mentioned in the literature" (Ellsworth, 2000 p. 43). Summarizing their review of theory and research on institutional structures, Tolbert and Zucker (1994) came to this conclusion:

> Probably the most important implication, from our perspective, is the need to develop more direct measures and better documentation of claims of the institutionalization of structures, since outcomes associated with a given structure are likely to depend on the stage or level of institutionalization.... For example, analyses examining the level of institutionalization of contemporary structures could use survey research, in which respondents were asked directly about the degree to which they perceived a given structure to be necessary for efficient organizational functioning. (p. 26)

Colbeck (2002) recommended that research in this area should include multiple indicators of institutionalization:

> By itself, a single indicator may signify true change—or simply a signal that a school is putting on a show of doing the fashionably "right" thing, while actually continuing business as usual.... Since institutionalization requires changes in rules, values, norms, beliefs, and behaviors, other schools or coalitions who wish to assess institutionalization of curricular reforms are encouraged to use multiple indicators in order to provide evidence of lasting change. (p. 6)

PURPOSE OF THE STUDY

- To determine actions that colleges and universities can take to institutionalize or strengthen their distance education programs.
- To identify factors influencing the institutionalization of distance education programs.
- To validate these factors by data collected from those who oversee distance education programs and from those who teach in them.
- To determine which factors are of greatest importance.
- To determine whether institutional role (leader or faculty), institutional level (undergraduate or graduate), or institutional locale (rural, suburban or urban) influences the importance of institutionalization factors.

METHOD

Participants

The sample consisted of 170 respondents representing two primary groups: *Distance Learning Faculty* teach courses via distance education at higher education institutions in the United States. *Distance Learning Leaders* are responsible for the administration or coordination of the distance education program at an institution of higher education. Respondents were further classified according to the academic level of the institution in which they were employed (associate, master's, or doctorate) and institutional locale (urban, suburban, or rural). Table 1 shows the breakdown of respondents by institutional classification:

Development of the Instrument

By expanding the scope of the literature review on institutionalization to include the disciplines of organizational behavior (Tolbert & Zucker, 1994), library science (Oldford, 2002), health care (Goodman & Steckler, 1989; Public Education Network, 2004), engineering (Colbeck, 2002), educational leadership (Aronsen & Horowitz, 2000), service learning

Table 1.   Institutional Classification of Respondents

Classification	Respondents
Institutional role	
Faculty	111
Leader	59
Institutional academic level	50
Associate	3*
Bachelor	59
Master/specialist	55
Doctor	3*
Unknown	
Institutional locale	60
Urban	52
Suburban	55
Rural	3*
Unknown	

Note: *Excluded from the data analysis for this classification.

(Furco, 1999; Kramer, 2000), and distance education (Levin, 2005; Phipps & Merisotis, 2000; WCET, 2000a), a fairly consistent list of factors began to emerge. After eliminating those items that were specific to disciplines other than distance education and rewording others to be relevant to distance education, a total of 30 institutionalization factors were identified (Piña, 2008). These factors were organized into five general topic areas: Planning, Organization, Resources, Personnel and Student Services.

The survey instrument was constructed to cover the five topic areas, with six items per area, for a total of 30 items. Following the example of Furco's (1999) and Kramer's (2000) rubrics on institutionalizing service learning, each factor was given a description of how it could be applied in an institutional setting. Table 2 illustrates the relationship between the five topic areas, 30 factors and 30 application items.

Each item was accompanied by a Likert-type scale. Respondents indicated the level of importance of that factor to the institutionalization of distance education: *Critical* = 1, *Important but not critical* = 2, *Not important* = 3, and *Not a consideration at all* = 4. The middle or neutral response was eliminated to address "neutral bias," the tendency for responses to be biased toward the middle (WebSurveyor, 2007). A preliminary paper-based draft of the survey instrument was pilot-tested at a technology conference with 12 professionals representative of the target audience. Results of the pilot test were that the 30 items were deemed appropriate; however, some of the wording of specific items was modified to be more concise.

An HTML version of the instrument was developed using SurveyMonkey software to be made available to respondents via a Web site. IP address information from respondents' computers was collected to prevent multiple submissions by the same user; however the information was aggregated to insure respondent confidentiality. Cronbach's alpha reliability testing across the 30 items yielded a coefficient of .87.

Data Analysis

Mean scores, standard deviations and item ranking were calculated for each of the 30 institutionalization factors for importance and implementation. Analysis of variance (ANOVA) was used to test for statistically significant differences between faculty and leaders, between associate, masters and doctoral institutions, and between urban, suburban and rural institutions. Alpha level for significance was set at $P < .05$. When significant differences among three different groups were discovered, ANOVA was followed by a Scheffé post hoc test for multiple comparisons.

Table 2. Topic Areas, Institutionalization Factors and Application Items

Topic Area	Factor	Item	Factor	Item
Planning	Institutional mission	Distance learning is compatible with institution mission/vision statements	Master plan	There is a specific master plan for distance learning
	Policies and procedures	Formal policies and procedures for distance learning have been adopted	Marketing	There is an aggressive marketing plan to promote distance learning
	Needs assessment	There is periodic assessment of faculty, student and institutional distance learning needs	Evaluation	There is a formal plan for ongoing evaluation of distance learning
Organization	Campuswide function	Distance learning is a campuswide function, not a dependent unit of a particular school, department or discipline	Centralized	Distance learning is coordinated by a single central entity, rather than run from many different departments.
	Collaboration	Distance learning staff collaborates regularly with other entities on campus to insure broad base support.	DL leadership authority	Distance learning director/coordinator has decision making authority
	Visibility	Distance learning is visibly recognized on the institution's web site, catalogue, bulletins or organizational chart	Communication	There is a formal mechanism for informing the campus community about distance learning activities
Resources	Instructional design support	Instructional design help to assist faculty to develop distance learning courses is available	Faculty tech support	The institution provides technical support for distance learning faculty
	Staff development	Comprehensive and on-going staff development in distance education is provided	Funding	The distance learning program and staff are permanent budget items funded by hard money
	Infrastructure	The campus hardware and software infrastructure can support distance learning systems	Course management system	Distance learning utilizes a course management system such as Blackboard

(Table continues no next page)

9

Table 2. (Continued)

Topic Area	Factor	Item	Factor	Item
Personnel	DL director	There is a director/coordinator whose primary responsibility is distance learning	Permanent staffing	Distance learning staff consists of permanent, rather than temporary, employees
	Full-time staff	Distance learning staff are assigned full-time to distance learning	Faculty participation	Faculty (especially faculty leaders) are actively recruited to teach distance learning courses
	Professional incentives	Professional incentives for teaching distance learning courses (e.g. positive evaluation for promotion/tenure) available	Financial incentives	Financial incentives for teaching distance learning courses (e.g. course development fees, royalties) are available
Student Services	Online registration	Students can register for, add and drop courses on line	Online library/research	Students can access a full range of library/research services on line
	Advising and counseling	Students have access to counselors and advisors without having to come to campus	Student tech support	The institution provides technical support for distance learning students
	Online degree	Students can complete an entire degree program via distance learning	Multiple disciplines	Distance learning courses are available in multiple disciplines

Table 3.   Mean Scores for Importance Across Five Topic Areas

Topic Area	Factors Per Topic	Faculty	Leaders	Total
Resources	6	1.28	1.32	1.30
Planning	6	1.51	1.45	1.50
Student services	6	1.54	1.50	1.52
Organization	6	1.71	1.58	1.68
Personnel	6	1.79	1.71	1.76
Total	30	1.57	1.51	1.55

RESULTS

Institutional Role

All respondents ($n = 170$) identified themselves as either distance education faculty or distance education leaders. Table 3, which shows mean scores for faculty and leaders across the five topic areas, reveals a high level of agreement by both groups as to the importance of each of the topic areas and their order of importance. ANOVA revealed no significant differences between faculty and leaders in any of the topic areas.

Table 4 reports mean scores, standard deviations, and rank orders for distance education faculty and leaders for all 30 factors. Both distance education faculty and leaders rated Infrastructure and Faculty Technology Support as the two most important factors. Faculty and leaders also ranked Online Library, Instructional Design Support, Student Technology Support, Online Registration, Institutional Mission, and Distance Learning Policy/Procedures as among their top 10 factors of importance. All 30 factors fell into the range of "critical" or "important" in both groups. None of these factors was found to be "of minor importance" or "not important."

ANOVA revealed significant differences between faculty and leaders in four of the 30 factors. Although Infrastructure was the highest rated factor for importance by both groups, the rating by faculty was significantly higher $F(1, 169) = 5.717, p = .018$. Faculty also rated Course Management System as significantly higher in importance than did leaders, $F(1, 169) = 5.015, p = .026$. Leaders rated Budget $F(1, 169) = 5.632, p = .019$ and Advisement $F(1, 169) = 9.885, p = .002$ significantly higher in importance.

Institutional Academic Level

Of the 167 respondents who listed the highest degree awarded by their institutions, 50 were at the associate degree level, 59 at the master's or

Table 4.   Mean Scores for Importance
for 30 Institutionalization Factors—Faculty and Leaders

Factor	Faculty (n = 111)			Leaders (n = 59)			Total (n = 170)		
	Mean	SD	Rank	Mean	SD	Rank	Mean	SD	Rank
Infrastructure	1.04	0.187	1	1.17	0.530	1	1.08	0.351	1
Faculty tech support	1.10	0.380	2	1.22	0.494	2	1.14	0.426	2
Online library/research	1.23	0.485	3	1.37	0.584	9	1.28	0.524	3
Instructional design support	1.32	0.559	5	1.27	0.582	5	1.31	0.566	4
Student tech support	1.32	0.504	5	1.34	0.512	6	1.32	0.506	5
Online registration	1.31	0.569	4	1.37	0.584	9	1.33	0.573	6
Institutional mission	1.38	0.557	9	1.24	0.536	4	1.33	0.552	6
Policies and procedures	1.32	0.489	5	1.36	0.550	8	1.34	0.510	8
Visibility	1.39	0.559	10	1.34	0.545	6	1.37	0.553	9
Budget	1.46	0.711	12	1.22	0.418	2	1.38	0.634	10
Course management system	1.34	0.625	8	1.59	0.812	19	1.43	0.704	11
Staff development	1.44	0.628	11	1.44	0.565	15	1.44	0.605	12
DL director	1.48	0.672	13	1.41	0.646	12	1.45	0.662	13
Master plan	1.50	0.645	15	1.41	0.561	12	1.47	0.617	14
Evaluation	1.49	0.601	14	1.46	0.625	17	1.48	0.608	15
Needs assessment	1.57	0.655	17	1.42	0.532	14	1.52	0.618	16
Permanent staffing	1.53	0.644	16	1.51	0.679	18	1.52	0.655	16
Collaboration	1.59	0.653	18	1.44	0.676	15	1.54	0.663	18
Advisement & counseling	1.69	0.685	20	1.37	0.522	9	1.58	0.650	19
Multiple disciplines	1.66	0.610	19	1.73	0.715	24	1.68	0.647	20
DL leadership authority	1.70	0.880	21	1.66	0.779	20	1.69	0.844	21
Communication	1.81	0.733	22	1.69	0.623	21	1.77	0.697	22
Campuswide function	1.85	0.844	25	1.69	0.793	21	1.79	0.828	23
Marketing	1.82	0.741	23	1.83	0.813	28	1.82	0.764	24
Professional incentives	1.82	0.765	23	1.85	0.847	29	1.83	0.792	25
Centralized	1.93	0.922	26	1.69	0.856	21	1.85	0.904	26
Faculty participation	1.94	0.766	27	1.78	0.696	25	1.88	0.744	27
Full-time staff	1.99	0.869	28	1.80	0.783	27	1.92	0.843	28
Online degrees	2.04	0.830	30	1.78	0.832	25	1.95	0.837	29
Financial incentives	1.99	0.847	28	1.88	0.853	30	1.95	0.848	29

specialist degree level, and 55 at the doctoral degree level ($n = 164$). Only three respondents reported that their institutions awarded the bachelor's as the highest degree, so they were excluded from this analysis.

ANOVA resulted in significant differences for Planning $F(2,163) = 3.869$, $p = .023$, Marketing $F(2,163) = 5.133$, $p = .007$, Recruiting Faculty $F(2,163) = 3.286$, $p = .040$, Professional Incentives $F(2,163) = 8.982$, $p < .001$, and Online Advisement $F(2,163) = 3.887$, $p = .022$. Scheffé post hoc test for multiple comparisons revealed that doctoral level institutions rated Planning ($p = .033$), Marketing ($p = .031$), Recruiting Faculty ($p = .040$), and Professional Incentives ($p < .001$) significantly higher than did associate level institutions. Master's level institutions rated Marketing ($p = .15$), Professional Incentives ($p = .009$), and Online Advisement ($p = .033$) as significantly more important than did associate level institutions. Significant effects were especially pronounced for the factor of professional incentives.

Institutional Locale

Of the 170 respondents, 167 identified their institutions as being located in either an urban ($n = 60$), suburban ($n = 52$), or rural ($n = 55$) setting. Significant differences were found for Advisement $F(2, 166) = 9.524$, $p < .001$ and Degree $F(2, 166) = 6.617$, $p = .002$. Scheffé post hoc analysis, reveals a large effect for online advisement, rural institutions ranking it significantly higher in importance than urban ($p < .001$) and suburban ($p = .004$). The importance of offering degrees via distance education was also shown to be significantly more important for rural institutions than for urban ($p = .003$) or suburban ($p = .039$).

CONCLUSIONS

The purpose of this study was to determine actions that colleges and universities can take to institutionalize their distance education programs. To accomplish this goal, 30 factors found to influence the institutionalization of innovations were identified from the literature of educational technology, distance education, and educational change. These factors were rated by distance education faculty and distance education leaders (directors and coordinators) as to their importance for influencing the institutionalization of distance education.

Results were analyzed and compared according to institutional role (distance education faculty or distance education leaders), academic level of the institution (associate, master's, or doctorate), and institutional locale (rural suburban or urban). All 30 factors were validated as indicators of institutionalization of distance education, rated at either the "critical" or "important" level. None of the factors was found to be at the level of "minor importance" or "not important." Validation of the factors held true across institutional role, academic level, and locale. This finding supports the literature identifying each of the factors as influencing institutionalization.

Although each of the 30 factors was validated, it is clear that not all factors were considered to be of equal importance. Having an adequate hardware and software infrastructure to support the distance education program was seen as paramount by all groups. A working system to deliver distance education, described by Boettcher and Kumar (2000) as "distance education's digital plant," finds broad support from the literature (e.g., Levin, 2005; WCET, 2000b). Rated nearly as highly overall as infrastructure, was the availability of technology support for distance education faculty and availability of online library resources for distance education students.

While there was not universal agreement among all groups with regards to the level of importance among all 30 factors, some trends did emerge within the study. The most consistently high-rated factors dealt with establishing technological capacity (technology infrastructure, online library access, and online registration access), support (faculty technology support, instructional design support, and student technology support), and policy (integration with the institution's mission, establishment of policies, and procedures for distance education, making distance education a permanent "hard money" budget item and maintaining a high level of visibility for the distance education program). These three categories closely resemble those identified by Boettcher and Kumar (2000) as required for programs that deliver online education: technology, organization, and support. This finding can provide guidance for those who wish to know where to start in the establishment, improvement, or institutionalization of their distance education programs.

At the other end of the spectrum, offering financial incentives for faculty to teach distance education courses was consistently rated at the bottom of the list of factors for both importance and implementation. This result must not be interpreted as meaning that financial incentives were deemed to be unimportant to institutionalizing distance education. Rather, it supports previous findings by Parker (2003) and Giannoni and Tesone (2003) that faculty value professional advancement and teaching resources higher than financial incentives.

Institutional Role

Although faculty and leaders are often seen as having very different views regarding innovations at their institutions (Smart, Kuh, & Tierney,

1997), results of this study indicate that distance education faculty and leaders showed a high level of agreement as to the importance of the various institutionalization factors and the ranking of importance of the factors. When the factors were grouped into the five categories of planning, organization, resources, personnel, and student services, faculty and leaders ranked them in identical order. Of the top 10 rated factors for both groups, 9 were found in common.

The few differences that existed between faculty and leaders can be explained by Selani and Harrington's research (2002), which found that faculty and leaders attach more importance to those areas in which they have regular contact. Since the course management system is used to deliver the course and is the primary interface that faculty have with the distance education program, it is not surprising that faculty rate it higher in importance than leaders. Faculty seldom deal with the management of the distance education budget or the registration and advisement of students. It is understandable, therefore, that leaders rated budget and online advisement higher in importance than faculty.

Academic Level

Institutions of higher education that award graduate degrees (master's, specialist, or doctorate) tended to show more similarities than differences with each other. However, distance education professionals at associate degree granting institutions demonstrated a number of differences from their graduate school peers. Those at associate-level institutions rated the factors of master planning for distance education, marketing the program, recruiting faculty to teach, providing professional incentives for faculty, and providing advisement via distance education for students, significantly lower in importance than those who worked for graduate level institutions.

A look at the two areas for which associate level colleges scored higher for implementation may provide clues as to their scores for importance. The successful implementation of visibility of distance education at associate institutions may contribute to less emphasis on marketing. The successful implementation of a centralized distance education program (as opposed to doctoral institutions, which tend to be divided into schools, colleges, and departments that provide their own independent services), may affect the perceived need for master planning at associate-level colleges.

Differences in the roles and expectations of faculty at associate-level colleges and graduate universities can account for the significant differences in the factors of faculty recruitment and professional incentives. At universities, promotion and tenure tends to be influenced greatly by the familiar "publish or perish" expectations of performing research, conference presentations, grant writing, advisement of master's theses and doctoral dissertations, and other professional and scholarly achievements. As indicated in this study, faculty are, by and large, not rewarded or credited professionally for engaging in distance education activities. This supports Schell's research, which finds that faculty at graduate institutions, whose promotion and tenure—if not employment—can be negatively influenced by developing distance education that pulls them away from scholarly activities (Schell, 2004). Faculty who teach at associate-level colleges tend to have a more exclusive teaching role and their promotion and tenure would be less likely to be affected negatively by distance education activities.

Institutional Locale

Distance education professionals at rural colleges and universities rated several of the factors differently than their peers at suburban and urban institutions. Being able to offer advisement and a full degree via distance education was seen as far more important for rural institutions than for suburban or urban. This can be understood in context of the nature of the rural college or university, which would normally have a much wider service area, with a much longer student commute than a typical suburban or urban campus. The more guidance and advisement students can get via online and other distance technologies, the less students would have to travel. The same holds true for distance degree programs. If students can complete their degrees online, by videoconference or other distance education methods, the more likely that they will be able to pursue higher education.

RECOMMENDATIONS

The findings of this study can be used to (a) determine how new distance education programs should be established; (b) evaluate existing distance education programs to determine strengths, weaknesses, and areas for improvement and focus; (c) assess the level of institutionalization of distance education in their organizations; and (d) make decisions that will lead to improvement and institutionalization of their distance education programs. This will enable institutions to avoid making decisions about distance education "without adequately considering the broader institutional context" (Boyd-Barrett, 2000, p. 1).

The findings of this study also indicate that distance education faculty and distance education leaders are concerned about similar things. This has positive implications for institutions seeking to institutionalize distance education. If distance education is established with attention given to the institutionalization factors, there is good potential for cooperation between those who direct the distance education program and those who teach in it. Both faculty and leadership input should be solicited in the development of distance education programs.

This study can also provide guidance for establishing priorities in the development or redevelopment of distance education programs. Attention should be given initially to technological capacity (technology infrastructure, online library access, and online registration access), support (faculty technology support, instructional design support, and student technology support) and policy (integration with the institution's mission, establishment of policies and procedures for distance education, making distance education a permanent "hard money" budget item, and maintaining a high level of visibility for the distance education program). All institutions should work toward establishing relevant professional incentives for faculty who teach at a distance, particularly at graduate level universities.

REFERENCES

Allen, I. E., & Seaman, J. (2007). *Online nation: Five years of growth in online learning.* Needham, MA: The Sloan Consortium.

Aronsen, J., & Horowitz, J. (2000). *How intersegmental collaborative projects become institutionalized: A portrait of the evolution and lasting effects of five California academic partnership projects.* Long Beach, CA: California State University Chancellor's Office.

Bear, M. P., & Nixon, T. (2006). *Bear's guide to earning degrees by distance learning* (16th ed.). Berkeley, CA: Ten Speed Press.

Boettcher, J. V., & Kumar, M. S. V. (2000). The other infrastructure: Distance education's digital plant. *Syllabus, 13*(10), 14-22.

Boyd-Barrett, O. (2000). Distance education provision by universities: How institutional contexts affect choices. *Information, Communication & Society, 3*(4), 474-493.

Carnevale, D. (2000). Faculty union opposes undergraduate degrees earned entirely through distance learning. *Chronicle of Higher Education, 46*(46), A32.

Clark, G. C. (1989). Distance education in United States schools. *Computing Teacher, 16*(6), 7-11.

Colbeck, C. L. (2002). Assessing institutionalization of curricular and pedagogical reform. *Research in Higher Education, 43*(4), 397-421.

Curry, B. K. (1992). Instituting enduring innovations: Achieving continuity of change in higher education. *ASHE-ERIC Higher Education Report No. 7.* Washington, DC: The George Washington University.

Ellsworth, J. B. (2000). *Surviving change: A survey of educational change models*. Syracuse, NY: ERIC Clearinghouse on Information and Technology.

Fullan, M., & Stiegelbauer, S. (1991). *The new meaning of educational change*. New York: Teachers College Press.

Furco, A. (1999). *Self-assessment rubric for the institutionalization of service learning in higher education*. Berkeley: Service Learning Research and Development Center, University of California, Berkeley.

Gersten, K., & Evans, L. (2004, July). *Online pedagogy: Catalyst for transforming the teaching-learning enterprise*. Paper presented at Syllabus 2004 Conference, San Francisco.

Giannoni, D. L., & Tesone, D. V. (2003). What academic administrators should know to attract senior level faculty members to online learning environments. *Online Journal of Distance Learning Administration, 6*(1).

Goodman, R., & Steckler, A. (1989). A model for the institutionalization of health promotion programs. *Family and Community Health, 11*(4), 63-78.

Gunawardena, C. N., & McIsaac, M. S. (2004). Distance education. In D. Jonassen (Ed.), *Handbook of research on educational communications and technology* (2nd ed., pp. 355-395). New York: Simon & Schuster/Macmillan.

Hunt, D. W., & Piña, A. A. (2004, March). *A journey from online courses to online degrees*. Paper presented at the Technology in Education (TechEd) Conference, Ontario, CA.

Jones, G. R. (2002). *Cyberschools: An education renaissance* (2nd ed.). Englewood, CO: IBooks.

Kanter, R. M. (1983). *The change masters: Innovation and entrepreneurship in the American corporation*. New York: Simon & Schuster.

Kotter, J. P. (1996). *Leading change*. Cambridge, MA: Harvard Business Press.

Kramer, M (2000). *Make it last forever: The institutionalization of service learning in America*. Washington, DC: Corporation for National and Community Service.

Levin, T. L. (2005). *Going the distance: A handbook for developing distance degree programs using television courses and telecommunications technologies*. Washington, DC: Annenberg/CPB Project and PBS Adult Learning Service. Retrieved January 26, 2005 from http://www.pbs.org/als/gtd/handbook/index.html

Levy, S. (2003). Six factors to consider when planning online distance learning. *Online Journal of Distance Learning Administration, 6*(1).

Noble, D. F. (2003). *Digital diploma mills: The automation of higher education*. New York: Monthly Review Press.

Oakley, B. (2004). The value of online learning: Perspectives from the University of Illinois at Springfield. In J.C. Moore (Ed.) *Elements of quality online education into the mainstream: Wisdom from the Sloan Consortium*. Needham, MA: The Sloan Consortium.

Oldford, R. (2002). Why institutionalization has failed. *Teacher Librarian, 29*(3), 8-15.

Olson, C. A. (2002). Leadership in online education: Strategies for effective online administration and governance. In K. E. Rudestam & J. Schoenholtz-Read (Eds.), *Handbook of online learning: Innovations in higher education and corporate training*. Thousand Oaks, CA: Sage.

Parker, A. (2003). Motivation and incentives for distance faculty. *Online Journal of Distance Learning Administration, 6*(3).

Phipps, R., & Merisotis, J. (2000). *Quality on the line: Benchmarks for success in Internet-based distance education.* Washington, DC: The Institute for Higher Education Policy.

Picciano, A. G. (2001). *Distance learning: Making connections across virtual time and space.* Upper Saddle River, NJ: Merrill/Prentice Hall.

Piña, A. A. (2008). Making e-learning permanent: What can institutions do? *Midwest Journal of Educational Communications and Technology 2*(1), 2-14.

Public Education Network. (2004). *Evaluation framework of institutionalization for school health programs.* Retrieved October 20, 2004, from http://www.publiceducation.org/sc-tools-survival-evalframe.asp

Rogers, E. M. (1995). *Diffusion of innovations* (5th ed.). New York: The Free Press.

Schell, G. P. (2004). Universities marginalize online courses. *Communications of the Association of Computer Machinery, 47*(7), 53-56.

Sellani, R. J., & Harrington, W. (2002). Addressing administrator/faculty conflict in an academic online environment. *Internet & Higher Education, 5*(2), 131-145.

Simonson, M., Smaldino, S., Albright, M., & Zvacek, S. (2006). *Teaching and learning at a distance: Foundations of distance education* (3rd ed.). Upper Saddle River, NJ: Prentice-Hall.

Smart, J. C., Kuh, G. D., & Tierney, G. (1997). The role of institutional cultures and decision approaches in promoting organizational effectiveness in two-year colleges. *The Journal of Higher Education, 68*(3), 256-281.

Surry, D W., & Brennan, J. P. (1998, February). *Diffusion of instructional innovations: Five important, unexplored questions.* Paper presented at the annual conference of the Association for Educational Communications & Technology. St. Louis, MO.

Surry, D. W., & Ely, D. P. (2002). Adoption, diffusion, implementation, and institutionalization of educational technology. In R. A. Reiser & J. V. Dempsey (Eds.), *Trends and issues in instructional design and technology* (pp. 104-111). Upper Saddle River, NJ: Merrill/Prentice Hall.

Taylor, J. C. (2001). Fifth generation distance education. *Higher Education Series Report No. 40.* Canberra, Australia: Australia Commonwealth Department of Education, Science and Training, Higher Education Division.

Tolbert, P. S., & Zucker, L. G. (1994). Institutional analyses of organizations: Legitimate but not institutionalized. *ISSR Working Papers in the Social Sciences, 6*(5). Los Angeles, CA: UCLA Institute for Social Science Research.

Verduin, J. R, & Clark, T. A. (1991). *Distance education: The foundations of effective practice.* San Francisco: Jossey-Bass.

WebSurveyor. (2007). *Survey design considerations: Recommendations for writing effective questionnaires.* Retrieved October 11, 2007, from http://www.websurveyor.com/pdf/designtips.pdf.

Western Cooperative for Educational Telecommunications. (2000a). *Statement of commitment by the regional accrediting commissions for the evaluation of electronically offered degree and certificate programs.* Boulder, CO: Author.

Western Cooperative for Educational Telecommunications. (2000b). *Best practices for electronically offered degree and certificate programs*. Boulder, CO: Author.

CHAPTER 2

ATTRIBUTES AND BARRIERS IMPACTING DIFFUSION OF ONLINE EDUCATION AT THE INSTITUTIONAL LEVEL

Considering Faculty Perceptions

Jason Neben
Concordia University Irvine

INTRODUCTION

The traditional model of face-to-face instruction continues to dominate the higher education landscape. However, over the past decade online education has entered the mainstream. Universities across the broad spectrum from state schools, to small private schools, to Ivy League schools are getting into the marketplace of online education offerings. Allen and Seaman (2013) report that over 6.7 million students, or 32% of total higher education enrollment, are taking at least one online course.

Online education is a subset of distance education. Schlosser and Simonson (2010) define distance education as "institutionally-based, formal education where the learning group is separated, and where interactive telecommunications systems are used to connect learners, resources, and instructors" (p. 1). Distance education is not new. It has its roots in

Beyond the Online Course: Leadership Perspectives on e-Learning
pp. 21–34
Copyright © 2016 by Information Age Publishing

the 19th century with correspondence courses. Simonson, Schlosser, and Orellana (2011) describe the evolution of distance education in three phases

> first, correspondence study, with its use of print-based instructional and communication media; second, the rise of the distance teaching universities and the use of analog mass media; and third, the widespread integration of distance education elements into most forms of education, and characterized by the use of digital instructional and communication technologies. (p. 131)

Online education, characterized by delivery of instruction using a learning management system via the Internet, has become the dominant platform for distance education in the third stage.

Unlike most technologies, online education, and distance education in general, is a disruptive innovation (Simonson, Smaldino, Albright, & Zvacek, 2012). An innovation is "an idea, practice, or object that is perceived as new by an individual or other unit or other unit of adoption" (Rogers, 2003, p. 12). A disruptive innovation may enter an environment and challenge the status quo by addressing a need the current technology is ignoring or not able to meet. Online education provides students access to academic programs they might not otherwise have, or schedule flexibility permitting participation without physical presence in a particular time and place. Innovations, whether disruptive in nature or not, present an individual with the choice to adopt or reject its use. As individuals across an organization or other populations choose to adopt, the use of the innovation spreads. Rogers' (2003) diffusion of innovation theory describes this as the innovation-decision process.

The diffusion of online education in higher education involves many stakeholders, including faculty. Faculty are at the core of the teaching and learning process directly impacting student achievement. Whether faculty choose to adopt or reject online education as a delivery model for instruction depends on many factors. Understanding these factors and the faculty perceptions of the impact these factors have on the diffusion process informs the educational community, including scholars and policy decision makers (Mitchell & Geva-May, 2009).

BACKGROUND

The rapidly changing higher education marketplace requires institutions to strategically consider how to enter the online market and the implications of such change. Nearly 70% of academic leaders report online learning as critical to the long-term strategy of the institution (Allen &

Seaman, 2013). Some administrators are even viewing online education as a necessity for survival in higher education (Lesht & Windes, 2011). This entrée into the online marketplace becomes extremely complex for small private institutions operating on thin profit margins, small endowments, and minimal amounts of reserve funds for the development costs needed to enter the online market.

Concordia University Irvine (CUI) was founded in 1972 as a parochial college committed to preparing professional church workers. A School of Education and School of Arts and Sciences were formed in 1988 and 5 years later the college became a university and joined a national system of nine other sister universities. In 1999 the original college was restructured and a School of Theology emerged. Three years later a School of Business and a School of Adult Studies were established, resulting in the five schools that currently make up the university.

About a decade ago the university invested in an online course management system and schools within the university began to independently explore using the course management system to deliver instruction. The School of Education was the first to offer a complete academic program online, beginning in 2003. The School of Arts and Sciences followed in 2008. The university has recently formally included an initiative to systematically expand online education as part of its strategic plan.

Efforts are escalating to carry out the initiative. An assistant provost position specifically tasked with expanding online education was created and filled. In this position, Doug Grove, with the support of the president and provost, acts as the primary change agent in the diffusion process at CUI. Additional human resources are being added and strategies for short and long-term growth are being investigated and developed.

Relevance

When attempting to diffuse online education across an institution, it is critically important for leadership to understand faculty perceptions. Faculty participation in online education will not increase substantially unless leadership minimizes barriers that inhibit faculty participation (Betts, 1998). For example, faculty may perceive online education as not aligned to their respective discipline contributing to breakdown of the innovation during implementation (Hannon, 2009). Using inclusive processes to gain buy-in, garnering commitment, developing a vision, and providing appropriate support to faculty during the implementation process promotes adoption of online education (Bremner, 2007). At CUI, Grove has emphasized that developing and communicating with faculty the institutional vision of online education is central to his role and responsibilities.

Since faculty are the direct connection to students, it is crucial to understand the perceptions of faculty when considering any major change to the teaching and learning process. Moore and Kearsley (1996) emphasize that faculty must remain a central figure in the transition from traditional teaching to distance education. Success of online education rests on the commitment of the faculty to develop and deliver online courses (Betts, 1998). When administrators are aware of particular faculty barriers to online education, targeted strategies, including effective policy development, can be implemented to increase motivation and mitigate barriers at their own institution (Howell, Saba, Lindsay, & Williams, 2004; Mitchell & Geva-May, 2009).

The expanded use of online education at CUI involves substantial change for all stakeholders, faculty and students being most affected. The change process is complex and teacher advocacy is a key factor to the initiation stage of successful change (Fullan, 1982, 1993; Fullan & Stiegelbauer, 1991). Actively engaging faculty in the change process involves understanding and responding to faculty perceptions about the adoption of online education. Rogers' (2003) diffusion theory emphasizes the importance of understanding the perceptions of potential adopters of an innovation, online education in this case, in the process of adopting an innovation.

THE CHALLENGE

Allen and Seaman (2013) report higher education faculty acceptance of online learning as valuable and legitimate at about 30%, a level that has remained relatively unchanged over the past decade. There is a widening gap between the view of academic leaders about online education as critical to the long-term strategy (almost 70%) and the faculty acceptance of online learning as valuable and legitimate (Allen & Seaman, 2013).

DIFFUSION OF INNOVATIONS THEORY

Rogers (2003) defines diffusion as "the process in which an innovation is communicated through certain channels over time among the members of a social system" (p. 5) Revealed in the definition are the four main elements of diffusion: an innovation, communication channels, time, and a social system. Diffusion theory has often been applied to the study of technology innovations (Sahin, 2006) and specifically used as the theoretical framework for studying diffusion of online education in higher education (Alhawiti, 2011; Bassett, 2012; Li, 2004). Eineke's (2004) study of online professional education demonstrated how the diffusion of innovations theory could be used as a successful structure to improve understanding of the adoption process and implementation of online education.

Diffusion of innovations theory is useful in many fields of study. Ellsworth (2001) summarized educational change theories through the lens of a change communication model. In doing so, he identified applications of change theory for educational practitioners. More specifically, Ellsworth constructed typical questions a practitioner might answer with an application of a theoretical framework. He proposed that diffusion theory could help address questions such as "What attributes can I build into the innovation or its implementation strategy to facilitate its acceptance by the intended adopter?" and "How can the presence or absence of these attributes affect the rate of acceptance by the intended adopter (or prevent acceptance altogether)?" (Ellsworth, 2001, p. 37).

Perceived Attributes of Innovations

All innovations are not equal when it comes to the rate at which members of the social system adopt their use. Some innovations may be adopted over a period of years while others may take decades. Rogers (2003) describes five attributes (relative advantage, compatibility, complexity, trialability, observability) of an innovation that contribute to the variance in rate of adoption. It is important to understand that these attributes are measured as perceptions of the potential individual adopter.

Relative advantage is defined as "the degree to which an innovation is perceived as better than the idea it supersedes" (Rogers, 2003, p. 15). An individual is more likely to adopt an innovation if she perceives it provides an advantage over current practice. What constitutes an advantage can vary with the potential adopter or the innovation. For instance, Alwahiti (2011) found that a majority of Saudi faculty viewed online education as a means to reach more students, indicating an advantage over traditional face-to-face instruction. The possible reasons for being able to reach more students could be due to geographic location, family time commitments, or flexibility in scheduling. The important factor in relative advantage contributing to the overall rate of adoption is that the potential adopter perceives some advantage. The reason for the advantage is not necessarily the focus. There is a direct, positive relationship between relative advantage and rate of adoption. The more an innovation is perceived as advantageous, the faster the rate of adoption (Rogers, 2003).

Compatibility is define as "the degree to which an innovation is perceived as being consistent with the existing values, past experiences, and
needs of potential adopters" (Rogers, 2003, p. 15). There can be different
reasons why a potential adopter may not find online education compatible with values, experiences, and needs. Some studies have found that faculty perceive online education as compatible with their values and current
teaching practice (Alwahiti, 2011; Li, 2004). It may only take one perceived incompatibility to cause a potential adopter of online education to
reject. Bruner (2007) found that some faculty considered online education incompatible with the mission of the institution. This perception
works against the rate of adoption of online education. As CUI faculty
member Tim Schumacher noted, "online education is compatible with
our mission, if it is intentionally done." This is a typical response. Faculty
at CUI believe that there must be an intentional and purposeful way that
online education can carry out the mission before they will engage. There
is a direct, positive relationship between compatibility and rate of adoption. The more an innovation is perceived as compatible with the social
system, the faster the rate of adoption (Rogers, 2003).

Complexity is defined as "the degree to which an innovation is perceived as difficult to understand and use" (Rogers, 2003, p. 16). For
example, a complex unclear process for developing e-learning environments was found to be an inhibitor for diffusion of online education at
one Australian university (Burch & Burnett, 2009). Dr. Grove has been
very attentive to faculty concerns about complexity at CUI. From the
beginning of CUI's online education initiative, an emphasis has been
placed on establishing a clear structure and process for faculty participation in online course development. This is likely to promote adoption.
The complexity attribute is different from the other four in that it has a
direct, negative relationship with rate of adoption. According to Rogers
(2003), the more complex an innovation is perceived, the slower the rate
of adoption. Innovations that are perceived as extremely complex are typically rejected altogether.

Trialability is defined as "the degree to which an innovation may be
experimented with on a limited basis." (Rogers, 2003, p. 16) Allowing an
individual or organization to test out a new idea can reduce doubt about
the innovation and promote adoption. In the case of online education,
this could mean time for faculty experimentation with the technology
tools used or time to participate in the course development process without mandate to teach in the online arena. According to Rogers (2003), if
an innovation is trialable its rate of adoption will increase.

Observability is defined as "the degree to which the results of an innovation are visible to others." (Rogers, 2003, p. 16) When a potential
adopter is able to observe the results of the use of an innovation, adoption

is more likely. It is encouraging when faculty observe their peers success-fully teach online (Lesht & Windes, 2011). People value the experiences of their peers and the sharing of positive information about an innovation's use promotes acceptance. Of course, the converse is true as well. If the observable results are negative, adoption is discouraged. If an innovation is perceived as observable and the observable results are positive, its rate of adoption will increase (Rogers, 2003).

Faculty members make value judgments about online education char-acterized by these five attributes. The end result may or may not be using online education as a method for teaching and learning. According to Rogers (2003), individuals progress through a series of stages when con-structing these opinions about an innovation. This series of stage is referred to as the innovation-decision process.

The Innovation-Decision Process

Rogers (2003) defines the innovation-decision process as

the process through which an individual (or other decision-making unit) passes from gaining initial knowledge of an innovation, to forming an atti-tude toward the innovation, to making a decision to adopt or reject, to implementation of the new idea and to confirmation of this decision. (p. 168)

The five stages of the innovation-decision process are knowledge, per-suasion, decision, implementation, and confirmation. Rogers cites the landmark study by Ryan and Goss (1943) as establishing that potential adopters of an innovation progress through a decision-making process. Ryan and Gross's study of Iowa corn farmers and hybrid seed adoption illustrated that adoption was not based on an impulse decision, but a pro-cess over time.

The knowledge stage is where an individual usually enters the innova-tion-decision process. Information about an innovation may be obtained actively or passively. Active seekers may have some sort of issue or prob-lem that current practices cannot address that prompts them to seek out a new idea or method to accomplish the task. For instance, educators have actively sought online education to serve populations in rural areas that cannot be served by traditional face-to-face instruction. Information may be received passively when a change agent seeking to encourage a shift in practice shares the new idea or method. For instance, when university leadership promotes online education to faculty as a means to deliver an existing program. In this case the faculty member is not seeking out knowledge on her own about the new idea stemming from a perceived or real need to address an issue or problem.

Knowledge acquisition by faculty at CUI was primarily by active seekers until relatively recently. For the past decade those faculty who have actively sought out to engage with online education are the ones who have developed and taught online courses. This has been changing, though, over the past year as leadership has begun to promote the use of online education.

Usually following discovery and knowledge acquisition, a potential adopter begins to form an attitude toward an innovation during the persuasion stage of the innovation-decision process. During this stage, the collective perception of the five innovation attributes contributes to the development of a favorable or unfavorable opinion of the innovation. Rogers (2003) states that relative advantage and compatibility have a greater influence on the formation of an attitude than the remaining three attributes. It is very common for a potential adopter to seek the opinion of or observe the use of the innovation by peers. Lesht and Windes (2011) concluded that, when unsure faculty observe other faculty being successful teaching online, it promotes engagement. Social reinforcement plays an important role in forming an attitude toward an innovation (Rogers, 2003). The attitude that is formed then contributes to the decision to adopt or reject. As a smaller higher education community, CUI faculty have a relatively close-knit community where social reinforcement is likely to play a substantial role in opinion formation.

Forming an attitude toward an innovation like online education typically results in a decision to adopt or reject it. This is described as the decision stage. Adoption is "a decision to make full use of an innovation as the best course of action available" (Rogers, 2003, p. 177). Most potential adopters of an innovation want to try it out, or observe someone else try it out, before making a decision. This creates a type of probationary period for the innovation (Rogers, 2003). Rejection is "a decision not to adopt an innovation" and can occur at any point in the innovation-decision process (Rogers, 2003, p. 177).

Typically following quickly after a decision to adopt, implementation of an innovation is characterized by observable actions by an individual to use the new idea. Most innovations will face problems and raise questions during the implementation stage. During this time adopters actively seek solutions to these problems and change agents promoting an innovation are typically tasked with providing technical support (Rogers, 2003). Again, rejection can occur at any point in the process.

Having adopted and implemented an innovation, or rejected it, the individual typically seeks to reinforce the decision with additional information in the confirmation stage (Rogers, 2003). The individual may be unsure about the decision, creating what Rogers refers to as dissonance, "an uncomfortable state of mind that an individual seeks to reduce or eliminate" (Rogers, 2003, p. 189). Adopters and rejecters both seek to mitigate any unsettled thoughts about the innovation. This may result in confirmation or reversal of a decision.

Passing through the innovation-decision process is not strictly linear. Rogers (2003) cautions that sharp distinctions between stages should not be anticipated. An individual is likely gaining knowledge about an innovation during the entire process, but certainly takes definitive actions that move away from a strictly knowledge acquisition phase. It is these behaviors that characterize and place the individual along the innovation-decision process continuum.

BARRIERS TO DISTANCE EDUCATION

Advances in technology have occurred faster and in greater frequency during the last decade than in previous decades. However, these advances do not necessarily translate into similar rates of online education adoption. Significant barriers to implementing distance education continue to exist and are well documented in the literature. Barriers may be related to institutional factors, technological issues, financial costs, pedagogical beliefs, or other factors.

Institutional Barriers

The literature reveals most barriers to implementation of distance education are related to institutional issues. Over the last 15 years studies have consistently identified lack of release time (Berge & Muilenburg, 2000; Betts, 1998; Birch & Burnett, 2009; Bollinger & Wasilik, 2009; Bruner, 2007; Haber & Mills, 2008; Lesht & Windes, 2011; Schifter, 2000; Seaman, 2009) and concerns related to allocation of faculty workload (Berge & Muilenburg, 2000; Betts, 1998; Bollinger & Wasilik, 2009; Bruner, 2007; Chen, 2009; Meyer, 2012) as prominent barriers to distance education. It should be noted, however, that at least one study (Birch & Burnett, 2009) indicated that interviews with participants revealed that "it may be more a matter of priorities than time, with some academics revealing that they can find time for things that are important to themselves and their career and those which they perceived to be rewarded such as research" (p. 11). Nevertheless, the overall time commitment, from training to course development to instruction, is perceived to be more for distance education than for traditional classroom education.

Institutional policy, or lack of institutional policy in many instances, contributes to established barriers. For example, studies have shown institutions not recognizing the teaching of online education courses as progress toward promotion or tenure in policy creates a barrier (Bolliger & Wasilik, 2009; Bruner, 2007; Howell et al., 2004). Likewise, unclear policies, or no policy at all regarding copyright and intellectual property, has been found as a barrier (Bolliger & Wasilik, 2009; Berge & Muilenburg, 2000). At CUI some faculty have expressed substantial concerns about intellectual property rights in the context of online education. One main concern is how long material in an online course might be used. There is a perception that material might be used too long and become irrelevant, possibly negatively affecting the reputation of a faculty member. Unless addressed by leadership in policy, this perception will inhibit adoption. Finally, lack of appropriate faculty compensation and reward systems in institutions is recognized in the literature as an important barrier (Berge & Muilenburg, 2000; Chen, 2009; Haber & Mills, 2008; Meyer, 2012).

Technological Barriers

Issues related to the technology associated with distance education make up another category of barriers. Effective online education involves many different skills than traditional classroom education from development through instruction. Not receiving the training needed for course development and instruction for online education has been shown to be a substantial barrier perceived by faculty (Berge & Muilenburg, 2000; Lesht & Windes, 2011; Mitchell & Geva-May, 2009; Schifter, 2000). In a 2010 study, Allen and Seaman reported that about 19% of chief academic officers indicated their institution provided no training for faculty teaching online. That percentage dropped to 6% 2 years later (Allen & Seaman, 2012), which is a promising indicator that training is improving. CUI is incorporating an in-house training protocol for instructors who teach online. It began with a needs assessment via an online teaching inventory of all faculty. Grove's office has established three levels of online teaching proficiency, identified where each faculty member resides, and planned training accordingly. This is likely to promote adoption.

Lack of technical support is one of the most frequently identified barriers for impeding the adoption of distance education (Betts, 1998; Berg & Muilenburg, 2000; Lesht & Windes, 2011; Schifter, 2000). The kind of support needed ranges from allocation of appropriate hardware and software to providing support for the many different technical skills needed for online education. Among others, online education involves interaction with the learning management system, converting print materials to electronic media, and using synchronous web-conferencing tools, all of which require initial specialized training and ongoing support. This is not limited to faculty support. Faculty perceives lack of student technical support as a barrier as well (Haber & Mills, 2008).

Financial Barriers

The lack of financial resources to meet the costs of implementing online education has been identified in the literature as a barrier to distance education (Berge & Muilenburg, 2000; Birch & Burnett, 2009; Chen, 2009; Schifter, 2000). There are substantial costs associated with the design and development of quality online education courses. Institutions may mitigate costs by adding responsibilities onto existing faculty. Meyer (2012) found additional responsibilities for faculty to be a major barrier to participation in distance education. This has been common practice for CUI, but that has changed with the establishment of online education as a strategic initiative. Substantial resources have been allocated to assist in mitigating these barriers.

Pedagogical Barriers

The literature reveals that pedagogical concerns are a major barrier to distance education. Over the last 15 years studies indicate that negative faculty perceptions about the quality of online education inhibit participation (Berge, 1998; Bolliger & Wasilik, 2009; Lesht & Windes, 2011; Meyer, 2012; Schifter, 2000; Seaman, 2009). The faculty perception of the quality of online education has not changed much over the past decade and it remains relatively low. Allen and Seaman (2013) report that less than one third (30.2%) of chief academic officers believe faculty accept the value and legitimacy of online education. Other pedagogical barriers include perceived incompatibility with a discipline (Hannon, 2009) and the desire to experience traditional face-to-face student-teacher interaction (Bruner, 2007; Haber & Mills, 2008; Lesht & Windes, 2011).

SUMMARY

While traditional classroom instruction continues to dominate higher education, online education is now mainstreamed across the United States. Institutions of all types are including online education in strategic plans, some even as a means of survival in an increasingly competitive market. Concordia University Irvine is a small, private, liberal arts institution investing substantial resources into online education as part of its strategic plan for growth, not just survival.

There are many factors and people that impact such an endeavor. One of the primary stakeholder groups in online education is faculty. How faculty perceive online education and the factors that promote or inhibit its use is central to successful implementation.

Rogers' (2003) diffusion theory principles of the innovation-decision process and perceived attributes provide a road map for leadership to follow in promoting faculty adoption of online education. Understanding faculty perceptions about the relative advantage, compatibility, complexity, trialability, and observability of online education informs decision makers seeking to increase adoption. CUI leadership must be attentive to faculty perceptions about these online education attributes in this strategic plan.

CUI leadership is attentive to diffusion theory concepts in the context of known barriers to online education. These barriers may be categorized as institutional, technological, financial, or pedagogical. Most barriers are institutional in nature, and for CUI this is no different. With a lack of centralized control and vision over the past decade there is a substantial lack of institutional policy in most areas relating directly to online education. While finances are always an issue, CUI has strategically allocated resources to address major financial barriers in hiring and for compensating existing personnel for online education development and delivery. An emphasis must be placed on addressing faculty perceptions of these barriers as faculty play the key role in institutional adoption.

REFERENCES

Allen, I. E., & Seaman, J. (2012). *Changing course: Ten years of tracking online education in the United States, 2011.* Needham, MA: Sloan Consortium.

Allen, I. E., & Seaman, J. (2013). *Changing course: Ten years of tracking online education in the United States.* Needham, MA: Sloan Consortium.

Alhawiti, M. M. (2011). *Faculty perceptions about attributes and barriers impacting the diffusion of online education in two Saudi universities* (Doctoral dissertation). Available from ProQuest Dissertations & Theses Full Text database. (UMI No. 3453898)

Bassett, P. (2012). Diffusion of online distance education at one liberal arts university (Doctoral dissertation). Retrieved from http://p8080-marps.library.nova.edu.ezproxylocal.library.nova.edu/MARPs/advancedss.aspx

Berge, Z. L., & Muilenburg, L. Y. (2000). Barriers to distance education as perceived by managers and administrators: Results of a survey. In M. Clay (Ed.),

Distance Learning Administration Annual 2000. Retrieved from http://emoderators.com/wp-content/uploads/Man_admin.pdf

Betts, K. S. (1998). An institutional overview: Factors influencing faculty participation in distance education in postsecondary education in the United States: An institutional study. *Online Journal of Distance Learning Administration, 1*(3). Retrieved from http://www.westga.edu/~distance/ojdla/fall13/betts13.html

Birch, D., & Burnett, B. (2009). Bringing academics on board: Encouraging institution-wide diffusion of e-learning environments. *Australasian Journal of Educational Technology, 25*(1), 117-134. Retrieved from http://www.ascilite.org.us/ajet/ajet25/birch.html

Bolliger, D. U., & Wasilik, O. (2009). Factors influencing faculty satisfaction with online teaching and learning in higher education. *Distance Education, 30*(1), 103–116. doi:10.1080/01587910902845949

Bremner, B. J. (2007). *Facilitating the adoption of online learning in educational organizations: A case study in a Canadian post secondary technical institute* (Doctoral dissertation). Retrieved from ProQuest Dissertations & Theses Full Text database.

Bruner, J. (2007). Factors motivating and inhibiting faculty in offering their courses via distance education. *Online Journal of Distance Learning Administration, 10*(2). Retrieved from http://www.westga.edu/~distance/ojdla/summer102/bruner102.htm

Chen, B. (2009). Barriers to adoption of technology-mediated distance education in higher-education institutions. *Quarterly Review of Distance Education, 10*(4), 333-338.

Eineke, K. R. (2004). *The diffusion of an innovation: Online professional education* (Doctoral dissertation) Retrieved from ProQuest Dissertations & Theses Full Text database. (UMI No. 3161309)

Ellsworth, J. B. (2001). *Surviving change: A survey of educational change models*. Syracuse, NY: ERIC Clearinghouse on Information & Technology.

Fullan, M. (1982). *The meaning of educational change*. New York, NY: Teachers College Press.

Fullan, M. G. (1993). *Change forces: Probing the depths of educational reform*. London, England: Falmer Press.

Fullan, M., & Stiegelbauer, S. (1991). *The new meaning of educational change* (2nd ed.). New York, NY: Teachers College Press.

Haber, J., & Mills, M. (2008). Perceptions of barriers concerning effective online teaching and policies: Florida community college faculty. *Community College Journal of Research and Practice, 32*(4-6), 266-283. doi:10.1080/10668920701884505

Hannon, J. (2009). Breaking down online teaching: Innovation and resistance. *Australasian Journal of Educational Technology, 25*(1), 14-29.

Howell, S. L., Saba, F., Lindsay, N. K., & Williams, P. B. (2004). Seven strategies for enabling faculty success in distance education. *The Internet and Higher Education, 7*(1), 33-49. doi:10.1016/j.iheduc.2003.11.005

Lesht, F., & Windes, D. L. (2011). Administrators' views on factors influencing full-time faculty members' participation in online education. *Online Journal of*

Distance Learning Administration, 14(4). Retrieved from http://www.westga.edu/~distance/ojdla/winter144/lesht_windes144.html

Li, Y. (2004). Faculty perceptions about attributes and barriers impacting diffusion of Web-based distance education (WBDE) at the China Agricultural University (Doctoral dissertation). Available from ProQuest Dissertations & Theses Full Text database. (UMI No. 3141422)

Meyer, M. (2012). *Overcoming barriers: How community college faculty successfully overcome barriers to participation in distance* education (Doctoral dissertation). Available from ProQuest Dissertations & Theses Full Text database. (UMI No. 3529747)

Mitchell, B., & Geva-May, I. (2009). Attitudes affecting online learning implementation in higher education institutions. *Journal of Distance Education, 23*(1), 71-88. Retrieved from http://www.jofde.ca/index.php/jde/article/view/43/835

Moore, M. G., & Kearsley, G. (1996). *Distance education: A systems view.* Belmont, CA: Wadsworth.

Rogers, E. M. (2003). *Diffusion of innovations.* New York, NY: Free Press.

Sahin, I. (2006). Detailed review of Rogers' diffusion of innovations theory and educational technology-related studies based on Rogers' theory. *Turkish Online Journal of Educational Technology, 5*(2). Retrieved from ProQuest Central.

Schifter, C. C. (2000). Faculty participation in asynchronous learning networks: A case study of motivating and inhibiting factors. *Journal of Asynchronous Learning Networks, 4*(1), 15-22.

Schlosser, L. A., & Simonson, M. (2010). *Distance education: Definition and glossary of terms* (3rd ed.). Charlotte, NC: Information Age.

Seaman, J. (2009). *Online learning as a strategic asset: The paradox of faculty voices—Views and experiences with online learning (Vol. 2).* Washington, DC: Association of Public Land-grant Universities. Retrieved from http://www.aplu.org/NetCommunity/Document.Doc?id=1879

Simonson, M., Schlosser, C., & Orellana, A. (2011). Distance education research: A review of the literature. *Journal of Computing in Higher Education, 23*(2-3), 124-142. doi:http://dx.doi.org/10.1007/s12528-011-9045-8

Simonson, M., Smaldino, S., Albright, M., & Zvacek, S. (2012). *Teaching and learning at a distance: Foundations of distance education* (5th ed.). Upper Saddle River, NJ: Merrill Prentice Hall.

CHAPTER 3

BARRIERS TO ADOPTION OF TECHNOLOGY-MEDIATED DISTANCE EDUCATION IN HIGHER EDUCATION INSTITUTIONS

Baiyun Chen
University of Central Florida

The purpose of the study was to empirically investigate the institutional approach to distance education, and examine whether the factors of concerns for program cost and faculty participation could statistically predict adoption of technology-mediated distance education (TMDE) among higher education institutions. It is elusive to base the determination of institutional decisions merely on existing descriptive statistics. Therefore, the author used the logistic regression method to explore the hypotheses, with controls for extraneous explanatory variables, such as institution type, graduate program availability, and degree of urbanization. Specifically, a binary logistic regression was modeled to analyze a number of barriers that might keep institutions from starting or expanding distance offerings. Two categories of barrier factors were analyzed. The program cost factors include program development costs and equipment maintaining costs. The faculty participation factors encompass concerns about faculty workload, lack of faculty interest, and lack of faculty rewards or incentives.

Beyond the Online Course: Leadership Perspectives on e-Learning
pp. 35–43

THEORETICAL FRAMEWORK

Access to postsecondary education is an issue of significant importance both to the individual and society in general. In the United States, estimates of the proportion of future jobs requiring postsecondary education range from 70 to 90% (Gladieux & Swail, 1999). The individuals with a postsecondary degree earn on average 50% more than high school graduates over the course of their lifetime (U.S. Bureau of Census, 1999). Also, increased educational attainments accrue benefits to society, including greater productivity, increased community services, enhanced civic life, and decreased reliance on government financial support (Institute for Higher Education Policy, 1998).

The rapid development of information technology and the Internet have generated broader opportunities for students to access postsecondary education. In the fall 2005 semester, more than 96% of the very largest higher education institutions (more than 15,000 total enrollments) had online distance offerings, and the enrollment in online courses reached nearly 3.2 million, up nearly 35% over the 2004 figures (Allen & Seaman, 2005, 2006). In 2007, approximately one-third of higher education institutions accounted for three-quarters of all online enrollments (Allen & Seaman, 2007).

While technology has expanded the opportunities for students to access higher education, it is interesting to note that a number of colleges and universities are still hesitant to offer technology-mediated distance education (TMDE), and there is a very uneven distribution of distance education offerings by type of institutions. The questions of interest for the current study focus on the institutional decision of distance education offering. What are the factors that impact a higher educational institution to adopt distance education? The factors in this study include concerns about program cost, faculty participation, and others.

Barriers to distance education exist both in the stakeholders of institution and faculty (Galusha, 1997). The primary institutional barrier is availability of funds, as cost will increase substantially due to utilization and maintenance of technology. Descriptive statistics show that the high cost for program development and maintenance is a significant barrier to widespread adoption of distance education (Allen & Seaman, 2007; National Postsecondary Education Cooperative, 2004; Waits & Lewis, 2003). In fall 2005, about two thirds of the very large institutions had online programs, compared to only about one sixth of the small institutions (Allen & Seaman, 2006). Moreover, the data from the Cost of Supporting Technology Services project show that for 2000-2001, the median spending on information technology was $1,299 for each student at the wealthiest colleges in the study. By contrast, the less endowed colleges showed a median spending of only $459 per student (Warburton & Chen, 2002). Thus, there is an institutional digital divide pertaining to the perceived gaps in access to technology capital among different types of institutions with regard to their funding availability.

Another important factor on institutional adoption of TMDE is faculty participation. Those institutions most engaged in online believe it is a barrier to more wide-spread adoption of online education (Allen & Seaman, 2007). Research has shown that barriers to teaching and learning at a distance often impede faculty from adapting to new educational opportunities. These barriers include technical expertise, faculty compensation and time, attitudes toward technology, and so on (Berge, 2002; Chen, Voorhees, & Rein, 2006). There is a critical need for regular training and support of faculty on the use of technology and adapting it to enrich their curriculum (Rodriguez, Gonzalez, & Cano, 1996).

Thus, two hypotheses on institution barriers and faculty barriers to TMDE adoption were derived based on the theoretical literature review:

Hypothesis 1. Controlling for institutional characteristics, institutions with fewer concerns about program cost are more likely to adopt TMDE than those with more concerns.

Hypothesis 2. Controlling for institutional characteristics, institutions with fewer concerns about faculty participation are more likely to adopt TMDE than those with more concerns.

METHODS

Empirical Data

The present study was a secondary data analytic research using the National Center for Education Statistics (NCES) public use dataset. The variables of the study come from a nationally representative survey of distance education, the Postsecondary Education Quick Information System (PEQIS), undertaken by the NCES in the academic year 2000-2001. Unfortunately, this is the most recent pubic dataset that the author was able to access. The survey panel employs a standing panel of 1,599 postsecondary education institutions. The panel includes institutions at the 4-year, 2-year, and less-than-2-year level, public and private colleges, and universities that award associate, baccalaureate, master's, and doctoral degrees. Among the eligible institutions, 1,500 responded to the survey, with a response rate of 94%. For the current analysis, 1,485 responses were valid for the selected variables, excluding 15 missing responses.

MEASURES

Adoption of TMDE

The dependent variable of this study is the adoption decision of TMDE of higher education institutions. The sample was divided into two groups based on adoption status. As illustrated in Table 1, the first group includes 1,111 institutions that offered TMDE in the academic year 2000-2001. The second group includes 121 institutions that did not offer TMDE in 2000-2001, but planned to offer it in the next 3 years (2001-2002 through 2003-2004), and 268 institutions that did not offer TMDE in 2000-2001, and did not plan to offer it in the next three years.

Institutional Characteristics

Institutional characteristics were controlled for in the analyses as five explanatory factors. The first controlling factor is institution type, created from a combination of level (2-year and 4-year) and control (public and private). The four types include: public 2-year, private 2-year, public 4-year, and private 4-year. The second controlling factor is the availability of graduate program. The third factor is based on the standard Carnegie classification code, indicating which level of programs the institution is offering, recorded as doctoral, master's, baccalaureate, associate, specialized, and other/missing. The fourth factor is the degree of urbanization, recorded as city, urban fringe, town/rural, and missing. And the last one is minority-serving institution.

Barriers to TMDE Adoption

The independent variables are barriers to TMDE adoption. In the survey, the participating institutions were asked to rate 15 factors that kept them from starting or expanding their distance education courses. In the

Table 1.   Adoption of TMDE by Type

Distance Ed Offering	Type (Institutional Type)				Total
	Public 2 Year	Private 2 Year	Public 4 Year	Private 4 Year	
Adopted	481	17	363	250	1,111
Not adopted	24	81	32	252	389
Total	505	98	395	502	1,500

current analysis, two major independent variables of 5 factors were selected from the 15 factors. The first one, program cost, is measured with two distinct factors: program development costs, and equipment failure/costs of maintaining equipment. The second variable, faculty participation, includes three factors. They are concerns about faculty workload, lack of faculty interest, and lack of faculty rewards or incentives. For each factor, the response categories are "not at all," "minor extent," "moderate extent," and "major extent."

Statistical Procedure

The analysis was done using the PEQIS dataset and SPSS software version 15.0. First, descriptive statistics were used to understand the sample and general information about barriers to distance education adoption. Then, considering the stratified, multistage sampling design of the dataset and the dependent factor as dichotomous, a binary logistic regression was selected for further analysis. With the institutional characteristics kept as constant, the regression was used to predict the institutional TMDE decisions based on two sets of perceived barrier variables.

RESULTS

Factor Descriptive

Table 2 shows the impact of the barrier factors to adoption of TMDE. About 30% of the participants scored "program development costs" as a factor of moderate extent. However, "equipment failure/cost" seems to be a less important factor and over 70% of the participants marked it as "minor extent" or "not at all." In the faculty participation factors, "concerns about faculty workload" outweighs the other two factors. About one third of the participants regarded the faculty workload as a moderate extent impact, while almost two thirds of the participants thought of faculty interest or reward as factors of minor extent or not at all important.

Binary Logistic Regression Analysis

The results of the binary logistic regression analysis support the hypotheses. The factors of program cost and faculty participation showed statistically significant associations with the institutional adoption of distance online courses ($p < .000$, $R^2 = .569$). The large positive regression

Table 2.   Descriptive on TMDE Adoption Factors

	Impact on Adoption of TMDE					
Factors	*Major Extent*	*Moderate Extent*	*Minor Extent*	*Not at All*	*Missing*	*Total*
Program Cost Factors						
Program development costs	24.11%	30.41%	25.99%	19.49%	0.47%	100%
Equipment failures/costs	9.51%	19.96%	32.08%	38.45%	0.47%	100%
Faculty Participation Factors						
Concerns about faculty workload	15.0%	32.69%	27.86%	24.45%	0.47%	100%
Lack of faculty interest	7.97%	25.99%	34.76%	31.28%	0.47%	100%
Lack of faculty rewards	13.48%	25.02%	30.38%	31.12%	0.6%	100%

coefficient suggests that these factors strongly influence the probability of the adoption decision. First, controlling for institutional characteristics such as institution type, location, and degree of urbanization, institutions with sufficient funding and few concerns about program cost are more likely to adopt TMDE than others. In particular, the adoption decision was associated with increased odds of concerns for program development cost (OR = 1.12; 95% CI = .60-2.11). In other words, for every one unit increase in program development cost, the odds of adoption distance education (versus not adopting) increased by a factor of 1.12.

Second, controlling for institutional characteristics, institutions with few concerns about faculty participation are more likely to adopt TMDE than other institutions. Specifically, whether to adopt distance education was associated with increased odds of concerns for faculty workload (OR = 3.02; 95% CI = 1.57 − 5.79), and lack of faculty incentives (OR = 2.97; 95% CI = 1.41 − 6.25). For every one unit increase in concerns for faculty workload, the odds of adoption distance education (versus not adopting) increased by a factor of 3.02, while for every one unit increase in concerns for lack of faculty incentives, such odds increased by a factor of 2.97.

Besides the hypotheses, it is noted that one of the controlling variables, institution type, has high associations with TMDE adoption. The public 4-year institutions have the highest odds to adopt distance education (OR = 17.62; 95% CI = 6.66 − 46.52). The public 2-year institutions have the second highest odds (OR = 7.91; 95% CI = 4.85 − 12.89). By contrast, the private institutions have much lower odds for TMDE adoption. Therefore, the results agreed to prior research that large, well-funded institutions have greater access to technology than smaller colleges with fewer resources do.

DISCUSSION AND CONCLUSIONS

This study explored associations between the institutional decision of adopting TMDE and the factors that keep them from starting or expanding distance course offerings. The empirical findings support the main hypotheses, including the significance of the program cost and the faculty participation in driving adoption.

Among all factors, program development costs, concerns for faculty workload, and lack of faculty rewards are significant barriers that prevent institutions from offering distance education. To address these factors and help more institutions start their online programs, federal and state education policy makers might allocate funding to encourage institutions and faculty to develop online courses. Other funding sources to roll out online learning initiatives are private foundations and commercial resources, such as Alfred P. Sloan Foundation, which has awarded grants to more than 100 colleges and universities during the past two decades (Parry, 2009).

On the other hand, institutions that are planning online offerings might be able to cut costs by taking advantage of new technologies. For instance, institutions could consider using open source software, such as Moodle, to reduce spending on course management systems. In terms of faculty participation, institution and faculty collaboration might be a way to avoid increasing faculty workload. Faculty members across the country can exchange and share courseware, instead of recreating the wheel. A number of world-class universities are offering free online courses to initiate collaborations. Examples are MIT Open Courseware, the University of California at Berkeley Webcasts courses, and the Open University's (UK) OpenLearn Learning Spaces. Free learning objects and course contents are available at multiple educational resource websites, such as Merlot (http://www.merlot.org/) and Jorum (http://www.jorum.ac.uk/).

The limitation of this research is that the PEQIS dataset was collected by the NCES in the academic year of 2000-2001. With the technology advances and an increasing need for alternative learning options, more universities are willing to embrace online education, compared to 8 years ago. Future research should seek a more recent database to reflect the most recent trends and situations in how higher education institutions are adopting technology-mediated distance education in a new Web 2.0 age when it is easier than ever before to create and share instructional materi-

als online. It will be interesting to see if the impact of the faculty participation factor on adopting distance education will change.

It is believed that student demand for online learning in the United
States is still growing (Allen & Seaman, 2007). This study addressed an
important issue of relationship between access to postsecondary education and the role of technology. It is expected that the results to be of
most value to academic administrators and education policymakers who
face the problem of designing postsecondary programs and expanding
access to higher education to a larger population. Understanding and
mitigating the barriers to TMDE adoption will motivate both institutions
and faculty to offer distance education, and better facilitate the opportunities for students to enroll in higher education.

REFERENCES

Allen, I. E., & Seaman, J. (2005). *Growing by degrees: Online education in the United States, 2005*. Newburyport, MA: Sloan Consortium. Retrieved from http://www.sloan-c.org/publications/survey/survey05.asp

Allen, I. E., & Seaman, J. (2006). *Making the grade: Online education in the United States, 2006*. Newburyport, MA: Sloan Consortium. Retrieved from http://www.aln.org/publications/freedownloads.asp

Allen, I. E., & Seaman, J. (2007). *Online nation: Five years of growth in online learning*. Newburyport, MA: Sloan Consortium. Retrieved from http://www.sloanconsortium.org/publications/survey/online_nation

Berge, Z. L. (2002). Barriers to distance education and training. *Quarterly Review of Distance Education, 3*(4), 409-418.

Chen, B., Voorhees, D., & Rein, D. W. (2006). Improving professional development for teaching online. *Journal of Computer Information Systems, 2*(1), 303-308.

Galusha, J. M. (1997). Barriers to learning in distance education [Electronic Ver-
sion]. *Interpersonal Computing and Technology*, 5, 6-14. Retrieved from http://www.emoderators.com/ipct-j/1997/n4/galusha.html

Gladieux, L., & Swail, W. S. (1999). *The virtual university & educational opportunity: Issues of equity and access for the next generation*. Washington, DC: The College Board.

Institute for Higher Education Policy. (1998). *Reaping the benefits: Defining the public and private value of going to college*. Washington, DC: Author.

National Postsecondary Education Cooperative. (2004). *How does technology affect access in postsecondary education? What do we really know? Report of the National Postsecondary Education Cooperative Working Group on Access-Technology*. Washington, DC: National Center for Education Statistics.

Parry, M. (2009, April 6). Sloan foundation ends major grant program for online education. *The Chronicle of Higher Education*. Retrieved from http://chronicle.com/daily/2009/04/15222n.htm

Rodriguez, C., Gonzalez, R. A., & Cano, N. (1996). *Improving utilization of the information highway by Hispanic-serving institutions*. San Antonio, TX: Hispanic Association of Colleges and Universities.

U.S. Bureau of Census. (1999). Educational attainment—Workers 18 years old and over by mean earnings, age, and sex: 1991 to 1998. *Current Population Survey*. Retrieved from http://www.census.gov/hhes/income/hisinc/p28.html

Waits, T., & Lewis, L. (2003). *Distance education at degree-granting postsecondary institutions: 2000-2001*. Washington: DC: National Center for Education Statistics.

Warburton, E. C., & Chen, X. (2002). *Teaching with technology: Use of telecommunications technology by postsecondary instructional faculty and staff* (NCES 2002-161). Washington, DC: National Center for Education Statistics.

CHAPTER 4

SIX BARRIERS CAUSING EDUCATORS TO RESIST TEACHING ONLINE, AND HOW INSTITUTIONS CAN BREAK THEM

Dana Gutman
Campus Management Corp

INTRODUCTION

In 2001, the South Dakota Alliance for Distance Education, partnered with the U.S. Department of Education's Star Schools Initiative, to host a 2-day workshop. This event, also known as the "conclave," allowed leading experts in the field of distance education, to discuss some of the barriers preventing online learning from gaining widespread prestige and acceptance from the academic community. One of the topics discussed at this workshop was the results gathered from an extensive evaluation process in which members of the conclave interviewed educators to assess their attitudes toward teaching online. Their findings reveal that educators feel significant apprehension about teaching in an online learning environment. This article will explore six of the major reasons educators resist teaching online, and propose solutions for overcoming each barrier.

Beyond the Online Course: Leadership Perspectives on e-Learning
pp. 45–52
Copyright © 2016 by Information Age Publishing

BARRIER 1: SALARY

It requires a major investment of time and energy for an instructor to create an engaging distance learning course, but for many faculty, moving a course from the traditional classroom into an electronic medium is considered part of the standard workload (Bower, 2001). However, translating a face-to-face class into an engaging online course requires pedagogical training that is inherently different from that of teachers who perform in a live classroom (Bower, 2001). Therefore, distance educators possess a unique set of knowledge, skills, and abilities that institutions should recognize by offering appropriate compensation, and providing low cost incentives such as awards and recognition. By valuing the role of online teachers, administrators will increase standards and performance in the field of distance education (Gold, 2001).

BARRIER 2: PROMOTION AND TENURE

According to Bower (2001), distance education classes are more time consuming to prepare than traditional courses, while instructional and operational costs are generally lower, yet faculty still receive less. In addition, time spent in developing distance learning courses is time not spent on other professional activities, which may be needed to be successful in the tenure process. This issue is particularly important for faculty at research universities who face high expectations in research and publication (Bower, 2001). When faculty members make contributions toward distance learning initiatives, their efforts should help them earn tenure rather than interfere with their duties and be a source of stress. The field of distance education should support individuals interested in learning about technical innovation and online pedagogy. In doing so, administrators attract leaders to the field of distance education who can then share their knowledge and expertise. This degree of commitment and contribution should help educators achieve promotion and tenure rather than work against them.

BARRIER 3: WORKLOAD

One of the reasons for expanding distance learning, and the use of technology, is to increase productivity and student enrollment. However, to maintain a high-quality learning environment, distance education courses should have no more than 25 students per classroom (Goodyear, Salmon, Spector, Steeples, & Tickner, 2001). Research suggests that intimate classroom discussions increase critical thinking, reflection, and interaction among learners (Goodyear et al., 2001). If institutions abide by this principle, administrators will need to hire more distance educators to keep up with the growing demand for online courses. The question remains, how many courses should a single educator be expected to handle? As mentioned, the role of an online instructor is different from a traditional classroom teacher; additional responsibilities include but are not limited to content facilitator, technologist, designer, manager/administrator, process facilitator, adviser/counselor, assessor, and researcher (Goodyear et al., 2001). Staying abreast of the latest technology and applying educational strategies effectively in an online learning environment requires a tremendous amount of time and effort. The problem is, if institutions provide faculty with release time to prepare their distance learning courses, they may need to demonstrate increased productivity through other means, such as increasing the student-faculty ratio (Bower, 2001). Research suggests that increasing class sizes so that fewer teachers would need to be hired and trained compromises quality of the learning experience (Lee, Paulus, Loboa, Phipps, Wyatt, Myers, & Mixer, 2010). By implementing team teaching, offering subscriptions to distance education journals, and providing time to attend training workshops and conferences, educators will be more efficient when it comes to designing courses, and thus require less release time to prepare.

BARRIER 4: TRAINING

Teachers must have the actual experience of online learning before they can be expected to be online teachers; otherwise, they simply map traditional practices onto the new medium (Gold, 2001; Lee et al., 2010). By training educators in an online learning environment how to integrate technology with pedagogical teaching strategies, they not only experience distance education as an end user, but they learn how to effectively design a digital curriculum.

In-service programs must offer convincing, no-nonsense, and ongoing training that deals with how to teach at a distance, not merely how to manipulate new instructional technology (Beaudoin, 1990). Specific content areas might include methods to establish and maintain effective communication, increasing interaction among students, strategies for encouraging individual and group motivation, planning and managing organizational details, developing an awareness of the time demands of distance delivered courses, techniques for adding visual components and audio, and how to access and integrate information from various sources (Bonk & Dennen, 2002; Gold, 2001).

Table 1.   Workshop Participants Training Experience and Needs

Survey Questions	No	Yes	Yes, Face-to-Face	Yes, Online	Yes, Either Type of Delivery
Does your institution have a formal training program in technology and online course development?	74.4%	25.6%			
Have you ever taken a course in technology and online course development?	65.8%	34.2%			
Do you want to take a course in technology and online course development?	2.6%	na	5.1%	30.8%	61.5%
Does your institution have a formal training program in teaching online?	94.9%	5.1%			
Have you ever taken a course in teaching online?	76.9%	23.1%			
Do you want to take a course in teaching online?	5.3%	na	0%	31.6%	63.2%

In a 2001 study, Gold investigated a 2-week faculty development pedagogical training course aimed at preparing teachers on how to operate effectively within an online educational environment. Before the workshop started, he conducted a survey to see what kind of training their institutions previously offered. Table 1 presents results from his questionnaire.

These data, along with the feedback gathered from the South Dakota Alliance for Distance Education, reveal an overwhelming desire for more training by educators. Faculty also express a need for more technical support and staff development in the areas of technical innovation and pedagogy.

In addition, Bonk and Dennen (2002) assert that a national system of teacher training emphasizing distance education should be considered, and mandatory training in theory and practice should be instituted as a condition of employment for new and continuing faculty. The myth that teaching from a distance is easier and requires less involvement from the teacher must be dispelled. As previously mentioned, teaching from a distance requires a set of knowledge, skills, and abilities inherently different from those used in a traditional classroom; by giving teachers the tools they need to perform successfully in a distance learning environment, the field of distance education will attract and retain talented professionals. It is precisely in the design and delivery of these new learning modes where the participation of competent and committed faculty is most critical (Beaudoin, 1990).

BARRIER 5: INTERPERSONAL RELATIONS

Personal interaction with students is one of the most gratifying aspects of teaching (Gold, 2001). For some, the lack of direct interpersonal contact with both students and faculty is an issue (Berge, 1998). In addition, the physical absence of the teacher makes it difficult to gauge the clarity of communication and understanding (Gold, 2001).

Online instructors have to be more outgoing, positive, and responsive to gain respect from their students (Gold, 2001). Mason identifies the three fundamental roles of a distance educator as organizational, social, and intellectual (1991). The organizational role involves setting the agenda, defining learning objectives, establishing a timetable, and explaining rules and procedures. Essentially, teachers must lay the groundwork for the discussion to begin. Their main social role is to create a friendly environment for the students. Good teachers often send out welcome messages, use a personal tone, and send prompt feedback with specific examples and references. Another important social role is modeling good intellectual behavior. Finally, the teacher must become the facilitator of the students' understanding. The teacher should focus on crucial points of discussions, ask questions, probe student responses, synthesize and summarize points, and help develop themes that link to the readings and class resources (Gold, 2001). Research suggests that these practices provide learners with a more satisfying learning experience and they feel more connected to their online teacher than they do in a face-to-face classroom (Oliver & Herrington, 2000).

Besides increasing the interaction between the teacher and student, it is also important to promote a community of practice among faculty (Bawane & Spector, 2009). Approaches to promote a community of practice for faculty include: involving them in developing courseware; permitting them to preview, purchase, and evaluate materials; engage them in pilot projects to test alternative delivery systems; and expose them to case studies of successful distance education activities. Their input can be encouraged through social networking, live and virtual meetings, committee work, and mentorship programs (Beaudoin, 1990; Bower, 2001).

One of the most critical aspects of an online course is introductions (Gold, 2001). Both the instructor and student should identify themselves within the discussion forum. By establishing a caring online presence and taking an interest in the students, this creates a positive atmosphere and a sense of student trust in the class (Bawane & Spector, 2009). The goals of these introductory posts are to exchange ideas, share information, and create a social environment where students feel comfortable interacting with each other. Another way to increase interaction among students is to encourage the exchange of informal conversation. A study of 80 college undergraduates found that this produced higher more complex levels of student participation (Ahern, Peck, & Laycock, 1992). These findings suggest that when online instructors are more informal and spontaneous in their commenting, students become more interactive with each other, compared to conditions where the instructor simply poses formal topic-centered statements or questions. Bonk and Dennen (2002) agree that the more teacher-centered the environment, the less student exploration, engagement, and interaction.

BARRIER 6: QUALITY

According to Bonk and Dennen (2004), many educators are still skeptical about the effectiveness of courses delivered from a distance, claiming that they are poor attempts to replace the teacher with technology, and offer students an easier way to earn credits without having to demonstrate mastery of learning outcomes. Even though these are myths, they could become a reality if distance educators do not strive toward continuously learning, evaluating, and improving their practices. The phenomenon of syllabism is an ever-present threat to the success of distance learning outcomes (Beaudoin, 1990). Syllabism is the tendency for students to focus only on what is prescribed in the syllabus. The outcomes may be a series of assignments that satisfy course requirements, but which result in very little learning. Students thus develop perfunctory answers to questions based solely on self-contained knowledge of the material, in which case the teacher is simply paid to check that the rules of the exercise are adequately followed (Beaudoin, 1990). When professors expect learners to solely refer to their syllabus and required readings, the student fails to authentically engage with the material. Without applying new information in a realistic context and without receiving feedback on correctness, the student never receives confirmation of mastery, but rather adheres to the course outline simply to earn a grade. Gold suggests that distance education courses stress learning rather than teaching, a constructivist approach based on the principle that the key to learning is what students do, not what teachers do (2001).

According to Beaudoin (1990), instructional personnel must be adept at facilitating students' learning through particular attention to process, unlike classroom-based teachers whose traditional role is largely confined to selecting and sharing content. The Institute for Higher Education Policy (2000) asserts that better instructional design and standards of success will increase acceptance for e-learning both within higher education as well as the surrounding community. From a constructivist point of view, learning is a search for meaning. To make meaning, students must focus on concrete situations and understand not only the facts but also the context in which these facts are placed (Gold, 2001). In addition to being adept at both content and process, faculty must know something about the potential of technology to facilitate learning and to enhance their own effectiveness (Beaudoin, 1990; Bower, 2001).

Two leaders in online pedagogy, Oliver (2000) and Paulsen (1995), focus on how Web tools foster student articulation, collaboration, intentional learning, and goal setting. They also connect these constructivist principles to Web-based resources such as bulletin boards, asynchronous conferencing, concept mapping, and survey tools that might be employed for student debates, reflection, cooperative group situations, role-play, brainstorming, special guest appearances, collaborative learning, and online discussions. According to Bonk and Dennen (2002) all of these strategies serve to enhance the quality of online learning environments.

CONCLUSION

While individual faculty members may have their own reasons to resist participating in the latest wave of distance education, there are several reasons why faculty in general resist distance education. Faculty have specifically expressed concerns for the adequacy of institutional support, the change in interpersonal relations, and quality.

Recognition, collaboration, technical support, online sharing of pedagogical practices, and instructional design assistance are all ways to increase faculty involvement and the adoption of web-based technologies in college teaching. Also, online educators have expressed a desire for more pedagogical tools, advice, and communities for their online teaching and learning efforts. By identifying these needs and the barriers that accompany them, professionals in the field of distance education can develop improvement strategies to overcome them.

REFERENCES

Ahern, T. C., Peck, K., & Laycock, M. (1992). The effects of teacher discourse in computer-mediated discussion. *Journal of Educational Computing Research, 8*(3), 291-309.

Bawane, J., & Spector, J. M. (2009). Prioritization of online instructor roles: Implications for competency-based teacher education programs. *Distance Education, 30*(3), 383-397.

Beaudoin, M. (1990). The instructor's changing role in distance education. *The American Journal of Distance Education, 4*(2).

Berge, Z. L. (1998). Barriers to online teaching in post-secondary Institutions: Can policy changes fix it? *Online Journal of Distance Learning Administration, 1*(2).

Bonk, C. J., & Dennen, V. (2004). Frameworks for research, design, benchmarks, training, and pedagogy in web-based distance education. In M. G. Moore & W. G. Anderson (Eds.), *Handbook of distance education* (pp. 329-346). Mahwah, NJ: Erlbaum.

Bower, B.L. (2001). Distance education: Facing the faculty challenge. *Online Journal of Distance Learning Administration, 4*(2).

Gold, S. (2001). A constructivist approach to online training for online teachers. *Journal of Asynchronous Learning Networks, 5*(1), 35-57.

Goodyear, P., Salmon G., Spector, J. M., Steeples, C., & Tickner, S. (2001). Competencies for online teaching: A special report. *Educational Technology Research and Development, 49*(1), 65-72.

Institute for Higher Education Policy. (2000). *Quality on the line: Benchmarks for success in Internet-based distance education.* Washington, DC: Author.

Lee, D., Paulus, T. M., Loboda, I., Phipps, G., Wyatt, T. H., Myers, C. R., & Mixer, S. J. (2010). Instructional design portfolio: A faculty development program for nurse educators learning to teach online. *TechTrends, 54*(6), 20-28.

Mason, R. (1991). Moderating educational computer conferencing. *DEOSNEWS, 1*(19), 1-11.

Oliver, R., & Herrington, J. (2000). Using situated learning as a design strategy for Web-based learning. In B. Abbey (Ed.), *Instructional and cognitive impacts of Web-based education* (pp. 178-191). Hershey, PA: Idea Group.

Paulsen, M. F. (1995). Moderating educational computer conferences. In Z. Berge & M. P. Collins (Eds.), *Computer-mediated communication and the on-line classroom in distance education* (pp. 81-90). Cresskill, NJ: Hampton Press.

CHAPTER 5

BRIDGING THE DIVIDE

Reconciling Administrator and Faculty Concerns Regarding Online Education

Leah E. Wickersham and Julie A. McElhany
Texas A&M University-Commerce

Online education opportunities continue to expand across the United States, as is evidenced at a regional institution in northeast Texas. Research literature supports that both administrators and faculty have concerns regarding online education. The authors conducted a study at this institution to investigate the concerns of university administrators toward online education and their attitudes concerning the establishment of institutional quality standards related to online education. Administrator and faculty concerns and suggestions for reconciling those concerns through faculty development opportunities were also investigated. Using a case study design, the authors conducted one-on-one interviews with the university administrators and distributed the Stages of Concern Questionnaire (SoCQ) to faculty to determine administrator and faculty concerns, respectively. The authors found that both faculty and administrators share similar concerns regarding online education and suggestions for meeting those concerns, although those concerns and suggestions are viewed from the unique role each plays at the institution. Effective communication between these two important institutional entities—administrators and faculty—is necessary to bridge the divide and reconcile administrator and faculty concerns regarding online education.

Beyond the Online Course: Leadership Perspectives on e-Learning
pp. 53–68

INTRODUCTION

Online education is considered one of the fastest growing educational enterprises in the United States. Over 3.9 million students were enrolled in at least one online course during the fall 2007 semester, a 12% increase over the number reported the previous year. Most institutions believe that the change in student demographics, student demand for more online course offerings, and the current state of the economy (i.e., the recent recession and past increases in gasoline prices) will have a positive impact on overall online enrollment, and the expectations of academic leaders are that these academic enrollments will continue their growth for at least another year. Considering these ever-increasing enrollments, administrators continue to have important decisions to make regarding online education at their institutions, and often "make decisions based on their understanding of faculty opinions" (Allen & Seaman, 2008, p. 6).

The success of online education programs hinges on the active and interdependent involvement of these two human resources—faculty and administrators (Olson & Hale, 2007). Administrators who develop successful online education programs do so by addressing the needs of faculty as they transition from traditional to online teaching (Zotti, 2005). Practices that support faculty in course development and delivery, while promoting participation in institutional decisions related to online programs, result in high levels of faculty satisfaction. Faculty who are on the front lines of the paradigm shift toward anyplace, anytime learning assess online learning effectiveness and leadership in terms of institutional support (Brown, 2003). Their participation in the policy development process is beneficial in informing administrators about concerns related to essential categories and elements of online education (Maguire, 2009). These essential categories or elements of quality online education include institutional support, course development and structure, student and faculty support, and evaluation and assessment. It is important to focus faculty development on these elements to help ensure quality online academic programs and at the same time recognize that these elements and the supporting faculty development are not enough. Faculty new to or veterans of teaching online approach online instruction with concerns regarding quality online course design, development, and delivery (Maguire, 2009). Administrators also have concerns relating to online education; however, their concerns are viewed through a slightly different lens. It is important to develop an understanding of both sides of these concerns in an attempt to develop a shared vision for online education as it relates to the design, development, and delivery of online courses to meet institutional standards of quality (Olson, & Hale, 2007).

PURPOSE OF STUDY

The information presented in this paper focuses on administrator concerns collected via one-on-one semistructured interviews as they relate to online course design, development, and delivery at a regional institution located in northeast Texas experiencing tremendous growth in online course development and offerings. The authors recently completed a study (Wickersham & McElhany, 2009) related to faculty concerns within the three academic colleges at the institution utilizing the Stages of Concern Questionnaire (SoCQ) with additional open-ended questions that concentrated on online course design, development, and delivery to determine areas needed for faculty development to assist in alleviating these concerns. A brief presentation of the faculty SoCQ data by college is presented; however, the main focus of this article is to present the administrators' responses to their concerns connected to online learning and make recommendations to assist in bridging the two sides for a shared vision of online education.

METHODOLOGY

The primary research questions addressed in this study focused on the concerns of university administrators toward online education and their attitudes toward the establishment of institutional quality standards related to online education. A secondary question compared administrator and faculty concerns and their suggestions for reconciling those concerns via faculty development opportunities.

A case study design was employed in order to gain deeper insight into administrator concerns as they related to online education, the need for the establishment of institutional standards of quality and importance of faculty development for online course design. A case study was the best method for addressing the research questions as it provides an opportunity to explore a "bounded system" or case over time (Creswell, 1998). Semistructured interviews using a nine-question administrator interview protocol were conducted with 16 out of a total of 24 academic department heads and four deans as a means of gaining information on faculty development and the development of online courses from their perspectives. Of the 24 academic department heads interviewed, only 8 had experience teaching an online course. The administrator interview protocol was made up of three sections with three open-ended questions in each section. The three sections focused on administrator concerns, institutional standards of quality for online courses, and faculty development needed relating to online course instructional design. The tape recorded interviews were transcribed and any identifying information was removed prior to engaging in the analysis of the interview data. The researchers followed a read-aloud protocol in order to look for patterns in the data and develop naturalistic generalizations via the analysis process. This level of analysis is referred to as inductive data analysis by Lincoln and Guba (1985). Qualitative techniques were followed for using the constant comparative method to compare data across categories and construct meaning as the researchers read the interview transcriptions, making notes, comments, and observations in the margins. The constant comparative method is used "a means for deriving (grounded theory), not simply a means for processing data" (Lincoln & Guba, 1985, p. 339).

"Categories were developed based on patterns that emerged from the reorganization of the data while drawing on the tacit knowledge of each researcher. Each pattern, or category, was given a unique color as a means of providing the researcher with a visual representation" (McElhany & Wickersham, 2009, p. 8). The categories derived from the reorganization and coding phase of the study were considered in relation to administrator concerns, institutional standards of quality for online courses, and faculty development needed related to online course instructional design. The researchers present the thick, rich descriptions of the case study findings along with conclusions and recommendations in narrative form.

FINDINGS

SoCQ Results by College

In order to determine faculty concerns as they relate to online education, the researchers administered the SoCQ. The SoCQ consists of 35 questions in relation to an innovation on a scale of 0 to 7 with options ranging from irrelevant to very true of me now. The SoCQ has strong reliability estimates (test/retest reliabilities range from .65 to .86) and internal consistency (alpha-coefficients range from .64 to .83) (Hall & Hord, 2001). The SoCQ is one of three instruments which together form what is known as the "Concerns-Based Adoption Model, a conceptual framework that describes, explains, and predicts probable behaviors throughout the change process" and that helps "educational leaders, coaches, and staff developers facilitate the process" (George, Hall, & Stiegelbauer, 2006, p. 4).

Of the 427 faculty who were surveyed, 118 faculty members returned a completed SoCQ questionnaire. Returned SoCQ questionnaires were grouped by each academic college within the university. The college of arts and sciences had a total of 39 faculty (31 full-time and 8 adjuncts) out of a total of 162 faculty return a completed questionnaire. Questionnaires were returned by 24 faculty (23 full-time and 1 adjunct) out of a total of 77 faculty from the college of business and technology. A total of 55 faculty (44 full-time and 11 adjuncts) out of a total of 188 faculty completed the SoCQ from the college of education and human services.

Peak stage scores for each stage of concern for the academic colleges combined were calculated to determine the level of intensity of concern for each of the seven stages. The intensity of concern for the university academic colleges combined is highest at Stage 0 at 94%, followed by Stage 2 at 76%, and Stage 1 at 66%. This indicated that the intensity of concern is highest at stages of concern related to "self" (Stages 0, 1, 2), which means faculty desire to know more about teaching online and how it will affect them personally.

Additionally, peak stage scores for each stage of concern were calculated for each of the three academic colleges separately to determine the level of intensity of concern for each of the seven stages of concern by college. The intensity of concern for the college of arts and Sciences faculty is highest at Stage 0 at 94%, followed by two stages of concern similar in intensity, Stage 2 at 76%, and Stage 1 at 72%. The intensity of concern for faculty who teach in the college of business and technology is highest at Stage 0 at 81%, followed by Stage 2 at 72% and Stage 1 at 67%. For faculty from the college of education and human services, the intensity of concern is highest at Stage 0 at 94%, followed by Stage 2 at 78%, and Stage 1 at 69%. Examination of these peak stage scores by college indicates that faculty from each of the three colleges have the greatest intensity of concern in stages of concern related to "self" (Stages 0, 1, 2). Table 1 presents intensity of concern data at each Stage of Concern for each of the three academic colleges.

Peak stage scores for the colleges combined, as well as each college separately, reveals that the intensity of concern is highest related to "self" (Stages 0, 1, 2). This indicates that faculty desire to know more about teaching online and how it will affect them personally. Despite the long

Table 1.   Intensity of Concern by Academic College

	Stage of Concern						
	0	1	2	3	4	5	6
College of education and human services	94%	69%	78%	56%	48%	48%	60%
College of business and technology	81%	72%	67%	60%	43%	44%	57%
College of arts and sciences	94%	72%	76%	60%	38%	31%	52%

history of online education at the institution, faculty as a whole have failed to move beyond the lowest level of concern.

Faculty Open-Ended Questionnaire Analysis

The SoCQ survey contained five open-ended questions related to faculty concerns toward online teaching. Faculty were asked to address their concerns and identify steps that could be taken to reduce those concerns to include what could be done from the administrative side and preference in the type and format of faculty development sessions offered targeted in assisting the improvement of both online course design and technical skills. Faculty were also asked about their perceptions of the development of standards of quality for online courses and to make recommendations for proceeding in the development of such standards. Questions were analyzed using the constant-comparative method as outlined by Lincoln and Guba (1985) with each unique idea or unit coded with a specific color developing into a category.

Faculty concerns related to online teaching do not differ from those of faculty at other institutions. The same issue surrounding the amount of time it takes to design, develop, and then teach a course online was a common response seen throughout the data. In addition, many faculty believe their course content will not translate well into the online learning environment. Faculty also carry with them the notion of the perceived lack of interaction in an online course versus that of a traditional course; however, this lack of interaction may be tied to poor design of the course, thereby failing to address this issue. Another concern noted by faculty is the fear of the popularity of online courses with administrators, seeing this as an opportunity to increase enrollment rather than cap it. Faculty also worry about student preparedness in regards to technology and the ability to be self-directed in learning, as many students perceive online learning to be "easy." Security, testing, and academic honesty were also areas noted by faculty as concerns. Above all, faculty are concerned about quality and they desire to know more about how to achieve that quality for teaching online to ensure their students are receiving the best education.

To reduce these concerns, faculty would like to see additional release time and support for the development of online courses. Support identified included initiating testing security measures such as proctored testing environments and/or exam guard software; enrollment caps to assist in the organization of the course and better time management; and the development of a course assessment tool to assist in determining if a course is suitable for the online environment. Faculty also identified orientation opportunities to better prepare students for success in the online learning environment. Type and format desired for faculty development sessions included small hands-on workshops with a focus on best practices for teaching online. Faculty also preferred one-on-one sessions targeted at specific issues, as opposed to scheduled face-to-face sessions, allowing many to learn in a way that best suits their style of learning. In addition to best practices, other topics identified by faculty for faculty development included assessment and evaluation, methods for student engagement, and incorporating other technologies such as Web 2.0 and synchronous/asynchronous communication technologies to further enhance the teaching and learning environment.

When asked about the need to develop quality standards for use in the design and development of online courses, faculty overwhelmingly agreed with this concept, adding that such standards would prove useful in establishing criteria, or a road map, for quality course design. Many believed the development of quality standards should remain at the department level, while some individuals desired a broader set of standards at the university level with room for customization at the department level. Faculty recommended that a committee comprised of a cross section of representatives across the institution, to include administrators, department heads, faculty with experience teaching online and faculty who do not teach online, students, and instructional technology staff provide input into the development of such standards. Faculty also suggested the committee investigates standards of quality for online education and course design at other institutions to assist with this process.

Administrator Interview Findings

The researchers interviewed the dean of the school of graduate studies and research and the academic deans of each of the three colleges at the university–the college of business & technology, the college of education and human services, and the college of arts and sciences. Additionally, the researchers interviewed 16 academic department heads from across the three academic colleges. The deans and academic department heads oversee both undergraduate and graduate online courses and programs. Of the 14 college of arts and sciences department heads, 8 were interviewed. The researchers interviewed 3 of the 5 department heads from the College of Business and Technology and 5 of the 6 department heads from the college of education and human services. The interview protocol questions were grouped into three sections: administrator concerns, institutional standards of quality for online courses, and faculty development needed related to online course instructional design. The findings of these interviews are presented by the three sections in the interview protocol.

Administrator Concerns

Administrators were asked three questions related to their concerns about offering online courses and/or programs at the university, asked for recommendations to their reduce concerns regarding offering online courses and programs, and asked whether or not they believe online instruction provides a quality learning experience for students. Analysis of the interview data revealed all administrators considered online instruction to be a quality learning experience for students; however, some verified their response by stating that quality for some online courses depended on the instructor, the design of the course, and/or implementation of some method of continuous improvement to ensure standards of quality are being met. Administrators expressed their concerns regarding the university offering online courses and/or programs and what it would take to reduce those concerns. The following categories representing their concerns emerged from the interview analysis: (1) barriers, (2) university and faculty preparedness, (3) student preparedness, (4) support and resources for faculty and students, (5) quality, and (6) communication.

Barriers

Concerns identified by the researchers as barriers refer to both internal and external barriers. One internal barrier discussed by several administrators could be classified as an epistemological barrier, in that some programs or courses simply did not fit the philosophy behind online education. It was questioned as to whether the content and/or nature of the course could be taught effectively online. For example, could science courses with associated labs or math courses be taught successfully in an online format? Another internal barrier identified related to the institution to include cost, course scheduling and availability, and how to provide tutorial assistance if needed.

External barriers are items outside of the control of the university, such as the economy and competition from profit and nonprofit organizations. The rise, fall, and rise again in gasoline prices combined with the promise of a cheap and quick associate's, bachelor's, master's or even a doctoral degree offered online without paying institutional fees and the ability to complete coursework in the comfort of one's home, provides great incentive for students to seek alternative routes for higher education. Additional external barriers identified by administrators included those related to student life and can be termed situational and dispositional. For example, situational barriers include a poor learning environment to complete an online course and/or lack of time to dedicate to an online course due to work or home responsibilities. Dispositional barriers are those that include a lack of a clear goal, inability to manage time properly, learning style differences, and the stress of multiple roles and/or motivation or attitude toward the content being taught.

University and Faculty Preparedness

Several administrators commented on the technological and human infrastructure of the university and its ability to support the demand for expanding online course and program development in order to meet the increasing demand of both the current and future student population for more online learning opportunities. In consideration of faculty preparedness, administrators acknowledged the need to support faculty in making the transition to the online environment. The university may be able to implement and maintain a technological infrastructure to support online learning; however, the infrastructure accomplishes little if the university does not provide an environment that prepares and supports its faculty to design and develop quality online courses. How faculty should be supported is a matter of debate. Many faculty believe in monetary incentive to develop and teach an online course, while administrators hold the belief that teaching, no matter the environment, is part of the job and not something that faculty should be "bribed" into doing. Also included in the university and faculty preparedness category, but somewhat tied to the internal institutional barrier addressed above, is the awareness of a need for broader availability of courses and diversity of scheduling to reach students in and out of state. Administrators acknowledged the lack of existence of a proper scheduling system and the need to develop one. One final concern expressed by the administrators interviewed related to the concept of sustainability. As the demand for online courses and programs will no doubt continue to rise, the infrastructure and technological support for faculty must be able to be sustained. This includes technology upgrades and resources for faculty such as quality computers, cameras, and other tools needed to develop an effective quality online course. Administrators believed that to sustain, the university has to determine continued sources of funding, both external and internal.

Student Preparedness

This category reflected student performance and student needs including technology skills and accessibility to technology. For example, online courses can be dynamic in nature in that they may incorporate video, audio, and synchronous learning tools that can provide course enrichment pieces that some faculty and administrators are concerned are missing from the online environment. In consideration of this concern, if students do not have the appropriate technology, such as high speed Internet access and computers with audio/video capabilities, their learning is affected as more time is spent on "fixing" the technological problems as opposed to learning with technology. The administration recognizes the fact that there is a high degree of motivation and self-directedness on the part of the online learner in order to be successful. A few administrators echoed the concern of the faculty regarding students' perceptions of the ease of completing online courses at their leisure and questioned how to dispel this false impression on the part of the student concerning the time and effort required to effectively engage in completing a course in the online learning environment.

Support and Resources for Faculty and Students

Administrators shared what they believed were some faculty perceptions related to offering online courses and programs. Some faculty may view online learning as a means of increasing enrollment at the university rather than a focus on quality instruction. Additionally, some faculty who have been teaching effectively in the traditional learning environment are reluctant to move their course to online delivery because of the fear of the time commitment and steep learning curve. Their belief is: if traditional instruction has been effective, why change? Why move a course online if it is going to require a change of philosophy as well as consumption of time? Finally, faculty perceive that there is a lack of socialization or interaction among students in the online learning environment, and that students do not make a connection to their university, leading to potential student retention issues. On the other hand, how should students be supported during this transition? Administrators acknowledged the need for training and support for both faculty and students. Additionally, in consideration of faculty perceptions, course development time and resources are needed to assist them in transitioning to online instruction. What those resources should be remains the question. Administrators recognize the importance of providing faculty with sufficient time to devote to both developing and teaching online courses; however, they are not ready to provide course "release time" as one measure of support. While both administrators and faculty alike are concerned about student preparedness for online learning, they did little in offering suggestions for addressing this concern.

Quality

One major concern of administrators regarding offering online courses and programs revolves around the concept of quality. Quality takes on multiple forms and meanings and brings into it the quality design of an online course as well as the value of the online learning experience in comparison to a traditional-based course. Some faculty and administrators wonder if rigor can be maintained in an online course, and question how learning can be measured in the online format. Also expressed were concerns regarding the student success rate in an online course, ways in which to manage the course, and assessment of the course for the purpose of continuous improvement. To date, no quality standards have been developed by the institution; however, administrators support this concept and similar to faculty, believe these standards should be developed from a broad-based perspective, customizable per content area and incorporate multiple stakeholders in the process of development.

Communication

The final category that emerged from the administrator interviews in relation to their concerns of online education, was that of communication. One aspect of communication identified by all administrators was the need for a greater flow of communication between academic department heads, deans, support entities within the university, faculty, and other key players. They addressed the potential need for reconsidering the structure of the university in addressing these types of academic concerns, and placing greater involvement of faculty and academic administrators in the decision making process relating to online education. Administrators held true to the belief that the institution needs to design and communicate both the vision of the role and priority of online education at the university. This vision, in turn, provides the driving force and rationale behind decisions made related to online education.

Institutional Standards of Quality for Online Courses

The second section of the interview protocol focused on level of awareness of institutional quality standards, who—if anyone—determines these quality standards, and the perceived level of input faculty members should provide in determining quality standards for online courses. Administrators were asked if they were aware of institutional quality standards. The majority of administrators said they were not aware of any quality standards established by the university; however, a few department heads shared that quality standards used were those provided by accrediting bodies for that discipline. The only measure of quality across disciplines is the annual course evaluation, which is used for both online course assessment and traditional course assessment. Some departments have implemented a common syllabus to ensure quality of instruction across all sections of a course.

Administrators were split on who they believed should be involved in deciding quality standards for online courses. Some identified the department of instructional technology and distance education (ITDE) as an authority in determining what needs to be included in an online course and what a quality online course should exemplify. Others believed standards should strictly come from the department because each discipline has their own unique needs and instructional approaches. Only one individual believed there should be no quality standards implemented for online courses and cited academic freedom as the reason, while others described a collaborative effort among departments, faculty, accrediting departments, and upper level administration as being the best approach for establishing these standards—a sentiment shared by the faculty.

The final question administrators were asked in this section related to the level of input they believed faculty members should provide in developing quality standards for online courses. Administrators recognized that faculty are the experts in their fields and thus value their input in establishing quality in online courses. They believed faculty should have a significant role in establishing standards while also obtaining departmental consensus on these standards of quality.

Faculty Development Related to Online Course Instructional Design

The final section of the interview protocol focused on questions related to faculty development needed for online course instructional design by the ITDE. Administrators were asked what formats—one-on-one, online or computer based sessions, workshops, or combination—they believed were most effective for faculty development sessions. Overwhelmingly, administrators believed that a combination of these approaches is the most effective method of providing training to faculty. Some responded that workshops or one-on-one sessions should be tailored to the specific discipline and/or the skill level of the specific faculty member.

When asked what types of faculty development sessions they would recommend be provided to their faculty, again they referenced department-specific training and to continue with the basics with how to work within the online course management system. They also desired to see sessions for developing audio enhanced instruction, technology troubleshooting, introductory sessions regarding new available technologies and software external to the course management system, creating videos, and opportunities to share, network and/or mentor with other faculty their technological abilities, pedagogical practices online, and instructional design tips.

The final question asked of administrators was the level of support they believed should be provided to faculty when developing and teaching an online course for the first time. Administrators repeated what they said previously regarding faculty needing resources and support for developing online courses and believed support and resources should be available to faculty at times convenient for faculty, as the need arises. Additional faculty support and resources identified by the administrators included the need for more personnel in the form of graduate assistants, instructional design, and technology support.

COMPARATIVE ANALYSIS OF RESULTS

Results from the administrator interviews echoed several faculty concerns and most likely concerns faced by other institutions going through similar online "growing pains." Administrators and faculty recognized the barriers faced by the institution in moving forward with online learning. These barriers included the level of preparedness of the university, faculty, and student for the technological infrastructure, logistical procedures such as scheduling, and methods to handle a different paradigm for teaching and learning. Administrators and faculty expressed concern about determining courses "fit" for an online environment and how to proceed with online course scheduling. The level of support provided to faculty and students was another concern that emerged from the administrator interviews. The support desired by faculty in the form of "release time" and/or monetary incentives were not the types of support administrators were willing to provide.

The issue of quality was raised by faculty in the study conducted by McElhany and Wickersham (2009) and again by the administrators interviewed for this article. Quality is scrutinized by many entities such as our coordinating boards and accrediting bodies and is not something relegated to just the online environment, but to teaching and learning as a whole. Administrators and faculty are responsible for providing evidence as to our students' growth and progress as a result of attending a university. However, when it comes to teaching an online course, quality is the first line of attack among those individuals opposing this medium. The authors of this study found this to be the case with both faculty and administrators alike. Both groups desired to see standards of quality developed and both were in agreement as to how this could be accomplished—via the collaboration of multiple entities, faculty, administrators, students and instructional technology staff while investigating standards established by other institutions. The last concern raised by administrators interviewed for this study was that of communication and how to involve faculty and administrators together in the decision making process.

CONCLUSIONS AND RECOMMENDATIONS

The university and administration must actively consider faculty concerns and suggestions for faculty development in order to assist the faculty and the institution in moving beyond "self" to the higher levels related to "impact," where the faculty member is able to give full and consistent attention to the curriculum and quality instruction.

Technology is not a one-time purchase. It is a budgetary item updated each year and serious consideration must be given to how and when to upgrade technology used by faculty, staff, and students alike. Commitments such as these provide faculty with some encouragement in knowing technological support will be available if and when the decision is made to teach online. Administrators must keep in mind that technology upgrades are more than a new computer. Additional technologies such as cameras, microphones, and software also assist faculty in truly enhancing the online learning experience.

It is recommended that the institution develop a procedure or matrix to assist departments in scheduling online courses and in determining courses fit for online learning by possibly identifying characteristics of both course content and of the online instructor. In this same vein, students enroll in online courses perceiving them as being easier than traditional classroom courses. Students must be provided with an orientation to the true online learning experience and the characteristics one must possess in order to be successful online. In addition, many students enroll in an online course technologically unprepared. They should be made aware of minimum technological requirements prior to enrolling, such as Internet access and speed and hardware/software capabilities.

A compromise should be reached via faculty and administrative dialog in determining the true need of support. For example, teaching online requires almost constant connection to the classroom to assist students one-on-one while also wearing multiple hats. The faculty member is not only the content or subject matter expert, but is now the first line of defense when it comes to student queries for technology troubleshooting. This could potentially add to the anxiety level of a faculty members who now realize their job description just had another line added to it—technological support. Providing faculty with support in the form of a graduate or teaching assistant may help to relieve this anxiety. Another recommendation is to make available consistent training and support for faculty from design through implementation of an online course so they know they are not alone in this process. A type of "just-in-time" support should be available to meet the needs and learning styles of individual faculty members. In addition, a comprehensive faculty development or training program is needed to assist faculty in moving beyond the mechanics of online course development to a focus on the curriculum and quality instruction.

> The faculty development program must enable faculty to see, experience, and integrate the many possibilities available for the development of quality courses. The program should be multitiered for the varied skill and knowledge levels of the faculty, and should provide for training at varied scheduled times and in varied delivery formats (small group, online, hands-on). (McElhany, 2007, p. 192)

These standards can provide a starting point for quality design and, coupled with the ongoing technology support provided by the administration, can hopefully alleviate some of the opposition toward online courses. Another recommendation in relation to quality is to ensure that best practices for assessment and evaluation are implemented. Assessment of student learning and course evaluations are two tools that can provide feedback as to the quality of course design; however, the current end-of-semester course evaluations typically focus on faculty performance as opposed to true student self-assessment of learning. In addition, an end-of-semester course evaluation is too little too late and it is recommended that strategies be implemented for the practice of formative evaluation in order to provide the instructor with information on quality design.

All too often, decisions are made by administrators regarding areas that will have a direct impact on faculty and students without the input of those individuals affected, causing frustration and distrust toward the administration. Giving faculty opportunity to provide input toward a decision, especially one with impact on faculty and students is a show of good faith and administrators may likely uncover aspects not currently in their thought process to assist them in making the best decision for all.

Both faculty and administrators have expressed similar concerns regarding online learning, ranging from standards for course development and delivery and the implementation of best practices for course and program assessment to providing effective support and training for both faculty and students. Concerns expressed by administrators and acknowledged by faculty as well as the recommendations offered by the authors are valid and valuable for the growth of online courses and programs. However, past decisions taken within this institution and other institutions have been based largely on the perspective of either faculty or administrators. Recognition of the uniqueness of the service of these two roles is important. Even greater in importance is reconciling the interdependence of these two entities. The concern perceptively voiced by administrators—communication—is the impetus for bridging the divide between administrators and faculty, resulting in online programs that are dynamic, effective, and vital. Communication that incorporates the knowledge and experience of faculty who serve on the front lines of online learning will promote faculty "buy in" and ownership, and will provide to administrators information and perspective related directly to those for whom both faculty and administrators have responsibility—online students.

REFERENCES

Allen, E., & Seaman, J. (2008). *Staying the course: Online education in the United States, 2008* (The Sloan Consortium. Babson Survey Research Group). Retrieved from http://www.sloanconsortium.org/publications/survey/pdf/staying_the_course.pdf

Brown, D. (Ed.). (2003). *Developing faculty to use technology: Programs and strategies to enhance teaching.* Bolton, MA: Ander.

Creswell, J. (1998). *Qualitative inquiry and research design: Choosing among five traditions.* Thousand Oaks, CA: SAGE.

George, A., Hall, G., & Stiegelbauer, S. (2006). *Measuring implementation in schools: The stages of concern questionnaire.* Austin, TX: Southwestern Educational Development Laboratory.

Hall, G., & Hord, S. (2001). *Implementing change: Patterns, principles, and potholes.* Boston, MA: Allyn & Bacon.

Lincoln, Y., & Guba, E. (1985). *Naturalistic inquiry.* Newbury Park, CA: SAGE.

Maguire, L. (2009). The faculty perspective regarding their role in distance education policymaking. *Online Journal of Distance Learning Administration, 12*(1). Retrieved from http://www.wetga.edu/~distance/ojdla/spring121/maguire121.html

Olson, J., & Hale, D. (2007). Administrators' attitudes toward web-based instruction across the UT System. *Online Journal of Distance Learning Administration, 10*(4). Retrieved from http://www.westga.edu/~ojdla/winter104/olson104.html

McElhany, J. A. (2007). *Interrelationships between faculty concerns and faculty development in the design, development, and delivery of online courses in select community colleges in Texas.* Doctoral dissertation, Texas A&M University-Commerce. (Publication No. AAT 3273643).

McElhany, J., & Wickersham, L. E. (2009). *Interrelationships between faculty concerns and faculty development in the design, development and delivery of online courses.* Manuscript submitted for publication.

Zotti, R. (2005, November). *Strategies for successful growth of online learning programs.* Presentation at the 11th Sloan-C International Conference on Asynchronous Learning Networks, Orlando, FL.

PART II

LEADING COURSE AND PROGRAM DESIGNS

CHAPTER 6

EXPERT INSTRUCTIONAL DESIGNER VOICES

Leadership Competencies Critical to Global Practice and Quality Online Learning Designs

Marcia L. Ashbaugh
University of Illinois

INTRODUCTION

The current economic challenge for students seeking to compete on a global scale with an advanced education has contributed to a continual rise in online enrollments (Allen & Seaman, 2010; Stern, 2009). However, Allen and Seaman (2012) reported that a persistent state of less than excellent online courses threatens to undermine the value of the educational opportunities afforded by the Internet. In spite of ongoing advances in instructional technologies, web-based higher academic pedagogies continued to demonstrate a lack of quality well into the new millennium (Means, Toyama, Murphy, Bakia, & Jones, 2009). The Means et al. (2009) study reported a perception of lower academic standards, a perception that was underscored with reports of an ongoing distrust in online courses by a majority of U.S. educators (Allen & Seaman, 2012). From an international perspective, Daniel (2007) referred to online pedagogies in India as "mostly rubbish" (Affordability section, para. 15), while Uysal and Kuzu (2009) reported a problem in Turkey of there being *no* online

Beyond the Online Course: Leadership Perspectives on e-Learning
pp. 71–101
Copyright © 2016 by Information Age Publishing

71

standards in existence. With due recognition of those making significant progress in improving the quality of online courses, there remains a question of whether enough is being done to meet growing learner demands.

Given the perceptions of lower quality pedagogies, the practice of designing products for online learning has been called into question in terms of the competencies and leadership of instructional designers needed to improve the situation (Beaudoin, 2007; Kowch, 2009; Naidu, 2007; Reeves, Herrington, & Oliver, 2004; Sims & Koszalka, 2008). This notion aligns with the business and trade industries where improvement of products has been inextricably linked to leadership. For example, after an earlier departure, Steve Jobs returned to Apple in 1997 and led an industry in re-envisioning ways of communicating information (Isaacson, 2011). Who can deny that his leadership resulted in exemplary products? From these observations, it was proposed that instructional design (ID) may likewise improve the quality of its products with applied leadership skills and attributes. To explore the assumption, a study was undertaken that would look for a potential connection between the quality of ID products and an instructional designer's leadership competencies as perceived by those in practice.

Often meaningful perceptions and insight will come through discourse, therefore, this was the method selected for exploring the issue of leadership's impact on quality. The in-depth interviews conducted with an international panel of expert practitioners resulted in themes that conveyed perceptions of practice from lived experiences. In the form of expressions from the participants, the findings extended the standards usually understood for ID and listed by groups such as the Association of Educational Communications and Technology, the International Board of Standards for Performance, Training, and Instruction, and others (Association of Educational Communications and Technology, 2012; International Board of Standards for Performance, Training, and Instruction, 2000; Larson & Lockee, 2009). Specifically, the participants identified competencies for designing online pedagogies with the added dimension of applied personal leadership characteristics deemed critical to high quality designs—competencies, attributes, and duties. In addition, specific instructional strategy components known to predict engagement (National Survey of Student Engagement, 2008) and learner satisfaction (Sims & Stork, 2007) framed a model for leading the online design process forward—strategy, vision, personality (interpersonal skills), productivity, emotional/psychological strength, values, and duties (mentoring). As a result of these findings, the goal of the study was satisfied: to determine that leadership from instructional designers has the potential for significant impact on the quality of online higher educational products.

BACKGROUND AND CONTEXT

Although standard ID competencies are well established for best practices, leadership competencies, per se, were nearly absent from the most common taxonomies (Association of Educational Communications and Technology, 2012; International Board of Standards for Performance, Training, and Instruction, 2000). While reviewing the cross-disciplinary literature, the topic of leadership as a characteristic of instructional designers was found to be just as scarce. There were, however, suggestions from a few that instructional designers may lead in the online educational transformation currently taking place by changing inappropriate or misapplied practices (Beaudoin, 2007; Kowch, 2009; Naidu, 2007; Reeves et al., 2004; Sims, 2006). Reports included ineffective and irrelevant design practices such as text-based lectures loaded into a course room, practice components, multiple choice quizzes and tests, a deck of slides for *learning enhancement*, a term paper—and not much more (Naidu, 2007). The notion of a misalignment of ID theory and online course designs resonated with Smith (in Fullan & Scott, 2009) who declared a *quiet crisis* in higher education from dependence on a model that "flies in the face of what we know about how people learn, the opportunities that technology presents to transform the educational enterprise and our historic record of failure with a rapidly diversifying population" (p. 20). In addition, Fullan and Scott (2009) observed a lack of leadership competency and experience in those expected to be change agents in education.

Questioning the design approach of adapting traditional course designs to the online environment was important because studies were beginning to show that people actually learn differently interacting with a computer than with a human interface (Dede, Dieterle, Clarke, Jass-Ketelhut, & Nelson, 2007; Spiro & DeSchryver, 2009). On-screen text and slideshows may not have been engaging the learner, yet various other multimedia affordances were showing promise to capture and hold attention (Thompson et al., 2011). Dede et al.'s (2007) study found positive learning outcomes from students connecting and learning in *new* ways—with computers, essentially a new *mode* of learning (Beaudoin, 2007). Later, Dede's (2011) explorations took him into mobile learning and the potential of engaging in learning in *new ways* with cell phones. The challenge for educators and producers of pedagogical materials is how to progress along the same continuum as the new paradigm of digital learning affordances and deliveries.

To explore the problem of quality in online course designs further, the small yet compelling study presented in this paper purposed to identify the critical ID competencies needed to produce effective designs for modern learning. Acting on the assumption that there may be a connection between leadership competencies—or characteristics in general—and an approach to the design process, a Delphi-style inquiry method of studying expert instructional design professionals in the context of practice was proposed and undertaken. Guiding the study were underlying questions: What is needed to improve quality in online courses? What characteristics of ID are lacking to meet global socio-educational demands? What competencies may be critical for designing effective pedagogies for a changing student body with diverse needs?

THEORETICAL FRAMEWORK

A literature review was conducted for purposes of grounding the phenomenological study in an identifiable theoretical framework. The review and analysis of a comprehensive body of scholarly work revealed that leadership theory encompasses copious philosophies, competencies, traits, attributes, attitudes, positions, and roles, which have been applied to a multitude of professions (Zenger & Folkman, 2009). With this complexity in mind, it seemed good to narrow the focus of the study to leadership competencies and attributes. Competency theory provided a relevant lens of exploration in that it was defined as behavioral demonstrations of knowledge, skill, and ability (Dooley et al., 2007). The definition was significant to the study as ID practice similarly demands multiple competencies (Larson & Lockee, 2009). Complicating the explication of these concepts, it was discovered during the literature analysis that both leadership and competency were described with an array of terms often used interchangeably. For example, competencies were also referred to as skills, abilities, or capabilities. Likewise, the term attributes included character, traits, emotions, temperament, or values. To mitigate obfuscation, and to gain a consensus of meaning for each term that would inform the study, the review resourced from a multi-disciplinary body of literary work. The cross-disciplinary approach was necessary, as the ID literature revealed a paucity of conceptualizations or theories of leadership in personal practice or of its impact on the field and its products (Kowch, 2009; Spillane, Halverson, & Diamond, 2004). Thus, a synthesis of theories framed the study being presented with multivariate characteristics of leadership categorized under competencies and attributes.

Leadership Competencies

A major predictor of work performance is competency, which enables the accomplishment of a desired or prescribed task (Dooley et al., 2007).

Through this lens, competency may be characterized as a category of leadership with multiple components, of which strategy, vision, personality (interpersonal skills), and productivity are defined below.

Strategy

It was widely reported that leaders are competent in developing a strategy that will include plans for the future (Scott, Coates, & Anderson, 2008). In other words, leaders are proactive in that they reflect on methods to prevent problems rather than wait for difficulties to happen. The Scott et al. (2008) study revealed that participants perceived leaders as engaging others in the process. In addition, leaders were said to collaborate for best possible solutions to not only current but unforeseen challenges. Others found that leaders know where to go for the answers or for the knowledge to create answers; they make the right connections in a network of colleagues and technology (Siemens, 2004; Sims, 2006).

Vision

A leader is commonly known to possess vision and, as such, is recognized as a visionary (Howard & Wellins, 2008). A leader also serves as a "steward of the vision" according to Sackney and Mergel (2007, p. 94). This person not only sees the vision, lives the vision through decisions, conveys the vision to others, enlivens others to the vision, promotes the vision but, at the same time, encourages others to share in the vision (Kouzes & Posner, 2007). As visionaries, leaders are expected to recognize innovation, forward-thinking, uniqueness, and "respond creatively to world conditions and the current state of their own society" (Greenleaf, 1977, p. 321). Scott et al. (2008) regarded this characteristic as having a capacity to see the *big picture* and to "read and respond to a continuously and rapidly changing external environment" (p. 11), a notion that may also be interpreted as possessing global competency (Reimers, 2009).

Personality

It was clear that leaders convey personality within the dynamics of human interaction. The notion resonated with a pervasive claim in literature that communication is the linchpin of all successful leadership (Sergiovanni & Corbally, 1984). Additionally, Sergiovanni and Corbally (1984) defined interpersonal competence as an essential force of leadership.

Moreover, demonstrations of genuineness stem from active communication. Kouzes and Posner (2007) described leaders as being caring, confident, and respectful to others. In contrast, Howard and Wellins (2008) cited the primary cause of failure by a large percentage of organizational leaders as the lack of interpersonal skills in their mentors. In other words, the essentials of being a leader were not being conveyed.

Productivity

Last, competency is evident in a leader's productivity; they understand how to work hard to achieve results. In fact, a study of leadership roles in virtual teams showed that learners preferred a producer (Chen, Wu, Yang, & Tsou, 2008), a leader who gets things done, over a visionary. In this capacity, leaders are expected to do what they say (Argyris & Schön, 1992) by converting words to action. In brief, results are produced by skillful leaders who have been trained in specific capacities, and work until the job is done.

Leadership Attributes

Emotional/Psychological

The category of attributes of leadership included emotional/psychological strength, which is interpreted, in one, as having confidence and displaying strength in diverse ways (Kirkpatrick & Locke, 1991). Through another lens, leaders are logical, make good choices, and, according to Kepner and Tregoe (1997), think rationally. Thus, the various ways of conveying emotional strength and psychological depth may be measured in how one thinks through and responds to challenges (Scott et al., 2008).

Values

Finally, an array of *values* described leadership, including one who operates from conscience (Walumbwa, Avolio, Gardner, Wernsing, & Peterson, 2008) and personal convictions, and is grounded in moral and ethical principles (Covey, 1989; Senge, 2006). With significance to one of this study's key assumptions, that leadership is a predictor of quality course designs, Walumbwa et al. (2008) put forth the notion that moral leadership is a predictor of "relevant organization outcomes" (p. 91).

When considered together, the leadership competencies listed above also describe the work of a designer or an ID team, and, consequently, provide a glimpse of how leadership may link to ID practice. Therefore, enhanced leadership competencies are proposed herein as factors in activating and maintaining quality, globally-accessed learning designs.

METHODOLOGY

Research Design

For exploration into the problem of quality in online pedagogical course designs, a phenomenological study engaged expert instructional designers—who shared a common interest in resolving a mutual problem within a defined social setting (Gelo, Braakman, & Benetka, 2008; Wenger, 1998)—to participate in a Delphi-style, narrative inquiry study. Drucker (1981) said, "It is the practitioner rather than the scholar who develops the discipline, who synthesizes experience into testable concepts, that is into theory, who codifies, who finds and tests new knowledge, and who teaches and sets the example" (p. 1). Thus, an idiographic strategy proffered a means of representing practitioner reality through retrospective inquiry. The approach aided in extracting deep or hidden meanings underlying a social phenomenon—as in how instructional designers perceived the pedagogical influence of leadership attributes in practice. In the end, consensus was sought from the panel members on an emerging model of leadership.

Understanding that experience impacts decision making in practice (Ertmer et al., 2008), experts were sought out for the study in order to discover what drives the critical decisions that impact pedagogical quality of online outputs. Following purposive selection from 610 Association of Educational Communications and Technology members solicited through e-mail, 7 respondents met the qualifications of at least 7 years' experience in ID, with 3 of those in online design (those selected actually averaged over 16 years' experience). Of the 7 who qualified, 6 completed the study. In addition, the group included both males and females from U.S. and Canadian universities. Sources of data included interview transcripts from research conversations, e-mails, personal documents, and institution-generated student evaluations. For analysis of findings, constant comparison analysis (Glaser & Strauss, 1977) was used to examine data until congruency was found in the units of meaning, or themes, identified. Subsequently, the interview data was corroborated for accuracy and relevance to personal documents—online course designs created by the participants.

Data Instrumentation and Collection

As the researcher and main instrument of collection (Seidman, 2006), I asked a series of questions that were each an expansion on the general question of which leadership competencies were deemed critical to effective online ID course development. To establish credibility, as well as to guide the study, a research protocol was first developed to organize the data collection procedure. The protocol called for three rounds of in-depth interviews during which the participants were asked the same 15 semistructured, open-ended questions. However, certain questions inspired important digressive thoughts; consequently, probing questions were added for eliciting clarification and deeper meaning.

Throughout the study, ID voices were captured in the context of daily practice in their respective institutions; therefore, all data and citations used in the following analysis are confined to these settings. It is hoped that the ideas recorded may resonate with others in similar situated contexts. In this way, the participating designers were asked to inform the study from a social constructivist perspective toward construction of meaning for a shared practice (Wenger, 1998). Experts often voice common experiences which, when made known, become triggers of change in a community of practice (Campbell et al., 2009). The methodology was indicative of a Sharma-Bryer and Fox (2008) study that described the typology as an exploration into the "ultimate essence of the experience" (p. 322) from interpreted narratives, which translates into an authentic documentation of participants' voices.

Additionally included in the research protocol were several tests of reliability. Because of the intimate nature of narrative research, and to minimize influence on the participant's responses, the research was conducted while practicing bracketing—a setting aside of one's personal beliefs and ideas (Moustakas, 1994). This is not always an easy task when involved in dialog, as a researcher will naturally insert her personality, interest, and investment in the topic into the interview dynamics (Onwuegbuzie, Leech, & Collins 2008). To the extent possible, though, bracketing was accomplished through active listening and by recording copious research notes in several journals, which later provided data for reflexivity (Kaplan, 2004). For example, one journal recorded perceptions of participants' emotional states, attitudes, and responsiveness to the questions or to the interviewer. Another journal recorded the research process, researcher emotions and attitudes, and the challenges of doing research.

Indicative of a Delphi study approach, group consensus on the competencies and characteristics named was attempted and achieved. In this way, reliability and accuracy of data were established by comparing participants' answers, then feeding those back to each participant for critical comments. In addition, inter-rater reliability was provided at the conclusion of the study by an external qualitative design expert, Laurie Bedford of Walden University, who corroborated all methodologies, tests, and findings. Although the study was small in terms of number of participants, the rich data from a group of experts in ID was, at the least, a great conversation re-starter of what has been before and is still considered an important characteristic for designers of online products—leadership.

ANALYSIS OF FINDINGS

For developing themes and theories from the data, a post hoc analysis of transcripts from over 14 hours of recorded narrative relied on NVivo9 software for a constant comparative analysis technique (Gelo et al., 2008). Phrases (units of meaning) from the transcribed data were labeled with descriptors found in the business, organizational, and educational literature. Initially, numerous phrases were coded using the general categories of leadership characteristics: competencies, attributes, and duties. However, further distillation generated the themes: strategy, vision, personality (interpersonal skills), productivity, emotional strength, values, and a duty to mentor or to pass on knowledge. The iterative process resulted in some phrases being reallocated; although, at times, the technique generated additional themes which, together, built the theories produced in the study. A list of themes, along with sample excerpts extracted from the data (abbreviated in most cases), are displayed in Table 1 to illustrate how phrases were organized into themes.

Since the context and focus of the study centered in the participants' daily experiences, an effort was made during the analysis phase to link the perceptions to practice. Various conceptions and perceptions comprise one's daily reality in terms of meanings and interpretations attached to the world in which one operates (Pratt, cited in Konings et al., 2005), as well as govern decisions in the work environment (Stein, Shephard, & Harris, 2011). To associate the leadership competencies and characteristics named as critical to quality course designs, participants' sample documents (online course designs) were evaluated using a modified Quality Matters rubric (Maryland Online, 2010) displayed in Table 2. Quality of the documents was determined from the positive ratings for course structures, including relevant and effective instructional strategies and components.

A second analysis looked for an alignment between measurable objectives, relevant assessments, instructional strategies, and authentic activities, a construct considered essential to quality academic designs (Bernard et al., 2009; Sims, 2011). Finally, a summary of ratings from student evaluations of completed courses, which accompanied the participant artifacts, found three major quality determinants present: opportunities for

**Table 1.   Example of Coded Phrases
and Development from In-Depth Interviews**

Theme	Excerpt Phrase	Participant
Strategy	Meet goals set by client: learning objectives, strategies, and personalized	P4
	Allow customer to be part of decisions	P5
	Collaborative team-building	P1
	Interactivity for digital learner	P1
	Offer client informed options	P2
	Synthesize best learning and ID theories; include real-world tasks in design	P3
Vision	Stay current	P5
	Backup designs with research	P1
	Partners with other educators to accept new approach	P3
Productivity	Quality control by team testing each element	P1
	Manage time, resources; meet deadlines, prioritize, produce good product	P6
Personality (inter-personal skills)	Satisfy customer through communication and provide solutions	P5
	They (the team) have fun	P1
	Provide expectations, build others up	P6
Emotional/psycho-logical strength	Accept other's ideas and go with, work with ideas of others (letting go of positional privilege)	P2
Values	Respect is foundation of leadership in design process	P2
	Accept consequences of decisions, self-leadership, self-regulation, self-management, self-discipline	P6
Duties (mentor)	Model collaboration (to faculty, team)	P6

engagement (NSSE, 2008), activities with learner-centeredness at the core (Sims & Stork, 2007), and overall student satisfaction with the courses.

Together, the results of the analyses not only identified aspects of practice deemed to be critical to its practitioners, they also suggested a relationship of leadership to higher quality pedagogies. As accuracy was considered paramount, general first impressions by the researcher of the participants' narratives, along with results of initial data analyses, were reported back to the participants in both verbal and written form for comments and elaboration. The corroborative step was completed before the third and final round of interviews and lent additional reliability to the study, as a more complete context of the research study's findings was illu-

**Table 2.   Ranking of Course Designs
by a Modified Quality Matters Rubric of Standards**

Categories/Standards	Percent of Points Possible
Learner Objectives	
2.3. The learning objectives are stated clearly and written from the students' perspective.	100
2.4. Instructions to students on how to meet the learning objectives are adequate and stated clearly.	90
2.5. The learning objectives address content mastery, critical thinking skills, and core learning skills.	90
2.1. The course learning objectives describe outcomes that are measurable.	80
Assessments and Measurements	
3.2. The course grading policy is stated clearly.	100
3.5. "Self-check" or practice assignments are provided, with timely feedback to students.	100
3.4. The assessment instruments selected are sequenced, varied, and appropriate to the content being assessed.	90
3.1. The types of assessments selected measure the stated learning objectives and are consistent with course activities and resources.	80
3.3. Specific and descriptive criteria are provided for the evaluation of students' work and participation.	73
Learner Engagement	
5.2. Learning activities foster instructor-student, content-student, and if appropriate to the course, student-student interaction.	93
5.4. The requirements for student interaction are clearly articulated.	90
5.1. The learning activities promote the achievement of the stated learning objectives.	87
5.3. Clear standards are set for instructor responsiveness and availability (turn-around time for e-mail, grade posting, etc.)	70

minated by each individual participant's situational perspective (Seidman, 2006). To capture the essence of their unique contributions to the study, a profile of each participant was developed and is located in Appendix A.

A MODEL OF LEADERSHIP FOR ID

Overall, the findings showed that a leadership mindset is positively associated with high quality work products when certain characteristics are in

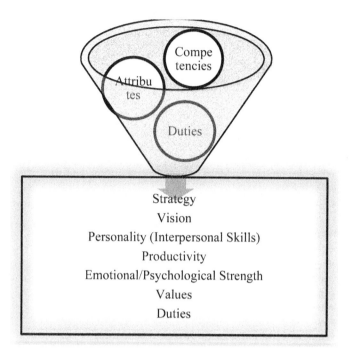

Figure 1.   Model of leadership for instructional design.

operation. When synthesized, the results formed a model of leadership for ID. The major categories of the model—competencies, attributes, and duties—as well as the themes listed in Table 1, are synthesized and displayed in graphic form in Figure 1. Subsequently, the model is more fully explicated in this section.

Strategy

When the study's participants discussed various aspects of strategy, two distinct subthemes were identified: overall design process strategy and instructional strategy for the design relevant to digital environments. It was articulated that it takes a leadership mindset to make (a) strategic decisions during the design process for the team to research best options for providing strict alignment of objectives to assessments, content, and activities; and (b) strategic decisions for the design structure to afford engagement with context-relevant learning flexible enough to adapt quickly to advancing technologies.

Design Process Strategy

The importance of the leadership competency of strategy for the design process resonated with Scott et al. (2008), who implied that leaders are competent in developing strategic, proactive plans for the future. In other words, leaders are adept at engaging others in the process to collaborate for best possible solutions to current and unforeseen problems and challenges. Dooley et al. (2007) concluded that this type of competency is evident during the creation and implementation of courses and in the critical decisions underpin high quality, effective, and relevant designs. In this capacity, leadership is essential to the building and functioning of the team for an efficacious design and development effort. Participant 6 stated this position on decision-making,

> Leadership really deals more with the types of decision that one has to make and the way that one makes and executes these decisions ... decision-making skill is definitely one of those leadership competencies ... as well as willingness to accept the consequences of your decisions ... you take responsibility for that and you don't shift it to someone else.

Another aspect of strategy is connectedness. The views of participants in this study were consistent with those (Siemens, 2004; Sims, 2006) who posited that leaders make the right connections in a network of colleagues and technology for expertly accomplishing the task at hand or anticipated. Likewise, Scott et al. (2008) posited that leaders know where to go for the answers or knowledge to create the answers to questions of design.

Collaboration with others in the field, as well as with those from other disciplines, adds a dimension of connectedness to practice from which springs inspiration for creating innovative and quality courses. Sims (2009) described a proactive mindset of collaboration and connectedness with each design stakeholder to ensure quality learning products as outcomes to ID efforts. Participant 1 stated,

> I think it's the leaders who can create and will create collaborative teams made up of people with diverse perspectives and talents, skills, and expertise ... the ones who will be developing the engaging, motivating, interactive, and effective learning environments for today's learners.

The study also found that a critical factor in producing quality courses is staying current with research in technologies and emerging learning theories. Connectedness and collaboration are not dissociative. One participant gave an illustration of an online research writing course he had written that resulted in a reported satisfying outcome for the learners. It required tailoring the course to the research he had done on current best practices for online learning and from collaborating with others who had already envisioned and/or designed a course like this. He also relied on media experts for the latest methods of presenting the course content; these were strategic leadership actions that resulted in an effective course. Summarizing this aspect of the strategy theme, Participant 3 expressed,

> you have to have a knowledge of the latest learning theories and the latest instructional design theories in order to be a leader. You also have to be able to implement those theories, individually and in concert with each other, to achieve best practice, instructional strategies, or instructional strategy design.

At the same time, online delivery requires letting go of outdated practices for effective learning. Participant 1 recognized this need,

> We've known ADDIE forever, we've known this model forever; but, the online models are different because it's a different delivery modality. So just get the most current research and information you can on what is best practices.

Design Structure Strategy

The second type of strategy linked to leadership competency was described as the ability to specify appropriate—research-based and contextual—instructional strategies with relevant learning components—to the student and to the environment, and having those align with the intended learning outcome. A depiction of this concept is conveyed in Figure 2 and articulated by Participant 6,

> We would tend to focus on, as far as basic axioms of instructional design, the one that objectives are measurable and that the objectives are aligned with the assessments, and the objectives and the assessments are aligned with the content ... allowing you to meet the objectives.

A related issue is the composition of the instructional strategy proposed for the design. Figure 3 is a compilation of the components identified by the study group as paramount to a quality online course: authentic tasks, interaction, learner-controlled tasks, problem solving, theory-based instruction, and values-based instruction. Together, the components provide a foundation of engagement and learner satisfaction through a contextualized and personalized learning approach posited by Sims and Stork (2007) as essential for effective online learning.

Extending the identification of strategic components in general, the expert designers' experiences paralleled examples of innovative approaches in the literature, such as social networking and mobile technologies (Velletsianos & Miller, 2008). Their perceptions underscored

Figure 2. Components of a well-designed online course structure.

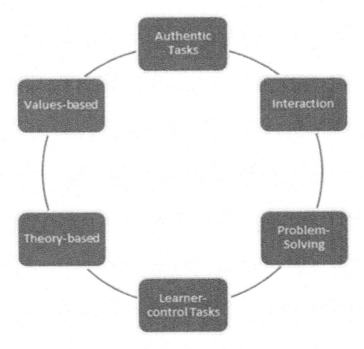

Figure 3.   Components of a well-designed online course instructional strategy.

Reimer's (2009) conclusions that instructional designers demonstrate competence—distributive, collaborative, and participatory leadership—by specifying nontraditional resources where appropriate for, in his study, an international student body. For example, The University of the People (www.universityopeople.org) requires its designers to select open source (free) textbooks, applications, and journals to expand access and affordability for their free online program. Participant 2 expressed her strategy as having the flexibility to see a future outcome through a unique point of view and to expand her own knowledge of design components and their potential as having, as she stated,

> the ability to recognize and work within the concepts of *different* and *better.*
> (Emphases added)

It is this kind of innovative and global thinking that demonstrates strategic leadership on the part of the instructional designers with an eye on the future.

Vision

Zenger and Folkman (2009) studied the effectiveness of leaders from a cross section of organizations and identified the characteristic of strategy in operation, which was summarized as, "to translate organizations [*sic*] vision and objectives into challenging and meaningful goals for others" (p. 70). The assumption is that business—and educational—institutions first develop a vision before a strategy. Likewise, instructional designers translate the vision and objectives of a client for an educational goal into a course design. From this perspective Participant 6 remarked, "I take information and I translate it into an environment that facilitates learning." During such pursuit, the instructional designer infuses a measure of his or her own vision for what may be the appropriate structure, strategy, affordance, and learning components for a high quality learning experience. Participant 6 interpreted this competency as, "the ability to see the big picture." With a similar perspective, Participant 1 likened the visionary role of an instructional designer to leading a sports team,

> it's having this quarterbacking skill, being able to read and see things two or three tasks ahead so that you … can foresee possible issues or challenges that are going to come up and try to get those taken care of before your team is at that level.

Second, a vision for the field and for education in general was viewed by one panel member as being aware of "contemporary" and "emerging technologies." Going beyond awareness to action, Participant 2 stated vision is,

> the ability to lead in the design ... implementation ... development of the new things that come along.

Instructional designers may envision and design for future trends in delivering education afforded by social networking technologies (Ashbaugh, in press). The findings in this present study confirmed that instructional designers demonstrate vision by specifying nontraditional resources, such as wikis (Baggio, 2008). However, having a vision for new pedagogies carries a responsibility to investigate its potential. One participant shared a story of experimentation with a wiki before she had gained a thorough understanding of how one works. Her embarrassment over not having learned enough about the technology was obvious as she told her story of "a disaster" in front of a classroom full of students. The lesson learned was that, while freely exploring innovation, designers need to resist prescribing new technologies before doing diligent research.

Personality (Interpersonal Skills)

For the design team, communication and meaningful dynamics are essential to a quality outcome and emanate from a leader's personality. Larson and Lockee (2009) considered interpersonal communication within diverse settings as vital although how to approach others in the intimate settings instructional designers often operate within requires the characteristics of personal leadership. The study participants related that instructional designers listen carefully to arguments by the team or clients and articulate decisions from a practical, firm position. Interpersonal skills afford designers of online pedagogies an opportunity to exhibit leadership by offering academic and relevant arguments for the design, strategic, and team decisions while taking responsibility for the final outcomes. This view of leadership in action was expressed by Participant 1 as being,

> able to communicate technological possibilities, letting people know what is possible with technology ... being able to be quite frank with them.

Participant 6 shared his experience with leading in creating positive team dynamics,

> I need to provide an atmosphere, a working atmosphere, that is not intimidating and that helps them feel that they can be creative, and that they can

inject their ideas and criticisms in areas that they see needs improvement, so that they can participate with this.

Another participant stressed the need for patience and partnership by working with clients to help them see a better way, through the lens of a professional, while acknowledging the clients' and the advising subject matter experts' unique contributions.

From a synthesis of the participants' perceptions on personality, it was apparent that the typical view of communication considered essential to leadership (Howard & Wellins, 2008)—ability to articulate—may not provide a broad enough understanding. Communication assumes various forms that stem from personality—interpersonal skills and attitude, ability to convey ideas and to practice reciprocity, and respect and honesty. Clearly, in this study it was shown that an instructional designer brings a unique personality to a design with a potential for leading in its quality outcome through each dynamic of interpersonal encounters.

Productivity

The study group named most of the known competencies of productivity associated with a good ID process such as: "meet deliverables," "lead in implementation," "time management," "know strengths of team," as well as motivating skillset improvement and keeping costs down. Often, the range of tasks involved in developing academic courses within client time and budget constraints (Moore & Kearsley, 2005) demands leading in hard work as well as finishing the job, in spite of limitations by institutions bent on following what Campbell et al. (2005) deemed cost-recovery models. In the context of preferring cost over quality, Participant 4 personally witnessed a less expensive approach to practice of relying on template-based design strategies. Considered an unproductive practice, she remarked,

> I understand why they were doing what they were doing ... but they could never reach real high quality doing what they were doing.

Ostensibly, there is an inherent quality of leadership that emanates from an inner desire for meeting goals, for getting the job done, and for completion without sacrificing relationships. Participant 6 viewed the motivational aspect of leadership as "set[ting] the course" while another Participant 1 summarized,

> [it's] using your inner relational skills to build positive, collaborative, cohesive teams to meet your deliverables ... plus you have to know how to moti-

vate them if you're going to get all this done ... and helping them honor and respect each other's skills and expertise.

From an end results perspective, Participant 1 added,

The lead instructional designer sets the tone for the team. If he or she is proficient, the end product will reflect that.

Emotional/Psychological Strength

A leader possesses or gains a measure of emotional or psychological strength, which is often displayed in intentional decisions made from self-confidence and strength of purpose, although this is not always an easy task when confronting inflexible institutions and faculty with entrenched epistemological ideas (Campbell et al., 2009). Conversely, participants in this study described experiences in which an inner strength was activated to lay aside personal preference in lieu of honoring a colleague or client's theories. This attribute was seen in the previous theme of strategy when a participant recognized an outdated practice and used a better approach. Maxwell (2007) considered leaders psychologically strong when they operate on the offensive and not the defensive, with openness to other ideas, opinions, and criticisms. On the other hand, Campbell et al. (2009) found instructional designers in moral conflict with client epistemologies and often without a sense of power to make changes. To this end, the study participants cited having "a lot of patience" and "being able to work with *it* [emphasis added]." Clearly, instructional designers are called upon to make complex, emotional decisions within a shifting learning environment while maintaining a rational approach (Kepner & Tregoe, 2007); and this study suggests they will need leadership strengths to succeed.

Values

One area of concern for instructional designers observed was operating from a set of personal values—for the entire spectrum of stakeholders, although, particularly for the learner. One particular participant in this study stressed his lived out values and perceived personal leadership in this way:

I think that, for a leader, it really involves who you are even more than what you do ... in the field of instructional design, I guess I'm looking at more character traits than competencies ... I would probably still hold honesty as the most important ... it's about honesty and integrity.

The personal perspective of leaders with values and the significant influence on design practice is echoed repeatedly in the literature and has been conceptualized as an individual having an inherent moral purpose (Fullan, 2001). Moreover, the Campbell et al. (2009) study revealed deeply held values in instructional designers who considered their practice a moral one with important social responsibility and influence, who "prefer[ed] to practice within a zone of moral coherence" (p. 660). For example, care is given to provide for the vulnerable, the disabled, and a multicultural learning community.

Duties

The theme of ID duties was discussed by participants mainly in the context of mentorship. With a sense of obligation to pass on knowledge gained through experience, instructional designers interpret the value of course designs to the client and to others through verbal and nonverbal interactions. In the process, there is a natural tendency to act as a mentor or instructor in the more complex nuances of design. As one participant stated about her experience with clients,

> You are educating at the same time that you are doing the design ... you have to double check on that all the time, that people actually understand what it is you're doing.

Adding a layered view to the mentoring process, Participant 2 articulated the need for acting in multiple capacities in her role as an instructional designer with faculty oversight,

> So, mentoring the junior people just in the basics of instructional design and how it works, sometimes on an individual level, sometimes they're working in the context of the larger project, so in the project of the team ... and sometimes I have teams of instructional designers, so it may be your journeyman instructional designer who is actually him or herself mentoring these juniors ... to help them mentor the juniors.

A perception of diminished status by instructional designers in a Rogers, Graham, and Mayes (2007) study implicated a field tasked with educating the world from a powerless position. Campbell et al. (2009) described study subjects' views on the designer's status as a "technician that primarily implements techniques and principles" (p. 661). The study participants (Campbell et al., 2009) described feelings of low respect and held perceptions of negative impact on their professional status and influence. It was argued in the study that instructional designers suffered from an historical view of leadership as one of a positional role. However, it is increasingly evident that individuals in any role benefit from a leadership perspective (Gressick & Derry, 2010; Kowch, 2009). Beaudoin (2007) supported the notion of distributed and multiple leadership roles as important to the future of instructional technology (p. 520). More than this, the ID demands regard for the earned role of leader (DeBlois, 2005). Similar to Campbell et al.'s studies (Campbell et al., 2005, 2009), DeBlois (2005) found that a majority of faculty and practicing instructional designers shared a perspective that includes a change agent and visionary role for leading the academy on what and how to prepare for a fluid educational world. Most significant to the conclusions offered in this paper, the participants in DeBlois' study linked success with embracing the leadership attributes needed for advancing the field. Therefore, instructional designers of higher academic online pedagogies are challenged to embrace the leadership competencies and approaches that underpin exemplary practice.

DISCUSSION

This study has shown that multiple competencies and leadership characteristics combine to create a quality product. Zenger and Folkman (2009) coded thousands of responses to their longitudinal survey study and arranged the findings into a model of five expressions of exemplary leadership—character, leading organizational change, focus on results, personal capability, and interpersonal skills. With close resemblance to their work, that which was critical for leading in quality design practice was summarized by Participant 1,

> Leadership competencies are, again, having a process, having a process that works; pulling together people, making sure that the interrelationship skills are there and working; knowing who to contact for help; again, using clear communication skills to convey the purpose and timelines, keeping them on the timelines; and, trying to build a collaborative team who have buy-in and ownership of this course.

In contrast to the Participant 1's more global perspective, Participant 3 stressed his view of technical skills as critical to quality. He stated,

> Unless you can implement best practice in instructional strategies, the online instruction, basically, remains back in the dark ages of instruction.... Looking at online course quality is figuring out which factors matter the most. And so when everything is said and done, leadership is about finding those factors.

Finally, Participant 2 summarized the study's findings with thoughts that underscore the significance and focus of the study: learners of the world and their futures,

> I do think that the leadership qualities are integral to the course design, to the student learning, to the outcomes that you're going to get, to future transfer ... not only in the subject matter content that you are doing, but also transfer in the instructional design principles and the educational precepts that are really important in higher education everywhere.

The evidence gathered in this study suggests that practicing instructional designers are capable of adopting and operationalizing leadership skills, abilities, and attitudes critical for improving course designs that equip future world citizens and leaders. As one participant expressed, "it's having a mindset." That mindset is broad and demands a new way of thinking. A new way of thinking or a new approach is often linked to those who lead, and just as often to the development of new or better products. As online education progresses, the burden of research is continuing to show that course structures and materials written for one type of learning situation need to be different than when learning in another—and since most instructional designers in practice today were trained for traditional requirements, they may need to be re-tooled for creating relevant and quality online products. In other words, instructional designers need a reorientation in thinking about designing for an evolutionary change in educational deliveries. This is because the literature increasingly called for a response to the demands of a new paradigm of learners for an instructional design vision that will encourage global collaboration among institutions (Durdu, Yalabik, & Cagiltay, 2009) and cultures (Reimers, 2009), through best-fit models and relevant curricula for quality online learning.

CONCLUSION AND FUTURE RESEARCH

Arguably, leadership is a controversial concept for the typical designer who has been trained for a supportive role (Campbell et al., 2009) with very little potential for leading on a personal or positional level (Gressick & Derry, 2010), let alone lead in a new way of learning. However, the seldom discussed notion of leadership for daily ID practice (Kowch, 2009) posited in this paper was intended to be an extension of a conversation started by leaders in the field during the last decade (Beaudoin, 2007; Naidu, 2007; and others) who called for leadership recognition for an effective ID practice. The experts whose voices are heard in this paper augmented the concerns of their predecessors by adding a compelling response: to identify and understand what will enhance the quality of learning events for students from any culture who are, or hope to be, engaged in e-learning.

It is hoped that this study creates a sense of urgency for developing new research streams; for infusing leadership competency training into advanced degree programs; for furthering inquiry into practitioners' perceptions of leadership's place in daily practice, and for broadening the research variables such as gender, ethnic, and geographic effects. There is a need for continued research into the underpinning factors of creating quality academic course designs. The critical nature of improving the structures for learning outcomes was highlighted by Participant 3, who warned that if quality does not become the focus of attention and dissemination in the field of online instructional design, "the majority of the instruction is going to remain inferior." One remedy to this indictment was suggested earlier by Hannum (2009) who admonished researchers to rigorously explore "variables that directly influence outcomes" (p. 173) of the online environment. Still others shared the need for continuing domain-specific research on strategies required in a modern learning environment (Bollettino & Bruderlein, 2008; Hong & Sullivan, 2009). Finally, Reimers (2009) promoted emergence of grassroots efforts to organize, define, and promote global competency throughout curricula—an ongoing challenge for leaders in instructional design.

To further this discussion, course designers and others are urged to pay attention to the powerful voices of experts in the field guiding this study for how increased leadership characteristics in practice will move the online education agenda forward toward more excellent products. It is further hoped that the conversation begun by instructional designers in the previous decades will gain renewed attention to the more critical elements of leadership and its role in the quality of online learning events.

APPENDIX A: PROFILES OF STUDY PARTICIPANTS

Participant 1 (P1)

A full-time professor who instructs at a U.S. university with significant online course offerings, P1 leads a teacher training department from both an instructional technology and educational leadership background. While bringing 12 years of experience to the study, P1's extensive knowledge in issues of quality course designs added credibility to the findings of this study. While filtering leadership through a lens of team leader, this participant emphasized interpersonal skills and knowledge of team skills in that role and focused on a leader's need for personal knowledge, skills, expertise, and proficiency. Design leadership competencies perceived by her included knowledge of current research on best practices and team-building. P1 was concerned with increasing student learning by aligning course strategies and activities with course and program outcomes. In addition, P1 expressed a belief that leadership decisions influence designs through knowledgeable choices for affordances such as appropriate technology and texts, as well as reliance on student feedback for improvement. Moreover, the experienced practitioner attributed a team-building, collaborative process to a successful practice of quality online course design.

Participant 2 (P2)

P2 is a full-time professor with teaching, training, and research duties for a Canadian university's educational technology department with 22 years of experience in the field. While filtering leadership through a lens of a team leader role, P2 emphasized leadership as a means to an end: creating effective learning (happy clients) through team collaboration and growth. She focused on a leader's ability to lead projects, giving clients informed options, and creating innovative, team-based designs. Design leadership competencies perceived by P2 included recognizing what is "different and better" as well as respectfully conveying the validity of instructional design principles underlying the recommendations offered to clients. Additionally, P2 was concerned with increasing student learning by advocating activity theory, mediation with tools, constructivist strategies, and authentic activities for metacognitive learning. With conviction, P2 acknowledged a leader's decisions influence designs through reliance on student involvement, students as "co-builders" of contextual, situational course topics and assessments. She believes that, ultimately, leaders impact student satisfaction in these ways.

Participant 3 (P3)

With over 7 years of experience practicing in the instructional design field, P3 added knowledge to this study from multiple perspectives and background in the e-learning industry. While completing a PhD in instructional technology (at a U.S. university), P3's extensive research in assessing quality of course designs lent valuable input. While filtering leadership through a lens of expertise in and application of instructional design theories, P3 emphasized influencing others toward improving quality of online instruction. He focused on a leader's ability to implement latest instructional design strategies for best practice. Design leadership competencies perceived by P3 included knowledge of current research, partnership with developers and instructors, and influence on many from a position of expertise and from evidence-based knowledge of best practices and approaches. Furthermore, P3 was concerned with increasing student learning by affording better and current technology-based strategies, and inclusion of real-world tasks in design affordances.

Participant 4 (P4)

P4 reported a semiretired status as an expert instructional designer with 20 years of experience in the field. As an adjunct online professor with a technical university, she instructed doctoral students, and was a frequent presenter at educational technology conferences worldwide. Although withdrawing from the study after two interviews, her valuable contributions to the study were included in the findings.

While filtering leadership through a lens of modeling behavior through patience in collaborating with the stakeholders, P4 emphasized understanding and aligning with institutional and students' educational goals to improve quality of online instruction. She strives for a course design that meets the needs of all learners, no matter their learning style or mode. Design leadership competencies perceived by P4 included knowledge of current research, as well as conference attendance and presentations as ways of being a "life-long learner" in the field. P4 was concerned with increasing student learning by affording good student interaction strategies in the course room.

Participant 5 (P5)

A director of a U.S. university learning center providing faculty development in instructional technology, P5 was working to improve his practice by seeking a PhD in the field. Quality of instructional design was the focus of his work, making him a particularly qualified candidate for this study. Although study participation was limited to the first interview due to scheduling conflicts, P5's important insights were included in the findings for RQ1.

Participant 6 (P6)

As dean of online studies and distinguished lecturer of graduate studies for a U.S. university, P6 contributed significantly from his 20 years of experience in the field of educational technology and design. The scholar presented compelling and passion-filled views on the study topic. While filtering leadership through a lens of both technical and foundational skills in instructional design systems, P6 emphasized honesty, interpersonal skills, and self-regulation as critical to improving quality of online instruction. He focused on a leader's ability to stay current in the latest instructional design strategies for effectively promoting student learning. Design leadership competencies perceived by P6 include setting objectives and relevant, measurable assessments grounded in the learner's context or situation, thus, a view toward "what the learner gets out of it." Moreover, P6 was concerned with increasing student learning by affording analysis and problem-solving strategies and activities through interaction and inclusion of real-world tasks in the design affordances.

REFERENCES

Allen, I. E., & Seaman, J. (2010). *Learning on demand: Online education in the United States, 2009*. Retrieved from http://www.sloan-c.org/publications/survey/pdf/learningondemand.pdf

Allen, I. E., & Seaman, J. (2012). *Going the distance: Online education in the United States, 2011*. Retrieved from http://www.onlinelearningsurvey.com/reports/goingthedistance.pdf

Argyris, C., & Schön, D. (1992). *Theory in practice: Increasing professional effectiveness*. San Francisco, CA: Jossey-Bass.

Ashbaugh, M. L. (2013). Leadership from ID (instructional design) for Web 2.0 adoption: Appropriate use of emerging technologies in online courses. In C. Wenkel & P. Blessinger (Eds.), *Increasing student engagement and retention in e-learning environments: Web 2.0 and blended learning technologies, Cutting edge technologies in higher education* (Vol. 7, pp. 17-56). Bingley, UK: Emerald.

Association of Educational Communications and Technology. (2012, July). Newly adopted AECT standards. *News Flash!*, 9-12. Retrieved from http://aect.site-ym.com/resource/resmgr/Newsletters/Current.pdf

Baggio, B. G. (2008). *Integrating social software into blended-learning courses: A Delphi study of instructional-design processes* (Doctoral dissertation). Capella University, Minneapolis, MN. Retrieved from http://proquest.umi.com/pqdweb?did=1492600541&sid=1&Fmt=2&cl ientId=79356&RQT=309&VName=PQD

Beaudoin, M. F. (2007). Distance education leadership: An appraisal of research and practice. In M. G. Moore (Ed.), *Handbook of distance education* (2nd ed., pp. 391-402). Mahwah, NJ: Erlbaum.

Bernard, R. M., Abrami, P. C., Borokhovski, E., Wade, C.A., Tamin, R. M., Surkes, M. A., & Bethel, E. C. (2009). A meta-analysis of three types of interaction treatments in distance education. *Review of Educational Research, 79*(3), 1243-1289. doi:10.3102/0034654309333844

Bollettino, V., & Bruderlein, C. (2008). Training humanitarian professionals at a distance: Testing the feasibility of distance learning with humanitarian professionals. *Distance Education, 29*(3), 269-287. doi:10.1080/01587910802395797

Campbell, K., Schwier, R., & Kenny, R. (2009). The critical, relational practice of instructional design in higher education: An emerging model of change agency. *Educational Technology Research & Development, 57*(5), 645-663. doi: 10.1007/s11423-007-9061-6

Campbell, K., Schwier, R., & Kenny, R. (2005). Agency of the instructional designer: Moral coherence and transformative social practice. *Australasian Journal of Educational Technology, 21*(2), 242-262.

Chen, C. J., Wu, J., Yang, S. C., & Tsou, H.-Y. (2008). Importance of diversified leadership roles in improving team effectiveness in a virtual collaboration learning environment. *Educational Technology & Society, 11*(1), 304-321. Retrieved from http://www.ifets.info/journals

Covey, S. R. (1989). *The 7 habits of highly effective people.* New York, NY: Simon & Schuster.

Daniel, J. (2007, February). *The expansion of higher education in the developing world: What can distance learning contribute?* Paper presented at the CHEA International Commission Conference, Washington, DC. Retrieved from http://www.col.org/resources/speeches/2007presentations/Pages/2007-02-01.aspx

DeBlois, P. (2005). Leadership in instructional technology and design: An interview. *EDUCAUSE Quarterly, 28*(4). Retrieved from http://www.educause.edu/EDUCAUSE+Quarterly/EDUCAUSEQuarterlyMagazineVolum/LeadershipinInstructionalTechn/157370

Dede, C. (2011). Emerging technologies, ubiquitous learning, and educational transformation. In *Towards Ubiquitous Learning: Proceedings of the 6th European Conference of Technology Enhanced Learning, EC-TEL 2011* (Vol. 6964, pp. 1-8). Retrieved from http://link.springer.com/chapter/10.1007%2F978-3-642-23985-4_1?LI=true

Dede, C., Dieterle, E., Clarke, J., Jass-Ketelhut, D., & Nelson, B. (2007). Media-based learning styles. In M. G. Moore (Ed.), *Handbook of distance education* (2nd ed., pp. 339-352). Mahwah, NJ: Erlbaum.

Dooley, K., Lindner, J., Telg, R., Irani, T., Moore, L., & Lundy, L. (2007). Road-map to measuring distance education instructional design competency. *Quarterly Review of Distance Education, 8*(2), 151-159. Retrieved from http://www.infoagepub.com/index.php?id=89&i=4

Drucker, P. (1981). *Why management consultants.* Retrieved from http://anoovaconsulting.biz/drucker.pdf

Durdu, P., Yalabik, N., & Cagiltay, K. (2009). A distributed online curriculum and courseware development model. *Educational Technology & Society, 12*(1), 230-248. Retrieved from http://www.ifets.info

Ertmer, P. A., Stepich, D. A., York, C. S., Stickman, A., Wu, X., Zurek, S., & Goktas, Y. (2008). How instructional design experts use knowledge and experience to solve ill-structured problems. *Performance Improvement Quarterly, 21*(1), 17-42.

Fullan, M. (2001). *Leading in a culture of change.* San Francisco, CA: Jossey-Bass.

Fullan, M., & Scott, G. (2009). *Turnaround leadership for higher education.* San Francisco, CA: Jossey-Bass.

Gelo, O., Braakmann, D., & Benetka, G. (2008). Quantitative and qualitative research: Beyond the debate. *Integrative Psychological & Behavioral Science*, *42*(3), 266-290. doi:10.1007/s12124-008-9078-3

Glaser, B. G., & Strauss A. L. (1977). *The discovery of grounded theory: Strategies for qualitative research* (8th ed.). Hawthorne, NY: Aldien de Gruyter.

Greenleaf, G. (1977). *Servant leadership: A journey into the nature of legitimate power and greatness/essays by Robert K. Greenleaf.* Mahwah, NJ: Paulist.

Gressick, J., & Derry, S. J. (2010). Distributed leadership in online groups. *Computer-Supported Collaborative Learning*, *5*, 211-236. doi: 10.1007/s11412-010-9086-4

Hannum, W. (2009). Moving distance education research forward. *Distance Education*, *30*(1), 171-173. doi: 10.1080/01587910902846020

Hong, H., & Sullivan, F. (2009). Towards an idea-centered, principle-based design approach to support learning as knowledge creation. *Educational Technology Research & Development*, *57*(5), 613-627. doi:10.1007/s11423-009-9122-0

Howard, A., & Wellins, R. S. (2008). *Global leadership forecast 2008 | 2009: Overcoming the shortfalls in developing leaders.* Retrieved from http://www.ddiworld.com/pdf/globalleadershipforecast2008-2009_ globalreport_ddi.pdf

Hout, M. (2012). Social and economic returns to college education in the United States. *Annual Review of Sociology*, *38*, 379-400. doi:10.1146/annurev.soc .012809.102503

International Board of Standards for Training, Performance and Instruction. (2000). *Instructional design competencies report.* Retrieved from http://www.ibstpi.org/downloads/InstructionalDesignCompetencies.pdf

Isaacson, W. (2011). *Steve Jobs.* New York, NY: Simon & Schuster.

Kaplan, C. (2004). *The invisible garment: 30 spiritual principles that weave the fabric of human life.* San Diego, CA: Jodere Group.

Kepner, C. H., & Tregoe, B. B. (1997). *The new rational manager: An updated edition for a new world.* Princeton, NJ: Princeton Research Press.

Kirkpatrick, S. A., & Locke, E. A. (1991). Leadership: Do traits matter? *Academy of Management Executive*, *5*(2), 48-60. Retrieved from http://journals .aomonline.org/amp

Könings, K. D., Brand-Gruwel, S., & van Merriënboer, J. J. G. (2005). Towards more powerful learning environments through combining the perspectives of designers, teachers, and students. *British Journal of Educational Psychology*, *75*, 645-660. doi:10.1348/000709905x43616

Kouzes, J. M., & Posner, B. Z. (2007). *The leadership challenge* (4th ed.). San Francisco, CA: Wiley.

Kowch, E. (2009). New capabilities for cyber charter school leadership: An emerging imperative for integrating educational technology and educational leadership knowledge. *TechTrends*, *53*(4), 41-48.

Larson, M. B., & Lockee, B. B. (2009). Preparing instructional designers for different career environments: A case study. *Educational Technology Research and Development 57*, 1-24. doi:10.1007/s11423-006-9031-4

Maryland Online. (2010). *Quality Matters rubric standards 2008-2010 edition with assigned point values (QM 2010).* Retrieved from http://qminstitute.org/home/Public%20Library/About%20QM/RubricStandards2008-2010.pdf

Maxwell, J. C. (2007). *The irrefutable of laws of leadership: Follow them and people will follow you* (Rev., 10th anniversary ed.). Nashville, TN: Thomas Nelson.

Means, B., Toyama, Y., Murphy, R., Bakia, M., & Jones, K. (2009). *Evaluation of evidence-based practices in online learning: A meta-analysis and review of online learning studies.* Washington, DC: U.S. Department of Education, Office of Planning, Evaluation, and Policy Development.

Moore, M., & Kearsley, G. (2005). *Distance education: A systems view* (2nd ed.). Belmont, CA: Thomson Wadsworth.

Moustakas, C. (1994). *Phenomenological research methods.* Thousand Oaks, CA: SAGE.

Naidu, S. (2007). Instructional designs for optimal learning. In M. G. Moore (Ed.), *Handbook of distance education* (2nd ed., pp. 247-258). Mahwah, NJ: Erlbaum.

National Survey of Student Engagement. (2008). *Promoting engagement for all students: The imperative to look within—2008 results.* Retrieved from http://nsse.iub.edu/NSSE_2008_ Results

Onwuegbuzie, A., Leech, N., & Collins, K. (2008). Interviewing the interpretive researcher: A method for addressing the crises of representation, legitimation, and praxis. *International Journal of Qualitative Methods, 7*(4), 1-17. Retrieved from http://ejournals.library.ualberta.ca/index.php/IJQM/article/view/1701/3818

Reeves, T. C., Herrington, J., & Oliver, R. (2004). A development research agenda for online collaborative learning. *Educational Technology Research & Development, 52*(4), 53-65.

Reimers, F. M. (2009). Leading for global competency. *Educational Leadership: Teaching for the 21st Century, 67*(1). Retrieved from http://www.ascd.org/publications/educational_leadership/sept09/vol67/num01/Leading_for_Global_-Competency.aspx

Rogers, P., Graham, C., & Mayes, C. (2007). Cultural competence and instructional design: Exploration research into the delivery of online instruction cross-culturally. *Educational Technology Research and Development, 55*(2), 197-217. doi:10.1007/s11423-007-9033-x

Sackney, L., & Mergel, B. (2007). Contemporary learning theories, instructional design and leadership. In J. M. Burger, C. Webber, & P. Klinck (Eds.), *Intelligent* Leadership (Vol. 11, pp. 67-98). doi:10.1007/978-1-4020-6022-9_5

Scott, G., Coates, H., & Anderson, M. (2008). *Learning leaders in times of change: Academic leadership capabilities for Australian higher education* [Report]. Melbourne, Australia: University of Western Sydney and Australian Council for Educational Research.

Seidman, I. (2006). *Interviewing as qualitative research: A guide for researchers in education and the social sciences* (3rd ed.). New York, NY: Teachers College Press.

Senge, P. (2006). *The fifth discipline: The art & practice of the learning organization.* New York, NY: Doubleday.

Sergiovanni, T. (2003). A cognitive approach to leadership. In B. Davies & J. West-Burnham (Eds.), *Handbook of educational leadership and management.* (pp. 12-16). New York, NY: Pearson/Longman.

Sergiovanni, T. (1984). Leadership and excellence in schooling. *Educational Leadership, 41*(5), 4, 6-13.

Siemens, G. (2004). *Connectivism: A learning theory for the digital age.* Retrieved from http://www.elearnspace.org/Articles/connectivism.htm

Sims, R. (2011). Reappraising design practice. In D. Holt, S. Segrave, & J. Cybulski (Eds.), *Professional education using e-simulations: Benefits of blended learning design* (pp. 25-40). Hershey, PA: IGI Global. doi:10.4018/978-1-61350-189-4.ch002

Sims, R. (2006). Beyond instructional design: Making learning design a reality. *Journal of Learning Design, 1*(2), 1-7. Retrieved from http://www.jld.qut.edu.au

Sims, R. (2009). From three-phase to proactive learning design: Creating effective online teaching and learning environments. In J. Willis (Ed.), *Constructivist instructional design (C-ID): Foundations, models, and practical examples* (pp. 379-391). Charlotte, NC: Information Age.

Sims, R. C., & Koszalka, T. A. (2008) Competencies for the new-age instructional designer. In J. M. Spector, M. D. Merrill, J. van Merriënboer, & M. P. Driscoll (Eds.) *Handbook of research on educational communications and technology* (3rd ed., pp. 569-575). New York, NY: Erlbaum.

Sims, R., & Stork, E. (2007, June). Design for contextual learning: Web-based environments that engage diverse learners. In J. Richardson & A. Ellis (Eds.), *Proceedings of AusWeb07.* Lismore, NSW: Southern Cross University. Retrieved from http://ausweb.scu.edu.au/aw07/papers/refereed/sims/index.html

Spillane, J. P., Halverson, R., & Diamond, J. B. (2004). Towards a theory of leadership practice: A distributed perspective. *Journal of Curriculum Studies, 36*(1), 3-34. doi:10.1080/0022027032 000106726

Spiro, R. J., & DeSchryver, M. (2009). Constructivism: When it's the wrong idea and when it's the only idea. In S. Tobias & T. M. Duffy (Eds.), *Constructivist instruction: Success or failure?* (pp. 106-123). New York, NY: Routledge.

Stein, S. J., Shephard, K., & Harris, I. (2011). Conceptions of e-learning and professional development for e-learning held by tertiary educators in New Zealand. *British Journal of Educational Technology, 42*(1),145-165. doi:10.1111/j.1467- 8535.2009.00997.x

Stern, A. (2009, October). Online education expanding, awaits innovation. *Reuters.* Retrieved from http://www.reuters.com/article/idUSTRE59047Z20091001

Thompson, D., Baranowski, T., Buday, R., Baranowski, J., Thompson, V., Jago, R., & Griffith, M. J. (2011). Serious video games for health how behavioral science guided the development of a serious video game. *Simulation Gaming, 41*(4), 587-606. doi:10.1177/1046878108328087

Uysal, O., & Kuzu, A. (2009). An investigation about quality standards for online education. In *Proceedings of the International Conference on Computational and Information Science 2009,* Houston, TX (pp. 328-332). Retrieved from http://portal.acm.org

Veletsianos, G., & Miller, C. (2008). Conversing with pedagogical agents: A phenomenological exploration of interacting with digital entities. *British Journal of Educational Technology, 39*(6), 969-986. doi:10.1111/j.1467-8535.2007.00797.x

Wenger, E. (1998). *Communities of practice: Learning, meaning and identity.* New York, NY: Cambridge University Press.

Walumbwa, F. O., Avolio, B. J., Gardner, W. L., Wernsing, T. S., & Peterson, S. J. (2008). Authentic leadership: Development and validation of a theory-based measure. *Journal of Management, 34*(1), 89-126. doi:10.1177/014920637308913

Zenger, J., & Folkman, J. (2009). *The extraordinary leader: Turning good managers into great leaders* (2nd ed.). New York, NY: McGraw-Hill.

CHAPTER 7

THREE LEVELS OF PLANNED E-LEARNING INTERACTIONS

A Framework for Grounding Research and the Design of e-Learning Programs

Atsusi "2c" Hirumi
University of Central Florida

Advances in technology offer a vast array of opportunities for facilitating elearning. However, difficulties may arise if e-learning research and design, including the use of emerging technologies, are based primarily on past practices, fads, or political agendas. This article describes refinements made to a framework for designing and sequencing e-learning interactions originally published in 2002 based on insights gained from a decade of application across settings. The updated framework adds neurobiological research on human learning as a theoretical foundation, and further distinguishes the relationship between learning theories, instructional strategies, planned e-learning interactions, and emerging technologies to guide future distance education research and practice.

There appear to be considerable discrepancies between rhetoric and practice in distance education. On one hand, much has been written about: (a) contemporary theories of human learning and their implications for education and instructional design (e.g., Driscoll, 2005; Schunk, 2012); (b) learner-centered psychological principles (APA, 1997) and

Beyond the Online Course: Leadership Perspectives on e-Learning
pp. 103–124
Copyright © 2016 by Information Age Publishing
All rights of reproduction in any form reserved.

examples of learner-centered instructional strategies (e.g., problem-based learning); (c) the virtues of experiential learning (e.g., Dewey, 1938; Kolb, 1984; Lindsey & Berger, 2009) and educating students in a manner that is consistent with what [science, technology, engineering and mathematics] professionals do in real life; and (d) the need to foster creativity and innovative thinking (Florida, 2002). On the other hand, we continue to see schools and teachers remunerated for high credit hour generation, and rewarded for high, and penalized for low standardized test scores that focus on the mastery of declarative knowledge. As a result, many online and hybrid, as well as conventional face-to-face courses continue to focus on transmitting content information and teaching to the test, perpetuating the use of teacher-directed instructional methods.

There are additional reasons online courses remain steeped in tradition. With little time, training, and resources, educators have little recourse but to do what they know best, and for many, that means using traditional teacher-directed methods and materials. Advances in technology also continue to increase access to e-learning opportunities, but do not necessarily improve the quality of the e-learning experience. Learning management systems such as Blackboard, Moodle, Canvas, and Desire2Learn, along with software applications such as Dreamweaver, Captivate, and Adobe Creative Suites, make it easier for people to create and post online instructional materials. Easier, however, does not mean better. There are now far more people designing online courses and course materials, with little to no formal preparation, practice, and experience in key areas such as, but not limited to, instructional design, multimedia development, and graphic design, resulting in greater variance in the quality of online course materials and, consequently, the quality of the online educational experience.

Another challenge facing distance educators and researchers is the seemingly unlimited ways one can integrate the use of technology to facilitate the array of interactions that may be planned to facilitate e-learning. New applications, based on Web 2.0 technologies and mobile computing, continue to emerge with the potential to enhance teaching and learning across settings (Ferdig, 2007; Pence, 2007; Simões & Gouveia, 2008, cited by Hartshorne & Ajjan, 2009). Literature on distance education also reveals a wide range of instructional strategies that may be used to facilitate e-learning (Hirumi, 2006). Clearly, e-learning is not a process that can be easily defined and readily conceived to facilitate research and development. Using emerging technologies can change the manner in which teachers and students interact with content and with each other, affording opportunities for teaching and learning that were not previously possible (Maloney, 2007). However, frameworks are necessary to

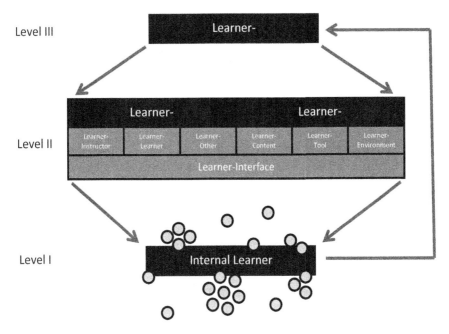

Figure 1.   Three levels for planning e-learning interactions.

help organize and apply our knowledge of research and theory, and properly integrate the use of emerging technologies to facilitate e-learning.

This article describes refinements made to a framework for designing and sequencing e-learning interactions based on a decade of insights gained from applying the framework in a variety of settings. It posits three primary levels of interactions that distinguish the framework and illustrate the relationship between learning theories, instructional strategies, and learner interactions with human and nonhuman resources that include the use of emerging technologies to facilitate e-learning. The original framework, first published in 2002, helped educators analyze, design, and sequence e-learning interactions (Hirumi, 2002a, 2002b). The second version further delineated Level II learner-nonhuman interactions by distinguishing learner-tool and learner-interface interactions (Hirumi, 2006). The third version (Hirumi, in press) elaborates on internal student-self interactions by recognizing how teams and groups of individuals may work together to construct knowledge and derive meaning during the learning process to facilitate cognition.

The framework continues to posit three basic levels of interactions and seven classes of Level II learner-human and learner nonhuman interactions. The latest version forwards the framework by including neurobiological research and theory on human learning, and elaborating on (a) the classes of Level I interactions that may be considered to drive the selection of Level II interactions, (b) the classes of Level III interactions that may be applied to guide the design and sequencing Level II interactions, and (c) the importance of aligning all three levels of interactions to guide research and practice. Over the past decade, advances in imagining technology and neuroscience research has revolutionized the way we treat disease states and physical traumas, and are leading to considerable insights into how and why people learn. Including neuroscience illustrates how physiological studies relate to existing psychological research and practice in human learning and instructional design. Elaborating Level I and Level III interactions further delineates the relationship between learning theories, instructional strategies, and planned e-learning interactions to help organize and guide research on e-learning interactions and the design of e-learning programs.

THREE LEVELS FOR PLANNING ELEARNING INTERACTIONS

The framework is based on three basic premises: (a) grounding research and the design of e-learning programs is necessary to systematically study and build a solid foundation for decision making and continuous improvement; (b) the alignment of theory, strategy and interactions is vital for contributing valid findings to the knowledge base, and (c) distinguishing three levels helps ensure alignment between learning theories, instructional strategies, and planned interactions.

While there is no substitute for practical experience, difficulties may occur if educators and educational researchers fail to ground their efforts in theory. When e-learning strategies and the uses of technology are based on past practices, fads, or political agendas, they represent "craft-based" approaches to instruction that are carved by one person or group of people for a specific situation. This is not to say that such activities are ineffective, only that they may not be applicable to circumstances beyond those in which they are employed. Grounding research and design in theory is vital so that e-learning environments may be systematically studied, continuously improved, and utilized effectively with similar populations across contexts.

Grounded design is "the systematic implementation of processes and procedures that are rooted in established theory and research in human learning" (Hannafin, Hannafin, Land, & Oliver, 1997, p.102). A grounded approach uses theory and research to make design decisions. It neither subscribes too, nor advocates any particular epistemology, but rather promotes alignment between theory and practice. Four conditions are basic to grounded design: (a) designs must be rooted in a defensible theoretical framework; (b) methods must be consistent with the outcome of research conducted to test, validate, or extend the theories upon which they are based; (c) designs must be generalizable to situations beyond the unique conditions in which they are being utilized; and (d) grounded designs and their frameworks must be validated iteratively through successive implementation (Hannifin et al., 1997).

According to the three level framework, educators and educational researchers should select an instructional strategy (Level III interactions) based on their values and beliefs about how and why people learn (Level I interactions). The selected strategy should then guide the design and sequencing of e-learning (Level II) interactions that are planned to stimulate or otherwise facilitate learning as defined by the designers' or researchers' (Level I) values and beliefs, bringing the process back full circle to ground e-learning research and design.

Level I: Internal Learner-Self Interactions

Internal learner-self interactions consist of the mental processes that constitute learning and the metacognitive processes that help individuals monitor and regulate their learning. Internal interactions may also consist of individual assessments of self-worth, self-competence, and online presence. Such internal interactions occur as individuals work by themselves as well as when they work in pairs, and in small or large groups to facilitate learning.

Table 1 depicts major classes of learning theories, including behavioral, cognitive, constructivist, and neurobiological theories, and identifies specific theories and lines of research associated with each class. As with many taxonomies, the boundaries of each category and the classification of objects and ideas (theories in this case) are not as clear-cut as they may appear. For example, some may view Bandura's (1986, 1997, 2001) social learning theory as behavioral in principle based on its focus on modeling and measuring overt behaviors. Others may view social learning theory as cognitive because it considers the internal mental processes of attention, memory, and motivation.

Space limitations prohibit an extended discussion on the history or development of each class of learning theory. Instead, an overview of each class is provided, including references to representative theories and prominent authors, and short descriptions of key concepts and principles to distinguish each class and relate them to Level III learner-instructional interactions.

**Table 1.   Major Classes of Learning Theories
and Related Theories and Lines of Research**

Major Classes of Theories	*Related Theories and Lines of Research*
Behavioral	• Connectionism (Thorndike, 1913a, 1913b, 1914, 1932) • Classical conditioning (Pavlov, 1927, 1928; Watson, 1913) • Operant conditioning (Skinner, 1938, 1953, 1954) • Contiguous conditioning (Guthrie, 1942, 1952, 1959)
Cognitive	• Meaningful reception learning (Ausubel, 1962, 1968; Mayer, 1977, 2003) • Conditions of learning (Gagné, 1974, 1977) • Cognitive information processing (Atkinson & Shiffrin, 1968) • Schema theory (Anderson, Spiro, & Anderson, 1978; Norman, 1982; Rumelhart, 1980) • Social learning theory (Bandura, 1986, 1997, 2001) • Attribution theory (Weiner, 1985, 1986)
Constructivist	• Genetic epistemology (Piaget, 1951, 1969) • Gestalt (Bower & Hilgard, 1981; Koffka, 1924) • Sociocultural learning (Bruner, 1964, 1983, 1990; Vygotsky, 1962, 1978) • Situated cognition (Cobb & Bowers, 1999; Greeno, 1989; Suchman, 1987) • Generative learning (Wittrock, 1974, 1985, 1990) • Community of practice (Lave & Wenger, 1998; Wenger, 1998)

Neuro-biological	• Brain-based learning (Caine, Caine, McClintic, & Klimek, 2005; Jensen, 2007)
	• Educational and cognitive neuroscience research on:
	  ○ Emotions (Damasio, 1994; Immordino-Yang & Faeth, 2010; LeDoux, 1996).
	  ○ Memory (Keele, Ivry, Mayr, Hazeltine, & Heuer, 2003; McClelland, 2000; Miller 2003)
	  ○ Attention (Corbetta & Shulman, 2002)
	  ○ Social cognition (Adolphs, 2003; Beer, 2009; Lieberman, 2007)
	  ○ Language (Caramazza, 1996; Dronkers, Wilkins, Van Valin, Redfern, & Jaeger, 2004; Hagoort, 2005)
	  ○ Creativity (Dietrich, 2004; Heilman, Nadeau, & Beversdorf, 2003; Neubauer, 2011)

Behavioral Learning Theories. Research and the behavioral theories on connectionism (Thorndike, 1913a, 1913b, 1914), classical conditioning (Pavlov, 1927, 1928), operant conditioning (Skinner, 1938, 1953), and contiguous conditioning (Guthrie, 1942, 1952, 1959) led to many of the fundamental principles that are now associated with behavioral learning. Behavioral theories viewed learning as a process of forming associations between stimuli and responses that result in relatively permanent changes in observable behavior. Behavioral learning theorists recognized that the brain processes information but since there was no way to measure such brain activity, they chose to focus their research on measurable overt behaviors.

Basic principles associated with respondent and operant behaviors, and reinforcement contingencies characterize behavioral explanations of how and why people learn. Respondent behaviors refer to behaviors that are elicited involuntarily in reaction to a stimulus. In contrast, operant behaviors are emitted by an organism's responses to his or her environment. Reinforcement contingencies explain how the antecedents of a response, also referred to as the contingent stimuli, either strengthen or weaken the relationship between the original (discriminative) stimulus and (operant) response.

Research, predominantly with animals and then generalized to humans, revealed a number of behavioral learning concepts and principles. Principles of operant conditioning indicate that positive and negative reinforcements may be used to strengthen a response, and how punishment and reinforcement removal may weaken a response. Behavioral research also demonstrates how shaping, chaining, discrimination learning, and fading work for teaching new behaviors (cf. Dricoll, 2005).

Cognitive Learning Theories. Frustrated with the limitations of behavioral learning theories, psychologists sought to put the "mind" back into human sciences (Bruner, 1990), leading to what is referred to as the cognitive revolution. A number of theories distinguish cognitive explanations of how and why people learn, including the theory of meaningful reception learning (Ausubel, 1962, 1968; Mayer, 1977, 2003), schema theory (Anderson et al., 1978; Norman, 1982; Rumelhart, 1998), and social learning theory (Bandura, 1986, 1997, 2001). Although their foci differ, each theory explains learning by the thought processes that govern behavior and measure changes in behavior as an indicator of internal cognitive processes. Models of cognitive information processing can be traced to Atkinson and Shiffrin's (1968) classic multistage theory of memory in which information undergoes a series of transformations before it is stored in long-term memory. The focus on the internal mental structures that process information and govern human learning and behavior distinguishes cognitive from behavioral and constructivist theories of human learning.

Constructivist Learning Theories. Constructivist learning theories assume that people construct knowledge based on their interpretations of the world. Reality is provisional and influenced by an individual's prior knowledge and experience. Like the other classes of learning theories, there is no single constructivist theory. One tradition comes from Gestalt theories of perception that focus on the ideas of closure, organization, and continuity (Bower & Hilgard, 1981). Gesalt psychologists suggest that people do not interpret pieces of information separately and that cognition imposes organization on the world (Koffka, 1924). Theories of intellectual and sociocultural development also contribute to the notion of constructivism. Developmental constructivists focus on how individuals construct knowledge through increasingly sophisticated methods of information representation and organization that are developed over time (e.g., Bruner, 1983, 1990; Piaget, 1951, 1969). In contrast, social constructivists depict learning as a socially mediated experience and concentrate on how groups construct knowledge and learn how to regulate their behaviors based on social and cultural interactions.

Research on situated cognition further distinguishes constructivist views on human learning. The idea that learning is affected by interactions between the person and the situation is not unique. Emphasis on the situation, however, differentiates constructivists, who see all thoughts residing in physical and social contexts, from cognitivists who view knowledge as something that resides within the learner. Situation cognition focuses on the relationship between the person and the situation (Cobb & Bowers, 1999). Situation cognition also addresses the notion that learning involves many processes, including motivation, and encourages researchers and practitioners to recognize the value of authentic learning activities and importance of experiential learning at schools and at work as well as online.

Perhaps the principles of constructivist learning that separate it from behavioral, cognitive, and neurobiological theories of human learning are best synthesized by the APA (1997) who list learner-centered psychological principles related to (a) cognitive and metacognitive, (b) motivational and affective, (c) developmental and social factors, and (d) individual differences.

Neurobiological Learning Theories. In distinct contrast to cognitive and constructivist learning theories that study the psychology of learning, neurobiological theories examine physiological changes to the brain and the central nervous system that govern human cognition and behavior. Over the past 5-10 years, advances in imaging technology have led to tremendous insights into how our brain functions, revolutionizing the way we treat both trauma and disease states. Brain research on healthy mental operations is now revealing neuromechanisms associated with sensory perception, learning, memory, imagination, and emotions that are of increasing relevance for educators and instructional designers.

From a cognitive neuroscience perspective, learning is viewed as the modulation of neurons: the formation and strengthening of synaptic connections through new and repeated thoughts and actions. Further discussion of the neuromechanisms associated with human learning goes beyond the purpose of this article. Instead, learning principles and key lines of cognitive neuroscience research, along with references to books and related professional organizations are listed to further distinguish neurobiological theories of human learning and guide future research and practice.

At this point, few have attempted to synthesize neuroscience research into comprehensive theories that explain human learning, with the exception of the 12 principles posited by Caine et al. (2005), and the seven principles proposed by Jensen (2007). While comprehensive theories remain rather limited, extensive lines of educational and cognitive neuroscience research are leading to insights on how and why people learn, including but not limited to studies on human development, memory, attention, language, social cognition, creativity, and emotions (referenced in Table 1). In turn, a growing number are authoring books that compile neuroscience research findings and discuss implications for learning and education (e.g., Sousa, 2011; Willis, 2006; Zull, 2011).

Theories posit principles for explaining phenomenon and provide a foundation for predicting cause-and-effect relationships. They offer contexts for interpreting observations and bridging the gap between research and practice. Theories also help organize research findings and establish a concrete basis for decision making and continuous improvement. Without theory, research may appear to be a disorganized collection of seemingly random data, and the use of technology and the design and sequencing of e-learning interactions may become reliant on individuals' intuition and experience, rather than years of research on teaching and learning. To base studies on theory, researchers must know the principles that distinguish major classes of learning theories. To make valid contributions to the knowledge base, researchers and practitioners must also select and apply instructional strategies, tools and techniques, and design e-learning interventions that are consistent with specified learning principles.

Level III: Learner-Instructional Interactions

Consistent with Driscoll's (2005) definition of instruction, learner-instruction interactions involve a deliberate arrangement of events to promote learning and facilitate the achievement of a set of learning objectives specified for an instructional unit, module, or lesson. The selection of an instructional strategy should be based on the designer's values and beliefs about how and why people learn (Level I interactions), and the instructional events posited by the strategy should guide the design and sequencing of human and nonhuman (Level II) interactions, that include the integration of tools and media used to facilitate each event.

A number of instructional strategies (defined as a comprehensive set of instructional events necessary to achieve a set of objectives specified for an instructional unit, module or lesson), may be applied to create teacher-directed or student-centered learning environments. In addition, a number of instructional tools and techniques have been specified for facilitating learning based on different theories. Table 2 lists instructional strategies along with tools and techniques that either stem from or are associated with the four major classes of theories distinguished by the framework.

In general, behavioral and cognitive instructional strategies are considered teacher-directed because the teacher typically specifies what is learned, how it's learned and how it's assessed. In contrast, constructivist instructional strategies require learners to direct their own learning. Radical constructivists may have learners defining their own objectives and assessments, but more pragmatic strategies may have learners working with the instructor to negotiate objectives and assessments. Neurobiological strategies, tools, and techniques are considered student centered because they recognize the importance of adapting goals, strategies, and assessments based on learners' knowledge, experience, and emotions.

It is important to note that instructional strategies do not necessarily fall into distinct teacher-directed or student-centered categories based on their theoretical orientation as depicted by Table 2. The extent to which an instructional strategy is considered teacher-directed or student-centered lies on a continuum and depends on the degree to which the teacher and the student take responsibility for specifying learning goals and objectives, learner assessments, and instructional/learning strategies. In other words, one can follow an instructional strategy based on cognitive information process theories of learning, such as Gagne's nine events of instruction, but can apply the strategy in a student-centered manner by allowing students to identify relevant learning objectives and giving them the responsibility of organizing and interacting with relevant stimulus information and selecting their own projects to elicit performance. Furthermore, it is apparent that the tools and techniques listed in column 3 are not necessarily unique to a particular class of learning theory. Rather, research related to each class may support the use of similar tools and techniques across theories.

Potential adaptations made during the application of an instructional strategy and use of tools and techniques across theories highlight the importance of understanding the foundation on which they are based. For instance, conducting research with a so-called constructivist learning environment that asks learners to work together to construct knowledge,

Table 2. Relating Instructional Strategies, Tools, and Techniques to Basic Instructional Approaches and Theoretical Orientations

Theoretical Orientation	Instructional Approach			
	Teacher Directed		Student-Centered	
	Behavioral	Cognitive	Neurobiological	Constructivist
Instructional strategies	• Elements of lesson design (Hunter, 1990) • Direct instruction (Joyce, Weil, & Showers, 1992)	• Nine events of instruction (Gagne, 1974, 1977) • 5 component lesson model (Dick, Carey, & Carey, 2009)	• Interplay strategy (Stapleton & Hirumi, 2011)	• Experiential learning (Kolb, 1984) • Learning by doing (Shank, Berman, & Macpherson, 1999) • Problem-based learning (Barrows, 1985) • 5E instructional model (BSCS, 2005; Bybee, 2002) • WebQuest (Dodge, 2007)
Instructional tools and techniques	• Task analysis • Behavioral objectives • Practice and feedback • Programmed instruction • Contingency contracts	• Message design • Rehearsal • Chunking • Mnemonics • Advanced organizers • Cognitive task analysis • Cognitive load • Self-regulated learning	• Evoking emotions • Positive climate • Sleep, nutrition, and movement • Active discussions • Simulation, role-playing, and immersion • Stimulating imagination • Graphics and multisensory learning	• Facilitating learning • Discovery and inquiry-based learning • Authentic/experiential learning • Collaborate learning • Cognitive apprenticeships • Scaffolding • Reflective teaching and learning

but does not situate learning tasks in their physical and social context would not lead to valid findings. Adaptations may also make it difficult to identify causes for success (or failure), or to attribute positive or negative results to a particular theory or on someone's interpretation and application of the theory. To properly ground e-learning practice, and to design and conduct rigorous studies that contribute to the knowledge base, the application of strategies, tools, and techniques must be consistent with the principles associated with selected theoretical frameworks.

Level II: Learner-Human and Learner-Nonhuman Interactions

Level II interactions occur between the learner and other human or nonhuman resources. According to the three level framework, the instructional events prescribed by the selected strategy should drive the design and sequencing of Level II interactions. The seven classes of Level II interactions, depicted in Figure 1, are based on review of taxonomies for classifying distance education interactions, including communication, purpose, activity, and tool-based frameworks (Hirumi, 2002a, 2002b) and refinements made to a separate framework originally posited by Reigeluth and Moore (1999) for comparing analyzing interactions for learning.

Learner-Interface Interactions. During e-learning, the graphical user interface may serve as the primary means of interaction with both human and nonhuman resources. Learners may utilize a graphical user interface to send and receive e-mail, post messages in wikis and blogs, or videoconference with the instructor and/or other learners. Learners will also use a graphical user interface to access lessons and content information posted in a learning management system. Hillman, Willis, and Gunawardena (1994) propose that a learner's degree of proficiency with a medium correlates positively with the degree of success the learner has in extracting information from that medium. Metros and Hedberg (2002) also note that poor interface design can place high cognitive demands on learners, taking their attention away from the subject matter.

Learner-Instructor Interactions. Learner-instructor interactions may be initiated by either the student or instructor during e-learning. The learner may interact with the instructor to ask and respond to questions, clarify and confirm learning outcomes/objectives, explain conditions, submit assignments, complete activities, monitor and evaluate teachers' performance, etc. Instructors, in turn, may interact with learners to establish learning outcomes/objectives; provide timely and appropriate feedback; facilitate information presentation; monitor and evaluate student performance; facilitate learning activities; initiate, maintain and facilitate discussions; and determine learning needs and preferences (Thach & Murphy, 1995).

Learner-Learner Interactions. Learner-learner interactions occur "between one learner and another learner, alone or in group settings, with or without the real-time presence of an instructor" (Moore, 1989, p. 4). Learner-learner interactions help groups and individuals construct knowledge and apply targeted skills. Typically, learner-learner interactions ask students to discuss important topics by using online discussion forums to share information, opinions, and insights. More involved forms of learner-learner interactions may ask students to work together to analyze and interpret data, and solve problems.

Learner-Other Human Interactions. Learner-other human interactions enable learners to acquire information from as well as work with experts or others who may or may not be a formal part of instruction. Online courses may ask learners to communicate with others outside of class to promote knowledge construction and social discourse (Bonk & King 1998). In K-12 education, such interactions may include exchanges with teaching assistants, electronic pen pals, peer mentors, and working professionals. Learner-other human interactions may occur online or face to face depending on the location, targeted outcomes, and desired experiences.

Learner-Content Interactions. Learner-content interactions may include learners accessing audio, video, text, and graphic representations of the subject matter. Multimedia such as YouTube videos and Podcasts may also be pushed to learners' cell phone or other mobile devices to facilitate e-learning. In a meta-analysis of three types of distance education treatments, Bernard et al. (2009) found that only student-content interactions contributed to higher achievement and attitudes, compared to student-student and student-teacher interactions. Similarly, in a test of Anderson's (2003) interaction equivalency theorem, Miyazoe and Anderson (2010) found that students ranked student-content interactions higher in order of importance than student-teacher or student-student interactions. Interestingly, such findings seem to be contrary to research on social presence and efforts to enhance learning by building communities of learners.

Learner-Tool Interactions. Learners may interact with tools both within and outside of the online learning environment to facilitate learning. Tools, such as electronic mail, discussion forums, chat, blogs, Twitter, and desktop video conferencing are typically integrated within learning management systems to facilitate learner-human interactions. Tools such as word processors, databases, spreadsheets, and document sharing programs may also be used to facilitate individual and team productivity. Outside of the virtual environment, learners may also be asked to use tools such as a microscope, building blocks, or other manipulatives to promote learning. Of particular interest may be tools such as video cameras and other recording devices that allow learners to generate and share their own content.

Learner-Environment Interactions. Learner- environment interactions occur when learners visit locations outside the virtual online environment. It's a common myth that in an online course all activities must occur online. Learners may be asked to seek or travel to specific locations to gather, observe, and otherwise interact with others and with external resources to complete prescribed learning activities. For example, nursing students may be asked go to a nearby hospital to refine their laboratory skills. It is true that such interactions may require considerable management. However, in some cases, learner-environment interactions may be essential for facilitating the development of specified skills and for promoting experiential learning.

APPLICATIONS OF THE THREE-LEVEL FRAMEWORK

As mentioned, the three level framework may be used to design and sequence e-learning interactions as well as to organize and guide e-learning research. Table 3 lists steps for applying the framework to design totally online courses (Hirumi, 2002a, 2002b, 2006, in press). The framework has also been used to design hybrid training (Hirumi, Bradford, & Rutherford, 2011) and to integrate the use of educational games (Hirumi, 2010).

Because the use of the framework to design training and educational programs is discussed in length in the cited references, the remainder of this article illustrates the application of the framework for analyzing and organizing existing research and for grounding the design of future investigations.

Analyzing and Organizing Research

In addition to designing and sequencing of e-learning interactions, the three level framework may be used to analyze and organize research on interactivity and e-learning, and to identify trends and issues for future study. Gaps in literature, along with trends and issues, may be found by asking questions such as: Which of the seven basic Level II interactions were addressed by the study? Was the design and sequencing of Level II interactions grounded in an explicit (Level III) instructional strategy and/ or (Level I) learning theory? If so, was the design and sequencing of Level

Table 3.   Six-Step Process for Designing and Sequencing eLearning Interactions

Step 1:	Identify essential experiences that are necessary for learners to achieve specified goals and objectives (optional);
Step 2:	Select a grounded instructional strategy (Level III interaction) based on specified objectives, learner characteristics, context, and epistemological beliefs;
Step 3:	Operationalize each event, embedding experiences identified in Step 1 and describing how the selected strategy will be applied during instruction;
Step 4:	Define the type of Level II interaction(s) that will be used to facilitate each event and analyze the quantity and quality of planned interactions;
Step 5:	Select the telecommunication tool(s) (e.g., chat, e-mail, bulletin board system) that will be used to facilitate each event based on the nature of the interaction; and
Step 6:	Analyze materials to determine frequency and quality of planned e-learning interactions and revise as necessary.

II interactions consistent with specified Level III strategy and/or Level I theory? How about the selection and integration of technology? Were they based on an explicit Level III strategy and/or Level I theory? Did the course apply more teacher or learner-centered instructional strategies? Was the instructional strategy (Level III interactions) congruent with the teachers', designers', and/or researchers' educational philosophy (values and beliefs about Level I interactions)? Several articles on e-learning are analyzed to demonstrate how the framework may be used to organize findings, identify issues, and guide future research.

Two studies referenced earlier illustrate how research on e-learning interactions may focus solely on Level II learner-human and learner-non-human interactions, and how considering Level I or Level III interactions may affect reported findings. The meta-analysis by Bernard et al. (2009) examined the relative value and strength of student-student, student-teacher, and student-content interactions in 77 studies and found that only student-content interactions contributed to higher levels of student achievement or improved attitudes. Likewise, Miyazoe and Anderson (2010) measured perceived levels of importance of 236 undergraduate students across four universities and found that learners ranked student-content interactions higher than student-teacher or student-student interactions. Based on the framework, the two may be classified as Level II studies that addressed only three of the seven Level II interactions (i.e., student-student, student-teacher, student-content). Further analysis based on the framework brings to question if the courses were distinguished by their Level III or Level I interactions, whether student-student interactions may have been of more value in courses that applied more learner-centered strategies based on constructivist learning principles than courses that may have been more teacher-directed and based on behavioral or cognitive learning theories. Certainly, questions regarding the influence of instructional strategy and theoretical orientation on perceived levels of importance and relative impact of specific learner human and learner nonhuman interactions may be raised for future research.

Studies examining the use of emerging technologies for distance education may also be analyzed and organized using the three level framework. Some studies focus on learner-tool (Level II) interactions and how they can facilitate other Level II interactions. For example, Augar, Raitman, and Zhou (2004) compared wikis and studied their use for facilitating ice breakers. Likewise, Godwin-Jones (2003) examined the nature of blogs and wikis and discussed how they could be used by teachers to communicate current events, class notes, and assignments, and by learners to facilitate team projects.

In comparison, others study learner-tool interactions and their use in facilitating alternative Level II interactions but do so in light of explicit Level I and/or Level III interactions. For instance, Beldarrain (2006) discussed the use of emerging Web 2.0 technologies for facilitating learner-learner, learner-teacher, and learner-content interactions and grounds the application of the tools on specific constructivist learning theories, such as situated cognition and communities of practice (Level I interactions). Similarly, Bruns and Humphreys (2005) examined how a wiki was used as a part of social constructivist pedagogical practice to facilitate learner-teacher, learner-learner, and learner-content interactions and advance information and communication technology literacy.

Together, the studies (examined above) illustrate how the framework may be used to analyze, organize, and help guide future research. By analyzing the six studies, it's evident that researchers may focus on a limited set of Level II interactions, and how one type of Level II interaction may affect other Level II interactions. It is also apparent that researchers may or may not relate or otherwise ground their studies on explicit learning theories. Applying the framework to analyze additional studies may reveal trends on what specific types of Level II learner-human and learner-nonhuman interactions are being studied, as well as the specific classes of Level III (instructional strategies) and Level I (learning theories) are being used to design e-learning to guide future research and practice.

SUMMARY

Published taxonomies reveal a plethora of interactions that may be used to facilitate e-learning. However, relatively little has been done to synthesize literature on—and delimit the relationships between—learning theories, instructional strategies, e-learning interactions, and the use of emerging technologies. This article described continuing advancements of a framework for grounding research and the design of e-learning interactions. The effectiveness of the proposed framework has been demonstrated in a number of practical situations (e.g., workshops and in the design of secondary school, undergraduate, and graduate e-learning programs), but much work remains. Further study is required to provide empirical evidence for its utility and to reduce the gap between rhetoric and practice in K-12 distance education.

REFERENCES

Adolphs, R. (2003). Cognitive neuroscience of human social behavior. *Nature Reviews Neuroscience, 3*, 165-178.

Anderson, R. C., Spiro, R. J., & Anderson, M. C. (1978). Schemata as scaffolding for the representation of information in connected discourse. *American Educational Research Journal, 15*, 433-440.

Anderson, T. (2003). Getting the mix right again: An updated and theoretical rationale for interactions. *The Interactional Review of Research in Open and Distance Learning, 4*(2). Retrieved from http://www.irrodl.org/index.php/irrodl/article/view/149/230

APA Work Group of the Board of Educational Affairs. (1997). *Learner-centered psychological principles: A framework for school reform and redesign.* Washington, DC: American Psychological Association.

Atkinson, R. C., & Shiffrin, R. M. (1968). Human memory: A proposed system and its control processes. In K. W. Spence & J. T. Spence (Eds.), *The psychology of learning and motivation* (Vol. 2, pp. 89-195). New York, NY: Academic Press.

Augar, N., Raitman, R., & Zhou, W. (2004). Teaching and learning online with wikis. *ASCILITE Proceedings.* Retrieved from http://www.ascilite.org.au/conferences/perth04/procs/augar.html

Ausubel, D. P. (1962). A subsumption theory of meaningful verbal learning. *Journal of General Psychology, 66*, 213-224.

Ausubel, D. P. (1968). *Educational psychology: A cognitive view.* New York, NY: Holt, Rinehart and Winston.

Bandura, A. (1986). *Social foundations of thought and action: A social-cognitive theory.* Englewood Cliffs, NJ: Prentice Hall.

Bandura, A. (1997). *Self-efficacy: The exercise of control.* New York, NY: Freeman.

Bandura, A. (2001). Social cognitive theory: An agentic perspective. *Annual Review of Psychology, 52*, 1-26.

Barrows, H. S. (1985). *How to design a problem based curriculum for the preclinical years.* New York, NY: Springer.

Beer, J. S. (2009). Social cognition. In M. S. Gazzaniga, R. B. Ivry, & G. R. Mangun (Eds.), *Cognitive neuroscience: The biology of the mind* (3rd ed.) (pp. 599-633). New York, NY: Norton.

Beldarrain, Y. (2006). Distance education trends: Integrating new technologies to foster student interaction and collaboration. *Distance Education, 27*(2), 139-153.

Bernard, M. R., Abrami, P. C., Borokhowski, E., Wade, C. A., Tamim, R. M., Surkes, M. A., & Bethel, E. C. (2009). A meta-analysis of three types of interaction treatments in distance education. *Review of Educational research, 79*(3), 1243-1289.

Bonk, C. J., & King, K. (Eds.). (1998). Computer conferencing and collaborative writing tools: Starting a dialogue about student dialogue. In *Electronic collaborators: Learner-centered technologies for literacy, apprenticeship, and discourse* (pp. 3-24). Mahwah, NJ: Erlbaum.

Bower, G. H., & Hilgard, E. R. (1981). *Theories of learning* (5th ed.). Englewood Cliffs, NJ: Prentice Hall.

Bruner, J. S. (1964). The course of cognitive growth. *American Psychologist, 19*, 1-15.

Bruner, J. S. (1983). *In search of mind.* New York, NY. Harper & Row.

Bruner, J. S. (1990). *Acts of meaning.* Cambridge, MA: Harvard University Press.

Bruns, A., & Humphreys, S. (2005). *Wikis in teaching and assessment: The M/Cyclopedia project.* Retrieved from http://portal.acm.org/citation.cfm?id=1104973 .1104976#abstract

BSCS Center for Professional Development. (2005). *Learning theory and the BSCS 5E instructional model.* Retrieved form http://www.bscs.org/library/handoutlearningtheory5E.pdf

Bybee, R. W. (Ed.). (2002). Scientific inquiry, student learning, and the science curriculum. In *Learning science and the science of learning* (pp. 25-36). Arlington, VA: NSTA Press.

Caine, R. N., Caine, G., McClintic, C., & Klimek, K. (2005). *12 brain/mind learning principles in action.* Thousand Oaks, CA: Corwin Press.

Caramazza, A. (1996). The brain's dictionary. *Nature, 380*, 485-486.

Cobb, P., & Bowers, J. (1999). Cognitive and situated learning perspectives in theory and practice. *Educational Researcher, 28*(2), 4-15.

Corbetta, M., & Shulman, G. L. (2002). Control of goal-directed and stimulus driven attention in the brain. *Nature Reviews Neuroscience, 3*, 201-25.

Damasio, A. R. (1994). *Descartes' error: Emotion, reason, and the human brain.* New York, NY: Putnam.

Dewey, J. (1938). *Experience and education.* New York, NY: Macmillan.

Dick, W., Carey, L., & Carey, J. O. (2009). *The systematic design of instruction* (7th ed.). Upper Saddle River, NJ: Pearson.

Dietrich, A. (2004). The cognitive neuroscience of creativity. *Psychonomic Bulletin Review, 11*(6), 1011-1026.

Dodge, B. (2007). *WebQuest.Org.* Retrieved from http://webquest.org/

Driscoll, M. P. (2005). *Psychology of learning* (3rd ed.). Needham Heights, MA: Allyn & Bacon.

Dronkers, N. E., Wilkins, D. P., Van Valin, R. D., Jr., Redfern, B. B., & Jaeger, J. J. (2004). Lesion analysis of the brain areas involved in language comprehension. *Cognition, 92*, 145-177.

Ferdig, R. (2007). Examining social software in teacher education. *Journal of Technology and Teacher Education, 15*(1), 5-10.

Florida, R. (2002). *The rise of the creative class*. New York, NY: Basic Books.

Gagné, R. M. (1977). *The conditions of learning* (3rd ed.). New York, NY: Holt, Rinehart, and Winston.

Gagné, R.M. (1974). *Principles of instructional design*. New York, NY: Holt, Rinehart and Winston.

Godwin-Jones, R. (2003). Emerging technologies, blogs, and wikis: Environments for online collaboration. *Language Learning & Technology, 7*, 12-16.

Guthrie, E. R. (1959). Association by contiguity. In S. Koch (Ed.). *Psychology: A study of a science* (Vol. 2, pp. 158-195). New York, NY: McGraw-Hill.

Guthrie, E. R. (1942). Conditioning. A theory of learning in terms of stimulus, response, and associations. In N. B. Henry (Ed.). *The psychology of learning: The forty-first yearbook of the National Society for the Study of Education, Part II* (pp. 17-60). Chicago, IL: University Press.

Guthrie, E. R. (1952). *The psychology of learning* (Rev. ed.). New York, NY: Harper & Brothers.

Greeno, J. G. (1989). A perspective on thinking. *American Psychologist, 44*, 134-141.

Hagoort, P. (2005). On Broca, brain, and binding: A new framework. *Trends in Cognitive Sciences, 9*, 416-423.

Hannafin, M. J., Hannafin, K. M., Land, S. M., & Oliver, K. (1997). Grounded practice and the design of constructivist learning environments. *Educational Technology Research & Development, 45*(3), 101-117.

Hartshorne, R., & Ajjan, H. (2009). Examining student decisions to adopt Web 2.0 technologies: Theory and empirical tests. *Journal for Computing in Higher Education, 21*(3), 183-198.

Heilman, K. M., Nadeau, S. E., & Beversdorf, D. O. (2003). Creative innovation: Possible brain mechanisms. *Neurocase, 9*(5), 369-379.

Hillman, D. C., Willis, D. J., & Gunawardena, C. N. (1994). Learner-interface interaction in distance education: an extension of contemporary models and strategies for practitioners. *The American Journal of Distance Education, 8*(2), 30-42.

Hirumi, A. (2002a). The design and sequencing of e-learning interactions: A grounded approach. *International Journal on E-Learning, 1*(1), 19-27.

Hirumi, A. (2002b). A framework for analyzing, designing and sequencing planned e-learning interactions. *Quarterly Review of Distance Education, 3*(2), 141-160.

Hirumi, A. (2006). A framework for analyzing and designing e-learning interactions. In C. Juwah (Ed.). *Interactivity and interactions in distance and online education* (pp. 46-72). London, England: Kogan Page.

Hirumi, A. (Ed.). (2010). A grounded approach to integrating games and facilitating game-based learning. In *Playing games in school: Using simulations and videogames for primary and secondary education* (pp. 229-248). Eugene, OR: International Society for Technology in Education.

Hirumi, A. (Ed.). (in press). Applying grounded instructional strategies to design and sequence elearning interactions. In *Designing grounded online and hybrid learning environments: Practical guidelines for educators and instructional designers.* Eugene, OR: International Society for Technology in Education.

Hirumi, A., Bradford, G., & Rutherford, L. (2011). Selecting delivery systems and media to facilitate blended learning: A systematic process based on skill level, content stability, cost and instructional strategy. *Journal for Online Learning and Teaching, 7*(4), 489-501.

Hunter, M. (1990). Lesson design helps achieve the goals of science instruction. *Educational Leadership, 48*(4), 79-81.

Immordinao-Yang, M. H. & Faeth, M. (2010). The role of emotion and skilled intuition in learning. In D. A. Sousa (Ed.). *Mind, brain, & education* (pp. 69-84). Bloomington, IN: Solution Tree.

Jensen, E. (2007). *Introduction to brain-compatible learning* (2nd ed.). Thousand Oaks, CA: Corwin Press.

Joyce, B., Weil, M., & Showers, B. (1992). *Models of teaching* (4th ed.). Needham Heights, MA: Allyn and Bacon.

Keele, S. W., Ivry, R., Mayr, U., Hazeltine, E., & Heuer, H. (2003). The cognitive and neural architecture of sequencing representation. *Psychological Review, 110*, 316-339.

Koffka, K. (1924). *The growth of mind* (R. M. Ogden, Trans.). London, England: Kegan Paul, Trench, Trubner.

Kolb, D. A. (1984). *Experiential learning: Experience as the source of learning and development.* Englewood Cliffs, NJ: Prentice-Hall.

Lave, J., & Wenger, E. (1998). *Communities of practice: Learning, meaning, and identity.* Cambridge, England: Cambridge University Press.

LeDoux, J. E. (1996). *The emotional brain: The mysterious underpinnings of emotional life.* New York, NY: Simon and Schuster.

Lieberman, M. D. (2007). Social cognitive neuroscience: A review of core processes. *Annual Review of Psychology, 58*, 259-289.

Lindsey, L., & Berger, N. (2009). Experiential approach to instruction. In C. M. Reigeluth & A. A. Carr-Chellman (Eds.). *Instructional-design theories and models: Building a common knowledge base* (Vol. 3, pp. 117-142). New York, NY: Routledge.

Maloney, E. (2007). What Web 2.0 can teach us about learning? *The Chronicle of Higher Education, 25*(18), B26.

Mayer, R. E. (2003). *Learning and instruction.* Upper Saddle River, NJ: Person.

Mayer, R. E. (1977). The sequencing of instruction and the concept of assimilation-to-schema. *Instructional Science, 6*, 369-388.

McClelland, J. L. (2000). Connectionist models of memory. In E. Tulving & F. I. M. Craik (Eds.). *The Oxford handbook of memory* (pp. 583-596). New York, NY: Oxford University Press.

Metros, S. & Hedberg, J. (2002). More than just a pretty (inter)face: The role of the graphical user interface in engaging online learners. *Quarterly Review of Distance Education, 3*(2), 141–60.

Miller, G. (2003). The cognitive revolution: A historical perspective. *Trends in Cognitive Sciences, 7*, 141-144.

Miyazoe, T., & Anderson, T. (2010). Empirical research on learners' perceptions: Interactions equivalency theorem in blended learning. *European Journal of Open, Distance and E-Learning*. Retrieved from http://www.eurodl.org/

Moore, M. G. (1989). Editorial: Three types of interaction. *The American Journal of Distance Education*, *3*(2), 1-6.

Norman, D. A. (1982). *Learning and memory*. San Francisco, CA: Freeman.

Neubauer, A. C. (2011). Where in the brain is creativity? Looking down on divergent thinking (Presidential Address). *International Society for the Study of Individual Differences*. Retrieved from http://www.youtube.com/watch?/y=dMTh9xoNWX4&feature=youtube

Pavlov, I. P. (1927). *Conditioned reflexes* (G. V. Anrep, Trans.). London, England: Oxford University Press.

Pavlov, I. P. (1928). *Lectures on conditioned reflexes* (W. H. Gantt, Trans.). New York, NY: International.

Pence, H. E. (2007). Preparing for the real web generation. *Journal of Educational Technology Systems, 35*(3), 347-356.

Piaget, J. (1969). *Science of education and the psychology of the child*. New York, NY: Viking.

Piaget, J. (1951). *Play, dreams, and imitation in childhood*. New York, NY: Norton.

Reigeluth, C. M., & Moore, J. (1999). Cognitive education and the cognitive domain. In C. M. Reigeluth (Ed.), *Instructional-design theories and models: A new paradigm of instructional theory* (Vol. 2, pp. 51-68). Mahwah, NJ: Erlbaum.

Rumelhart, D. E. (1980). Schemata: The building blocks of cognition. In R. J. Spiro, B. C. Bruce, & W. F. Brewer (Eds.). *Theoretical issues in reading comprehension* (pp. 33-58). Hillsdale, NJ: Erlbaum.

Schunk, D. (2012). *Learning theories: An educational perspective* (6th ed.). Boston, MA: Allyn & Bacon.

Shank, R. C., Berman, T. R., & Macpherson, K. A. (1992). Learning by doing. In C. M. Reigeluth (Ed.). *Instructional design theories and models: A new paradigm of instructional theory* (pp. 161-179). Hillsdale, NJ: Erlbaum.

Simões, L., & Gouveia, L. (2008, March-April). *Web 2.0 and higher education: Pedagogical implications on higher education: New challenges and emerging roles for human and social development*. Paper presented at the 4th International Barcelona Conference on Higher Education Technical University of Catalonia (UPC).

Skinner, B. F. (1938). *The behavior of organisms*. New York, NY: Appleton-Century-Crofts.

Skinner, B. F. (1953). *Science and human behavior*. New York, NY: Free Press.

Skinner, B. F. (1954). The science of learning and the art of teaching. *Harvard Educational Review, 24*, 86-97.

Sousa, D. A. (2011). *How the brain learners* (4th ed.). Thousand Oaks, CA: Corwin.

Stapleton, C., & Hirumi, A. (2011). Interplay instructional strategy: Learning by engaging interactive entertainment conventions. In M. Shaughnessy & S. Fulgham (Eds.). *Pedagogical models: The discipline of online teaching* (pp. 183-211). Hauppauge, NY: Nova Science.

Suchman, L. (1987). *Plan and situated actions: The problem of human-machine communications*. Cambridge, England: Cambridge University Press.

Thach, E. C., & Murphy, K. L. (1995). Competencies for distance education professionals. *Educational Technology Research and Development, 43*(1), 57-79.

Thorndike, E. L. (1913a). *Educational psychology: Vol. 1. The original nature of man*. New York, NY: Teachers College Press.

Thorndike, E. L. (1913b). *Educational psychology: Vol. 2. The psychology of learning*. New York, NY: Teachers College Press.

Thorndike, E. L. (1914). *Educational psychology: Vol. 3. Mental work and fatigue and individual differences and their causes*. New York, NY: Teachers College Press.

Thorndike, E. L. (1932). *The fundamentals of learning*. New York: Teachers College Press.

Vygotsky, L. (1962). *Thought and language*. Cambridge, MA: MIT Press.

Vygotsky, L. (1978). *Mind in society: The development of higher psychological processes*. Cambridge, MA: Harvard University Press.

Watson, J. B. (1913). Psychology as the behaviorist views it. *Psychological Review, 20*, 158-177.

Weiner, B. (1986). *An attributional theory of motivation and emotion*. New York, NY: Springer-Verlag.

Weiner, B. (1985). An attributional theory of achievement motivation and emotion. *Psychological Review, 92*, 548-573.

Wenger, E. (1998). *Communities of practice: Learning, meaning and identity*. New York, NY: Cambridge University Press.

Willis, J. (2006). *Research-based strategies to ignite student learning: Insights from a neurologist and classroom teacher*. Alexandria, VA: Association for Supervision and Curriculum Development.

Wittrock, M. C. (1974). Learning as a generative process. *Educational Psychologist, 11*(2), 87-95.

Wittrock, M. C. (1985). Teaching learners generative strategies for enhancing reading comprehension. *Theory into Practice, 24*(2), 123-126.

Wittrock, M. C. (1990). Generative processes of comprehension. *Educational Psychologist, 24*, 345-376.

Zull, J. E. (2011). *From brain to mind: Using neuroscience to guide change in education*. Sterling, VA: Stylus.

CHAPTER 8

KEY INTERACTIONS FOR ONLINE PROGRAMS BETWEEN FACULTY, STUDENTS, TECHNOLOGIES, AND EDUCATIONAL INSTITUTIONS

A Holistic Framework

Jomon Aliyas Paul and Justin Daniel Cochran
Kennesaw State University

Online education is becoming increasingly popular among both traditional and nontraditional students. Students gravitate to the flexibility of online courses, which allows them to work around jobs, family, and other responsibilities. While online program growth continues, these programs present several new challenges to educational institutions and their successful implementation requires a clear understanding of several factors that are at the root of these challenges. We propose 2 intuitive relational diagrams featuring roles and interaction among faculty, student, technology, and institution that could serve as a conceptual framework for developing successful online education programs.

Beyond the Online Course: Leadership Perspectives on e-Learning
pp. 125–145

INTRODUCTION

The popularity of online education is ever increasing with almost 4.3 million undergraduate students taking at least one distance education course (National Center for Education Statistics, 2011) per year. About 0.8 million of these students took their entire program through distance education (National Center for Education Statistics, 2011). Some factors related to this trend include student demand for flexible schedules, increased course availability, and increased student enrollment options. Online programs serve as a great opportunity for educational institutions to grow their educational programs. However, the success of an online program ultimately depends on the ability of the faculty and institution to provide quality online education (Allen & Seaman, 2006). Extant literature has emphasized on the importance of faculty, educational institution, and technology for attaining online education success. However, it has left out several key interactions between these entities from this discussion, in addition to student responsibilities (Finch & Jacobs, 2012; Mayadas, 1997; McLean, 2005; Thompson, 2003).

We believe that while these four components (institution, student, faculty, and technology) are necessary and important as single entities for delivering and utilizing online education, the larger risks and rewards for online education occur where these components intersect. This article attempts to develop a framework to aid in understanding the significance of the key interactions between these four components and their relevance to online programs by reviewing previous research in online education and bringing it together to represent a more holistic view of online education. Specifically, we develop two relational diagrams that could serve as the conceptual framework for online programs. Further, we discuss challenges in successfully achieving and maintaining the aforementioned interactions and provide examples from extant literature and our personal experiences for successful implementation of online education. We examine additional relationships *within* the components that serve as additional opportunities and risks to institutions. For instance, student-student interactions beyond the classroom in the form of professor evaluations on noninstitution websites, e-mail and phone communication, sharing of work from previously enrolled online courses, etc., need to be considered when developing online programs. These can have significant positive as well as negative implications on the quality and success of the online programs offered by an institution.

CONCEPTUAL FRAMEWORK

We propose a relational diagram that presents the interactions between four primary components (institution, faculty, student, and technology) that have a significant impact on online education (Figure 1). This does not discount the responsibilities of the components on their own (such as faculty members maintaining their expertise over time). In Figure 1, we show six pairwise relationships between components. We attempt to bring together diverse and focused research articles in online education to create a more comprehensive and holistic conceptual model for online programs. To accomplish this, we first highlight challenges that exist with the interactions between key components (students, faculty, technology, and institution) from an online program perspective. Then, we present some mechanisms for resolving these challenges based on investigation of extant literature. Finally, we propose a second relational model that builds on the basic assumptions of the first model (Figure 2).

STUDENT ↔ FACULTY

Perhaps the most important interaction that takes place at an institution is between the students and faculty. In an online environment, the importance of this interaction is no less important. Research has shown that about 55% of communication happens nonverbally (through facial expression and body language), about 38% is tone (called "vocal liking"), and about 7% is verbal (Mehrabian, 1972, 1981). As a consequence, two

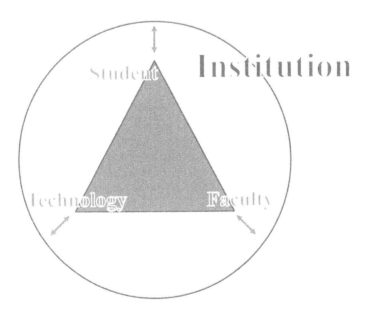

Figure 1.   Macro view of online education components.

major components of communication are limited in many online courses—tone and facial expression/body language. We can probably think of cases where nonverbal communication is not a key aspect of our communication (e.g., e-mail, instant messaging), but we often are more comfortable in those situations because we have an initial impression of the other parties. In a new relationship, such as that between a student and a faculty member in an online class, there may not be that "first impression" to rely on as a substitute for nonverbal and tone aspects of communication. Fortunately, in an online course, there are some steps that both the student and the faculty can take to help overcome the limitations to communication found in many courses.

Course Development

The first step to combating the limitations of communication that are often found in online courses is a thorough course development process. Course development should focus on both course content and delivery of instruction. Specifically, course content should be accurate, current and cover all the concepts students are expected to learn when taking the course (Zhu, Payette, & DeZure, 2003).

Interaction and Feedback

Interaction and feedback are important behaviors influencing student motivation and involvement. Faculty concern and communication with students helps those students get through rough times and continue working (Chickering & Ehrmann, 1996). It is important for instructors to actively engage their students to promote advanced understanding, rather than allowing students to be passive consumers of information (McKeachie & Svinicki, 2005). Immediacy, presence, and feedback are each important aspects of the student-faculty interactions.

Verbally immediate behavior by instructors has been found to positively affect student performance. This can be achieved through initiation of discussions (Arend, 2009), asking questions, using self-disclosure, addressing students by names, using inclusive personal pronouns, responding frequently to students, offering praise, and communicating attentiveness (Arbaugh, 2001; J. D. Baker, 2004; McAlister, 2001; O'Sullivan, Hunt, & Lippert, 2004).

Presence has been found to positively impact student learning, cognition, and motivation. Methodical design, establishment of time parameters and group norms via conventions of netiquette, and facilitation of discourse (C. Baker, 2010), and weekly announcements are excellent ways of achieving presence as an online instructor.

Students need chances to reflect on what they have learned, what they still need to know, and how they might assess themselves. This can be achieved effectively via prompt faculty feedback. Instructor feedback has been shown to improve student involvement in discussions (Meyer, 2007), enhance student motivation for learning, and stimulate student interest in class (Mory, 1992). Pyke and Sherlock (2010) have classified feedback into three types: corrective, motivational, and technology-oriented. Corrective feedback, the most important of the three, should not be restricted to grading/verification of student work, but should also help students better understand the concepts and guide them in correcting their work (Kulhavy & Stock, 1989). Motivational feedback, unlike corrective feedback (which is task oriented), is aimed at motivating the student towards better performance.

Communicate Expectations

Setting expectations is an important step for a faculty member to make in an online course. These expectations should not only communicate the deliverables for the course, but also the nature of the interaction between faculty and students and between the students. This is more critical for those students who may have a tendency to shirk preparation and lack a willingness to exert themselves since self-motivation can be more difficult in an online environment. Expecting students to perform well has been found to be a self-fulfilling prophecy. This includes an emphasis on time on task, clear communication of the assessment criteria, et cetera (iNA-COL, 2010). Since there is no face-to-face interaction between faculty and students, taking the time to stress these aspects can improve online education success. In other words, students may not feel the same pressure to perform up to expectations when they are not physically standing in front of a faculty member. Finally, given the "distance" of the relationship between students, as well as the pseudo-anonymity students have in online classes, setting a clear communication etiquette policy is wise.

Assessment of Student Learning

To take advantage of the relationship established between faculty and students in online classes, the students need to believe that the course assesses their knowledge accurately and appropriately. This may seem like an obvious point, but it is relatively easy to lose alignment between course objectives, course content, and course assessments in an online course. There also may not be as many opportunities to clarify the links between objectives, content, and assessment in an online class. So additional care should be taken to ensure the students understand the connections.

Additionally, students need to believe in the integrity of the course. There is a perception that it is easier to cheat in an online class, which may have negative effects on the commitment of enrolled students as well as undermine the credibility of the institution. Results of a study suggest that 73.6% of the students in the sample held the perception that it is easier to cheat in an online versus a traditional course (King, Guyette, & Piotrowski, 2009). Prevention or reduction of fraud is possible if chances of the fraud triangle (opportunity, incentive, and rationalization) are reduced (Wells, 1997).

Some possible activities to decrease the likelihood of cheating (and improve the perception of the integrity of the course) are algorithmic/numerical assignments that require a process to reach the solution, discussions, proctored exams, and team projects. One effective way of achieving this is through assignment of a significant number of activities with minimum weight because having only a few activities with large weights might facilitate the fraud triangle. Other practices that have been shown to deter cheating in online classes include the following: providing students with an academic honesty policy (Olt, 2002), clear communication by the faculty on consequences of cheating (Chapman, Davis, Toy, & Wright, 2004), electronic submission of assignments (McMurtry, 2001), and proctored tests that include randomized questions (Serwatka, 2003; Shuey, 2002; Vachris, 1999).

STUDENT ↔ TECHNOLOGY

While there is an obvious relationship between the student and the technologies they must utilize in an online class, there is much variability in the satisfaction of the students with this relationship. Some students will find the technology requirements for online courses to be rather elementary, while others (often nontraditional students) may have more struggles and frustrations. As a result, online programs should take some steps to improve the relationship between students and technology required for their online courses.

Student-Centered and Intuitive Systems

Technology adoption should be done keeping in mind the frequent interactions that numerous students enrolling in online programs will have with the system selected. Since the technology is a delivery mechanism for course content and repository for accepting student work, it should be intuitive for students to use and have an effective and accessible help system. This is particularly important for online courses because help desk support may not be available at the hours when students are doing their work for online classes. Students today are highly familiar with popular web-based software that undergoes constant evaluation and frequent improvements—and they are expecting similar ease of use and intuitive design from their online course technologies.

Technology Orientation for Students

While students have different skill levels with technology, success of an online student nonetheless depends to a considerable extent not only on learning and assessment, but also on these technological skills. Furthermore, while it is appealing to have intuitive systems with which students interact, the reality is that the improvement cycle time for learning management systems and class technologies is much slower than technologies provided to the broader consumer base (e.g., Amazon.com, Facebook). As a result, students often need training in the basic skills of file management, sending and checking e-mails, locating course materials, accessing discussion posts, using chat rooms, et cetera. (Mandernach, Gonzales, & Garrett, 2006). A good tool for helping students gain the necessary technology skills is an institution mandatory online student success course (Beyrer, 2010). This should ideally use rich demonstrations, like screen capture and video, to demonstrate the necessary skills for online courses.

Technology is essentially a double-edged sword, bringing great benefits to students while potentially introducing increased risks for misuse. For example, increased use of technology has been shown to increase the risk of plagiarism, cheating, and discourteous behavior among students (Glenn, 2008). These risks need to be factored in carefully in all the technology-related decisions made by institutions and faculty.

STUDENT ↔ INSTITUTION

In the traditional institutional setting, the student is able to leverage the possibility for face-to-face communication through the option of physically entering institution buildings, allowing the benefits of face-to-face communication such as body language and real-time interaction. In most cases, an electronic or online substitute is not offered, making many of the administrative tasks the student must undertake more difficult and time consuming. For instance, tasks like student advising or even acquiring a student identification card can require physical presence on campus. Even processes such as applying for financial aid that are increasingly computer based are often significantly easier when real-time interaction is possible.

Of course, administrative processes and requirements are not the only significant interactions between institution and students. Students in entirely online environments are not able to participate in institution activities at the same level and richness as students that physically attend campus. For instance, institutions are not likely to offer academic and social clubs for online students, or any tools to facilitate this type of participation in the institution. While online students likely realize they are willingly foregoing these possibilities, institutions could take additional steps to accommodate these students. In fact, there may be tangible benefits for the institution in terms of student persistence, a commonly acknowledged problem of online education (McGivney, 2009), through provision of tools for involving online students in broader institution activities.

While they may be challenging, there are some steps that institutions can take to enhance the relationship between itself (administrative employees) and the online students.

Student Advising and Other Support Services

Mayadas has stated the importance of having a good student advising system available to online students (1997). This should include advisors that are well versed in the differences that may be encountered in online courses in general so that they can assist students in deciding which delivery methods suit them best. Advisors should also be able to guide students regarding total number of courses they can handle during a semester given there may be some differences in the time commitment required for online classes. In other words, while online courses are considered to be more flexible, the increased responsibility on the student for active learning may lead to a greater time commitment. This knowledge can be critical for students that work full time. Advisors should also help students set reasonable expectations for taking online courses. Other student support structures include providing students with information about programs, admission requirements, tuition and fees, books and supplies, technical and proctoring requirements, availability of hands-on training, how to use services like interlibrary loans, campus libraries (Merisotis & Phipps, 2000), credit transfers, placement testing, financial aid counseling, et cetera. Consequently, as online programs grow at individual institutions, it is important to have staff that can cater to the unique needs of the online student that may be far away from campus, as well as technologies that support effective asynchronous and synchronous communication with students.

Career Services Offerings

In most cases, students are attending institutions to increase their knowledge and skills so that they are more attractive to the workplace. For students that operate entirely online, they generally do not have the same access to career services offerings, like resume help, cover letter coaching, job postings, and other helpful resources. Given that their career is often driving their continued education, institutions can provide great value to online students by leveraging some of the same communication technologies that courses use. The provision of this service will go a long way to fostering a long term connection with the student, especially when career services can match that student with an employer. Several examples of a virtual career centers that aim to help online students receive the same career development support as traditional on campus students are available (California State University-Fullerton, 2011; University of Central Florida, 2011).

Institution Engagement and Immersion Offerings

Institutions recognize the benefits of student and alumni commitment reaped through student persistence (prior to graduation) and monetary (and other) contributions back to the institution upon completion. Forward-thinking institutions will recognize an opportunity with a growing number of online students that are graduating, but may have difficulty encouraging the same level of contributions from students that do not have the broader on-campus immersive experiences. These alumni are no less important to the institution, and institutions should take steps to engage students in deeper extracurricular experiences for both the positive effects it will have on the online student population and the potential rewards it will bring for fundraising. While achieving the same level of immersion for online students as resident and traditional students may not be possible, it does not mean that these opportunities should not be identified and provided (Glenn, 2008). Fortunately, free technologies like Google Hangouts and Skype, and licensed technologies like Adobe Connect and Blackboard Collaborate, will allow institutions to have richer interactions with students, both present and former.

Support Services for Students

One of the greatest burdens on faculty in online environments comes from dealing with student issues beyond the content of the course itself. Institutions can mitigate the issues associated with student needs beyond the course by providing support resources for students. In particular, students need access to general support services and to technical support. Student failure in online courses can be generally attributed to the following: unreasonable expectations, lack of technological know-how, inappropriate online communication etiquette, poor time management skills, lack of experience working on team projects with members at different locations, and inadequate opportunities to evaluate online versus traditional learning environment suitability before registering for actual courses. These challenges can be overcome through development of mandatory online student success courses to become eligible for online education (Beyrer, 2010).

Additionally, institutions should ensure students have constant information technology support online and by phone (even 24 hours if needed), and easy access to software upgrades (Mayadas, 1997). In addition, frequent updates on changes in system requirements, web browsers etc. should be provided to students to reduce frustrations and avoid any handicap to student performance. While these services are targeted for students, they greatly reduce the burden on faculty when properly advertised to students. Faculty are often ill-equipped to handle technical and student success issues, and lack of support at the institutional level for these needs reduces greatly the satisfaction of faculty teaching online.

Faculty ↔ Technology

Given the technology-dependence of delivering online courses, faculty have to ramp up their understanding of available technologies to keep pace with improvements that improve the overall experience for online students. There are a number of ways that faculty can keep pace with technology, starting with a sincere interest in looking for ways to increase the richness of their course offerings. Without a desire for some experimentation with technology and a willingness to tinker, faculty commonly have difficulty improving the quality of their online courses. Fortunately, there are some avenues to assist faculty in their interactions with technology for online environments.

Instructor Training and Technological Know-How

Many institutions have in place specific technology training resources, which is fortunate given that instructor training is critical to online learning outcomes. Technically prepared faculty have been found to spend more time on actual teaching than on the technical aspects as compared to less prepared faculty (De Gagne & Walters, 2009) since the technology presumably becomes second nature with more understanding.

Continuous Technology Improvement

For faculty, the good news is that software that supports both the creation of content and the delivery of online courses is becoming both more sophisticated and easier to use. Where producing online videos just a few years ago required a studio, expensive equipment, and staff to shoot and edit the footage, faculty can now use a wide variety of video devices and produce their own videos inexpensively with relative ease on their own computer using tools like Camtasia Studio (2011) and Panopto (2011). There are many tools that capture activity on computer screens in a manner similar to the classroom whiteboard, like Blackboard Collaborate (2013). Additionally, most tools export content to standard formats that reduce the number of compatibility issues that can arise in online environments. Perhaps the most fortunate aspect of this continual improvement is that the ease-of-use qualities of these tools is outpacing their complexity, meaning faculty can use technology more intuitively with less need for training. This aspect also encourages faculty to explore more on their own.

FACULTY ↔ INSTITUTION

Beyond technology-specific support for faculty, institutions can assist individual faculty efforts in online education by providing an umbrella of services at a broader level. Among these offerings are administrative and monetary support, pedagogical support, and mechanisms to ensure ethical learning.

Administrative and Monetary Support

Faculty satisfaction is one of the five pillars of a quality online education (Mayadas, 1997). For years, faculty who set off in the direction of online education felt isolated and alone in figuring out the details of offering a course virtually. This has led numerous faculty to avoid the hassle and stick with traditional classroom teaching in many cases. The institution can take steps to facilitate development and teaching of online courses by providing the appropriate administrative direction and staff to complete the necessary paperwork or other hurdles. Additionally, to encourage greater faculty participation, institutions have often offered monetary incentives to faculty developing online courses as subject matter experts and to those teaching them. Such incentives have been shown to encourage online teaching (Betts, 1998; Jones & Moller, 2002; Rockwell, Schauer, Fritz, & Marx, 1999; C. Schifter, 2002; C. C. Schifter, 2002). Other similar incentives include consideration of online efforts during tenure and promotion evaluations. This has been shown to improve the level of job satisfaction as well as the amount of support and recognition faculty receive from peers (Bonk, 2001; Parisot, 1997; Rockwell et al., 1999).

Pedagogical Support

Given the variations of assignments, assessments, and general engagement of students in an online environment, faculty are often stepping out of their comfort zone when designing and teaching online courses. Institutions can help alleviate some of the anxiety that comes with this shift by providing expertise in online course design and teaching in the form of instructional designers. Modern instructional designers focus much more on virtual delivery of content, assessment, and assignments than in years past. This makes trained instructional designers invaluable to faculty members since instructional designers can discuss pedagogical issues and partner with faculty to help develop some of the course content (while leaving the subject expertise to the faculty).

Mechanisms to Ensure Ethical Learning

Perhaps still the most problematic concern or fear in online environments is the potential for unethical behavior by students. While this is a valid concern (in online and face-to-face environments), there are a number of mechanisms available to help deal with this concern. Among these are proctoring, course design, and technology solutions.

In some cases, faculty still wish to give final exams in person. To give students flexibility, while still issuing a photo-verified final exam, many institutions offer proctoring options. Of course, certification of proctors is critical for promoting ethical learning. Since it can be difficult to check every proctoring center, the institution should provide support services to faculty in terms of verifying the proctor information. According to Koch (2000), "fear of lawsuits, time required to handle cheating incidents, lack of institutional rewards for catching cheating, [et cetera], are all listed as rationalizations for this behavior" (p. 753). Institutions also must support and motivate faculty to report and take action against academic dishonesty. It is in the best long term interests of the institution to police and punish academic dishonesty because not doing so only worsens the problem and also leads to a gradual substitution/demotion of courses less susceptible to cheating practices by those more prone to it (Gresham's Law).

Institutions can also support faculty by providing integrity checks for faculty. These tools have become readily available from a variety of sources, such as Turnitin (http://turnitin.com/) and SafeAssign (http://www.safeassign.com). While expensive, they provide more confidence that homework submissions are unique to a student, that writing is not plagiarized, and that assignments across time are also legitimate. These systems also send a signal to students that their work is being monitored for cheating, which in itself is a deterrent from academic dishonesty.

INSTITUTION ↔ TECHNOLOGY

Since online offerings are technology-dependent, it is critical for the university to provide the infrastructure necessary to deliver content to students in a reliable and fast manner. Institutions without the proper infrastructure and support of technologies will have frustrated users, both faculty and students. In fact, online education programs at institutions that are not simply equipped with technology, but are pro-technology overall have been shown to be more successful (Clark, Holstrom, & Millacci, 2009).

However, institutions do not have unlimited resources for building technology infrastructure, especially during phases of rapid growth. At institutions where there is a heterogeneous expansion of online programs, the technology acquisition process is even more difficult. Some colleges or departments within the institution may be more "mature" with online education and have different technology needs than colleges just entering into online instruction. There can be substantially different technology requirements for leveraging large amounts of video and audio files versus more text-based course offerings. As a result, there can be a continual struggle to determine whether to adopt technology in different areas of the institution or institutionwide, and when that decision should be made.

Many of these decisions are at times simplified, for better or worse, by institution technology decision models (e.g., centralized, federated, or decentralized models). In other words, a structured acquisition process may reduce the options considered during selection decisions.

In some cases, institutions may have development capabilities on campus to help construct tools to support online education. For instance, instead of a marketplace solution for housing videos produced by students, institutions may choose to develop their own solution that is designed for the particular needs of the institution audience. Of course, not all institutions will have development capabilities or resources on that level and purchasing technology may be the only option.

While much of this discussion is related to how the institution will support the technology needs for online education, there is also a missed opportunity by the institution to leverage technology to understand more about their online programs. Part of this is due to the limitations of the systems that are available to institutions off-the-shelf to collect usage data and other indicators of technology use. There can also be compliance concerns about collecting certain data about students that must be thoroughly evaluated. However, in many cases, there is simply a lack of strategy for how data could be leveraged to better serve the students, faculty, and how to gauge future technology purchases.

THE IMPACT OF CROSS POLLINATION

To this point, we have discussed a framework that leverages the most commonly examined and researched aspects of online education. These, however, are not the only relationships present in institutional settings. In this section, our focus is on examining the potential positives and negatives of "cross-pollination," or communication within the components.

The framework portrayed by Figure 1 presents a traditional view of roles for each of the four components (students, faculty, institution, and technology), but is not adequate in light of technological advancements that have enabled much higher interaction within the student, faculty, and technology communities. Cross-pollination is in essence a "back channel" communication within each group. We believe this model (Figure 2) extends to fit increasingly integrated and social communication environments, which are beginning to have a real impact in online education. This view is critical in any dialogue about online education especially among administrators.

Cross-Pollination

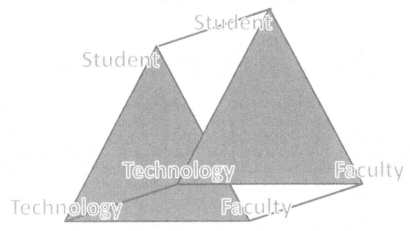

Figure 2.   Cross-pollination of students, technologies, and faculty.

STUDENT ↔ STUDENT

There are two primary interactions between students outside of classes that can influence online programs: direct and indirect. Direct communication between students often occurs between former and current classmates in a manner similar to traditional settings, albeit more likely to occur through various communication technologies. Students discuss the class experience, which professors to choose for upcoming courses, and tips for success. Students will commonly use telephones, e-mail, face-to-face meetings (where possible) or tools like Facebook for direct communication (Facebook can also be an indirect tool depending on the user's privacy settings). There are positives and negatives of this interaction. For example, they may share assignments across terms, making the use of plagiarism check systems even more important when appropriate. They could also challenge the integrity of the online course, undermining the demand for the course or future integrity for the course. However, they may also reinforce expectations for online classes, the skills and dedication necessary and additional learning benefits that they gained in an online environment.

Indirect communication also occurs in the online environment through tools like Twitter, RateMyProfessor.com, and MyEdu.com. These tools can be both beneficial and damaging for the institution or individual faculty. This is a primary motivation for encouraging faculty members to ensure that their classes are of high quality and their relationship with students in the course is positive and effective. With the various communication tools available today, negative word of mouth can reach much farther and enough poor experiences can quickly damage the perception of overall program quality. It is not clear if the most motivated commenters are negative for these tools and there are also concerns about their validity due to possibilities of abuse of these tools (Otto, Sanford, & Ross, 2008).

The primary means to ensure positive outcomes from student-student interactions beyond courses and on the broader Internet is to maintain high quality (and continually improve) in online courses across the board. Institutions should also undertake an initiative to monitor public channels for indications of poor quality and publicly make efforts to remedy complaints where pertinent. This type of brand monitoring is common in the corporate setting, and should be included in brand management for institutions as well.

FACULTY ↔ FACULTY

Faculty are obviously on the frontlines of education, and in online environments where techniques and technologies are continually changing and hopefully improving, they are a primary source for hands-on knowledge. A common problem in many institutions is a lack of communication between faculty about the classroom experience (e.g., new ideas, failed efforts, etc.), and this is compounded in environments where online classes are taught by off-campus faculty. These faculty are often reluctant to share their experience and "lessons learned" with others for several reasons. They may not have a good connection to the traditional institution faculty, they may not have the best tools to communicate their experiences or give feedback to others, or they may believe their ideas are not novel.

There are several real benefits to facilitating communication about online teaching between faculty. Faculty are able to transition more smoothly from a face-to-face to online classroom with fellow faculty support. It helps faculty learn about new techniques and experiences other faculty had when they incorporated it in their courses. It reinforces faculty faith in methods of instruction they use and it also provides faculty with moral support and space for airing frustration when facing similar problems as other faculty (Kyei-Blankson & Keengwe, 2011).

Of course, negative word of mouth can spread about the online teaching experience as well. The institution is often well served by implementing communication structures among the faculty to help monitor and alleviate concerns as well as promote successes. Some possible avenues for encouraging communication are committees, faculty surveys, brownbags, and/or newsletters devoted to online learning. These tools can help encourage buy-in from faculty while communicating to administration what aspects need improvement. Additionally, these tools can also bridge the gap between online faculty and face-to-face faculty that are skeptical of online teaching.

TECHNOLOGY ↔ TECHNOLOGY

Students' expectations of technology in online programs are heavily influenced by their broader technology experiences with smartphones, social networking, and even their personal computers. They expect applications to work seamlessly, have richness and clarity, be simple to use, and at times fun. They often do not realize the amount of resources required to create these experiences (like those created by Apple for example), or the limited budget at institutions to develop software. Thus far, learning management systems are improving with each iteration, but are still much less intuitive than popular systems and websites frequented by students today. Nonetheless, these marketplace systems and websites set student (and faculty) expectations and online programs need to continue to chase the experiences that students are seeking, technologywise.

Given that the target is always moving, and the absence of a single system that delivers learning content in a way that compares to the students' broader experiences, institutions need to consider ways to integrate technologies as seamlessly as possible. There are tools available to allow students to have video and audio discussions, for example, but these systems often require the students to leave the learning management system and learn a new interface. This experience, while still an improvement, is not seamless and results in some dissatisfaction for the students (and faculty). Additionally, much of the material in online classes is "stuck" within the particular course. Students must manually move the content to their personal devices to have it available after the close of the course at the end of the semester, so their submitted work may be difficult to access. A better structure would enable students to leverage a "cloud storage" option so that they can access material in years to come much like previous generations kept notebooks on a shelf for reference.

Ultimately, there will be learning management systems that are more intuitive and more closely match user expectations. In the meantime, institutions should take advantage of opportunities to integrate technologies to make the online learning experience richer and less "clunky." It is admittedly not an easy process, and will be full of tradeoffs due to limited resources, but the goal should be to get away from numerous siloed systems.

CONCLUSION

Successful online education is critical to success of the institution, teaching faculty, and careers of the students. Increasingly, growth of the educational programs at institutions to a large extent depends on its ability to provide a quality online education. Quality of the online education offered, in turn, depends on the understanding by institution administration, faculty, and students about their roles and responsibilities. In this article, we have presented some of the most important pieces of the online education puzzle and have framed the discussion in terms of the key interactions that need to be bolstered and managed for rolling out successful online programs. The understanding of the interactions between components (students, faculty, institution, and technology), underlying challenges, methods to overcome them, as well as the cross-pollination that occurs between components (students, faculty members, and technologies) should benefit institutions already running online education programs as well as those that are planning to plunge into this enticing market in the near future by recognizing that the various components cannot be treated independently.

There are several directions that future research could pursue. For instance, empirical studies to check effectiveness of tools and techniques suggested for successful implementation of various interactions discussed in this study is a matter worthy of future research (for example, effectiveness of software to prevent academic dishonesty like Turnitin and Safe-Assign). Student retention continues to be a serious issue affecting online programs, which might be due to lack of intrinsic and extrinsic student motivations. Faculty-student and student-institution interactions need to account for these issues when designing and evaluating online courses and programs. Research on mechanisms that could better prepare students prior to enrolling in an online program is notably lacking as well.

REFERENCES

Allen, I. E., & Seaman, J. (2006). *Making the grade: Online education in the United States.* Needham, MA: The Sloan Consortium.

Arbaugh, J. B. (2001). How instructor immediacy behaviors affect student satisfaction and learning in web-based courses. *Business Communication Quarterly, 64*(4), 42-54.

Arend, B. (2009). Encouraging critical thinking in online threaded discussions. *The Journal of Educators Online, 6*(1), 1-23.

Baker, C. (2010). The impact of instructor immediacy and presence for online student affective learning, cognition and motivation. *The Journal of Educators Online, 7*(1), 1-30.

Baker, J. D. (2004). An investigation of relationships among instructor immediacy and affective and cognitive learning in the online classroom. *The Internet and Higher Education, 7*(1), 1-13.

Betts, K. S. (1998). An institutional overview: Factors influencing faculty participation in distance education in postsecondary education in the United States: An institutional study. *Online Journal of Distance Learning Administration, 1*(3).

Beyrer, G. M. D. (2010). Online student success: Making a difference. *MERLOT Journal of Online Learning and Teaching, 6*(1).

Blackboard Collaborate. (2013). Retrieved from http://www.blackboard.com/platforms/
collaborate/overview.aspx

Bonk, C. J. (2001). *Online teaching in an online world.* Bloomington, IN: CourseShare.com.

California State University-Fullerton. (2011). Virtual Career Center. Retrieved from http://campusapps2.fullerton.edu/Career/students/
jobSearch/Chapter1/TitanConnection.aspx

Camtasia Studio. (2011). Retrieved October 20, 2011, from http://www.techsmith.com/camtasia/

Chapman, K., Davis, R., Toy, D., & Wright, L. (2004). Academic integrity in the business school environment: I'll get by with a little help from my friends. *Journal of Marketing Education, 26,* 236-249.

Chickering, A. W., & Ehrmann, S. C. (1996). Implementing the seven principles: Technology as lever. *AAHE Bulletin,* 3-6.

Clark, M., Holstrom, L., & Millacci, A. M. (2009). University of Cincinnati: Case study of online student success. *Journal of Asynchronous Learning Networks, 13*(3), 49-55.

De Gagne, J. C., & Walters, K. (2009). Online teaching experience: A qualitative metasynthesis (QMS). *MERLOT Journal of Online Learning and Teaching, 5*(4), 577-589.

Finch, D., & Jacobs, K. (2012, October). Online education: Best practices to promote learning. *Proceedings of the Human Factors and Ergonomics Society 56th Annual Meeting.* Boston, MA.

Glenn, M. (2008). Future of higher education: How technology will shape learning. Austin, TX: Economist Intelligence Unit white paper, sponsored by the New Media Consortium.

iNACOL. (2010). *National standards for quality online teaching.* Vienna, VA: Author.

Jones, A. E., & Moller, L. (2002). A comparison of continuing education and resident faculty attitudes towards using distance education in a higher education institution in Pennsylvania. *College and University Media Review, 9*(1), 11-37.

King, C., Guyette, R., & Piotrowski, C. (2009). Online exams and cheating: an empirical analysis of business students' views. *The Journal of Educators Online, 6*(1), 1-11.

Koch, K. (2000). Cheating in schools. *The CQ Researcher, 10*(32), 745-768.

Kulhavy, R. W., & Stock, W. A. (1989). Feedback in written instruction: The place of response certitude. *Educational Psychology Review, 1*(4), 279-308.

Kyei-Blankson, L., & Keengwe, L. (2011). Faculty-faculty interactions in online learning environments. *International Journal of Information and Communication Technology Education, 7*(3), 25-33.

Mandernach, B. J., Gonzales, R. L., & Garrett, A. L. (2006). An examination of online instructor presence via threaded discussion participation. *Journal of Online Learning and Teaching, 2*(4), 248-260.

Mayadas, F. (1997). *The 5 pillars.* Retrieved from http://www.sloan-c.org/5pillars

McAlister, G. (2001). *Computer-mediated immediacy: A new construct in teacher-student communication for computer-mediated distance education* (Unpublished doctoral dissertation). Regent University, Virginia Beach, VA.

McGivney, R. J. (2009). *Adult student persistence in online education: Developing a model to understand the factors that affect adult student persistence in a course.* Amherst, MA: University of Massachusetts-Amherst.

McKeachie, W. J., & Svinicki, M. (2005). *McKeachie's teaching tips: Strategies, research and theory for college and university teachers.* Boston, MA: Houghton-Mifflin.

McLean, J. (2005). Addressing faculty concerns about distance learning. *Online Journal of Distance Learning Administration, 8*(4).

McMurtry, K. (2001). E-cheating: Combating a 21st century challenge. *THE Journal Online: Technological Horizons in Education.* Retrieved from http://thejournal.com/Articles/2001/11/01/echeating-Combating-a-21st-Century-Challenge.aspx

Mehrabian, A. (1972). *Nonverbal communication.* Chicago, IL: Aldine Atherton.

Mehrabian, A. (1981). *Silent messages.* Belmont, CA: Wadsworth.

Merisotis, J. P., & Phipps, R. A. (2000). *Quality on the line: Benchmarks for success in Internet-based distance education.* Washington, DC: Institute for Higher Education Policy.

Meyer, K. A. (2007). Does feedback influence student postings to online discussions? *The Journal of Educators Online, 4*(1), 1-17.

Mory, E. H. (1992). The use of informational feedback in instruction: Implications for future research. *Educational Technology Research & Development, 40*(3), 5-20.

National Center for Education Statistics. (2011). *The condition of education 2011 (NCES 2011-033).* Retrieved from http://nces.ed.gov/fastfacts/display.asp?id =80

O'Sullivan, P. B., Hunt, S. K., & Lippert, L. R. (2004). Mediated immediacy: A language of affiliation in a technological age. *Journal of Language and Social Psychology, 23*(4), 464-490.

Olt, M. (2002). Ethics and distance education: strategies for minimizing academic dishonesty in online assessment. *Online Journal of Distance Learning Administration, 5*(3).

Otto, J., Sanford, D. A., & Ross, D. N. (2008). Does ratemyprofessor.com really rate my professor? *Assessment & Evaluation in Higher Education, 33*, 355-368.

Panopto. (2011). Retrieved October 20, 2011, from http://www.panopto.com/

Parisot, A. H. (1997). Distance education as a catalyst for engaging teaching in the community college: Implications for institutional policy. *New Directions for Community Colleges, 99*, 5-13.

Pyke, J. G., & Sherlock, J. J. (2010). A closer look at instructor-student feedback online: A case study analysis of the types and frequency. *MERLOT Journal of Online Learning and Teaching, 6*(1), 110-119.

Rockwell, S. K., Schauer, J., Fritz, S. M., & Marx, D. B. (1999). Incentives and obstacles influencing higher education faculty and administrators to teach via distance. *Online Journal of Distance Learning Administration, 2*(3).

Schifter, C. (2002). Perception differences about participating in distance education. *Online Journal of Distance Learning Administration, 5*(1).

Schifter, C. C. (2002). Faculty motivators and inhibitors for participation in distance education. *Education Technology, 40*(2), 43-46.

Serwatka, J. A. (2003). Assessment in on-line CIS courses. *Journal of Computer Information Systems, 44*(1), 16-20.

Shuey, S. (2002). Assessing online learning in higher education. *Journal of Instruction Delivery Systems, 16*(2), 13-18.

Thompson, M. M. (2003). *Faculty satisfaction in the online teaching-learning environment*. Needham, MA: Sloan Center for Online Education.

University of Central Florida. (2011). Virtual Career Center. Retrieved October 19, 2011, from http://www.career.ucf.edu/categories/Students/91_13.aspx

Vachris, M. A. (1999). Teaching principles of economics without chalk and talk: The experience of CNU online. *Journal of Economic Education, 30*(3), 292-303.

Wells, J. T. (1997). *Occupational fraud abuse*: Austin, TX: Obsidian.

Zhu, E., Payette, P., & DeZure, D. (2003). *An introduction to teaching online*. Ann Arbor, MI: University of Michigan.

CHAPTER 9

UNIVERSAL COURSE SHELL TEMPLATE DESIGN AND IMPLEMENTATION TO ENHANCE STUDENT OUTCOMES IN ONLINE COURSEWORK

Arthur J. Borgemenke, William C. Holt, and Wade W. Fish
Texas A&M University-Commerce

Instructors are continually looking for means to improve outcomes for students in online courses. This article examines the instructional design of courses to determine if consistent components implemented in a recently established online master's degree program can produce significant student outcomes. The authors detail the construction and implementation of a universal course shell template in an online master's program. The program faculty perceptions about the success of the universal shell in online courses are discussed. The rationale underpinning the template implementation is examined in light of program faculty and student reflections.

INTRODUCTION

According to the U.S. Department of Education (USDE), online learning is one of the fastest growing trends in educational uses of technology (USDE, 2009). While debate continues about the effectiveness of online instruction compared to traditional face-to-face class, this meta-analysis

Beyond the Online Course: Leadership Perspectives on e-Learning
pp. 147–157
Copyright © 2016 by Information Age Publishing
147

by the USDE of 51 study effects, mostly in older learners, found that students who took all or part of their class online performed better than those taking the same course through traditional instruction. The study also did not find a significant effect by learner type. While this meta-analysis did not identify online learning as a superior medium, it did note that online learning is much more conducive to the expansion of learning time than is face-to-face instruction.

Educators face new challenges as instruction is increasingly delivered online in asynchronous formats (Dabbagh, 2000). As online instruction expands in scope, instructors search for means to maintain rigor and content via nontraditional course delivery (Cooper, 2000). Online instruction can add another level of cognitive loading if the student must relearn how to access course components as they matriculate through their program of study. Students' cognitive loading may be lessened when course components are presented with consistency and designed with clarity in mind.

PURPOSE

This article describes the implementation of a universal course shell template in a graduate studies program from faculty perspectives regarding improvements in program goals and student outcomes. The authors participated in the migration of a traditionally delivered principal preparation program to full online course delivery. The universal course shell template is reviewed to determine if it benefits students and instructors alike in providing a more user-friendly interface with the professor and the course content. Instructors explore seeing student engagement with the course content taking place sooner because they do not need to relearn the format of the digital learning interface.

RATIONALE

Instructional design is a critical concept in the development of university courses, particularly in intensive and shorter term courses such as those utilized by the Texas A&M University-Commerce Educational Administration program. Chen (2007) found a blended approach of objectivist-constructivist design to be the most effective in these intensive programs. This design encourages the learner to take responsibility for his or her learning while allowing the instructor to serve as facilitator and concurrently set specific learning objectives for the class. Students in this blended approach had a positive learning experience and were highly satisfied with their learning outcomes (Chen). Snyder (2009) suggested that new instructional design theories are needed using the current technologies and web tools available to enhance learning among adult learners. She combined elements of three fields of study—learning communities, adult learning theory, and constructivism—to propose a new instructional design theory that supports a sense of community and achieves the goals of the instructional program.

LITERATURE REVIEW

It is widely recognized that teaching online requires different skills as opposed to teaching in a traditional classroom. One of those skills is course and program development in the online environment. According to Caplan (2004), online course development is complex and it is not reasonable to expect high caliber online courses to be developed by just one or two instructors. Many universities now bring faculty and support staff together to develop online programs and courses. Hixon (2008) studied four instructor teams collaborating in online course development and identified several important commonalities, including flexibility, ownership of the process, and communication between team members.

Course Quality Design Factors

A number of course design factors can improve student learning and satisfaction in the online environment. Miller (2012) contended that professors can improve engagement, completion, and success by fine-tuning course shells to make them simple to navigate and understand. She also noted that students do not indicate distress when a course works well; the mechanics of course operation fade into the background if they do not present a problem.

Since online instruction is relatively new for many students, it is imperative that clear expectations for the class be established by a number of measures. Dykman and Davis (2008) asserted that many students do not know what to expect or even how to behave in an online course, so the professor must tell them what to do. A well-developed syllabus including the course description, technical requirements and university policies, and class procedures creates the foundation. These authors also contended the professor should be prepared to answer questions to the entire group in well-thought-out, consistent responses. Careful communication of expectations and documentation right from the beginning are mandatory for effective online instruction (Dykman & Davis).

Another characteristic of quality course development is consistency in design. To increase the comfort level of students, all courses in a program should have a similar look and feel (Dykman & Davis, 2008). This uniformity makes the software much easier to navigate and less threatening or confusing. Online courses are more difficult to change during the term once students have learned the system and expectations. These courses need similar design, organization, and structure across the modules within the course and within the coursework in a program.

In addition to consistency, an established structure of learning such as course modules of defined length helps to simplify course organization for students. Swan (2012) found that using modules was important in navigation of the course. This study found that when modules were consistent within the course, students believed they learned more and were more satisfied. Swan concluded that the nature of online courses makes it more likely students will get lost or confused if the course is not easily navigated.

Component Design Efficacy

How to design quality online courses using available components to enhance learning is a question posed by staff members charged with developing both course content and instructional tools. In a meta-analysis of 99 studies comparing online and face-to-face courses, the USDE (2009) identified several statistically significant characteristics of effective online courses. While the incorporation of multiple media does not singularly enhance learning, the learner's ability to control the learning media is important. The clearest recommendation for practice came from the incorporation of mechanisms that promote student reflection and self-monitoring of understanding. Simulations and more complex evaluation strategies were also more effective than simple multiple-choice quizzes to enhance learning. Individualization and feedback was found to be effective in some studies also. Group learning may also be more effective as students scaffold for one another to enhance learning (USDE). The following components reflect the findings of the USDE analysis and represent the best practices currently being utilized in quality online instruction.

The homepage often provides orientation to the course. Chen (2007) found that good orientation plays a critical role in an online course. The homepage must be deliberately designed to ensure students are familiar with the learning tools and resources. This feature often contains various components including unit introductions, announcements, and reminders. Miller (2012) found frequent homepage posts improve the appearance of the course and help engage learners. Enhanced homepages are not typically time consuming to professors and lead to improved student success and completion. Homepages may also link to a question-and-answer feature and an announcement board to communicate with all students. Revere and Kovach (2011) contended that status updates—links, pictures, and videos—keep online students connected throughout the course.

Discussion is an essential dimension of human learning. Within asynchronous online courses, the discussion board essentially replaces face-to-face interaction in the brick and mortar classroom. Andresen (2009) contended that, while the online discussion forum has its limitations, it is able to generate the critical dimensions of learning found in the traditional classroom. He suggested the primary goal of the discussion forum is to enhance higher levels of learning. The professor must design and evaluate appropriate participation in the discussion forum to achieve this end. The role of the instructor must also change from the traditional classroom to facilitate higher order discussion and not simply serve as the sage to answer questions. The research of Nandi, Hamilton, and Harland (2012) encouraged a blended student-centered and instructor-centered discussion format where instructors post answers, guiding questions and hints to encourage deeper learning. Students should be required to participate substantively with specific goals. A grading rubric is particularly important in this feature to set expectations and provide some equity in grading (Fisher, 2010).

The development of group tasks is an instructional strategy to increase interaction among peers and to encourage engagement. Brindley, Blaschke, and Walti (2009) made a strong argument for small group collaborative learning in online courses. These researchers saw a strong relationship between these experiences and teamwork skills as well as deeper learning. They also showed a close link to learner satisfaction and retention. Revere and Kovach (2011) believed collaboration technologies could facilitate synchronous coursework and foster camaraderie. These authors suggested that online environments that encourage sharing of personal information foster cohesion and support both social and cognitive engagement. Even simple posting of introductions allows online students to learn about each other early in the course and to develop a sense of community. A number of collaboration software applications exist to create this environment including Google Docs, Facebook, and VoiceThread.

This component of teaching and learning should be part of any learning process, but is critical in the online classroom to ensure success. Fisher (2010) noted the importance of feedback in guiding the writing process to avoid student confusion and apprehension. He encouraged the instructor to provide detailed syllabi, explicit instructions, assessment criteria, and coaching to enhance learning. Most learning management systems provide multiple venues for information and feedback, including syllabus, announcements, dropboxes, and e-mail (Fisher, 2010). Grading rubrics provide a tool that delineates the specific expectations or criteria that will be used to assess a student's performance. Solan and Linardopoulos (2011) believed that rubrics are particularly important in online learning since there is typically less opportunity for the students and instructors to interact one to one. Rubrics reduce the element of surprise for students and allow them time to think about how they will be evaluated and what a completed assignment should look like.

INSTRUCTIONAL DESIGN PROCESS

The first step faculty took toward the universal course shell implementation was to identify features that would be provided within each program's online course. The participants strove to build online courses that provided a standardized and familiar feel for students. This was initiated without neglecting the unique positive attributes of each faculty member that complemented specific learning objectives and instructor strengths in respective courses.

Through input from program faculty, the identified components of this consistent course shell presentation included the course syllabi, course home page, and module agendas. Further uniform protocol that was agreed upon by instructors revolved around assignment submission, discussion forum procedures, and methods for communication between instructor and student.

Universal Course Shell Template Components

Syllabus. One of the most important components of the universal course shell template design is establishing consistent syllabi throughout all courses in the program of study. Students not only find course syllabi within the same location of each program course shell, but all syllabi contain the same sections and section order regardless of the course. Sections contained in all course syllabi within program courses include instructor contact information, course information, course requirements, course assignments, course calendar, technology requirements, and university specific procedures and polices.

Course descriptions and student learning outcomes are included within the course information section of all program course syllabi. Within the course requirement section of the course syllabus, students are provided with information pertaining to the design of the course and assignment descriptions complemented with specific grading rubrics. While the previously mentioned course syllabi sections are specific to the unique needs of each course, the remaining two sections, technology requirements and university-specific procedures and policies, provide verbiage consistent across all program course syllabi. University-specific procedures and policies remind students about guidelines for the Office of Student Disability Resources and Services, scholarly expectations, dropping the class, incomplete grades, and academic honesty.

Course Homepage. Based upon the notion that "first impression is everything," our universal course shell template provides a course home page that is student/user friendly, providing relevant information that is easy to navigate without providing too many resources that confuse the learner. Our course shells are designed with the assumption that a learner has never taken an online course before, which caters toward these attributes. Resources included within our universally designed course home pages include a welcome video, links to course announcements, program information, grade book, course syllabus, and technical support.

When students enter their online course shell for the first time, they are prompted to view a welcome video that highlights how to successfully navigate through the course. This video remains on the course front page throughout the duration of the course in case learners need to go back and review instructions.

While not wanting to provide too many announcements in risk of saturating the importance, this method of communication effectively serves as a means to prompt students to proceed to particular agendas in addition to reminding learners about assignment due dates. Course announcements also allow the instructor to communicate relevant modifications to course content and manage "troubleshooting" issues that may suddenly occur throughout the course.

The course homepage within each course shell is a program information link where students can obtain relevant information pertaining to the master's program that may be beyond the scope of a particular course. Resources within this program information link include our updated student handbook, degree plan, internship packet, upcoming TExES Examination tutoring sessions and graduation application protocol. There is also a discussion thread link where students can ask nonconfidential questions pertaining to these program related items.

A student lounge link within the course homepage provides students an opportunity to become familiar with and practice using the discussion form tool by posting a message introducing themselves to their new classmates. Furthermore, these new learners to a course can practice responding to classmate posts.

Student Grading. The grade book is an essential component of our universal course shell design that allows students to efficiently monitor and manage their course grades. Within each assignment link in the grade book, students are able to obtain feedback by clicking their linked numerical assignment grade. All faculty members within our program strive to provide constructive feedback to students within 72 hours of assignment due dates. Program course grade books are linked to assignment drop boxes, which allow assignment submissions to link directly to the grade book.

Other universal components to the course shell homepage include links to the course syllabus, library, e-mail, student lounge, and technical support. The technical support page is especially important for students if the course instructor is unable to resolve specific technical situations experienced by the student.

Course Content and Assignments

The majority of our program courses align within a 7-week course format. All weekly course content is housed under corresponding module agenda links. Modules for all courses within our program are designed to begin on a Monday and conclude the following midnight Sunday in order to deter confusion regarding assignment due dates. Within each module agenda, students are able to view a particular module overview, module learning outcomes, module resources and module assignment instructions. This module outline is consistent across all courses.

Multimedia. Our instructors often embed a module video within the overview section where they walk students through important concepts and reminders pertaining to the specific agenda. Reading material and videos are linked within the resources section of module agenda where students are able to retrieve easily.

Student Discussion Responses. A discussion forum link is often provided within a module that allows students to post a response to a designated activity specifically tied to the agenda's learning outcomes. Module discussion forums are often broken into groups of 7 to 10 in order to enhance student-to-student interaction. Students are encouraged to post an initial response to a module discussion question by Thursday of a particular week and provide constructive feedback to at least two of their classmates through the following Sunday.

Student Assignments. Module assignment activity links are also provided within a particular module agenda where students are prompted to submit via a dropbox feature that is directly linked to the course grade book. Grading rubrics are embedded into each module discussion forum and assignment link in order to remind students of the necessary criteria for success. One common practice that aligns with the universal course design is for assignments to become due at the final date of each module.

Student Q & A. Each module has a module question-and-answer link for students to ask nonconfidential questions, allowing all students to view previous questions and responses within a timely manner housed under one forum. Students are also provided the opportunity to address a class-mate's question if they can effectively address the issue.

SUMMARY AND IMPLICATIONS

The graduate program described in this article has had various compo-nents of the universal course shell template in place for approximately two years. Direct measurement of the success of the universal course shell template can be difficult to gauge. Anecdotally, students and adjunct instructors report that the courses have a better look and feel. A more practical approach to gauging the effect of this initiative might be exam-ining program goals and outcomes.

The program described in this article implemented the new online compressed model in hopes of increasing student enrollment. The pro-gram has experienced explosive student growth since the 2009-2010 semesters. The number of students enrolled and actively taking courses in the program has swelled by more than 400% during that time period. This is a result of a program reorganization that took place beginning in late 2011. The anecdotal faculty perceptions about the reasons for the large increase are many.

- The program was migrated to fully online status and courses were shortened to 7 weeks in length.
- The number of semester credit hours required to complete the master's degree and principals certification courses was lowered from 36 to 30.
- The amount of time that students need to complete the program has been shortened by several months in length.
- The program completion rate has risen significantly.
- The first-time student passing percentage on the state of Texas school administrator certification examination is now greater than 95%.

Using these metrics to gauge the initiative, the implementation of the universal course shell template in the Educational Administrative pro-gram can be called at least a promising best practice.

REFERENCES

Andresen, M. A. (2009). Asynchronous discussion forums: Success factors, outcomes, assessments, and limitations. *Educational Technology & Society, 12*(1), 249-257. Retrieved from http://www.ifets.info/abstract.php?art_id=923

Brindley, J. E., Blaschke, L. M., & Walti, C. (2009). Creating effective collaborative learning groups in an online environment. *International Review of Research in Open and Distance Learning, 10*(3), 1-18. Retrieved from http://www.irrodl.org/index.php/irrodl/article/view/675/1313

Caplan, D. (2004). The development of online courses. In T. Anderson & F. Elloumi (Eds.), *Theory and practice of online learning.* Athabasca, Alberta, Canada: Athabasca University. Retrieved from http://cde.athabascau.ca/online_book/

Chen, S. J. (2007). Instructional design strategies for intensive online courses: An objectivist-constructivist blended approach. *Journal of Interactive Online Learning, 6*(1), 72-86. Retrieved from http://www.ncolr.org/jiol/issues/viewarticle.cfm?volID=6&IssueID=19&ArticleID=100&Source=2

Cooper, L. (2000). On-line courses tips for making them work. *Technological Horizons in Education Journal, 27*(8), 87-92.

Dabbagh, N. H. (2000). The challenges of interfacing between face-to-face and online instruction. *Tech Trends, 44*(6), 37-42.

Dykman, C. A., & Davis, C. K. (2008). Online education forum: Part two—Teaching online versus teaching conventionally. *Journal of Information Systems Education, 19*(2), 157-164. Retrieved from http://www.jise.appstate.edu/Issues/19/V19N2P157-abs.pdf

Fisher, C. (2010). Discussion, participation and feedback in online courses. *Proceedings of the Information Systems Educators Conference, 27*(1382). Retrieved from http://proc.isecon.org/2010/pdf/1382.pdf

Hixon, E. (2008). Team-based online course development: A case study of collaboration models. *Online Journal of Distance Learning Administration, 11*(4). Retrieved from http://www.westga.edu/~distance/ojdla/winter114/hixon114.html

Miller, J. M. (2012). *Finding what works online: Online course features that encourage engagement, completion, and success* (Doctoral dissertation). Retrieved from California State University Northridge ScholarWorks website: http://scholarworks.csun.edu/handle/10211.2/1062

Nandi, D., Hamilton, M., & Harland, J. (2012). Evaluating the quality of interaction in asynchronous discussion forums in fully online courses. *Distance Education, 33*(1), 5-30. doi:10.1080/01587919.2012.667957

Revere, L., & Kovach, J. V. (2011). Online technologies for engaged learning: A meaningful synthesis for educators. *Quarterly Review of Distance Education, 12*(2), 113-124.

Snyder, M. M. (2009). Instructional-design theory to guide the creation of online learning communities for adults. *TechTrends, 53*(1), 48-56. doi:10.1007/s11528-009-0237-2

Swan, K. (2001). Virtual interaction: Design factors affecting student satisfaction and perceived learning in asynchronous online courses. *Distance Education,*

22, 306-331. Retrieved from www.rcet.org/research/publications/interactivity.pdf

Solan, A. M., & Linardopoulos, N. (2011). Development, implementation, and evaluation of a grading rubric for online discussions. *MERLOT Journal of Online Learning and Teaching, 7*(4). Retrieved from http://jolt.merlot.org/vol7no4/linardopoulos_1211.htm

U.S. Department of Education, Office of Planning, Evaluation, and Policy Development. (2009). *Evaluation of evidence-based practices in online learning: A meta-analysis and review of online learning studies.* Retrieved from U.S. Department of Education website: www.ed.gov/about/offices/list/opepd/ppss/reports.html

CHAPTER 10

KNOWLEDGE BUILDING IN AN ONLINE COHORT

Mary E. Engstrom, Susan A. Santo, and Rosanne M. Yost
University of South Dakota

This study sought to understand how an online cohort in a master's program, comprised of teachers from the same school district, constructed knowledge about instructional theories and practices. Participants in this descriptive study included 10 teachers from the same rural school district. Data collection consisted of a focus group and written survey. Four constructs guided the development of questions: collaboration, learning community, course design, and individual factors. Findings showed that cohort members drew on one another's strength to support their collective learning throughout the program. One unexpected finding was the role that face-to-face, informal study groups played in support knowledge construction and technology skill building.

KNOWLEDGE BUILDING IN AN ONLINE COHORT

Studies of face-to-face, blended, and online graduate education cohorts have established the importance of a cohort model to the learning process (Conrad, 2005; Maher, 2005; Wenzlaff & Wieseman, 2004). Lawrence (2002) defined a cohort as "a small group of learners who complete an entire program of study as a single unit" (p. 83). Due to its close-knit nature, a cohort has a strong potential to become a learning community whose members acquire, use, and share their collective knowledge (Brown

Beyond the Online Course: Leadership Perspectives on e-Learning
pp. 159–181
Copyright © 2016 by Information Age Publishing
159

& Duguid, 2000). How does an online cohort in a master's program, comprised of teachers from the same school district who were approached to complete a degree in instructional technology, construct knowledge?

While the notion of a master's cohort is not unique, we found ourselves in a unique situation in which 10 teachers from the same public school district became a cohort group and completed a master of science degree in instructional technology. Furthermore, in the case of this particular cohort group, the opportunity to complete a master's degree came to them; they didn't seek it out. The state had a federal Teacher Quality Enhancement (TQE) grant that focused on professional development through cohort programs for teachers. The purpose of this TQE grant initiative was to increase the number of teachers in the state with master's degrees in either instructional technology or in curriculum and instruction. The MS program was approved for this initiative by the grant's executive team and the state secretary of education. Teachers in this particular school district were invited to form a cohort because the school district was recognized for its innovations with technology.

This study sought to understand how the online cohort in this master's program, comprised of teachers from the same school district, constructed knowledge about instructional theories and practices. Our program uses a social-constructivist paradigm in which the instructor, rather than transmitting knowledge and being seen as the sole authority on the course, is more of a facilitator. Discussions, collaborative work, and real-life projects are an essential aspect of this approach. Social constructivism is based on the work of Vygotsky (1978), who developed the idea that cognition is related to social interaction and learning involves the integration of learners into a learning community. According to Jonassen (1999), social constructivism assumes that knowledge is "socially co-constructed by learners based on their interpretations of experiences in the world" (p. 217).

REVIEW OF THE LITERATURE

Knowledge can be defined as being "composed of those insights and understandings that give meaning to information and data... Knowledge originates in the minds of knowing subjects, who evaluate and interpret it in the light of the framework provided by their experiences, values, culture, and learning" (Sallis & Jones, 2002, p. 9). Knowledge building and learning communities are closely connected concepts (Garrison, Anderson, & Archer, 2000; Lawrence, 2002; Ubon & Kimble, 2002). For the purpose of this study and based on the readings, we defined *knowledge building* as an active attempt to understand experiences and create meaning through collaboration and discussion, "whereby ideas are negotiated, concepts evolve, meanings are agreed upon, and knowledge is constructed" (Swan et al., 2000, p. 380). We defined *learning community* as "a general sense of connection, belonging, and comfort that develops over time among members of a group who share purpose or commitment to a common goal" (Conrad, 2005, p. 2).

Garrison and colleagues (2000) used the phrase *community of inquiry* to describe learning in an online environment. This community exists through the interaction of three elements: cognitive presence (how learners construct meaning and knowledge through collaborative communication), social presence (ability of learners to present themselves as "real people," a sense of group commitment), and teaching presence (designing the educational experience and acting as a facilitator). All three are needed for a successful community that can go beyond simply transmitting information. Learners can be "questioning but engaging, expressive but responsive, skeptical but respectful, and challenging but supportive" (p. 96). The authors concluded that knowledge acquisition is essential for building understanding and maintaining a learning community. Swan and colleagues (2000) identified three similar factors that contribute to successful online learning: consistency in course design, connection to online community through the encouragement of the instructor, and knowledge building through frequent course discussion.

Lawrence (2002) stated that one way of co-creating knowledge is for students to share stories of their own experiences and perspectives. This leads to a deeper understanding: "The knowledge that is co-created is greater than the sum of each individual member's knowledge" (p. 85). All learners are responsible for the growth of every member of the community; helping one person helps the group to succeed. To build knowledge, they need to share expertise with each other and discuss ideas and perspectives. A group will be more willing to consider multiple perspectives if provided by other members than if only the authority figure (i.e., the teacher) provides it. Knowledge construction takes place through social interaction. Informal opportunities may lead to exploring ideas students are not sure about and obtaining assistance from other classmates.

Knowlton (2001) stated that the use of good online pedagogy and facilitation of students' knowledge building in online discussions (as opposed to lecturing in an online discussion) promotes higher order thinking. Knowlton stated:

> Knowledge construction is best accomplished through collaboration. In general, students learn through the give-and-take among classmates. That is, as students write contributions to discussions, they learn what it is that they are trying to say. The replies that they receive from their classmates further this learning. (Knowledge Construction heading, ¶2)

In addition, Knowlton, Knowlton, and Davis (2000) stated:

> When students share ideas in a discussion, they receive feedback on those ideas. Often this feedback from classmates will cause cognitive dissonance for the student because it conflicts with their original views. The dissonance encourages students to revise their views and test their revised views in light of further peer review among the class. (as cited in Knowlton, 2001, Knowledge Construction heading, ¶2)

Bober and Dennon (2001) used the term *intersubjectivity* to refer to the collaborative exchange and mutual understanding that promotes knowledge construction. The authors stated that achieving intersubjectivity and knowledge construction in online or blended courses "goes hand in hand with the development of a sense of community amongst learners" (p. 249). A learner-centered environment promotes intersubjectivity and fosters community building. Several student- and course-based factors influence the development of an online community. They include the following:

1. Tapping students' personal and professional experiences, motivation, and their learning preferences
2. The nature of the class (survey, core, elective, etc.)
3. Program pacing. "Community building must take into account the 'collegiality' of student relationships, not the least of which is their prior experience as classmates and/or project partners, and the likelihood that they will continue to work together on a formal or informal basis" (p. 247).

Lawrence (2002) pointed out that while all cohorts have a common goal, this does not automatically make them learning communities. Such a community can only develop over an extended period of time as members develop respect for each other's strengths, similarities, and differences, become comfortable with one another, and form bonds. When all contributions are valued, students are willing to change their opinions, and commitment to the group grows; thus students have the potential to cocreate knowledge.

Maher (2005) looked at what it meant to belong to a cohort and how that influenced students' relationships with one another and with the instructor. She collected data from a face-to-face cohort of 13 students in their first year of their master's program. Four themes emerged related to learning community: seeing peers as part of their family, seeing peers as part of a task-oriented team, a comfort zone or mindset of being accepted, and being able to learn through small group participation. The strength and the meaning of cohort membership evolved over time and students had initially underestimated the influence of the cohort model on their learning. Potthoff, Batenhorst, Fredrickson, and Tracy (2001), in a qualitative analysis of electronic portfolios of a face-to-face master's cohort group, identified the family theme as the most powerful and also recognized faculty support as important.

Wenzlaff and Wieseman (2004) looked at a blended learning master's program in curriculum for a cohort of 22 K-12 teachers. Teachers emphasized that the cohort helped in three ways: creating a learning community that made them better teachers, having professors create a safe space for students to engage in reflection, and establishing a collaborative culture helped them to broaden their perspectives.

METHODOLOGY

The setting for this descriptive study of an online cohort was a master's degree program in instructional technology in a school of education at a midwestern state university. The 36 credit hour program had a core of 24 credit hours and two specialty tracks consisting of 12 credit hours: K-12 education and training and development. A unique feature of this program was its selection for inclusion in the "Master's Degree Cohorts" initiative of a federal Teacher Quality Enhancement grant awarded to the state. The purpose of this grant was to increase the number of teachers in the state with master's degrees in technology (with a classroom focus) or in curriculum and instruction. One third of tuition costs were paid by the grant, one third was paid by the school district, and one third was paid by the students. A special course rotation was designed for this cohort in which the sequence of courses was spread out over 2 years (four semesters and two summer sessions), with students completing an average of six credit hours per semester.

Participants

All 10 participants in this study were teachers in the same rural school district who were invited to enroll in the MS program. Faculty from the program visited with interested teachers at their school site to provide a program overview, share the proposed 2-year sequence of courses, and answer any questions. Nine females and one male participant from this group applied and were admitted to the program. They all selected the K-12 specialty track. The *semi-closed cohort* (Basom, 1993, as cited in Potthoff et al., 2001) was comprised of middle school and elementary teachers, the

majority of whom were mid-career or veteran teachers. They were apprehensive about returning to school and completing the work expected of
students pursuing graduate-level work.

Cohort Program Design

The program used a social cognitive and constructivist philosophy that
emphasized a collaborative approach to learning, authentic and real-life
projects, and a balance of theoretical and skills-based courses. Cohort
participants were placed in self-contained or *closed* (Basom, 1993, as cited
in Potthoff et al., 2001) sections for the first semester of the program, in
an effort to ease their orientation into graduate level work and to create a
learning community based on collaboration and collegiality. Learning
experiences in the two courses taught during the first semester used a
blended approach (a combination of face-to-face and distance-based
interaction). From the second semester on, the cohort became a semi-
closed one in which others, outside of this cohort group, could enroll in
the course(s).

WebCT was the course management system used for online learning.
Interaction in all courses consisted primarily of asynchronous discussions.
Synchronous chat sessions also took place in several courses, and most
courses utilized individual and small group or collaborative assignments.
An interactive television (ITV) system was also used during the first
semester of the program for weekly orientation/Q&A sessions. The face-
to-face course sessions took place both on campus and at the school district site, which were separated by a distance of about 200 miles. In addition, face-to-face group advising sessions were held once a semester at
either the cohort school site or the university location. These informal
sessions (which always included sharing food!) guided students as they
synthesized knowledge gained from the program for their oral (electronic
portfolio) defense. The electronic portfolio defense was one of two summative program assessments whereby students demonstrated competency
around key program knowledge and skills.

Research Design

This descriptive study used a focus group and written survey to develop
"converging lines of inquiry" (Yin, 1994, p. 92). In addition to the use of
multiple data collection procedures, triangulation was achieved through a
peer review of the draft report.

A limitation of this study is the small number of students in our cohort. One suggestion for future research is to repeat this study with additional, larger cohorts.

Another limitation includes the researcher's biases and values. In a qualitative study, the researcher(s) must interpret complex, multidimensional evidence and the data will, to some extent, "reflect the notion of *researcher as instrument*" (Leedy & Ormrod, 2001, p. 162).

Data Collection

Data collection in this research study consisted of two phases. First, a focus group session was held at the district site. All 10 participants were invited to participate in this session and 5 (4 females and 1 male) were able to attend the 1-hour semistructured discussion. The researchers used a set of 10 general questions to gather students' perceptions of agents of knowledge building within the cohort program based on the research literature. An initial table of constructs was drafted, based on the literature review, to guide in the development of the questions. The five constructs included: collaboration, learning community, course design, interactions with the instructor, and individual factors.

Examples of questions were:

1. What did it mean to be a cohort group working on your master's degree together?
2. What role did cohort members play in helping you construct knowledge in the master's program?
3. What role did others play in helping you construct knowledge in the master's program?

One researcher served as the moderator and the other two recorded responses verbatim. Additional probes were asked by all three researchers. Focus group responses were transcribed and responses were organized, by common themes, within the draft constructs.

The second phase consisted of a written survey which allowed the researchers to explore the identified themes in more detail. For example, the following survey items correspond to the three focus group questions provided earlier:

1. Our cohort group drew upon one another's strengths to support our collective learning throughout the program.

2. The cohort group added to my knowledge of integrating technology to support student learning.
3. I frequently participated in informal study group sessions (face-to-face) with other cohort members.

Forty-nine of the 50 survey items used a 6-point Likert scale including a "not applicable" or "not sure" option. Forty-seven of the items used a scale ranging from *strongly agree* to *strongly disagree* (along with a *not applicable* option). The two items that asked participants to rate the level of knowledge building and level of community in their cohort used a scale ranging from *very high* to *very low* (along with a *not sure* option). The last survey item was an open-ended question. The 50-item survey was mailed to the 10 participants and all surveys were returned. Responses were kept anonymous.

Data Analysis

The original five constructs were collapsed into four during data analysis. It became apparent that the small number of items under interactions with faculty overlapped with the course design items, and thus they were merged into the course design category. The researchers set an arbitrary standard of 8 out of 10 people (80%) with responses of "agree" or "strongly agree" on survey items as positive indicators. Survey items for which seven or fewer people selected "agree" or "strongly agree" as responses were considered problematic. Qualitative comments included in the focus group and written survey were used to shed light on some of the findings and are included where applicable.

Collaboration

The study sought to understand how cohort members worked collaboratively to construct knowledge both within and outside their courses. Cohort members drew upon one another's strengths to support their collective learning throughout the program. This theme emerged in both data sets.

The cohort agreed that small group projects/assignments (in both content and skills classes) were important sources of knowledge building. Projects/assignments were viewed as "real life" applications that allowed students to "focus their work—real classroom work—around their curriculum." They also reported that there was a benefit of knowing each other for working on group projects. This allowed the students to share ideas with one another and "talk over the backyard fence." In this same vein, instructors were perceived as encouraging students to collaborate with one another.

The students liked having others outside their cohort in their classes after the first semester, because it "forced them" to use the online communication technologies more. In other words, they had to use online communication tools to complete projects/assignments when placed in small groups with classmates who were not a part of their cohort. In addition, students reported that the semi-closed nature of their courses allowed them to network with other teachers. As one student commented in the focus group session, "I got to meet some of those people at a state conference."

The internship, a program requirement, was also viewed as an agent for promoting knowledge building. The Internship requirement involved gaining direct work experience through the application of program coursework.

The students frequently participated in informal (face-to-face) study group sessions, on their own initiative, with their cohort members. The cohort members selected their study group partners based on professional respect and convenience. For example, those who worked in the same building or on a common time schedule were more likely to choose each other as partners. Most students agreed that their informal study group drew upon one another's strengths to support their collective learning throughout the program; this theme was present in both data sets. However, a few students rarely participated in such groups.

One problem area emerged under the collaboration theme. The response rate fell just below our set standard with regard to the extent that the Internship promoted collaboration with other professionals. Even though one requirement of the Internship includes working collaboratively with other professionals, only seven of the ten participants agreed that this practical experience promoted such collaboration.

Learning Community

All participants reported that the cohort model successfully promoted knowledge building among the cohort members. They agreed that the group increased their knowledge of K-12 student learning, teaching methods, and integrating technology to support student learning. Students perceived that their sharing of outside resources promoted knowledge building. They reported that the cohort members supported and encouraged one another. One comment on the survey explained: "The cohort model was an excellent way to build knowledge and a learning community. It helped in building confidence and also with basic questions that arose, therefore decreasing frustration and building a support system."

They felt a sense of trust and safety within their cohort and also reported being committed to the success of all cohort members in the program. The notion of support and encouragement was a strong theme in the focus group session. It also emerged in the open-ended survey item:

> The support of colleagues was so beneficial. In my study group, two of us lost loved ones, one of us left the country to adopt a baby, and one of us had a daughter [undergo] surgery. We were there for each other—not sure I would have made it without the cohort.

The participants would not only choose to be part of *a* cohort again, they would choose to be part of *this* cohort again.

A few areas did not meet our standards. For example, one question asked students to rate the level of knowledge building in their cohort. Seven of 10 rated the level of knowledge building in their cohort group as very high or high, and 3 of 10 as average. None of the participants indicated that this level was low or that they were unsure of the level of knowledge building in their cohort group. In regard to learning community, 7 of 10 rated the level of community in their cohort group as high or very high, while 3 respondents indicated an average level of community among their group. None rated it as low. It should be noted that one participant referred to herself as an "independent learner" during the focus group session; she indicated a preference for working on her own.

Seven of 10 people agreed that cohort members challenged one another's ideas and beliefs within and outside of the courses. In other words, this took place online and in the face-to-face study groups. When looking strictly at online discussion contributions, however, only 6 of 10 agreed that they sometimes changed their own beliefs about teaching and learning and no one strongly agreed with this statement. Three respondents replied "N" (neutral) to this question and one disagreed.

Course Design

Students agreed that communication (facilitator-student, student-student, discussions, and chats) in courses promoted knowledge building and a sense of community. They agreed that instructor facilitation of discussion, including sharing of outside resources, promoted their individual knowledge building, and reported that instructor feedback on assignments was effective in helping them build knowledge. In addition, the use of small group (collaborative) assignments was effective and encouraged a sense of community among the cohort.

Students appreciated the assignments and projects that allowed for a theory to practice connection. One comment made in the focus group stressed this: "Because this was an entire Masters degree program [as opposed to a professional development workshop], we learned the entire foundation, the theory behind [using technology to support student learning]." Many students addressed the real-life focus of the course work as a benefit of the program. "The instructors set up good projects and assignments that were focused on real-life learning; we had choices. We could pick and choose projects we could really use in our classrooms."

Students agreed that the cohort model successfully promoted a learning community among the cohort members and that socializing during face-to-face sessions with instructors contributed to the development of a learning community. As one student stated in the focus group, "Making us come to campus for face-to-face sessions made us get to know [the faculty] and made us more comfortable with you. It was easier to talk to you then."

WebCT was viewed as an effective tool for building an online learning community, although students did have to adjust to an online learning environment initially. Learning how "everything worked online" and improving time management skills were common themes that emerged in this context.

A number of problem areas emerged, falling just below our standard. Seven of 10 participants agreed: student facilitation of discussion promoted their individual knowledge building; face-to-face course meetings contributed to the development of a learning community; interaction with professors during courses was a strong factor in promoting their knowledge building; instructors encouraged students to ask questions about things that they didn't understand; and group advising sessions with faculty members contributed to their sense of belonging to a professional cohort. Two people were neutral and one person disagreed.

Individual Factors

The cohort members agreed that their comfort level with colleagues was a factor in joining the cohort. They also agreed that their respect for other colleagues in the cohort, as professional educators, was a factor in joining the cohort, and that their respect for their colleagues grew over the course of the program. They felt that they grew professionally during this cohort experience. Cohort members felt responsible for their own knowledge building and for the knowledge building of everyone in the group. They also agreed that they assumed responsibility for contacting instructors when questions or problems arose.

DISCUSSION AND RECOMMENDATIONS

This online case study sheds light on issues that may emerge in an online cohort comprised of teachers from the same school district. Teaching often occurs in isolation; class schedules and room size/arrangement do not often lend themselves to a collaborative approach to teaching in most K-12 school districts. Thus it was not anticipated that this cohort would form a strong learning community outside of the online environment, and the fact that they did so influenced their perception of the program, the role of instructors, and their role as learners.

Collaboration

Collaboration was found to be valued by the majority of the cohort, who even formed their own small study groups (not a requirement) to study together, help one another learn technology skills, and work on group projects. The informal study groups served as a "community of inquiry" (Garrison et al., 2000) as much knowledge acquisition was perceived to occur in these informal sessions. Lawrence (2002) stressed the importance of sharing expertise and discussing perspectives in the knowledge building process, and the informal study groups functioned in this context. As one person commented on the survey, "[Our] cohort supported and respected each other. All were there to help others with their weaknesses and were willing to share their strengths." Sharing expertise within the study group context emerged as a strong theme in the focus group discussion; students were aware of one another's areas of content and technology expertise and used them to their advantage. This was expressed as both a benefit and a constraint of cohort membership:

> Maybe we didn't try to learn on our own as much as we could have or should have. That was a constraint. It was easy to fall back/rely on others. If I got stuck while trying to learn something, it was easy to just give up and wait until the group got together and try to figure it out together at that time.

Bober and Dennon (2001) discuss how prior relationships as students can help to build collegiality and a sense of community. Although the cohort initially had no experience with one another as graduate students, they did see each other as fellow professionals within the same school district. This is both a benefit and a constraint for members of cohorts. The benefit is that they have the opportunity to learn more about one another, including their learning styles, strengths, and weaknesses. One student explained it this way in the focus group session: "It took us a while to understand how to work with one another because we didn't work together here at school. It took us a while to learn each others' learning styles." The biggest constraint may be the fact that the cohort members have to maintain positive relationships with one another as professional colleagues who will continue working in the same small, rural school district. This concern was voiced on the written survey: "The only downfall [of a cohort group] is when some members don't do their readings, assignments, etc. and then expect you to update and help them at the drop of a hat. The positives outweigh the negatives, though."

One culminating requirement of our MS program is an Internship which involves gaining direct work experience through the application of program coursework. Students in this cohort group chose to complete this requirement within their own school district by completing a project outside the scope of their responsibility as classroom teachers. One Internship project consisted of four cohort members working with building level colleagues to create a set of technology standards for elementary students in the district. Another project involved an individual cohort member designing and developing a staff development program on an electronic assessment software program. A third (individual) project resulted in the development of a new online Health course. The study revealed that collaboration with other professionals, which is supposed to be an integral part of the Internship experience, was not always taking place. This might reflect an advising issue, as dissatisfaction with one faculty member's role as an advisor was mentioned in both sets of data. This will be addressed in more detail in the course design discussion.

Learning Community

This cohort experienced the typical group norming process in the first semester of the program, initially serving as "cheerleaders" for one another in online discussions. Instructors had to push them to move beyond this role into that of critical friend. They also focused on comparing one another's grades in the first semester of the program. This was a source of stress for many of the students. One student helped the others put this initial anxiety into perspective by saying, "Whether [the overachiever in the group] gets the 'A' and we get a 'B', we still get the same degree."

Regarding the issue of learning community, participants felt that cohort members supported one another. Although they also agreed that the cohort model successfully promoted knowledge building, it was problematic that only 60% agreed they sometimes changed their own beliefs based on other's online discussion comments. Knowledge construction is supposed to involve the give and take of ideas, and it would be expected that some beliefs would be changed based on evidence and knowledge of other students. According to Knowlton (2001), feedback from other students during a discussion should lead to cognitive dissonance, which encourages students to revise their views and form new knowledge.

This cohort group demonstrated the four themes that Maher (2005) identified in a study of a face-to-face master's cohort: seeing peers as part of their family, seeing peers as part of a task-oriented team, a comfort zone or mindset of being accepted, and being able to learn through small group participation. It may be that the small study groups played such a large role in the students' knowledge building process that their online interactions in courses took a back seat to their weekly face-to-face study sessions.

Course Design

Although participants agreed in general that communication in courses promoted a learning community and knowledge building, on several of the more specific survey questions regarding these issues, fewer students agreed. For example, 30% did not see student facilitation of instruction, face-to-face course meetings, general interaction with instructors, or group advising sessions as promoting knowledge building and community. These responses may have been influenced by both the social constructivist nature of the program and the role that the informal study groups played in students' learning. In other words, students' prior formal learning experiences may have utilized a more traditional, teacher-centered approach. This idea emerged in the focus group session, during a discussion on ways in which this master's program differed from other forms of professional development they've experienced. All participants agreed that this was much harder than typical school-based professional development programs, because "you do not just 'do it'—just don't rush through and do [the workshop]. It was real work for your classroom; the two were integrated."

The fact that the small study groups served as the nucleus of the learning community may have also influenced the perceived role of instructors in the knowledge building process. Garrison and colleagues (2000) report that community exists through the interaction of three elements: cognitive presence, social presence, and teaching presence. The structure and purpose of the students' small study groups attended to these three elements. However, it should be noted that one person perceived the general interaction with instructors as a person-specific issue. The student commented on the survey: "The instructor made a huge difference. Depending on the class, [the instructor] determined how much knowledge building was promoted." Most of the face-to-face course meetings served as question and answer sessions, and the group advising sessions served to clarify program requirements.

Clear preferences regarding the use of online pedagogy and facilitation of students' knowledge building in online discussions (Knowlton, 2001) emerged in the focus group session. Students expressed frustration with the lack of consistency in online discussion practices (Swan et al., 2000) across courses. When asked how the design of the program influenced their learning, all participants agreed with this student's comment: "It depended on the professor; some professors only counted the number of times you responded [to a post]. Others focused on the *quality* of the posts." Cohort members liked the opportunity presented in some classes to assume the role of a discussion facilitator for one of the weekly online discussions.

It also emerged during the focus group discussion that a summer course on multimedia production was found to be much too short for students to be able to master the technology skills to the degree that they wanted (at that time, it ran only four weeks). Faculty need to work together more to determine what should be taught in this course and how it should be taught. Students were helping each other in their face-to-face study groups, with more skilled students helping those having difficulty. This caused them some frustration. Problems also emerged regarding access to software and hardware. In the future we need to work closely with the school district's technology directors to make sure needed software applications and hardware are available to the students. Finally, students expressed dissatisfaction with one professor as an advisor.

Individual Factors

In terms of individual factors, students were quite positive. They felt that they grew professionally during this experience and felt responsible not only for their own knowledge building but for that of other students. One theme that emerged during the focus group session was a sense of ownership over their learning. While only one third of tuition costs were paid by the students, making the degree program affordable, this individual contribution was also valued. As one person stated in the focus group session, "It was my choice to complete this program. I was paying for it; no [administrator] made me take it."

The concept of a cohort as family (Maher, 2005) was very evident in this group. The self-directed nature of these 10 teachers and colleagues, most of whom were veteran teachers, allowed them to form a strong and meaningful bond as a cohort and as small study groups. The three benefits of cohorts presented by Wenzlaff and Wieseman (2004) were present in this group.

First, their learning community made them better teachers. During the focus group session, the participants provided examples of how they now differentiate instruction to meet students' needs, use real-life learning experiences, and integrate technology to support student learning. Second, one course in particular, which focused on personal and organizational change, was highly regarded as an opportunity for the students to "become more reflective personally and professionally." Finally, the collaborative nature of the informal study groups influenced the members to broaden their perspectives.

Recommendations

These practical recommendations are designed for those who want to set up a cohort comprised of teachers from the same school district.

1. Recognize that online cohort members from the same school district are not likely to limit their learning and community involvement to the online environment. This has instructional design implications for the program. One possibility is to create a semi-closed cohort and assign group projects in which cohort members are consistently paired with noncohort members to complete assignments. Another option is to create a closed cohort for such a group and discuss options for creating a learning community within and beyond the online environment.

2. Provide a program orientation. Explain the cohort online model to learners so that they can make an informed decision about participating in such a group. In addition, discuss philosophical basis of the program in detail. Discuss privacy issues regarding sharing of grades. Finally, make all program requirements clear to the students.

3. Ensure, as a department, consistency across courses in terms of course design and online discussion protocols. This includes a willingness for faculty to share effective discussion facilitation practices with one another. Develop a consistent base across courses for grading participation in online discussions. Adopting a rubric for use by all instructors may be helpful.

4. Establish an ongoing relationship with the administrators at the school site to garner their support of the program. Work collabora-

tively to develop solutions regarding access to needed hardware and software.

5. Select advisors for cohort programs with care. Advisors should be able to establish and maintain a good rapport with students at a distance.

6. For students who indicate a preference for working individually, counsel them to consider other program delivery options.

REFERENCES

Bober, M. J., & Dennen, V.P. (2001). Intersubjectivity: Facilitating knowledge construction in online environments. *Education Media International, 38*(4), 241-250.

Brown, J. S., & Duguid, P. (2000). *The social life of information*. Boston: Harvard Business School Press.

Conrad, D. (2005). Building and maintaining community in cohort-based online learning. *Journal of Distance Education, 20*(1), 1-20.

Garrison, D. R., Anderson, T., & Archer, W. (2000). Critical inquiry in a text-based environment: Computer conferencing in higher education. *The Internet and Higher Education, 2*(2-3), 87-105.

Jonassen, D. (1999). Designing constructivist learning environments. In C. M. Reigeluth (Ed.), *Instructional-design theories and models: A new paradigm of instructional theory* (Vol. 2, pp. 215-239). Mahwah, NJ: Erlbaum.

Knowlton, D. S. (2001, April). Promoting durable knowledge construction through online discussion. *Proceedings of the annual Mid-South Instructional Technology Conference*, Murfreesboro, TN, (ERIC Document Reproduction Service No. ED 463 724).

Lawrence, R. L. (2002). A small circle of friends: Cohort groups as learning communities. *New Directions for Adult and Continuing Education, 95*, 83-92.

Leedy, P. D., & Ormrod, J. E. (2001). *Practical research: Planning and design*. Upper Saddle River, NJ: Prentice-Hall.

Maher, M. (2005). The evolving meaning and influence of cohort membership. *Innovative Higher Education, 30*(3), 195-211.

Pothoff, D., Batenhorst, E., Fredrickson, S., & Tracy, G. (2001). Learning about cohorts: A Masters degree program for teachers. *Action in Teacher Education, 23*(2), 36-42.

Sallis, E., & Jones, G. (2002). *Knowledge management in education: Enhancing learning and education*. Sterling, VA: Stylus.

Swan, K., Shea, P., Fredericksen, E., Pickett, A., Pelz, W., & Maher, G. (2000). Building knowledge building communities: Consistency, contact, and communication in the virtual classroom. *Journal of Educational Computing Research, 23*(4), 359-383.

Ubon, A. N., & Kimble, C. (2002, March). Knowledge management in online distance education. *Proceedings of the 3rd International Conference Networked Learn-*

ing (pp. 465-473), University of Sheffield, United Kingdom. Retrieved March 15, 2007, from http://www.cs.york.ac.uk/mis/docs/km_in_olde.pdf

Vygotsky, L. (1978). *Mind in society*. London, England: Harvard University Press.

Wenzlaff, T. L., & Wieseman, K. C. (2004). Teachers need teachers to grow. *Teacher Education Quarterly, 31*(2), 113-124.

Yin, R. (1994). *Case study research: Designs and methods*. Thousand Oaks, CA: SAGE.

KNOWLEDGE BUILDING IN AN ONLINE COHORT SURVEY

Directions:

Part 1: Collaboration

1. I knew the other Chamberlain cohort members, as professional colleagues, before entering this program.

    ☐ SD   ☐ D   ☐ N   ☐ A   ☐ SA   ☐ DNA

2. Our cohort group drew upon one another's strengths to support our collective learning throughout the program.

    ☐ SD   ☐ D   ☐ N   ☐ A   ☐ SA   ☐ DNA

3. I frequently participated in informal study group sessions (face-to-face) with other cohort members.

    ☐ SD   ☐ D   ☐ N   ☐ A   ☐ SA   ☐ DNA

4. I selected as informal study group partners those Chamberlain cohort colleagues for whom I held professional respect.

    ☐ SD   ☐ D   ☐ N   ☐ A   ☐ SA   ☐ DNA

5. I selected my informal study group partners based on convenience (same building, common time schedules, etc.).

    ☐ SD   ☐ D   ☐ N   ☐ A   ☐ SA   ☐ DNA

6. My informal study group drew upon one another's strengths to support our collective learning throughout the program.

    ☐ SD   ☐ D   ☐ N   ☐ A   ☐ SA   ☐ DNA

7. Small group projects/assignments in "content" courses (Learning Principles, Instructional Design, Social & Philosophical Foundations of Ed., etc.) were an important source of knowledge building for me.

    ☐ SD   ☐ D   ☐ N   ☐ A   ☐ SA   ☐ DNA

8. Small group projects/assignments in "skills" courses (Multimedia, Web Page Design, etc.) were an important source of knowledge building for me.

    □ SD   □ D   □ N   □ A   □ SA   □ DNA

9. Small group projects/assignments in "content" courses (Learning Principles, Instructional Design, Social & Philosophical Foundations of Ed., etc.) encouraged a sense of community among the cohort.

    □ SD   □ D   □ N   □ A   □ SA   □ DNA

10. Small group projects/assignments in "skills" courses (Multimedia, Web Page Design, etc.) encouraged a sense of community among the cohort.

    □ SD   □ D   □ N   □ A   □ SA   □ DNA

11. Instructors encouraged students to collaborate with one another.

    □ SD   □ D   □ N   □ A   □ SA   □ DNA

12. The Internship requirement was an important source of knowledge building for me.

    □ SD   □ D   □ N   □ A   □ SA   □ DNA

13. The Internship requirement promoted collaboration with other professionals.

    □ SD   □ D   □ N   □ A   □ SA   □ DNA

Part 2: Learning Community

14. The TET cohort model successfully promoted knowledge building among the cohort members.

    □ SD   □ D   □ N   □ A   □ SA   □ DNA

15. Cohort members supported and encouraged one another.

    □ SD   □ D   □ N   □ A   □ SA   □ DNA

16. Cohort members challenged one another's ideas and beliefs.

    □ SD   □ D   □ N   □ A   □ SA   □ DNA

17. Sometimes I changed my viewpoint on issues based on others' online discussion contributions.

    □ SD   □ D   □ N   □ A   □ SA   □ DNA

18. Sometimes I changed my beliefs about teaching and learning based on others' online discussion contributions.

   ☐ SD   ☐ D   ☐ N   ☐ A   ☐ SA   ☐ DNA

19. Students shared outside resources that promoted knowledge building (i.e.: provided web sites, titles of articles, conferences, etc.)

   ☐ SD   ☐ D   ☐ N   ☐ A   ☐ SA   ☐ DNA

20. The cohort group increased my knowledge of K-12 student learning.

   ☐ SD   ☐ D   ☐ N   ☐ A   ☐ SA   ☐ DNA

21. The cohort group added to my knowledge of teaching methods.

   ☐ SD   ☐ D   ☐ N   ☐ A   ☐ SA   ☐ DNA

22. The cohort group added to my knowledge of integrating technology to support student learning.

   ☐ SD   ☐ D   ☐ N   ☐ A   ☐ SA   ☐ DNA

23. I was committed to the success of all cohort members in the program.

   ☐ SD   ☐ D   ☐ N   ☐ A   ☐ SA   ☐ DNA

24. I would choose to be a part of **a** cohort again.

   ☐ SD   ☐ D   ☐ N   ☐ A   ☐ SA   ☐ DNA

25. I would choose to be part of **this** cohort group again.

   ☐ SD   ☐ D   ☐ N   ☐ A   ☐ SA   ☐ DNA

26. If knowledge building is "(our definition goes here)," how would you rate the level of knowledge building in your cohort group?

   (need a different response scale for this item)

27. If community is "our definition goes here," how would you rate the level of community in your cohort group?

   (need a different response scale for this item)

Part 3: Course Design

28. Online discussions in courses encouraged a sense of community among the cohort.

   ☐ SD   ☐ D   ☐ N   ☐ A   ☐ SA   ☐ DNA

29. Online chat sessions in courses encouraged a sense of community among the cohort.

□ SD   □ D   □ N   □ A   □ SA   □ DNA

30. Student-to-student communication in courses promoted knowledge building.

□ SD   □ D   □ N   □ A   □ SA   □ DNA

31. Instructor facilitation of discussion promoted my individual knowledge building.

□ SD   □ D   □ N   □ A   □ SA   □ DNA

32. Student facilitation of discussion promoted my individual knowledge building.

□ SD   □ D   □ N   □ A   □ SA   □ DNA

33. Instructors encouraged students to work in small groups when it was appropriate.

□ SD   □ D   □ N   □ A   □ SA   □ DNA

34. Small group work in courses encouraged a sense of community among the cohort.

□ SD   □ D   □ N   □ A   □ SA   □ DNA

35. Instructors shared outside resources that promoted knowledge building (i.e., provided Web sites, titles of articles, conferences, etc.).

□ SD   □ D   □ N   □ A   □ SA   □ DNA

36. WebCT was an effective tool for building an online learning community.

□ SD   □ D   □ N   □ A   □ SA   □ DNA

37. The face-to-face course meetings contributed to the development of a learning community.

□ SD   □ D   □ N   □ A   □ SA   □ DNA

38. Sharing food at face-to-face sessions contributed to the development of a learning community.

□ SD   □ D   □ N   □ A   □ SA   □ DNA

Part 4: Interactions With the Instructor

39. Instructor-student communication in courses led to my individual knowledge building.

    □ SD   □ D   □ N   □ A   □ SA   □ DNA

40. Interaction with professors during courses was a strong factor in promoting my knowledge building.

    □ SD   □ D   □ N   □ A   □ SA   □ DNA

41. Instructor feedback on assignments was effective in helping me build knowledge.

    □ SD   □ D   □ N   □ A   □ SA   □ DNA

42. Instructors encouraged students to ask questions about things they didn't understand.

    □ SD   □ D   □ N   □ A   □ SA   □ DNA

43. Group advising sessions with faculty members contributed to my sense of belonging to a professional cohort.

    □ SD   □ D   □ N   □ A   □ SA   □ DNA

44. The TET cohort model successfully promoted a learning community among the cohort members.

    □ SD   □ D   □ N   □ A   □ SA   □ DNA

Part 5: Individual Factors

45. My comfort level with my Chamberlain colleagues was a factor in joining the MS TET cohort group.

    □ SD   □ D   □ N   □ A   □ SA   □ DNA

46. My respect for other Chamberlain cohort colleagues, as professional educators, was a factor in joining the MS TET cohort group.

    □ SD   □ D   □ N   □ A   □ SA   □ DNA

47. My respect for other Chamberlain cohort colleagues, as professional educators, grew over the course of the program.

    □ SD   □ D   □ N   □ A   □ SA   □ DNA

48. I grew professionally during this cohort experience.

    □ SD   □ D   □ N   □ A   □ SA   □ DNA

49. I was actively involved with my cohort group.

    □ SD   □ D   □ N   □ A   □ SA   □ DNA

50. I felt responsible for my own **knowledge building**.

    □ SD   □ D   □ N   □ A   □ SA   □ DNA

51. I felt responsible for the **knowledge building** of everyone in my cohort group.

    □ SD   □ D   □ N   □ A   □ SA   □ DNA

52. My level of activity/engagement in courses was typically greater than that of other cohort members.

    □ SD   □ D   □ N   □ A   □ SA   □ DNA

53. My level of activity/engagement in courses was typically the same that of other cohort members.

    □ SD   □ D   □ N   □ A   □ SA   □ DNA

54. I assumed responsibility for contacting instructors when questions or problems arose.

    □ SD   □ D   □ N   □ A   □ SA   □ DNA

---

55. Now that you have completed the MS TET program as a cohort member, what is your opinion of the cohort model as a way to build both knowledge and a learning community?

56. You can use the space below to provide any additional comments.

Thank you for completing this survey.
Please return this survey in the enclosed stamped, addressed envelope to:

Mary Engstrom
USD School of Education
414 E. Clark St.
Vermillion, SD 57069

CHAPTER 11

CONVERTING A CONVENTIONAL UNIVERSITY TO A DUAL MODE INSTITUTION

The Case of the University of Botswana

Ontiretse S. Tau
University of Botswana

A dual mode institution provides educational courses by both the conventional, on-campus mode and by distance education. This article discusses the challenges encountered during introduction of distance education at the University of Botswana (UB). At the UB, introduction of distance education was piecemeal and left the Distance Education Unit disconnected from the academic mainstream and unable to fully implement its mandate to convert university programs to the distance education mode. The UB experience is used to identify important factors that can guide the process of converting to a dual mode university.

BACKGROUND

Botswana gained independence from Great Britain in 1966. Since then, national development has taken place through a series of 5- to 6-year

Beyond the Online Course: Leadership Perspectives on e-Learning
pp. 183–194

development plans. In 1997, Botswana enacted the Long Term Vision for Botswana, commonly called "Vision 2016" which identifies goals for the first 50 years of independence. One of these important goals is that by the year 2016 Botswana should be "an educated and informed nation." Expansion of education is recognized as a key element in the strategy for realizing the Vision, and increased access to higher education is critical to achievement of this goal. Diversification of the modes of delivery of higher education thus became an important factor in achieving the Vision.

EDUCATION IN BOTSWANA

The University of Botswana has its origins in the Pius XII Catholic University, in Lesotho, which registered its first students in 1946. Twenty years later it became the University of Bechuanaland, Basotholand, and Swaziland (UBBS), serving the three southern African British colonies that became the independent nations of Botswana, Lesotho, and Swaziland. After the three countries attained their independence in 1966, the university was renamed University of Botswana, Lesotho, and Swaziland (UBLS), and had campuses in all three countries. In 1975, when Lesotho established a national university, UBLS became the University of Botswana and Swaziland (UBS). In 1982, when the University of Swaziland was established, UBS became the University of Botswana (UB). UB, a government-supported university, is the only comprehensive university in Botswana, and thus has a mandate to meet the educational needs of the country (University of Botswana, 2006a, p. 7).

During the first decade of independence, the Botswana government concentrated on expansion of access to primary and secondary education, and the number of primary schools increased from 376 in 1978 to 647 in 1991. Table 1 shows the increase in enrollment in primary, secondary, and tertiary education in Botswana from 1978 to 1997. It can be seen that enrollment in primary and secondary schools increased rapidly during this period. The University of Botswana also expanded, in response to the increasing number of secondary school graduates. By 2005-2006 total university enrollment was over 15,500 students (University of Botswana, 2006, 7b).

However, even with the rapid growth of UB, the demand for university education far outstripped existing resources. The university realized that it could not meet the national demand for higher education if it relied solely on the conventional mode of delivery, namely campus-based, face-to-face education. For example, out of a total of 19,372 students who completed Form Five in the year 2000, 7,710 (approximately 40%) were

**Table 1.   Enrollment in Primary, Secondary,
and Tertiary Education in Botswana from 1978 to 1991**

Type of School	Year and Enrollment Numbers		
	1978	1991	1997
Elementary	145,459	292,233	322,268
Junior Secondary	13,765	55,430	76,045
Senior Secondary	2,250	13,057	40,031
University	860	3,567	8,007

Source: Republic of Botswana (2003, pp.144, 149, 159).

Table 2.   2001 Tertiary Institution's Intake

Tertiary Institution	Intake	%*
University of Botswana	4,335	22
Vocational and technical institutions	2,815	14
Colleges of education	560	3
Total intake	7,710	40
Year 2000 total senior secondary output	19,372	

Source: Republic of Botswana (2003, pp.144, 149, 159).
*Percent of total senior secondary school graduates.

admitted into a postsecondary education institution including the University of Botswana, vocational and technical institutions, and Colleges of
Education (Republic of Botswana, 2003). The demand for postsecondary
training and education far exceeded available places (Table 2). Thus, UB
seriously considered offering some of its programs through the distance
mode in order to increase access to a university education.

DEVELOPMENT OF DISTANCE EDUCATION IN BOTSWANA

Botswana's initial involvement in distance education was in 1960-1965,
when some Batswana teachers were enrolled in the Salisbury Correspondence College in Rhodesia (Jones, n.d.). These teachers, who were sponsored by the Colonial Government, received distance education
preservice training through the college.

This preindependence experience provided a basis for the first
attempt by the government of the young republic to provide distance
education. From 1968-1973, the Botswana Government sponsored a dis-

tance education program designed to improve teaching skills of 700 primary school teachers. This was a 1-off 2-year in-service course which comprised three residential periods of intensive instruction followed by individual study (Jones, n.d.).

The first full-fledged distance education institution in Botswana was the Botswana Extension College (BEC), established in 1973. BEC offered distance education courses at the secondary-school level. The programs offered were mainly print-based self-instructional materials, supplemented by broadcast radio and face-to-face sessions at study centers or weekend residential schools. BEC was incorporated into the Ministry of Education's new Department of Non-formal Education in 1978 and in 1996 became the Botswana College of Distance and Open Learning (BOCODOL) in 1996 (Republic of Botswana, 1994).

The second institution in Botswana to offer distance education was the University College of Botswana (a college of UBLS), through its Division of Extra Mural Services (DEMS). From 1971-1979, DEMS provided community education through an alternative mode to face-to-face teaching, namely that of broadcast radio (Jones, n. d.). UB offered formal distance education from 1979 with the introduction of the diploma in theology (discontinued in 1990), followed by the certificate in adult education in 1983 (Youngman, 1991). The certificate in adult education was offered through the Institute of Adult Education (IAE), which had taken the place of the Department of Extra Mural Services in 1978 (Youngman, 1991, p. 8). Each of these activities involved a single program that was initiated and offered by a single department.

The university recognized the role that distance education could play in increasing access to university education. In 1991, the Institute of Adult Education was divided into two separate entities, the Department of Adult Education, a teaching department in the Faculty of Education, and the Centre for Continuing Education (CCE), which was to be an outreach arm of the University as a whole. The CCE was to have within it a Distance Education Unit, which would be responsible for converting the programs of the university into the distance education mode. It was envisioned that the University would then offer its programs through both modes, the conventional and distance education, and would thus become a dual mode institution.

CHALLENGES OF A DUAL MODE INSTITUTION

Historically, universities have used either of two main models. In one model, fully integrated teaching staff are expected to teach in both the traditional and distance programs. In the other model, most staff teach in either traditional or distance programs, but not both (Chick, 1992). These models have changed and slowly given way to other structures. Rumble and Latchem (2004) point out that the models are "fluid, transmuting and converging" (p. 134).

The basic structure of most dual mode universities requires that the distance education unit or department has responsibility for coordinating all aspects of distance education programs. The functions carried out by this unit or department include: development of educational materials, distribution of these materials, tutoring and counseling students, maintaining student records, and assessment or accreditation (categorization by Perraton, 2004). The processes involved in delivery of an academic program by distance education require both business and specific subject area skills. This skill and knowledge requirement is foreign to the governance and management of conventional university academic programs. A conflict thus arises between academic freedom and the necessity for maintaining effective educational delivery mechanisms. According to Rumble (1981):

> There is a need for a clear definition of the interrelationships between two broad areas, one of which is more in the nature of a business enterprise requiring appropriate management techniques and a hierarchical structure of management and control, while the other is more in the nature of traditionally conceived academic areas, in which the staff expect a style of management or governance reflecting traditional forms of management in conventional universities. A major issue confronting distance-teaching universities is the reconciliation of these two tendencies. (p. 179)

Because of the complex interdependence between the subject matter and business requirements of a distance learning program, there is need for constant administrative supervision. Renwick (1992) argued that "dual mode universities have to acknowledge that their distance education activities must be managed in ways that are foreign to most face-to-face teaching responsibilities." Renwick further reiterates Rumble's call "to find ways of combining management and academic principles" (p. 149).

Writing about the experience of the University of Zambia, a dual mode institution, Siaciwena (1997) indicates that the distance education unit experienced problems arising from the integrated structure of distance education at that University. In an effort to resolve operational problems, a new model of distance education was created. The new model entails "an autonomous distance education unit which was responsible for the organization, administration and coordination of all distance learning courses offered by various teaching departments" (p. 57). The greatest challenge to conventional universities that want to become dual mode institutions is developing appropriate organizational structures that effectively facilitate distance education.

INTRODUCING DISTANCE EDUCATION INTO THE UNIVERSITY OF BOTSWANA

The decision of UB to introduce distance education came in 1991 with the creation of the Centre for Continuing Education (CCE), which had one specialized unit, the Distance Education Unit (DEU). However, when the CCE founding director took office in 1994, he divided the center into four units: the already existing Distance Education Unit, a new Extra-Mural Unit (EMU) responsible for part-time evening classes and short, noncredit courses, a new Public Education Unit (PEU) which provided general public education and awareness on different issues through seminars and public lectures, and a new support unit, the Technical Support Unit (University of Botswana, 1996).

This restructuring decreased visibility of the Distance Education Unit within the university. Furthermore, the divisions were not statutory, so all of the Units lacked autonomy. Even though its mandate was large, the DEU had a weak organizational structure that prevented effective implementation of the mandate. Recommendations from the DEU staff for the Unit to be upgraded to the status of a department within the structure of the university were not adopted (Tau, 2002).

In summary, the internal structure of the Unit, and its place within the Centre for Continuing Education, meant that the needs of the DEU were filtered through the center, a process that severely hampered the ability of the DEU to live up to the expectations of its stakeholders.

The approaches used by institutions to introduce distance education are as varied as the institutions themselves. Nonetheless, a number of factors have been identified as affecting the success of distance education in a dual mode university. Croft (1992) identified four conditions that would ensure successful implementation of distance education in a dual mode institution: it should be an administrative unit with significant authority; it should have cooperation from other units; it should have a well-trained staff; and it should have secured sound funding. Ntloedibe-Kuswani and Tau (2006) argue that it is important for institutions planning to introduce distance education to first conduct a front-end analysis so that the institution is prepared to address potential challenges that might negatively impact the success and quality of distance education.

However, many institutions have followed a piecemeal approach in which the introduction of distance education was not sufficiently planned, either structurally or operationally. Banathy (1992) and Robinson (2004) have concluded that the incremental approach to the reform of educational systems has not worked well, and this approach has contributed to the challenges of converting a conventional university into a dual mode institution. The Distance Education Unit at UB was created with a mandate to increase access to the University of Botswana. UB failed to appreciate the fact that the unit would have to function together with the other subsystems and be fully integrated into the University in order to achieve its goals.

The mandate required the Distance Education Unit to work collaboratively with the teaching departments to convert existing university programs into the distance mode. DEU would provide expertise in distance education as well as the day-to-day administration of programs, while the teaching department would be responsible for content and quality assurance. The goal was to take existing university programs to as wide a community as possible and thus increase access to a university education.

Implementation of the mandate became a serious challenge for the unit. There was no framework to guide and facilitate the process. The unit could not convince the academic departments of the university to offer programs through the distance education mode. Resistance has been attributed primarily to a heavy staff workload and lack of interest in distance education. The absence of a formal policy also meant that there was no requirement for academic departments to convert their programs to the distance education mode (Tau, 2002). In addition, the support functions needed to provide distance education (academic services, financial services, student affairs, library services and/or others), were only marginally informed about their roles and about the expectations and special needs of distance learners. In short, the new unit was not recognized and did not receive sufficient support within the university.

The multiplicity of departments and units that must be involved in providing a distance education course makes it imperative for a carefully formulated implementation strategy to be in place, with active support at all levels within the University. Albrecht and Bardsley (1994), writing about the planning process, note that it must be carefully designed and supported by all those who will be involved. This is essential, they write, "so that the leadership and all other participants have involvement with and confidence in the process. Without full participation, the process will be incomplete and likely to fail, no matter how well it is diagrammed from beginning to end" (p. 68).

Introduction of a distance education program can be initiated by a teaching department, or following a request from a stakeholder, such as a ministry. For example, the Botswana Ministry of Education perceived a need to upgrade teaching skills of primary school teachers, and approached UB for assistance in meeting this need. In 1994, the Revised National Policy on Education sought to improve the quality of primary education, which the country regards as foundational to the education of its citizens. The Ministry of Education intended to change the minimum requirement for teaching at the primary school level from a certificate to a diploma in primary education. The ministry concluded that the skills of 10,000 teachers (certificate in primary school holders) needed to be upgraded to diploma (Republic of Botswana, 1994). Other than through distance education, there was no other way to accomplish this within a reasonable time.

The UB Distance Education Unit regarded this request as being in line with its mandate to increase access to university education. However, the enthusiasm of the unit was not shared by the Department of Primary Education, which could provide an academic home for the program. The department had its own priorities and distance education at that time was not one of them. In addition, the department did not have the resources needed to embark on a new activity of such a large scale. Since the DEU was unable to persuade the department to provide the academic home for the program, CCE together with the Ministry of Education had to devise alternative means to offer the needed program by distance mode. The program was run collaboratively with the Department of Teacher Training and Development with students registered as bona fide students of the four colleges of primary education.

From the systemic context of UB, what emerged was that the process of creating the Distance Education Unit had not been carried through to completion. UB had attempted to develop distance education programs without the needed supportive structures. One aspect of this was the absence of an implementation strategy or policy to guide, which would create new structures and align existing ones to the mandate of the DEU. The critical relationships needed to facilitating the work of the Unit did not exist. Most importantly, there was no effective relationship between DEU and teaching departments whose courses and programs would be converted into the distance education mode. There was thus a call to go back to the drawing board and reconceptualize the whole organizational structure of CCE including DEU (Tau, 2002).

Thus, development of the Distance Education Unit was slow, hampered by:

1. Ignorance of the unit's mandate by the rest of UB, particularly the teaching departments which were expected to work collaboratively with DEU to develop distance education programs;

2. Lack of an implementation framework and/or a poorly articulated strategy;

3. Lack of an effective organizational structure both within the unit and in relation to the university faculties and teaching departments.

In response to a seemingly ineffective Distance Education Unit, the UB in October 2000 commissioned a consultancy to undertake a comprehensive review of CCE in order to "redefine its vision, operations, priorities, and to develop a modus operandi that is fully compatible with both national and university planning developments" (Nhundu, 2005, p. 1). The main findings of the consultancy were that the main barrier to increasing access to university education through CCE included a policy vacuum and marginalization of CCE within the University. A corollary problem was that CCE's relationship with the Faculties was under-developed (Yerbury, Dunlop, & Glackman, 2001). Tau's study (2002), conducted in late 1999, came to similar conclusions in that it identified the lack of an implementation strategy to guide the work of DEU as one of the major flaws that negatively affected the quality of its work. This vacuum had a negative impact on the development of effective relationships between DEU and other components of UB, and led to the minimal success of the DEU in carrying out its mandate, particularly during the early stages of its development.

To implement the recommendation of the external review of CCE, a restructuring process was initiated. The purpose was to redefine the center's vision, operations, procedures, and priorities so as to make it fully compatible with both national and university development plans. Along with this restructuring exercise, the UB Distance Education Mainstreaming Policy was approved in 2005. The mainstreaming policy attempts to fill the policy gap that has impeded provision of distance education since the creation of the center with a "specialised Distance Education Unit" in 1991. The policy provides the framework within which University functions that should take part in the distance education process will operate. It also creates some critical structures needed for the development of programs and courses. These structures help to define the relationship of the Department of Distance Education with Faculties and teaching departments. It attempts to mainstream distance education in the university system.

However, the new structure that has resulted from restructuring does not suggest a radical change from the status quo except that the status of the DEU is elevated to a department within CCE; instead of four units, CCE now has two departments: the Department of Distance Education and the Department of Extra-mural and Public Education (University of Botswana, 2006c). The author contends that as long as the Department of Distance Education is located within another unit of the university and not within its academic structure of university faculties, some of the limitations, such as competing for resources and having its needs filtered through the center, are likely to persist.

In spite of the many challenges that the unit has faced since its creation, it has forged ahead. By January 2007, the Department of Distance Education offered eight academic programs, including four business degree and four diploma programs, while one master's, two bachelors degree, and one diploma programs are under development. Besides, the relationship with the faculties and teaching departments has improved, guided by the mainstreaming policy. Furthermore, some departments have identified the need to offer some of their programs through distance education and are in the process of doing so; they include two bachelor's degree programs: bachelor of information and library studies and bachelor of primary education.

CONCLUSION

Failure to be systemic in its approach to the introduction of distance education at UB meant that:

1. Distance education as a subsystem was introduced into a system that was not ready for it.
2. The Distance Education Unit as a subsystem of UB was not aligned with the rest of the UB academic structure.
3. As a result, DEU could not perform the process of providing education at a distance to the optimum level.

The long, meandering route that the dual mode University of Botswana took in order to arrive at a point of relative success was not necessary and could have been avoided if a systems view and approach had been used to introduce distance education. The processes of providing education at a distance are cross-functional; as such, all necessary functions should be fully integrated within the university. The organizational structure and the relational arrangements among the departments can limit or expedite the delivery of distance education, thus directly impacting its success or failure.

For a distance education enterprise to work in a dual mode university, the process of converting the institution should be informed, among others, by the following considerations:

1. The university should conduct a front-end analysis to guide all the decisions including that of the distance education model to be adopted.

2. The organizational structure that is devised should ensure that the distance education unit will not be isolated from the academic mainstream;

3. An implementation framework should be developed to guide the process.

4. A systems approach must be used to ensure that all the other units and departments of the university that will have a role in the process of distance education provision are fully informed and readied for the endeavor.

REFERENCES

Albrecht, R., & Bardsley, G. (1994). Strategic planning and academic planning for distance education. In B. Willis (Ed.), *Distance education: Strategies and tools* (pp. 67-86). Englewood Cliffs, NJ: Educational Technology Publications.

Banathy, B. H. (1992). Comprehensive systems design in education: Design in pursuit of the ideal. *Educational Technology, 32*, 33-35.

Chick, J. (1992). The New England Model in theory and practice. In I. Mugridge (Ed.), *Perspectives on distance education in single and dual mode universities* (pp. 33-48). Vancouver, British Columbia, Canada: The Commonwealth of Learning.

Croft, M. (1992). Single or dual mode: Challenges and choices for the future of education. In I. Mugridge (Ed.), *Perspectives on distance education: Distance education in single and dual mode universities* (pp. 49-62). Vancouver, British Columbia, Canada: Commonwealth of Learning.

Jones, K. (n.d.). *A survey of distance education provision in Botswana.* Gaborone: Institute of Adult Education, University of Botswana.

Nhundu, T.J. (2005). *Centre for Continuing Education: Restructuring proposal.* Gaborone: University of Botswana.

Ntloedibe-Kuswani, G. S., & Tau, O. S. (2006, September). Distance education as an instructional innovation in conventional institutions: What a challenge. *Proceedings of the 22nd ICDE World Conference on Distance Education* (pp. 3-6). Rio de Janeiro, Brazil.

Perraton, H., & Lentell, H. (2004). *Policy for open and distance learning.* London, England: RoutledgeFalmer.

Renwick, W. (1992). Distance education in dual mode universities. In I. Mugridge (Ed.), *Perspectives on distance education: Distance education in single and dual mode universities* (pp. 141-152). Vancouver, British Columbia, Canada: Commonwealth of Learning.

Republic of Botswana. (1994). *Government paper No. 2 of 1994: The revised national policy on Education.* Gaborone, Botswana: Ministry of Education.

Republic of Botswana. (2003). *Education statistics 2001.* Gaborone: Central Statistics Office, Department of Printing and Publishing Services.

Robinson, B. (2004). Governance, accreditation and quality assurance in open and distance education. In H. Perraton & H. Lentell (Eds.), *Policy for open and distance learning* (pp. 181-206). London, England: RoutledgeFalmer.

Rumble, G., & Latchem, C. (2004). Organizational models for open and distance learning. In H. Perraton & H. Lentell (Eds.), *Policy for open and distance learning: World review of distance education and open learning* (Vol. 4, pp. 117-140). London, England: RoutledgeFalmer.

Rumble, G. (1981). Organization and decision-making. In A. Kaye & G. Rumble (Eds.), *Distance teaching for higher education* (pp. 179-199). London, England: Croom Helm.

Siaciwena, R. (1997). Organisational changes at the University of Zambia. *Open Learning, 12,* 57-61.

Tau, O. S. (2002). *An analysis of distance education at the University of Botswana from a systems perspective*. (Doctoral dissertation, Northern Illinois University, 2002). Ann Arbor, MI: UMI Dissertation Services.

University of Botswana. (1996). *CCE proposals for the NDP 8*. Gaborone, Botswana: Centre for Continuing Education.

University of Botswana. (2006a). *University of Botswana calendar 2006-2007*. Gaborone, Botswana: Office of the Deputy Vice Chancellor.

University of Botswana. (2006b). *Fact book, May 2005/06*. Gaborone: Botswana: Department of Institutional Planning. Retrieved July, 2006, from http://www.ub.bw/about/fact book2006.pdf

University of Botswana. (2006c). Restructuring of the Centre for Continuing Education document. Gaborone: Botswana: Office of the Deputy Vice Chancellor.

Yerbury, J. C., Dunlop, C. C., & Glackman, W. (2001). *External review: Centre for Continuing Education, University of Botswana final report* (Prepared by Simon Fraser University External Review Team). Gaborone, Botswana: University of Botswana.

Youngman, F. (1991, March). *Distance education in Botswana*. Paper presented at the seminar on Distance Education, Broadcasting and Adult Education. Windhoek, Namibia.

PART III

LEADING THE DEVELOPMENT
AND SUPPORT OF ONLINE STUDENTS

CHAPTER 12

SUPPORTING THE DISTANT STUDENT

The Effect of ARCS-Based Strategies on Confidence and Performance

Jason Bond Huett
University of West Georgia

Leslie Moller
University of South Dakota

Jon Young
University of North Texas

Marty Bray
Forsynth County Schools

Kimberly Cleaves Huett
University of West Georgia

The purpose of this research was to manipulate the component of confidence found in Keller's ARCS Model to enhance the confidence and performance of undergraduate students enrolled in an online course at a Texas University. This experiment used SAM Office 2003 and WebCT for the delivery of the tactics, strategies, confidence-enhancing e-mails (CEE), and course content. The students were trained to use the Microsoft Access database program for 5-and-one-half weeks. The results indicated that the treat-

Beyond the Online Course: Leadership Perspectives on e-Learning
pp. 197–216

ment group showed no statistically significant gains over the control group for the variable of learner confidence. The treatment group did statistically significantly better than the control group on the posttest.

INTRODUCTION

Motivation is a highly important aspect of learning. Means, Jonassen, and Dwyer (1997) cited studies showing that motivation accounted for 16% to 38% of the variations in overall student achievement. However, an extensive review of the literature leads one to concur that there is a noted lack of research concerning the motivational needs of learners (Astleitner & Keller, 1995; Gabrielle, 2003; Means et al., 1997; Shellnut, Knowlton & Savage, 1999; J. Visser & Keller, 1990).

This is particularly true with computer-based and distance instruction. Keller (1999a) noted that self-directed learning environments posed greater challenges to learner motivation than their face-to-face counterparts. Song and Keller (2001) advised that continued problems with learner motivation in Web or site-based computer-assisted instruction (CAI) were often the result of incorrect assumptions on the part of instructional designers that motivation, if taken into account at all, was assumed to be already present in the CAI. They also noted that with the widespread use of computers in education, one could no longer depend on the "novelty effect" of technology to stimulate learner motivation.

Distance education environments provide unique challenges for instructors and designers who wish to motivate students. Traditional distance learning models stress the independence of the learner (Downs & Moller, 1999; Moore, 1989) and the privatization of the learning environment (Keegan, 1986; Moller et. al. 2005). Such student-centered, independent learning requires a strong sense of motivation and confidence.

Keller's ARCS Model and Previous Studies

To stimulate and manage student motivation to learn, Keller (1987a, 1987b, 1987c) created the ARCS Model of Motivation. ARCS stands for Attention, Relevance, Confidence, and Satisfaction and serves as the framework for the confidence-enhancing tactics found in this study.

Keller's ARCS model enjoys wide support in the literature, and a number of researchers attest to its reliability and validity in many different learning and design contexts. The ARCS model is an attempt to synthesize behavioral, cognitive, and affective learning theories and demonstrate that learner motivation can be influenced through external conditions such as instructional materials (Moller, 1993). The ARCS model was initially predicated on the *expectancy value theory* based on the work of Tolman (1932) and Lewin (1938). The expectancy value theory essentially states that learners pursue activities they value and in which they expect to succeed (Keller, 1987c).

ARCS research can be found concerning the traditional classroom (Bickford, 1989; Klein & Freitag, 1992; Means et al., 1997; Moller, 1993; Naime-Diefenbach, 1991; Small & Gluck, 1994; J. Visser & Keller, 1990), computer assisted instruction (Asteitner & Keller, 1995; Bohlin & Milheim, 1994; ChanLin, 1994; Lee & Boling, 1996; Shelnut, Knowlton & Savage, 1999; Song, 1998; Song & Keller, 1999; Suzuki & Keller, 1996), blended learning environments (Gabrielle, 2003), and online, distant, and Web-based classrooms (Chyung, 2001; Huett, 2006; Song, 2000; L. Visser, 1998). In fact, Means et al. (1997) called Keller's ARCS model the "only coherent and comprehensive instructional design model accommodating motivation" (p. 5).

While Keller (1987a) believes that "motivational interventions can be focused within a general category or specific subcategory of the model" (p. 6), there is insufficient evidence to support claims that learner motivation can be isolated or compartmentalized into separate categories. Studies of ARCS-enhanced instructional materials have returned inconsistent results on the individual subsections as well as on the overall measure of learner motivation (Babe, 1995; Gabrielle, 2003; Moller, 1993; Naime-Diefenbach, 1991). In addition, Means et al. (1997) found that "there is inconsistent evidence that each of the factors operates independently, that learners' motivations can be decomposed and isolated, or that changes in one motivational state have an inconsequential effect on others" (p.6).

CONFIDENCE

Confidence has been described as an inherent personality trait (McKinney, 1960). However, confidence is generally accepted as situation-specific, and it can therefore be manipulated by internal and external factors (Keller, 1979; Moller, 1993). In his development of social learning theory, Rotter (1954) argued that people have a tendency to ascribe their failures or successes to internal or external factors: he found that people tend to pursue that which brings about the most rewarding consequence, which he called *expectancy*. Bandura (1977, 1986) elaborated on this concept when he explained that individuals' expectancy is related to their estimate of the outcome of a given behavior. He used the term *self-efficacy* to describe the belief that one's abilities and knowledge are sufficient to be successful at a given task: learners who expect to succeed demonstrate more confidence than learners who expect to fail. However, a learner may still possess confidence without the guarantee of success, as long as the challenge is "within acceptable boundaries" (Naime-Diefenbach, 1991, p. 12).

Building on the work of Rotter, Bandura, and others, Keller defines confidence as "helping the learners believe/feel that they will succeed and control their success" (Keller, 1987a, p. 2). Confidence is the interplay between desire for success and fear of failure. These opposing forces vie for control over the learning experience. To better understand the role of confidence in the ARCS model, it helps to examine what Keller and Suzuki (1988) characterize as its three most important dimensions: perceived competence, perceived control, and expectancy for success.

Perceived Competence

The extent to which learners feel they are able or unable to learn is perceived confidence. Learners who believe in their potential success are more likely to exert the effort required to be successful. Despite the fact that learner expectations are not always realistically aligned with their abilities, expectations can still positively influence outcomes (Bickford, 1989).

Students with a poor perception of their abilities may become anxious and perform less well than their counterparts with higher confidence in their abilities (Naime-Diefenbach, 1991). Moller (1993) describes learners with high anxiety as often "misdirecting effort from learning to task-irrelevant concerns. Learners high in anxiety are often low in self-esteem and, as such, avoid evaluative situations" (p. 7). In contrast, learners with normal anxiety levels feel more confident and motivated in situations where they must be evaluated.

Perceived Control

When learners believe their efforts and decisions have real consequences, they feel more confident (Bandura, 1977; Keller & Suzuki, 1988). This fosters a higher internal locus of control and a greater sense of self-pride and accomplishment (Moller, 1993). In contrast, learners who believe luck or other uncontrollable outside forces are in charge of their successes or failures tend to feel more helpless and unconfident, and perform at lower levels.

According to Keller and Suzuki (1988), "features in the instruction that promote feelings of personal control over outcomes will help develop confidence and persistence" (p. 405). This is supported by researchers such as Carroll (1963), Bloom (1976), and Kinzie and Sullivan (1989), who recommend allowing learners to control the pace of instruction. However, research is mixed about how much control is actually beneficial to learners (Klein & Keller, 1990). Steinberg (1989) cited numerous studies showing that learners with little prior knowledge of the subject matter were likely to perform poorly with increased learner control.

Keller (1987a) suggests one strategy for fostering control is to give students knowledge of what is expected of them. However, this is not enough to guarantee confidence: while learners may understand what steps are necessary to complete an assigned task, without the confidence in their ability to successfully complete those tasks, they may not perform as well as they should (Moller, 1993).

Expectancy for Success

Learners' expectations or beliefs can influence outcomes. If the learner believes he will be successful at a given task, such belief may result in greater effort expended and improve success. Learners with such expectancy for success also possess higher motivation than learners who expect failure (Naime-Diefenbach, 1991). Conversely, the learner who expects failure may evince learned helplessness (Keller, 1979; Seligman, 1975). Once taken hold, learned helplessness can be a powerful impediment to success.

In summary, in order to help learners overcome learned helplessness and other self-fulfilling prophecies, it is necessary for instructional designers to consider learner anxiety and provide for instruction that helps boost learner confidence, making them feel competent, in control, and successful. While fear of failure can strongly affect motivation in traditional learning environments, it may be an even greater factor in distance education (L. Visser, 1998). Even with highly motivated students, the isolation of the learner, an unfamiliar distance environment, the technology required in distance courses, and the distance separating learner and instructor have an effect on learner confidence. The concept of perceived control may be particularly relevant to distance learning environments. Roblyer (1999) found that students who chose distance education classes over face-to-face classes often did so out of a greater desire or need for control over their own learning outcomes. Studies have shown that technology brings with it new attitudes and anxiety levels that can have a direct effect on confidence (Yaghi & Ghaith, 2002). The instructor of the distant course may need to be especially concerned with increasing and maintaining learner confidence.

The major focus of this study was to determine whether confidence could be specifically targeted for improvement and whether improvements in confidence would translate into performance gains. The underlying assumptions are that confidence is a highly important aspect of motivation, that it can be manipulated through external factors, and that it has an effect on learner performance.

METHOD

This study was conducted over a period of approximately 5-and-one-half weeks. The purposes of this research were to: (a) determine if there were statistically significant increases in confidence levels of online learners using systematically designed confidence tactics based on Keller's ARCS model; and (b) determine if the tactics also produced a statistically significant increase or change in academic performance.

Within the ARCS model, confidence can be increased (Keller 1987a, 1987b) by examining learning requirements (LR) to give students knowledge of what is expected of them. Confidence can also be increased by providing for success opportunities (SO) that are meaningful, are challenging, bolster achievement, and avoid boredom. Lastly, to improve confidence, Keller advocates a sense of personal control (PC) where the learner is allowed as much control of the learning experience as possible. Following Keller's (1999a, 1999b) advice, the confidence-enhancing tactics were designed to be appropriate for the audience, the delivery system and the course, to be in line with course objectives and assessments, to be integrated with instruction (provide a minimal level of disruption to the learning process), to be cost-effective, and to fit within the time constraints of the class.

Participants

The subjects in this study were undergraduate students enrolled at a Texas university rated Carnegie Doctoral/Research Universities—Extensive. Subjects were enrolled in multiple sections of an online, freshman-level, for-credit computer course. All enrolled subjects in all sections were combined into a single pool and then were selected for the treatment or control group using a table of random numbers matched to the last four digits of their student IDs. They were then assigned to either the treatment or the control group sections in WebCT and SAM Office 2003.

The initial sample consisted of 81 (treatment $n = 41$; control $n = 40$) total students and included 37 males (treatment $n = 18$; control $n = 19$) and 44 females (treatment $n = 23$; control $n = 21$). Ages ranged from 18 to 31. Student-reported ethnicities were in line with university-reported demographics concerning the campus undergraduate population as a whole.

Variables

The independent variable (treatment) consisted of ARCS confidence tactics (see Table 1) distributed through SAM Office 2003 and through confidence-enhancing e-mail messages in the WebCT environment (see Figure 1). The two main dependent variables under investigation were confidence and academic performance.

Instruments

The instruments used in the study were the Instructional Materials Motivation Survey (IMMS) survey and a posttest, and both were delivered in a web-based format at a distance. Both the IMMS survey and the posttest were delivered immediately following the treatment around the middle of the semester. Created by Keller (1993), the IMMS was used to gauge the motivational effect of instructional materials. It was designed to assess the four components of the ARCS model, as well as an overall motivation score. In this case, an individual measure of learner confidence was highlighted. In this study, the IMMS was found to have a total reliability alpha of .93 based on the obtained scores. The reliability alpha for computed scores of the individual subsection of confidence in this study was .85.

Academic performance was measured using an identical posttest automatically generated by SAM Office 2003 after students completed the training/instructional materials. The posttest consisted of an interactive performance-based simulation that tested what the students had learned concerning Microsoft Access. Given the nature of the posttest and the propriety restrictions of the software, a copy of the outcome measure cannot be provided. However, a sample screen shot from the posttest is included (see Figure 2). For this study, the posttest was found to have a total reliability alpha of .86 based on obtained scores.

Research Design

This study used a true experimental, posttest-only, control-group design, and was undertaken using quantitative methods. Given the nature

Table 1. Confidence Tactics (CT)

CT Components	Treatment Group	Control
LR1: Are there clear statements, in terms of observable behaviors, of what is expected of the learners?	Objectives were stated in *SAM* at the beginning of each lesson and restated on guide-sheets. Reminders were stated in the confidence-enhancing e-mails (CEE). In addition, a performance exercise (see SO1) served to familiarize learners with what was expected of them.	Objectives were not stated, and a pretest was not provided.
LR2: Is there a means for learners to write their own goals or objectives?	SAM 2003 is a self-contained simulation environment, so this was not an option.	SAM 2003 is a self-contained simulation environment, so this was not an option.
SO1: Multiple entry points: Provide a pretest and multiple entry points into the instructional material.	The treatment group received a performance exercise that determined the level of expertise the learner brought to each exercise, and this allowed for the learner to enter the training/instructional material at differing points. Each learner received training/instructional materials only in areas of demonstrated deficiency. Learners were reminded of this in the CEEs.	The control group received no such pretest/performance exercise and was required to take all of the training/instructional material regardless of previous knowledge, experience or expertise.
SO2: Is the content organized in a clear, easy-to-follow sequence?	The content was organized in a pretest-training-posttest sequence. The treatment group received a statement with each lesson assuring them the material was clear and easy-to-follow along with directions highlighting how to proceed through the pretest-training-posttest sequence. Learners were reminded of this in the CEEs.	This group received no such explanation.
SO3: Are the tasks sequenced from simple to difficult within the material?	Materials in SAM 2003 follow a logical sequence and are generally sequenced from easy to more difficult in each lesson. However, only the treatment group received a statement assuring them of this fact. Learners were reminded of this in the CEEs.	The tasks were sequenced from simple to difficult; however, the control group received no statement.
SO4: Is the overall challenge level appropriate for this audience?	Yes, but only in the treatment group was this stated to the learner. Learners were reminded of this in the CEEs.	Yes, but not stated.
SO5: Are the materials free of "trick" or excessively difficult questions or exercises?	Yes, but only this version stated this fact to the learner, and learners were reminded of this in the CEEs.	Yes, but this fact was not stated.

	Treatment	Control
SO6: Are the exercises consistent with the objectives?	Yes, however, only this version stated the objectives to the learner before beginning. Learners were also reminded of this in the CEEs.	Yes, but objectives were not stated.
SO7: Are there methods for self-evaluation?	Yes, SAM 2003 was set to display simple feedback for each task (e.g., correct or incorrect). Results were also displayed at the end of each exam as a percentage (e.g., 90% correct). Learners were reminded of this in the CEEs.	No feedback was provided, and no results were displayed.
PC1: Are learners given choices in sequencing? Can they sequence their study of different parts of the material?	All exercises in each module were presented at once, and learners were able to approach the lessons in any order they chose. Learners were reminded of this in the CEEs.	Learners were given the lessons in a particular sequence, one-at-a-time, with a specific due date.
PC2: Are learners allowed to go at their own pace?	Self-pacing was allowed with a due date established clearly up front, and all assignments were opened at the same time and stayed open until the due date with no time-limits for self-pacing. Learners were reminded of this in the CEEs.	Each exercise was timed. The time-limit was decided as follows: (a) examine the time it took for the students in the previous semester to complete exercises, (b) select the longest time for completion, and (c) add thirty minutes. The control group had ample time to complete the exercises but was not informed of this. Every control group subject finished each exercise before time had expired.
PC3: Are learners given opportunities to create their own exercises or methods of demonstrating competency?	Learners were given the opportunity for demonstrating further competency by creating their own exercises (such as an *Access* database) for extra credit or to take the place of a low test score. Learners were reminded of this in the CEEs.	Learners were given no such opportunity.
PC4: Are learners given choice over study location?	Yes—this was an Internet-based class. Learners were reminded of this in the CEEs.	Yes—this was an Internet-based class.

Table continues on next page.

Table 1 (Continued)

CT Components	Treatment Group	Control
PC5: Are learners given the opportunity to record comments on how the materials could be made more interesting?	A blog and threaded discussion concerning the materials was set up to allow for comments. Learners were encouraged to participate in the CEEs.	There was no access to a blog or threaded discussion about materials.
PC6: Are learners given the opportunity for feedback and practice in a "low risk" environment where it is acceptable to make mistakes and learn from them?	On the pretest, training, and posttest, learners were given feedback regarding performance and were allowed multiple attempts at the posttest. They were reminded about these multiple attempts at the beginning of each exercise and in the CEEs. Only the first attempt was used to gather data to measure and compare performance.	The control group received no pretest, one timed attempt at the training with minimal computer-generated feedback, and one attempt at the posttest with no feedback concerning final performance.

Note: Adapted from Moller (1993) and Moller and Russell (1994). LR = Learning Requirements, SO = Success Opportunities, PC = Personal Control, CEE = Confidence-Enhancing E-mail.

206

Figure 1.   Example of confidence-enhancing e-mail with comments.

of this study, adopting a pretest/posttest model was inappropriate. In this study, an initial performance exercise (similar in concept to a pretest) was used as a confidence treatment. There were also concerns about potential test effects and the short delay between a complimentary pretest and posttest; this led to the decision to use a posttest-only design (Gall, Gall, & Borg, 2003).

The control group received none of the confidence-building tactics. The treatment group received confidence tactics (see Table 1) through SAM Office 2003 and through confidence-enhancing e-mails in WebCT (see Figure 1). Participation in this study was voluntary.

Treatment was provided in four steps:

1.   The instructor selected *SAM Office 2003*'s simulation of *Microsoft Access* to be used for the duration of this experiment and *WebCT* for the delivery of confidence-enhancing emails (CEE).

2.   As outlined in Table 1, the instructor modified SAM Office 2003's Access simulation by incorporating the interventions and tactics

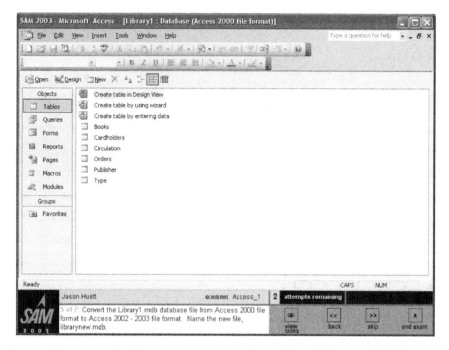

Figure 2.   Screen shot from posttest measure (reproduced with permission from Course Technology).

based on the component of confidence in Keller's ARCS model for the treatment group.

3. The instructor composed supplementary CEEs (see Figure 1) to help disseminate the remaining confidence-enhancing tactics based on Keller's ARCS model for the treatment group.

4. The instructor presented the materials, with and without modification, to the respective treatment and control groups.

The attention, relevance, and satisfaction components of the ARCS model were not intentionally incorporated into the design of this study in order to better isolate the variable of confidence in question.

Distance Education Software

SAM (Skill Assessment Manager) provides training scenarios for Microsoft Office in a lifelike, simulated environment designed to replicate Microsoft Office 2003. In the case of this study, the students were trained to use the Access database program for about 5-and-one-half weeks.

Three semesters of prior surveys indicated that Access was the Microsoft Office program with which students were least familiar. Therefore, Access was chosen to help control for any variance in student ability. The SAM software is widely distributed to universities across the country and claims to have served hundreds of thousands of students and educators since its inception in 1998 (Course Technology, 2005). WebCT, along with SAM, is another widely used distance learning application.

RESULTS

Research Question 1: Will the confidence tactics used in this study produce statistically significant differences between the control group and the treatment group in terms of learner confidence as measured by the IMMS?

The results indicated there was not a statistically significant difference between the treatment and control groups for confidence as measured by the IMMS (p = .080). However, the reported effect size (d = .41) and estimated power (.53) at alpha .05 cannot be dismissed as insignificant. Further study is warranted before a definitive conclusion can be drawn. The means, standard deviations, skewness and kurtosis values, effect size, and approximate power for the confidence variable are reported in Table 2.

Research Question 2: Will the confidence tactics used in this study produce statistically significant differences between the control group and the treatment group in terms of learner performance as based on posttest scores automatically generated in SAM Office 2003?

The posttest showed a statistically significant difference in performance between the treatment and control groups (p < .001) with a

Table 2.   Results for the Confidence Subsection of the IMMS

Section	N	Mean	SD	Skewness	Kurtosis	p	Effect Size (d)	Approx. Power (p = .05)	Approx. Power (p = .01)
Treatment	35	31.77	7.276	−.607	−.207	.080	.41	.53	.27
Control	37	28.70	7.356	−.159	−.641				
Total	72	30.19	7.428	−.348	−.619				

Table 3.   Results for Posttest Measure

Section	N	Mean	ST	Skewness	Kurtosis	p	Effect Size (d)	Approx. Power (p = .05)	Approx. Power (p = .01)
Treatment	30	93.40	5.43189	−.702	.002	< .001	1	.98	.91
Control	26	86.10	7.38568	−.865	1.730				
Total	56	90.0	7.33922	−.896	1.354				

reported effect size of $(d = 1)$ at alpha .05 for the posttest score. This can be interpreted to mean that the treatment group $(n = 30)$, on average, scored approximately one standard deviation above the average mean of the control group $(n = 26)$. Results are reported in Table 3.

DISCUSSION

Students in the treatment group did not seem to find the designed tactics especially confidence-enhancing during the Access training. Similar to Moller's (1993) findings, there seem to be at least three potential explanations: (a) The ARCS model is ineffective for improving learner confidence; (b) the confidence tactics and methods used in this study were implemented improperly or were somehow inappropriate for these subjects; and/or (c) the differences in confidence were too small to measure or were immeasurable with the instrument (IMMS).

Taking each of these possible explanations in turn, there are insufficient data to suggest that the ARCS model is somehow flawed or incomplete when it comes to addressing learner confidence. The model has shown an ability to increase learner confidence even when confidence was not the focus of the researchers' investigations. The question is not whether the model, as a whole, can produce increases. It is whether the individual subsection of confidence can be targeted as a valid, independent construct that produces consistent results. One could argue that this study's results suggest that independently targeting confidence for improvement may more difficult than the ARCS model would lead one to believe. This could potentially require a rethinking of the ARCS model as a series of interdependent (and not independent) constructs for improving motivation (Babe, 1995). Further study is warranted before conclusions can be drawn, but the results of this study continue to challenge researchers' assumptions (Keller, 1987a; Naime-Diefenbach, 1991) that individual components of the ARCS model can be isolated for improvement.

The second possible explanation for the lack of a statistically significant difference in confidence is that the confidence tactics used in this study were ineffective or implemented improperly. This is a possibility. Through informal surveys, e-mails, and discussion board postings, some treatment group subjects indicated that they found some of the confidence tactics used in this study more effective than others—particularly those related to personal control. Researchers have linked increases in learner control to increases in confidence (and positive attitudes of learners) as well as decreases in learner anxiety (Bandura, 1977; Keller & Suzuki, 1988; Kinzie, 1990; Kinzie & Sullivan, 1989; Moller & Russell, 1994). However, some members of the control group indicated an appreciation for the strict structure, deadlines and pacing. Also, a majority of treatment group students (64%) who were given personal control to complete the assignments at any time during the 5-and-one-half-week window waited until the last 72 hours to "cram in" most of the assignments before they were due. Only 24% of the treatment group finished the required assignments before the last week. There is no real way of knowing how such procrastination affected the confidence levels of the treatment group, but one can imagine that procrastination brings with it an increase in learner anxiety. Anxiety has an inverse relationship to confidence, so the effect on confidence levels was probably not a positive one.

In this study, a comprehensive approach to improving confidence was taken where several tactics were applied in one treatment. As a result, any differences in the study (or lack thereof) could be the result of effects of any of the individual manipulations (or combinations thereof), and there is no clear way of determining to what extent each tactic may have contributed to any differences found. However, this was not the goal of the study. While it would be ideal to conduct dozens of studies, each isolating only one confidence tactic, this is not practical. And, given the nature of new distance learning software packages (which often allow for extensive customization of the learning environment), such a multifaceted "approach" to improving confidence may have its place. In retrospect, it would have also been potentially beneficial to use an instrument to get a baseline measure of learner confidence before applying the treatment. Getting a read on how confident learners were before beginning instruction would have helped more clearly explain any changes in motivation. Such a measure is recommended for future studies.

Third, another way of stating differences may be too small to measure is to say perhaps the IMMS survey is not sensitive enough to detect short-term changes. While no current research indicates that the IMMS survey is a poor or weak measure of learner confidence, it seems possible that this survey may not be sensitive enough to detect short-term changes. Perhaps the confidence enhancements are producing a desired effect, but the survey cannot consistently detect the changes over the short-term. Given the protean motivational nature of learners over time, the survey would need to be highly sensitive or delivered at precisely the right time to accurately reflect learner changes in confidence. Over a brief period, learners may not even be aware enough of a change to report it accurately. Again, further study is warranted.

Performance

The data showed that the students in the treatment group outperformed the control group on the posttest measure for this particular study. This is in line with previous research findings that suggest increases in motivation can translate into increases in performance or achievement (Bickford, 1989; Gabrielle, 2003; Song & Keller, 2001). Because of the multiple tactics applied in the treatment, specific explanations of changes are as difficult to pinpoint for performance as for confidence. One cannot say with certainty that any particular aspect of the treatment was effective. It might be more appropriate to say that this multiple-tactic approach to increasing performance may have merit and is worth further study.

Additional Analysis

It seems confounding that, for this study, the confidence tactics did not produce a noted increase in learner confidence but did seem to have an effect on performance. In an attempt to further explain these findings, analysis of the individual subsections of the IMMS was conducted. For this study, there were differences noted for attention ($p = .015$, $d = .57$), relevance ($p = .001$, $d = .75$), satisfaction ($p = .002$, $d = .72$), and overall motivation ($p = .002$, $d = .72$), but not confidence ($p = .080$, $d = .41$). The reliability alphas for computed scores of the individual subsections in this study were as follows: attention (.86), relevance (.80), satisfaction (.86), and overall motivation (.92).

One particular reason for the noted increases in A, R, S, and total motivation in this study may be an overlap of the confidence tactics and confidence-enhancing e-mails into the attention, relevance and satisfaction components. For instance, providing the treatment group the opportunity to create their own exercises or methods of demonstrating competency and allowing the treatment group access to a blog and threaded discussion for comments may have enhanced attention or even relevance. Tactics such as these might stimulate the learner's curiosity to think of ideas for improvement that increase feelings of "connectedness," or relevance, to the material.

Simply receiving the e-mails might serve to gain learner attention. The concern, verbal praise, and goal reminders expressed in the messages may have served to increase learner satisfaction and improved their sense of connectedness (relevance) to the subject matter. Again, this study highlights some of the challenges faced in trying to isolate confidence for independent enhancement.

Perhaps the most important finding in this additional analysis was that overall motivation was enhanced in learners through the application of external factors. That was the belief which initially guided this study and, despite any disagreement about the validity of the independent components of the ARCS model, the model, as a whole, was apparently effective in this study for increasing overall learner motivation and performance.

CONCLUSION

It appears that this comprehensive approach to using the ARCS model shows a possibility for addressing some of the motivational needs and performance concerns of online students. Although this initial study should not be generalized beyond undergraduates enrolled in the online, entry-level computer application course using the SAM Office 2003 software at the university in this study, the apparent positive performance and overall motivation results should encourage continued study.

REFERENCES

Astleitner, H., & Keller, J. (1995). A model for motivationally adaptive computer-assisted instruction. *Journal of Research on Computing in Education, 27*(3), 270-280.

Babe, T. (1995). *The validation of relevance as an independent dimension of the ARCS motivational model of instructional design.* Unpublished doctoral dissertation, The Pennsylvania State University, University Park.

Bandura, A. (1977). *Social learning theory.* Englewood Cliffs, NJ: Prentice-Hall.

Bandura, A. (1986). *Social foundations of thought and action: A social cognitive theory.* Englewood Cliffs, NJ: Prentice Hall.

Bickford, N. (1989). *The systematic application of principles of motivation to the design of printed instructional materials.* Unpublished doctoral dissertation, Florida State University, Tallahassee.

Bloom, B. S. (1976). *Human characteristics and school learning.* New York: McGraw-Hill.

Bohlin, R., & Milhelm, W. (1994, February). *Applications of an adult motivational instructional design model.* Paper presented at the Association for Educational Communications and Technology, Nashville, TN.

Carroll, J. B. (1963). A model of school learning. *Teachers College Record, 64,* 723-733.

ChanLin, L. (1994). *A case for assessing motivation from learning a computer-assisted instruction.* (ERIC Document Reproductions Service No. ED376 803)

Chyung, S. Y. (2001). Systematic and systemic approaches to reducing attrition rates in online higher education. *American Journal of Distance Education, 15*(3), 36-49.

Course Technology. Retrieved March 3, 2005, from http://samcentral.course.com/sam_2003.cfm

Downs, M., & Moller, L. (1999). Experiences of students, teachers, and administrators in a distance education Course. *International Journal of Educational Technology, 1*(2). Retrieved October 1, 2004, from http://www.ao.uiuc.edu/ijet/v1n2/downs/index.html

Gabrielle, D. (2003). *The effects of technology-mediated instructional strategies on motivation, performance, and self-directed learning.* Unpublished doctoral dissertation, Florida State University, Tallahassee.

Gall, M. D., Gall, J. P., & Borg, W. R. (2003). *Educational research: An introduction.* (7th ed.). Boston: Allyn and Bacon.

Huett, J. (2006). *The effects of ARCS-based confidence strategies on learner confidence and performance in distance education.* Unpublished doctoral dissertation, University of North Texas, Denton.

Keegan, D. (1986). *The foundations of distance education.* London, England: Croom-Helm.

Keller, J. M. (1979). Motivation and instructional design: A theoretical perspective. *Journal of Instructional Development, 2,* 26-34.

Keller, J. M. (1987a). Strategies for stimulating the motivation to learn. *Performance & Instruction, 26*(8), 1-7.

Keller, J. M. (1987b). The systematic process of motivational design. *Performance & Instruction, 26*(9), 1-8.

Keller, J. M. (1987c). Development and use of the ARCS model of motivational design. *Journal of Instructional Development, 10*(3), 2-10.

Keller, J. M. (1993). *Manual for instructional materials motivational survey (IMMS).* Tallahassee, FL.

Keller, J. M. (1999a). Motivation in cyber learning environments. *International Journal of Educational Technology, 1*(1), 7-30.

Keller, J. M. (1999b). Using the ARCS motivational design process in computer-based instruction and distance education. *New Directions for Teaching and Learning, 78,* 39-47.

Keller, J. M., & Suzuki, K. (1988). Use of the ARCS motivation model in courseware design. In D. H. Jonassen (Ed.), *Instructional designs for microcomputer courseware* (pp. 401-434). Hillsdale, NJ: Erlbaum.

Kinzie, M. B. (1990). Requirements and benefits of effective interactive instruction: Learner control, self-regulation, and continuing motivation. *Educational Technology Research & Development, 38*(1), 5-21.

Kinzie, A B., & Sullivan, H. (1989). Continuing motivation, learner control, and CAI. *Educational Technology Research and Development, 37*(2), 5-14.

Klein, J. D., & Freitag, E. T. (1992). Training students to utilize self-motivational strategies. *Educational Technology, 32*(3), 44-48.

Klein, J. D., & Keller, J. M. (1990). Influence of student ability, locus of control, and type of instructional control on performance and confidence. *The Journal of Educational Research, 83*(3), 140-146.

Lee, S., & Boling, E. (1996). *Motivational screen design guidelines for effective computer-mediated instruction.* Paper presented at the Association for Educational Communications and Technology, Indianapolis, IN.

Lewin, K. (1938). *The conceptual representation and the measurement of psychological forces.* Durham, NC: Duke University Press.

McKinney, F. (1960). *The psychology of personal adjustments: Students' introduction to mental hygiene.* London, England: Wiley.

Means, T., Jonassen, D., & Dwyer, F. (1997). Enhancing relevance: Embedded ARCS strategies vs. purpose. *Educational Technology Research and Development, 45*, 5-17.

Moller, L. (1993). *The effects of confidence building strategies on learner motivation and achievement.* Unpublished doctoral dissertation, Purdue University, West Lafayette.

Moller, L., Huett, J., Holder, D., Young, J., Harvey, D., & Godshalk, V. (2005). Examining the impact of motivation on learning communities. *Quarterly Review of Distance Education, 6*(2), 137-143.

Moller, L., & Russell, J. (1994). An application the ARCS model confidence building strategies. *Performance Improvement Quarterly, 7*(4), 54-69.

Moore, M. G. (1989). Three types of interaction. *The American Journal of Distance Education, 3*(2), 1-6.

Naime-Diefenbach, B. (1991). *Validation of attention and confidence as independent components of the ARCS motivational model.* Unpublished doctoral dissertation, Florida State University, Tallahassee.

Roblyer, M. D. (1999). Is choice important in distance learning? A study of student motives for taking Internet-based courses at the high school and community college levels. *Journal of Research on Computing in Education, 32*(1), 157-171.

Rotter, J. B. (1954). *Social learning and clinical psychology.* New York: Prentice-Hall.

Seligman, M. (1975). *Helplessness: On depression, development and death.* San Francisco: Freeman.

Shellnut, B., Knowlton, A., & Savage, T. (1999). Applying the ARCS model to the design and development of computer-based modules for manufacturing engineering courses. *Educational Technology, Research and Development, 47*, 100-110.

Small, R. V., & Gluck, M. (1994). The relationship of motivational conditions to effective instructional attributes: A magnitude scaling approach. *Educational Technology, 34*(8), 33-40.

Song, S. H. (1998). *The effects of motivationally adaptive computer-assisted instruction developed through the ARCS model.* Unpublished doctoral dissertation, Florida State University, Tallahassee.

Song, S. H. (2000). Research issues of motivation in web-based instruction. *Quarterly Review of Distance Education, 1*(3), 225-229.

Song, S. H., & Keller, J. M. (1999, February). *The ARCS model for developing motivationally-adaptive computer-assisted instruction.* Paper presented at the Association for Educational Communications and Technology, Houston, TX.

Song, S. H., & Keller, J. M. (2001). Effectiveness of motivationally adaptive computer-assisted instruction on the dynamic aspects of motivation. *Educational Technology, Research & Development, 49,* 5-22.

Steinberg, E. R. (1989). Cognition and learner control: A literature review, 1977-88. *Journal of Computer-Based Instruction 16*(4), 117-124.

Suzuki, K., & Keller, J.M. (1996, August). *Applications of the ARCS model in computer-based instruction in Japan.* Annual meeting of the Japanese Educational Technology Association, Kanazawa, Japan.

Tolman, E. C. (1932). *Purposive behaviour in animals and men.* New York: Appleton-Century.

Visser, J., & Keller, J. M. (1990). The clinical use of motivational messages: An inquiry into the validity of the ARCS model of motivational design. *Instructional Science, 19,* 467-500.

Visser, L. (1998). *The development of motivational communication in distance education support.* Den Haag, The Netherlands: CIP- Gegevens Koninklijke Bibliotheek.

Yaghi, H., & Ghaith, G. (2002). Correlates of computing confidence among teachers in an international setting. *Computers in the Schools, 19,* 81-94.

CHAPTER 13

ONLINE INSTRUCTION

Student Satisfaction, Kudos, and Pet Peeves

C. Eugene Walker and Erika Kelly
University of Oklahoma

Widespread availability of computers and the Internet provide considerable enrichment in terms of variety of material and formats for presentation over what was possible with the old correspondence courses. As a result, a large number of universities have begun to offer an extensive list of online courses in various programs. We set out to answer the question about student satisfaction with online distance learning by surveying the undergraduate and graduate students taking online courses in the College of Liberal Studies of the University of Oklahoma. The survey was sent to a total of 767 students who had participated in an online course lasting either 8 or 16 weeks in the College of Liberal Studies at the University of Oklahoma. Students were contacted and requested to participate in the survey at the end of each 8-week and 16-week course. A total of 304 students participated in this survey producing a participation rate of 40%. Overall the results of this survey indicated that the students were very satisfied with the format, the nature and amount of the work required, as well as with the assessment of their work and grading.

Beyond the Online Course: Leadership Perspectives on e-Learning
pp. 217–231
Copyright © 2016 by Information Age Publishing
217

INTRODUCTION

Distance education, in one form or another, has been around at least since the nineteenth century, when colleges began to offer instruction through correspondence courses. Over the years various media have been employed to facilitate distance education, including radio, television, and more recently computers and the Internet (Phipps & Merisotis, 1999). While design flaws have frequently been pointed out in the research in this area, there is a pretty substantial accumulation of evidence indicating that distance education produces results equivalent to face-to-face classroom instruction in many areas (e.g., Russell, 1999). While there are advantages and disadvantages to online instruction, student satisfaction is generally good (e.g., Johnson, Killion, & Oomen, 2005). While barriers and problems with online teaching have been investigated (e.g., Berge, 1998), widespread availability of computers and the Internet provide considerable enrichment in terms of variety of material and formats for presentation over what was possible with the old correspondence courses. As a result, a large number of universities have begun to offer an extensive list of online courses in various programs. It is now possible at many institutions to obtain training through the doctoral level entirely online. Many faculty providing instruction in these courses have been doing so for 10 or 15 years (Bonk, Maher, & Halpenny, 2001). A question of concern to such faculty is, "How are we doing?" There are two ways to answer this question. One is to evaluate student achievement using various assessment procedures to determine the amount learned in such courses and, when possible, to compare this achievement with that of students in on campus face-to-face classes. A second approach to answering this question is the topic of the present article. This approach has to do with student satisfaction. What factors in online courses do students consider important in enhancing their learning? What characteristics of online instruction do they specifically single out as the most important benefits of such instruction and what are their top pet peeves about online instruction? We set out to answer the above questions by surveying the undergraduate and graduate students taking online courses in the College of Liberal Studies of the University of Oklahoma. The University of Oklahoma has been a pioneer in distance education. In 1960, the College of Liberal Studies at the University of Oklahoma was established and, over the years, had extensive offerings of courses leading to a bachelor's and master's degree (begun in 1967) in liberal studies. As computers and the Internet became readily accessible, the university switched its format from correspondence with intensive on-campus seminars to totally online offerings for most courses and programs. The first online courses in this program were offered in 1997. It seemed appropriate at this point to survey students regarding their attitudes regarding effectiveness of the program.

METHODS

Following a review of the literature and a careful examination of the format employed for most online courses in the College of Liberal Studies, a survey was prepared for administration to students taking such courses. It was determined that the survey must be brief and easily accessible in order to obtain student cooperation. Previous attempts at routine evaluation of these courses had resulted in a very low rate of participation by students. The survey employed appears as Appendix A at the end of this article. The majority of the courses offered by the College of Liberal Studies are organized in four units that the student completes in either 8 or 16 weeks. Each unit typically has a required reading from the course textbook, as well as library and Internet research. Based on this, the student writes two to three essays on assigned topics covering the material. Each unit also involves one phase of preparation of an overall paper called the "course spanning paper" that is due at the end. In most of the courses, no standardized or objective tests are used, rather each of the essays and papers receives a grade and the final grade for the course is dependent on performance on these writing tasks. The survey employed in this investigation was specifically prepared to mirror the course structure employed in the College of Liberal Studies.

The survey was first administered as a pilot study to summer school students in 2005. Student response to the survey was very good and there did not appear to be any problems with ambiguity or understanding the questions. Thus, it was determined to use the same instrument in a more extensive survey for the fall semester of 2005. Two additional questions were added at this point to facilitate data analysis—students were asked to indicate their gender and whether they were undergraduate or graduate students. Students were contacted and requested to participate in the survey at the end of each 8-week and 16-week course. A total of 48 different undergraduate and 24 graduate courses, many with multiple sections, were included in the survey. Responses to the survey were anonymous. Trent Gabert, associate dean of the College of Liberal Studies, sent an e-mail letter to all students informing them of the survey and encouraging them to participate in order for instructors in the college to understand student attitudes better and improve the quality of courses. The instructors in the courses were also requested to encourage their students to participate. Two follow-up reminders were sent via e-mail to all students encouraging them to participate if they had not already done so.

ANALYSIS

Data for Questions 1-15 were expressed in percentages. In addition, the raw data for these items were analyzed using a MANOVA. The data were also subjected to a regression analysis which was performed between overall satisfaction with the online program (Question 15) as the dependent variable and the 12 questions regarding specific student satisfaction as the independent variables. The open-ended questions: "16. The best thing (kudos) about OU online courses is (list 2 or 3)" and "17. The worst thing (pet peeves) about OU online courses is (list 2 or 3)" were subjected to a qualitative analysis. Three graduate student judges independently read all of the responses for Questions 16 and 17. As they read the responses, they made a list of categories into which they thought it would be possible to classify the comments. After each had read the comments and created categories independently, they met and in conference settled on a final list of categories for each question. They then reread each item classifying it into the appropriate category. Items for which two or three of the raters agreed were considered classified. Comments not so classified were discussed in conference and classified by consensus. Only 4 of the 782 total responses had to be classified by conference.

RESULTS

The survey was sent to a total of 767 students who had participated in an online course lasting either 8 or 16 weeks in the College of Liberal Studies at the University of Oklahoma. Responses were anonymous and were made via a specially prepared website. A total of 304 students participated in this survey producing a participation rate of 40%. While we had hoped for a better participation rate, 40% was considered acceptable for a strictly voluntary and anonymous survey.

A MANOVA was conducted on Questions 3-15 regarding student satisfaction using data from Questions 1 and 2 to categorize respondents. Questions 7, 8, 9, and 13 had significant MANOVA models. Question 7 had a significant MANOVA of $F(3, 241) = 10.53, p < .0001$. Review of the analysis of variance indicated that degree was a significant contributor of differences, $F(1, 241) = 23.86, p < .0001$. The Bonferroni t test revealed that undergraduate students ($M = 4.2831$) enjoyed sharing their work with other students more than did graduate students ($M = 3.1139$). Question 8 had a significant MANOVA of $F(3, 241) = 10.76, p < .0001$. Examination of the analysis of variance indicated that degree was a significant contributor of differences, $F(1, 241) = 31.85, p < .0001$. The Bonferroni t test revealed that undergraduate students ($M = 3.1265$) ideally preferred feedback in a shorter amount of time than did graduate students (M = 4.6203). Question 9 had a significant MANOVA of $F(3, 241)$ = 18.28, p < .0001. Inspection of the analysis of variance indicated that degree was a significant contributor of differences, $F(1, 241)$ = 47.11, p < .0001. The Bonferroni t test revealed that undergraduate students (M = 5.1386) realistically preferred feedback in a shorter amount of time than did graduate students (M = 7.3544). Question 13 had a significant MANOVA of $F(3, 241)$ = 2.85, p = 0.0382. A look at the analysis of variance indicated that degree was a significant contributor of differences, $F(1, 241)$ = 6.46, p = 0.0117. The Bonferroni t test revealed that graduate students (M = 2.3165) were less satisfied with an 8-week-long course than were undergraduates (M = 2.0482). In addition, there was a significant interaction between degree and gender, $F(1, 241)$ = 4.12, p = 0.0434. Examination of the means revealed that undergraduate females (M = 2.1885) and graduate females (M = 2.1875) were equivalent in their satisfaction with the 8-week courses. However, male undergraduates (M = 1.8545) were more satisfied with the 8-week courses than were male graduate students (M = 2.5143).

Table 1 presents the percentages of students selecting each option for each of Questions 1-15. Figures 3 and 4 display the frequencies for the categories employed to classify the responses having to do with what was the best thing (kudos) about online courses and what was the worst thing (pet peeves) about such courses.

A standard multiple regression was performed between overall satisfaction with the online program (Question 15) as the dependent variable and the 12 questions regarding specific student satisfaction as the independent variables. The linear combination of the specific satisfaction variables were significantly related to the overall satisfaction variable, $F(12, 138)$ = 7.19, p < .0. The multiple correlation coefficient was .62, indicating that approximately 38% of the variance of the overall satisfaction with the program in the sample can be accounted for by the linear combination of specific satisfaction measures.

Only four of the independent variables (Question 3, 8, 9, and 13) contributed significantly to prediction of overall satisfaction. Satisfaction with reading assignments (Question 3) contributed significantly to the prediction of overall satisfaction (β = 0.21, p = 0.01). Ideal time for feedback (Question 8) contributed significantly to the prediction of overall satisfaction (β = 0.05, p = 0.06). Realistic time for feedback (Question 9) contributed significantly to the prediction of overall satisfaction (β = −0.06, p = 0.02). Satisfaction with the 8-week program (Question 13) contributed significantly to the prediction of overall satisfaction (β = 0.10, p = 0.05).

Regressions analyses examining the predictive qualities of gender, as well as degree were also conducted. Gender was not a significant predictor of overall satisfaction, $F(1, 297) = 1.88$, $p = 0.1709$. Neither was degree a significant predictor of overall satisfaction, $F(1, 297) = 0.88$, $p = 0.3501$.

DISCUSSION

The main effects of the MANOVA reveal relatively minor differences in which undergraduates enjoyed interaction with their classmates slightly more and wanted quicker feedback on their assignments than did graduate students. The significant interaction on Question 13 dealing with 8-week courses reveals that undergraduate males were more satisfied with 8-week courses than were graduate student males. This result must be interpreted with caution because very few 8-week courses are offered for graduate students and these are primarily during summer sessions. Overall, students were very satisfied with 8-week courses. Given the small number of minor differences revealed by the MANOVA, we determined to present the data for the individual items on the survey for the whole group rather than breaking it down by gender or class level.

Data for survey items 1-15 are shown in Table 1. Questions 1 and 2 were included to obtain data for classification purposes in performing the MANOVA. The data indicate good participation in the survey by males and females as well as by undergraduate and graduate students

Examination of Questions 3, 4, 5, and 6 indicated that students found the basic components and format of the courses useful in enhancing their learning. They were somewhat more positive with respect to the reading assignments and the short essay assignments than they were for the Internet assignments and the major course spanning term paper, however, they were basically positive about all of these activities.

One of the disadvantages cited with respect to online instruction is that there is no opportunity for interaction with classmates. To make up for this, some instructors use chat sessions, discussion boards, or encourage class members to e-mail selected assignments to each other for comment and interaction. Question 7 indicates that the students were only mildly pleased with such opportunities. Recall that earlier results from the MANOVA indicated that undergraduate students were slightly more positive about such interactions. Anecdotally, however, some students commented that they were too busy and did not want to hear from other students.

A crucial aspect of online courses has to do with the promptness of feedback to students. Question 8 indicated that most students would prefer to have feedback within 2 to 3 days. However, Question 9 indicated 5 to 7 days is acceptable. Recall that the MANOVA revealed that undergrad-

**Table 1.   Responses to Survey Questions 1-15
Expressed in Percentages**

1. Please indicate whether you are:	*Response Percent*	*Response Total*
Female	**64.8**	**197**
Male	35.2	107
Total Respondents		**304**
(skipped this question)		0

2. What degree are you obtaining?	*Response Percent*	*Response Total*
Undergraduate	**60.9**	**185**
Graduate	39.1	119
Total Respondents		**304**
(skipped this question)		0

3. I found the reading assignments useful in enhancing my learning.	*Response Percent*	*Response Total*
Strongly agree	27.6	84
Agree	**61.2**	**186**
Neutral	8.2	25
Disagree	2	6
Strongly disagree	0.7	2
Not applicable	0.3	1
Total Respondents		**304**
(skipped this question)		0

4. I found the essay assignments useful in enhancing my learning.	*Response Percent*	*Response Total*
Strongly agree	30.6	93
Agree	**56.6**	**172**
Neutral	9.5	29
Disagree	2.3	7
Strongly disagree	0.7	2
Not applicable	0.3	1
Total Respondents		304
(skipped this question)		0

5. I found the Internet assignments useful in enhancing my learning.	*Response Percent*	*Response Total*
Strongly agree	25.4	77
Agree	**48.5**	**147**
Neutral	16.2	49
Disagree	4.3	13
Strongly disagree	1.7	5
Not applicable	4	12
Total respondents		303
(skipped this question)		1

(Table continues on next page)

Table 1   (Continued)

6. I found the course spanning final paper assignment useful in enhancing my learning.	Response Percent	Response Total
Strongly agree	24.5	74
Agree	**48.7**	**147**
Neutral	14.9	45
Disagree	5.6	17
Strongly disagree	1	3
Not applicable	5.3	16
Total Respondents		302
(skipped this question)		2

7. I enjoyed sharing my work with and getting comments from other students in courses.	Response Percent	Response Total
Strongly agree	6.9	21
Agree	20.4	62
Neutral	29.9	91
Disagree	8.2	25
Strongly disagree	3	9
Not applicable	**31.6**	**96**
Total Respondents		304
(skipped this question)		0

8. In an online course, the professor should provide prompt feedback on completed assignments. Ideally feedback should be received within how many days?	Response Percent	Response Total
1	6.6	20
2	25.5	77
3	**29.8**	**90**
4	8.6	26
5	11.6	35
6	0	0
7	14.6	44
8	0	0
9	0	0
10	2	6
Other	1.3	4
Total Respondents		302
(skipped this question)		2

9. Realistically, feedback should never be later than how many days?	Response Percent	Response Total
1	0.3	1
2	5.6	17
3	13	39
4	11.3	34
5	20.6	62
6	3	9
7	**20.9**	**63**
8	4.7	14
9	1	3
10	16.9	51
Other	2.7	8
Total Respondents		301
(skipped this question)		3

(Table continues on next page)

Table 1   (Continued)

10. Overall the instructor grading in the courses I have taken online has been fair.	Response Percent	Response Total
Strongly agree	37.4	113
Agree	**52**	**157**
Neutral	8.6	26
Disagree	2	6
Strongly disagree	0	0
Total Respondents		302
(skipped this question)		2

11. Evaluation in the online courses I have taken has been too subjective.	Response Percent	Response Total
Strongly agree	1.7	5
Agree	9.9	30
Neutral	**48**	**145**
Disagree	34.1	103
Strongly disagree	6.3	19
Total Respondents		302
(skipped this question)		2

12. I would prefer an objective test in addition to the more subjective forms of evaluation.	Response Percent	Response Total
Strongly agree	2.4	7
Agree	12.5	37
Neutral	31.3	93
Disagree	**40.4**	**120**
Strongly disagree	13.5	40
Total Respondents		297
(skipped this question)		7

13. I found 8-week courses long enough to adequately cover the course material.	Response Percent	Response Total
Strongly agree	19.7	59
Agree	**46.5**	**139**
Neutral	10.7	32
Disagree	7	21
Strongly disagree	3	9
Not applicable	13	39
Total Respondents		299
(skipped this question)		5

14. The amount of work required for the online courses I have taken has been.	Response Percent	Response Total
Very excessive	3	9
Excessive	24	72
About right	**73**	**219**
Too little	0	0
Far too little	0	0
Total Respondents		300
(skipped this question)		4

(Table continues on next page)

Table 1   (Continued)

15. Overall my experience with online courses at OU has been.	Response Percent	Response Total
Very positive	**49.8**	**149**
Positive	42.5	127
Neutral	4.7	14
Negative	2.7	8
Very negative	0.3	1
Total Respondents		299
(skipped this question)		5

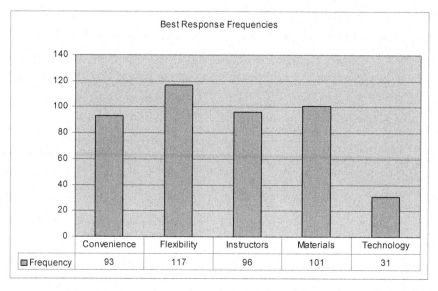

Figure 1.   Kudos or best feature of online courses reported in frequencies.

uates, who tend to take courses in 8 weeks, prefer slightly quicker feedback than students in general.

The majority of the courses offered by the College of Liberal Studies employ a series of essays and papers for evaluation and assigning grades. No objective tests are administered. Since grading of student essays is a highly subjective endeavor, we were interested in surveying the students regarding their attitude toward this aspect of online courses. Examination of the results for Questions 10 and 11 indicated that students did not regard the grades assigned to them as being overly subjective or unfair. In addition, Question 12 indicated that they did not think an objective test would be desirable as a part of the course.

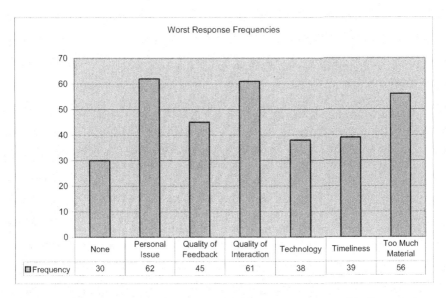

Figure 2.   Pet peeves or worst features of online courses reported in frequencies.

Eight weeks is relatively short period of time in which to complete an entire course online. Our concern with this issue led us to include Question 13. In spite of the panic that students often experience with deadlines in courses of that duration, the majority of the students in the survey were of the opinion that 8 weeks was long enough to adequately cover the course material.

Question 14 dealt with the amount of work required for the online courses. Overwhelmingly, these students felt that the amount of work demanded was about right. Interestingly, none thought that too little work was required.

Responses to Question 15 indicated an extremely high level of satisfaction with the online experience the students had. Thus, overall the results of this survey indicated that the students were very satisfied with the format, the nature and amount of the work required, and with the assessment of their work and grading.

Figures 1 and 2 present summary data for the open-ended questions (16 & 17) on the survey. Over 99% of the responses were assigned to a category on the first attempt and all were successfully classified in conference. Examination of Figure 1 indicates that the flexibility of online courses was the most attractive feature. Typical responses in this category were, "Online courses work very well with people working full time" and "I can do the work in my own time."

Instructors and materials were rated very highly. Typical comments included "Great instructors," "The interaction with OU professors is top notch!" and "The books are not things I would read for pleasure but I find them very engaging once I read them for the courses."

Convenience was also very high on the list. Typical responses in this category were "I can do it all from home and as a single mom that is my most important factor" and "I get to attend OU and still live in my home-town!"

Finally students mentioned the use of technology. However, this was much less important than the others. Items mentioned were the course Web site, e-mail, and message boards.

Examination of Figure 2 indicated that personal issues topped the list of pet peeves. This category consisted of specific complaints about a particular instructor or a problem with a particular assignment.

The second most frequent pet peeve involved the quality of interaction. This had to do with the students feeling isolated because they were not able to meet their professor or classmates face-to-face. Typical comments were, "I would like to personally meet the professors" and "I wish there was more interaction among students." It should be recalled from the data earlier presented that there was not major dissatisfaction with this aspect of the course. However, for those who had pet peeves, this was one that was frequently mentioned. The same could be said for the third most common pet peeve which refers to too much material. Typical responses in this category were, "Way too much reading and essays. It's more than a full time job" and, "Having to write so many darned papers!" However again, it should be recalled that the majority of students felt the amount of material was "about right" in the data presented earlier.

Quality and timeliness of feedback appeared as significant pet peeves. Typical responses in this category were, "Feedback wasn't constructive enough to improve" and, "The feedback is minimal."

Technology was a significant source of pet peeves. This category referred mainly to difficulties of dealing with computer programs, Internet sites, broken links, and similar problems.

Finally, 30% of the respondents insisted that they had no pet peeves regarding the online experience. It is rather surprising that such a substantial number would have no complaints at all, however, this agrees with the overall satisfaction data presented earlier. Typical comments were "I cannot honestly think of one negative thing about the online courses" and "I'm pleased."

Examination of the results of the regression analysis indicates that this analysis did not provide significant insight beyond what was obtained via the MANOVA; however, the results did confirm the earlier results in terms of general outcome.

The data in this report provide evidence of a high level of satisfaction with online courses as well as provide insight into the features that students find particularly helpful or detrimental. It should be pointed out that the current data are limited to the particular courses studied at one university. They may or may not generalize to other settings, though as pointed out in the introduction, students in other settings have positively endorsed distance and online instruction.

ACKNOWLEDGMENT

This investigation was supported by a grant from the College of Liberal Studies of the University of Oklahoma.

REFERENCES

Bonk, C., Maher, E., & Halpenny, B. (2001). *Online teaching in an online world.* Retrieved June 19, 2006, from the Indiana University Research Park website: http://www.courseshare.com/reports.php

Berge, Z. L. (1998) Barriers to online teaching in post-secondary institutions. *Online Journal of Distance Education Administration, 1*(2). Retrieved November 10, 2006, from http://emoderators.com/barriers

Johnson, J., Killion, J., & Oomen, J. (2005). Student satisfaction in the virtual classroom. *The Internet Journal of Allied Health Sciences and Practice, 3*(2). Retrieved June 19, 2006, from http://ijahsp.nova.edu/articles/vol3num2/johnston.htm

Phipps, R., & Merisotis, J. (1999). *What's the difference: A review of contemporary research on the effectiveness of distance learning in higher education.* Washington, DC: Institute for Higher Education Policy. Retrieved June 19, 2006, from http://www.eguana.net/organizations.php3?action=printContentItem&orgid=104&typeID= 906&itemID=9249&User_Session=6b7e3512ae3559ed724f62501e8762e7

Russell, T. (1999). *The no significant difference phenomenon.* Raleigh: North Carolina State University.

APPENDIX A:
OU COLLEGE OF LIBERAL STUDIES ONLINE COURSE SURVEY

1. Please indicate whether you are:

Female__   Male __

2. What degree are you obtaining:

Undergraduate__   Graduate __

3. I found the reading assignments useful in enhancing my learning.

Strongly   Agree__   Neutral__   Disagree__   Strongly   Not
agree__   disagree __   applicable__

4. I found the essay assignments useful in enhancing my learning.

Strongly   Agree__   Neutral__   Disagree__   Strongly   Not
agree__   disagree__   applicable__

5. I found the Internet assignments useful in enhancing my learning.

Strongly   Agree__   Neutral__   Disagree__   Strongly   Not
agree__   disagree__   applicable__

6. I found the course spanning final paper assignment useful in enhancing my learning.

Strongly   Agree__   Neutral__   Disagree__   Strongly   Not
agree__   disagree__   applicable__

7. I enjoyed sharing my work with and getting comments from other students in courses.

Strongly   Agree__   Neutral__   Disagree__   Strongly   Not
agree__   disagree__   applicable__

8. In an online course, the professor should provide prompt feedback on completed assignments. Ideally feedback should be received within how many days?

1__   2__   3__   4__   5__   6__   7__   8__   9__   10__   Other__

9. Realistically, feedback should never be later than how many days?

1__   2__   3__   4__   5__   6__   7__   8__   9__   10__   Other__

10. Overall the instructor grading in the courses I have taken online has been fair.

Strongly   Agree__   Neutral__   Disagree__   Strongly
agree__   disagree__

11. Evaluation in the online courses I have taken has been too subjective.

Strongly   Agree__   Neutral__   Disagree__   Strongly
agree__   disagree__

12. I would prefer an objective test in addition to the more subjective forms of evaluation.

Strongly   Agree__   Neutral__   Disagree__   Strongly
agree__   disagree__

13. If you were in an 8 weeks course, was it long enough to adequately cover the course material.

Strongly agree__   Agree__   Neutral__   Disagree__   Strongly disagree__   Not applicable__

14. The amount of work required for the online courses I have taken has been.

Very excessive__   Excessive__   About right__   Too little__   Far too little__

15. Overall my experience with online courses at OU has been.

Very positive__   Positive__   Neutral__   Negative__   Very negative__

16. The best thing (kudos) about OU online courses is (list 2 or 3):

17. The worst thing (pet peeves) about OU online courses is (list 2 or 3).

Thank you very much for your participation. College of Liberal Studies, University of Oklahoma.

CHAPTER 14

ASSISTIVE TECHNOLOGY

Enhancing the Life Skills of Students With Learning Disabilities

Aries Cobb
Baldwin-Wallace College

INTRODUCTION

The goal of this study was to explore and report how behavior therapists and applied behavior analysts used data derived from the Child Behavioral Checklist (CBCL) and the Parent-Infant Relationship Global Assessment Scale (PIR-GAS) to prescribe assistive technology to increase the overall psychological well-being of early childhood students, ranging in age from 3 to 5 years. The CBCL is a tool that parents, teachers, clinicians, and therapists who know the child rate a child's problem behaviors and competencies (Achenbach, 1991). The PIR-GAS is a scale of infant-parent relationship adaptation, raging from "well-adapted" to "dangerously impaired" (Aoki, Zeanah, Heller, & Bakshi, 2002, p. 493). Applied behavior analysis (ABA) is an active ingredient that assists preschool aged students to develop creativity and learn basic skills, such as speaking, listening, controlling emotions, et cetera. In this study, applied behavior analysis was conducted using assistive technology (AT) to enhance the

Beyond the Online Course: Leadership Perspectives on e-Learning
pp. 233–247

233

learning and life skills of clients with learning disabilities. AT can help autistic children achieve their highest potential regardless of their inborn abilities (Hasselbring & Glaser, 2000; Smaldino, Lowther, & Russell, 2008; Tinker, 2001).

ASSISTIVE TECHNOLOGY

In the field of instructional technology (IT), special education, and in ABA, the varying definitions of AT are as follows: (a) "Any item, piece of equipment, or product system, whether acquired commercially, modified, or customized, that is used to increase, maintain, or improve functional capabilities of individuals with disabilities" (Assistive Technology Act, 2004, p. 1); (b) devices and software designed specifically for those with learning or physical disabilities (Smaldino, Lowther, & Russell, 2008); and (c) AT has powerful tools that support physically challenged students with equal opportunities to more fully participate in the teaching-learning process (Hager & Smith, 2003).

In this study, the researcher takes each definition into account and focuses on studying the impact of the computer, mediating hardware, and software used by disabled students in learning environment. The research suggests that students that use AT display positive effects for psychological health when compared to other children in the program who do not use AT (Cavanaugh, 2002; Hasselbring & William-Glaser, 2000; Khek, Lim, & Zhong, 2006; Smaldino et al., 2008, 2012). Moreover, this body of research refers to the IT devices as a system of positive reinforcement used to help students learn. In this study the use of AT plays an important role in behavior management and enhancement of life skills for the overall education of students with learning disabilities.

ASSISTIVE TECHNOLOGY USED
BY APPLIED BEHAVIOR ANALYSTS

In the areas of applied behavior analysis and special education, there are sets of technologies and computerized equipment that are used to assist children in the learning process. The list of technological devices and/or assistive technology used by behavior therapists as a treatment for children with special needs includes simple magnifiers, pointers, alternative input/output devices, touch screens, voice recognition systems, graphic organizing software, and special cognitive software (Khek et al., 2006).

In this study, the treatment group used AT to improve language and motor delays in children 3 to 5 years of age. Evaluating researchers have

**Table 1.   Assistive Technology Devices
for Specific Learning Disabilities**

AT Device	Type of Motor Skill and/or Learning Disability
Click-N-Type	Students that do not have the use of their fingers or do not have fine motor skills
Word Talk	Students that are visually impaired and/or have a form of a reading disability
Let Me Type	Students with cognitive disabilities or learning disabilities (e.g., dyslexia)
Next Talk	Students who are deaf or hard of hearing (auditory impairments) or are sound sensitive
Click and Speak	Students with visual impairments, cognitive disabilities
Power Talk	Students with cognitive disabilities and visual impairments

Source: Adapted from The Ohio State University, College of Education & Human Ecology, Ideal Group (n.d.).

documented that, when AT is used for children with special needs, properly designed instruction contributes enormously to its effectiveness, especially in the case of autism (Cavanaugh, 2002; Smaldino et al., 2008). When used correctly for students with special needs, AT tends to create a learning environment that promotes enhanced operant procedures, positive self-growth, increased motor skills, and effective oral communication (Cavanaugh, 2002; Khek et al., 2006; Smaldino et al., 2008, 2012). In conjunction with the application of AT, educational therapists have found various technological devices to be effective in specific types of learning disability. Table 1 provides a list of practical uses of assistive technology devices for specific learning disabilities.

SPECIAL INSTRUCTIONAL INTERVENTIONS:
REGULAR CLASSROOM

Children with disabilities need special instructional interventions that will eventually result in their improved understanding, learning function, and self-confidence with which they merit inclusion in the regular classroom. Multiple reports indicate that the number of students with disabilities enrolled in K-12 schools has steadily increased since the passage of P.L. 94-142: Education of All Handicapped Children Act (Reed & Lahm, 2004). Children with mental disabilities have a great opportunity to learn when presented with high-structured learning situations (Smaldino et al., 2008). The EDU-AT-TECH program provides students with disabilities with appropriately structured instruction that helps them to develop positive learning constructs. In this study, the researcher states and discusses the benefits of the EDU-AT-TECH program and how the participants learn as a result of AT and structured instruction. Through the use of AT, many students with learning disabilities are found to decrease their isolation and demonstrate their increasing ability to become participants in regular classes (Cavanaugh, 2002).

LITERATURE REVIEW

The uses of IT and AT in education are not new phenomena. IT not only brings exciting treatment based on real-world problems into the classroom but also provides scaffolding to enhance learning (Hitchcock, 2001; Tinker, 2001). IT has increased the psychological health of global communities that include teachers using IT as a treatment for behaviors on a student's individual education plan (Salomon, 1993). This technology gives students and teachers collaborative feedback, reflection, and revision. AT also expands learning opportunities for both teachers and students (Bransford, Brown, & Cocking, 1999).

Computer-Assisted Instruction and Computer-Managed Instruction

In this study, the uses of computer-assisted instruction and computer-managed instruction are briefly outlined. The two treatments are used together with ABA to decrease the effects of language and speech delays in children with learning disabilities. In other words, the EDU-AT-TECH program uses AT in the form of computer-assisted instruction and computer-managed instruction as treatment for children with autism. Computer-assisted instruction refers to the use of technology to aid teaching and learning in the classroom (Cobb, 2009). Computer-managed instruction refers to the use of computer systems to manage information about learner performance and learning resources and to then prescribe and control individual lessons (Smaldino et al., 2012). Students who participate in tutorial drill, practice, and games tend to outperform students who do not use such interventions (Cobb, 2009; Morrison, 2001; Slavin, 2008). In addition, ABA teachers that use a combination of computer-assisted instruction and computer-managed instruction tend to use computer systems to manage information about learner performance and learning resources and to then prescribe and control individual lessons (Smaldino et al., 2008). By contrast, there has been a new shift toward a software design model which is characterized by a consistent presentation of voice prompts to promote interaction with audio in the form of voice and sound (Lewis & Doorlag, 1999).

Computer Multimedia and Learning Disabilities

Computer multimedia is a computer hardware/software system for the composition and display of presentations that incorporate text audio, still, and motion images (Smaldino et al., 2008). In this study, the researcher determined whether computer mediated hardware and software used by disabled students in a learning environment assist in improving their overall psychological well-being. Instructional Technology was used as a tool to improve instruction for students with learning disabilities.

Technology Productive Tools: Augmentative Technology

Technology-productive tools consist of computer software that enables people to work more effectively and efficiently (Blackhurst & Koorland, 1995). IT and quality teaching increase the psychological well-being of students in the EDU-AT-TECH program. For example, voice recognition software with transcription capabilities can assist students with special needs who are physically unable to type using a keyboard (Hasselbring & Glaser, 2000).

Augmentative technology uses voice prompts to teach students that demonstrate developmental language delays in how to communicate at home and in the school environment, as well as in learning life skills. The technological cognitive code base in the device reduces a student's dependence on others to perform such simple tasks as reading, writing, and listening. In addition, there are various types of software available that can provide immediate feedback to the student, and also offer an individualized learning environment. Furthermore, the data analysis driven method employed by ABA identifies behavior that is displayed and improved by the student as a vital component of overall success by tracking reinforcement and improved behavior in terms of performance objectives (Margolis & Michaels, 1994).

Education and Students With Learning Disabilities

AT's high standards provide benefits for students with learning disabilities. It improves student self-confidence and academic performance.

This study includes documentation of observable behavior displayed by clients that the behavior therapist is able to describe and categorize in order to form a report. Such reports show that AT can increase students' enthusiasm to learn. Students with mild learning disabilities often demonstrate higher-level performance and attention to detail when working on multimedia projects than they normally exhibit (Hasselbring & Glaser, 2000). As a result, their interest in academic endeavors is enhanced. In 2005, a nationwide population of approximately 70,000,000 pre-K-12 students who had been identified as having special needs was the driving initiative for the Individuals with Disabilities Education Act, which focused on students with disabilities that needed to be taught and brought to the same high standards as students without disabilities (U.S. Department of Education, 2006).

Innovative advantages in technology have assisted teachers to better meet the special needs of students with learning or physical disabilities, as well as students who have language delays. The values of using technology for diverse type of learners have been established and individualized education programs are now being created for students with special needs by integrating assistive technology into classroom instructional practices. Today's applied behavior analysis can be used as a resource for specialized software and digital tools to create, maintain, and report student individualized education programs as well as to provide overall management, behavioral analysis, behavior therapy, and support of students with special needs. This program was created to meet the needs of the children with learning disabilities that are entitled to receive behavior therapy to meet their learning needs.

Learning Centers

New technologies also serve to increase the current and future compatibility of classrooms in adapting to accommodate special needs learners. Learning centers can be equipped with assistive technology or digital devices and software designed specifically for children and adolescents with learning or special disabilities. The technology enables students to control the rate of speech delivery. A computer screen is used so they can better read the results of a database. The treatment allows students to perform a search by using a voice synthesizer, to have the printed page remade to meet their needs or to enable them to take notes in class through an electronic storage device that can later print out the document in Braille (Smaldino et al., 2008). The behavior therapists in the study made accommodations for the learners by offering user-centered selection of text and graphics for design options for the AT.

Hearing Impaired Learners and Visually Impaired Learners

Behavior therapists at EDU-AT-TECH use technique alternatives with special needs learners by providing handouts using notes for hearing impaired learners and using audio recording for visually impaired learners. Thus, the treatment can improve the learning of all students. Students diagnosed with visual impairments require different kinds of learning materials such as appropriate audio devices; adjusted instruction for exceptional learners; and prescription of technology, media, and materials. Applied behavior analysis uses assistive strategies for students with disabilities. AT is beneficial to the clients because assistive technology enhances learning.

EDU-AT-TECH Clients

In Table 2 and Table 3, the outcomes of EDU-AT-TECH clients are presented by age, and by age and gender. EDU-AT-TECH was initiated in July 2007. Ninety-six EDU-AT-TECH clients consented to participate in Invest in Children's external evaluation of the overall initiative. A total of 63.5% of the clients were male and 36.5% of the clients were female.

Table 2.   EDU-AT-TECH Clients by Gender

	Gender	Frequency	Percent
Valid	Male	61	63.5
	Female	35	36.5
	Total	96	100.0

Table 3.   EDU-AT-TECH Clients by Age and Gender

Male	N	Valid	61
		Missing	0
	M		28.0768
	SD		7.63888
Female	N	Valid	35
		Missing	0
	M		27.6729
	SD		8.89107

Table 4.   Parent/Guardian Consent
for Study Participation in Invest in Children

N	Frequency	Percent	Valid Percent
Valid	1	1.0	1.0
0	21	21.9	21.9
1	74	77.1	77.1
Total	96	100.0	100.0

Table 5.   Number and Reason for Continuing
or Discontinuing the EDU-AT-TECH Program

Reason In or Not in Program		Frequency	Percent	Valid Percent
Valid	1	26	27.1	34.2
	2	37	38.5	48.7
	3	2	2.1	2.6
	4	5	5.2	6.6
	5	6	6.3	7.9
	Total	76	79.2	100.0
Missing	System	20	20.8	
Total		96	100.0	

Note: 1 = Treatment completed satisfactorily; 2 = Noncompletion: Family withdrew child from service; 3 = Noncompletion: Child transitioned to other program; 4 = Noncompletion: Child aged out (> 48 months); 5 = Noncompletion: Family moved residence.

The mean age of the 61 male EDU-AT-TECH clients that participated in the program was 28 months, and the median age of the 35 female EDU-AT-TECH clients was also 28 months.

Table 4 represents data collected about the total number of parents that wished to be involved in Invest in Children's external evaluation process. There were 96 EDU-AT-TECH clients enrolled in the program. Parents had the option of giving consent to be contacted during the evaluation process: 21.9% of the parents and/or caregivers indicated that they did not want to be contacted in regards to the evaluation of their child. By contrast, 77.1% of the parents and/or caregivers wanted to have contact with the provider regarding the evaluation of their child.

Table 5 is the data representation of the total number of clients that had a closed case in the EDU-AT-TECH program. Details of the data representation are discussed following the table.

Table 6.   Reference Resources

		Frequency	Percent	Valid Percent	Cumulative Percent
Valid		1	1.0	1.0	1.0
		10	10.4	10.4	
1		2	2.1	2.1	13.5
2					
3		3	3.1	3.1	16.7
4		11	11.5	11.5	28.1
5		69	71.9	71.9	100.0
	Total	96	100.0	100.0	

Note: 1= Self-parent (SP); 2 = medical provider (MP); 3 = social science organization (SSOOA or other agency); 4 = home service coordinator (own agency); 5 = HMG service coordinator (other agency or HMGSCOA).

Of the total number of EDU-AT-TECH clients in the EDU-AT-TECH program, 79.2% cases were closed, and the analysis of the data suggests that 27.1% of the cases were closed with treatment program completed satisfactorily; 38.5% of the cases were closed for noncompletion because a family member withdrew the client from the EDU-AT-TECH service; 2.1% of the clients' cases were closed for noncompletion because the child transitioned to another program outside of the agency; 5.2% of client cases were closed because of noncompletion because the child aged out of the program at 48 months; and finally, 6.3% of the cases were closed for noncompletion because the family moved residence.

Table 6 is an analysis of how clients were referred to the EDU-AT-TECH program. The types of referral were self/parent, medical provider, social service organization/other agency, home service coordinator, and HMG service coordinator.

The data in Table 6 show that there are nine identified reference referral resources for the EDU-AT-TECH clients for Learning Disability Services: 10.4% of referrals are derived from parents, 2.1% of all referrals are from medical providers, 3.1% of the referrals are from a social service organization that are outside of the EDU-AT-TECH agency, 11.5% of the clients are referred by the Home Service Coordinator (Targeted ABA Program or Own Agency), and 71.9% of all referrals are from Home Service Coordinator (other agency).

Table 7 provides a presentation of the paired sample statistics and/or *t* test. The statistics are used to compare the assessment scores and group performance on a pretest and posttest of EDU-AT-TECH clients.

Table 7 contains the paired *t*-test used to compare the EDU-AT-TECH client assessment scores and group performance on a pretest and posttest.

Table 7.   Paired Sample Statistics

	Pairs	Mean	N	SD	Std. Error Mean
Pair 1	CBCLi.1	58.61	61	11.046	1.414
	CBCLi.2	51.48	61	10.563	1.353
Pair 2	CBCLe.1	68.87	61	12.428	1.591
	CBCLe.2	57.64	61	10.950	1.402
Pair 3	CBCLt.1	65.62	61	10.903	1.396
	CBCLt.2	55.21	61	10.154	1.300
Pair 4	PIRc1.1	68.88	68	13.856	1.680
	PIRc1.2	75.69	68	12.228	1.483

For instance, the assessment that is administered to the client is known as the CBCL. The CBCL is a standardized psychometric measure which records the behavioral problems and competencies of the children aged 1 1/2 to 5 years, as reported by their parents or others such as a guardian.

The CBCL has three main scales. The checklist is composed of 113 items that are all scored on a 3-item scale: 0 = *not true,* 1 = *somewhat true,* and 2 = *very true.* A parent or parents or guardian completes the CBCL. The instrument provides three scores: (a) a total score (CBCLt), (b) scores on internalizing behaviors (CBCLi; fearful, shy, anxious, and inhibited), and (c) externalizing behaviors (CBCLe; aggressive, antisocial, and undercontrolled).

A checklist is the form of the instrument. The method of delivery is a self-report. The CBCL has relevance to injury. In other words, the instrument is used to assess behaviors that may be associated with injury in children.

PIR-GAS is an assessment scale for children under the age of 6 that focuses on the overall quality of the child-parent relationship. In the assessment, the parent-child relationships are described by a range of ability to adapt, from "well adapted" to "severely impaired": The PIR-GAS scores range from 90, indicating a well-adapted relationship, to 10, indicating a severely impaired relationship. Stressors affect relationships described by scores in the middle range of 50 but still maintain some adaptive qualities (Billings & Moos, 1985).

Additionally, the PIR-GAS has been shown to share concurrent validity with the Achenbach CBCL for children ages 1.5 through 5 by providing answers to the following two questions: (a) Do children with autism spectrum disorders show improved functioning following treatment? (b) Does the use of AT and behavior therapy lead to differing levels of improve-

Table 8.   Paired Sample Correlation

	Pairs	N	Correlation	Sig.
Pair 1	CBCLi.1 & CBCLi.2	61	.373	.003
Pair 2	CBCLe.1 & CBCLe.2	61	.398	.001
Pair 3	CBCLt.1 & CBCLt.2	61	.321	.012
Pair 4	PIRc1.1 & PIRc1.2	68	.615	.000

ment in the symptoms exhibited by the children? The study also provides information that may prove useful to agencies in enhancing their current strategies for working with students with learning disabilities (Cripps & Zyromski, 2009).

In Table 8, the paired sample correlation of the performances of EDU-AT-TECH clients' statistical correlations are identified and discussed.

Table 8 shows the EDU-AT-TECH clients' mean and of a set of scores for each assessment, which is as follows: CBCLi 1 is 58.61, CBCLi 2 is 51.48, CBCLe1 is 68.87, CBCLe2 is 57.64, CBCLt1 is 65.62, CBCLt2 is 55.21, PIRc1.1 is 68.88, and PIRc1.2 is 75.69.

There is a strong correlation between increase in client overall psychological well-being when behavior therapists and/or teachers administer both the pretest and posttest and use the data to provide interventions for the client.

Table 9 provides a presentation of the statistical analysis of pretest and posttest CBCL scores. Significant differences are identified and discussed.

Table 9 shows that there is a significant difference in means between pretest and posttest CBCL scores, indicating improvement on all three scales: (a) CBCLi 1 and CBCLi2, (b) CBCLe1 and CBCLe2, and (c) CBCLt1 and CBCLt2. For example, with the PIR-GAS, there is a statistically significant increase in posttest scores, indicating improvement.

Table 10 represents an analysis of group statistics of pretests and posttests. The group statistics are discussed in Table 10.

Table 10 shows that there is an increase in post scores for the CBCLi, CBCLe, CBCLt, and the PIRc1.

CONCLUSIONS

The EDU-AT-TECH program was developed to address the needs of children from birth to 5 years of age that show signs of autism spectrum disorder issues. The Educational Assistive Technology program was developed to increase parent participation in the evaluation process, rate

Table 9. Paired Samples Test

| | Paired Differences | | | | | | | |
| | Mean | SD | Std. Error Mean | 95% Confidence Interval of the Difference | | t | df | Sig. (2 tailed) |
Pairs				Lower	Upper			
Pair 1 CBCLi.1- CBCLi.2	7.131	12.109	1.550	4.030	10.232	4.600	60	.000
Pair 2 CBCLe.1- CBCLe.2	11.230	12.881	1.649	7.931	14.528	6.809	60	.000
Pair 3 CBCLt.1- CBCLt.2	10.410	12.287	1.573	7.263	13.557	6.617	60	.000
Pair 4 PIRc1.1- PIRc1.2	−6.809	11.543	1.400	−9.603	−4.015	−4.864	67	.000

Table 10. Group Statistics

	Date.2 >= DATE.MDY(01,01,2 010) (FILTER)	N	Mean	SD	Std. Error Mean
CBCLi_diff	2010 before	29	-2.8621	12.67654	2.35397
	2011 after	32	-11.0000	10.30189	1.82113
CBCLe_diff	2010 before	29	-7.7931	13.63394	2.53176
	2011 after	32	-14.3438	11.49645	2.03230
CBCLt_diff	2010 before	29	-6.5517	12.69867	2.35808
	2011 after	32	-13.9063	10.95551	1.93668
PIRc1_diff	2010 before	29	2.9310	12.10056	2.24702
	2011 after	39	9.6923	10.34447	1.65644

significant behavior problems identified by the therapist to increase children's success rate in school. The EDU-AT-TECH program has the following significant and/or positive outcomes: (a) There is a statistically significant increase in PIR-GAS posttest scores, indicating improvement. (b) There is a significant difference in means between pretest and posttest CBCL scores, indicating improvement on all three scales. (c) There is a strong relationship between increase in client overall psychological well-

EDU-AT-TECH Pilot Satisfaction through First Quarter 2011

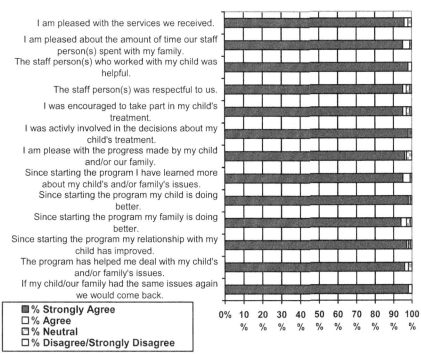

Figure 1.   Satisfaction survey results.

being when behavior therapists administer both the pretest and posttest and use the data to provide interventions for the client.

By contrast, there are three main areas where EDU-AT-TECH may want to devise a plan for improvement: (a) In the future, researchers may want to see if there is a correlation between parental consent and clients who withdraw from the program. These data could be useful in maintaining enrollment in the program; (b) researchers would like to decrease the number of students that withdraw transition, age out, and move out of the program; and (c) researchers will need to track parent participation in the evaluation process. With more parent and guardian involvement in the program, the more likely children will complete the program and gain a list of skills to live healthier lives.

REFERENCES

Assistive Technology Act, 2004. (29 U.S.C. Sec 2202(2).

Achenbach, T. M. (1991). *Manual for the child behavior checklist/4-18 and 1991 profile*. Burlington, VT: University of Vermont, Department of Psychiatry.

Aoki, Y., Zeanah, C. H., Heller, S. S., & Bakshi, S. (2002). Parent-infant relationship global assessment scale: A study of its predictive validity. *Psychiatry & Clinical Neurosciences. 56*(5), 493-497.

Billings, A. G., & Moos, R. H. (1985). Life stressor and social resources affect post treatment outcomes among depressed patients. *Journal of Abnormal Psychology, 94*(2), 140-153.

Blackhurst, A. E., & Koorland, M. A. (1995). Computer-assisted constant time delay prompting to teach abbreviation spelling to adolescents with mild learning disabilities. *Journal of Special Education Technology, 12*(30), 1-11.

Bransford, J. D., Brown, A. L., & Cocking, R. R. (Eds.). *How people learn: Brain, mind, experience, and school*. Washington, DC: National Academy Press.

Cavanaugh, T. (2002). *The need for assistive technology in education technology*. Retrieved from http://www.aace.org/pubs/etr/issue2/cavanaugh.cfm

Cobb, A. (2009). *Improving African American student achievement in reading with computer-assisted instruction and CL* (Unpublished doctoral dissertation). Nova Southeastern University, Fort Lauderdale, FL.

Cripps, K., & Zyromski, B. (2009). Southern adolescents' psychological well-being and perceived parental involvement: Implications for parental involvement in middle schools. *Research in Middle Level Education Online, 33*(4), 1-13.

Hager, R. M., & Smith, D. (2003). *The public school's special education system as a funding source: The cutting edge*. Retrieved from http://www.nls.org/pdf/special-ed-booklet-03.pdf

Hasselbring, T. S., & Glaser, C. H. W. (2000). *Use of computer technology to help students with special needs*. Retrieved www.familiestogetherinc.org/.../COMPUTERTECHNEEDS.pdf

Hitchcock, C. (2001). Balanced instructional support and challenge in universally designed learning environment. *Journal of Special Educational Technology, 16*(4), 23-30.

Khek, C., Lim, J., & Zhong, Y. (2006). Facilitation students with special needs in mainstream schools: An exploratory study of assistive learning technologies (ALT). *International Journal of Web-based Learning and Teaching Technologies, 1*(3), 56-74.

Lewis, R., & Doorlag, D. (1999). *Teaching special students in general education classrooms* (5th ed.). Upper Saddle River, NJ: Prentice Hall.

Margolis, V., & Michaels, C. (1994). Technology: The personal computer as a resource tool. In C. A. Michaels (Ed.), *Transition strategies for persons with learning disabilities* (pp. 239-269), San Diego, CA: Singular.

Morrison, P. A. (2001). *The emerging digital divide: A demographic perspective on our nation's future*. Santa Monica, CA: RAND.

The Ohio State University, College of Education & Human Ecology, Ideal Group (n.d.). Free assistive technology software. Retrieved from http://wac.osu.edu/conferences/emrc08/free_at.html

Reed, P., & Lahm, E. (2004). *Assessing student needs for assistive technology: A resource manual for school district teams*. Retrieved from http://www.wati.org/content/supports/free/pdf/ASNAT4thEditionDec08.pdf

Salomon, G. (1993). No distribution without individuals' cognition: A dynamic international view. In G. Salomon (Ed.), *Distributed cognitions psychological and educational considerations* (pp. 111-138). New York, NY: Cambridge University Press.

Slavin, R. E. (2008). What works? Issues in synthesizing education program evaluations. *Educational Researcher, 37*(1), 5-14.

Smaldino, S. E., Lowther, D. L., & Russell, J. D. (2008). Instructional technology and media for learning (9th ed.). Upper Saddle River, NJ: Prentice Hall.

Smaldino, S. E., Lowther, D. L., & Russell, J. D. (2012). *Instructional technology and media for learning* (10th ed.). Upper Saddle River, NJ: Prentice Hall.

Tinker, R. (2001). Future technologies for special learners. *Journal of Special Education Technology, 16*(4). Retrieved from http://jset.unlv.edu/16.4/tinker/first.html

U.S. Department of Education (2006). Special education and rehabilitative services. Retrieved from http://www2.ed.gov/about/overview/budget/budget07/summary/edlite-section2b.html

CHAPTER 15

SUPERVISION ON SITE

A Critical Factor in the Online Facilitated Internship

Kaye B. Dotson and Hui Bian
East Carolina University

Online education is increasingly prevalent in graduate schools of teacher education. Questions arise, however, as to the effectiveness of the online facilitated graduate internship. This article examines perspectives of librarian site supervisors within online supported internships. Perspectives in regard to program support and self-perceived readiness to supervise interns within an online facilitated graduate program were the focus of this study. A web-based survey was distributed to site supervisors who had previously served an online facilitated internship. Findings point to responsive program improvement for graduate educators to enhance support of on-site supervisors and interns to strengthen the online facilitated internship.

INTRODUCTION

Across the nation, schools of education are receiving criticisms for inadequate preparation of the nation's teachers (Wagner, 2008). Although teaching learners to teach is not an easy task, colleges and universities

Beyond the Online Course: Leadership Perspectives on e-Learning
pp. 249–264

continue to strive to produce graduates who are prepared to contribute and to succeed in various teaching positions. A review of higher education, both nationally and internationally, shows that graduate programs widely embrace the concept of the traditional clinical experience. For future school librarians the clinical experience offers a unique opportunity for providing an avenue to experience professional work while continuing to have access to academic support.

The teaching and learning of library science skills in real-life context offers the opportunity for graduate schools to do a more effective job in the preparation of future professional school librarians (Stefl-Mabry, Dequoy, & Stevens, 2012). The American Library Association Core Competences of Librarianship, American Association of School Librarians Standards for Initial Preparation of School Librarians, International Society for Technology in Education, the National Board for Professional Teaching Standards, and the North Carolina Department of Public Instruction Standards for the Master of Library Science Degree/School Library Media Coordinator License together provide clear guidelines for library science programs to address the issue of clinical competencies. The university program under review for this study, the master of library science program, firmly advocates the value of the clinical experience as reflected in the literature (Ball, 2008; Jurkowski, Antrim, & Robins, 2005; Shannon, 2008). This study was initiated to gather data to improve the program's clinical experience, the professional internship, specifically a distance learning facilitated internship.

The program under review by the researchers is completely online and is based on goals and objectives established by the department of library science (DLS) faculty through the curriculum development process. This process evolved through systematic planning by the department of library science curriculum committee in response to requirements for licensure from the state Department of Public Instruction (DPI) and the Standards for Initial Preparation of School Librarians designed by the American Library Association/American Association of School Librarians. Based on the program goals and objectives, the curriculum addresses the theory, principles, values and practices necessary for American Association of School Librarians students to succeed in their professional library careers. The master of library science program fosters curricular goals and objectives through a variety of educational experiences, culminating in the capstone clinical experience, the professional internship. The internship is a crucial, culminating link between theory and practice. This complex activity provides the means by which individuals may become critically conscious of themselves as professionals, applying theory gained in coursework in the totality of a real-life experience (Brown, Collins, &

Duguid, 1989; Lave & Wenger, 1991). An effective, on-site credentialed librarian as supervisor is essential to the process.

Technology in Library Science Internships

Technology played a strong role in this study, which focuses upon the need for support of site supervisors by university programs, as the program under review is offered entirely online. The course management system BlackBoard was used for the online facilitated internship. Discussion threads, blogs, video, and online evaluation and assessment formats were used. Coursework may be effectively adapted to the online arena, breaking conventional teaching modes and making advantageous use of rapidly expanding technology in allowing teacher and student to communicate, exchange work, pursue evaluation/assessment, and generally provide solid core subject education (Guoying, Shunxing, & Jiyue, 2005). However, concerns remain with the internship component. The clinical experience, the crucial link between theory and practice, is perhaps the most difficult program component to supervise and facilitate in an online environment (Dotson, 2010). Particular attention and effort are required to maintain contact and support with and for site supervisors who are working in distant schools and sites. The goal of this study was to understand the perspectives of supervisors who have experienced an online supported internship. Understanding these perceptions and making advantageous use of the technology available today is essential for continuing program improvement. The perspectives of the site supervisor role were examined through the lenses of situated cognition theory and the precede-proceed model.

THEORETICAL FRAMEWORK

Situated Cognition

This examination of the site supervisor role through the lens of situated cognition theory is based upon the perception that learning is constituted through the sharing of purposeful activity (Brown et al., 1989) in the preparation and practice of future school librarians. Situated cognition offers a theoretical foundation for examination of the role of the site supervisor for teaching and learning in the real world context.

Through a professional internship in a real-life setting, interns gain experience, hone skills, and test professional dispositions under the supervision of trained and certified site supervisors. Students are able to assimilate what is learned in coursework more thoroughly when they are able to see it in real-life practice (Ball, 2008; Daix & Epps, 2001; Feldman et al., 2009; Kelsey & Ramaswamy, 2004; Vecchio, 1987). Learning, in both theory and practice, promotes the social construction of knowledge related to a particular field of study (Brown, Collins, & Duguid, 1989). Theorists posit that placing learners in programs conducted within the professional field, under direct supervision, leads to effective development of professional competency and success (Berry, 2005; Brown et al., 1989; Kirshner & Whitson, 1997). During internships, interns are guided to inquire, think critically, gain knowledge, draw conclusions, make informed decisions, apply knowledge to new situations, and create new knowledge under the direction of both a university supervisor and a site supervisor. The interns gain understanding through a process of both inquiry and practice (American Association of School Librarians, 2010).

Research supports the value of an internship within the graduate study program intentionally incorporating inquiry, increased freedom and professional responsibility with the guidance of on-site supervisors (Ball, 2008; Brown et al., 1989; Dotson, 2010; Jurkowski et al., 2005; Kirshner & Whitson, 1997, Shannon, 2008). Site supervision is probably the most important component of the internship (Feldman et al., 2009; Kelsey & Ramaswamy, 2005).

Educators, as professionals involved in the preparation of future school librarians, face challenges in providing clear and visible guidance to the students they teach, particularly in online programs. Data has affirmed that university supervisors and site supervisors are the primary sources of support for interns engaged in fieldwork (Dotson, 2010). University supervisors observe, mentor, and guide from a distance to help develop the skills and dispositions needed in exemplary librarians (Jones & Bush, 2009). In contrast, site supervisors serve daily directing and guiding interns face to face. Ongoing interaction between site supervisor and academic institution is essential to assure that all participants have a clear understanding of the goals and process, in order to provide the most challenging and varied experience to the intern within the professional setting (Callison, 1985; Orchowski, 2005). Close interaction and open communication are hallmarks of an effective internship program (Dixon, Cunningham, Sagas, Kent, & Turner, 2005; Orchowski, 2005).

A critical component to any successful internship experience is the site supervisor. The site supervisor is an "in-person" facilitator, mentor, and model in the practice and inquiry process. Internship site supervisors monitor student progress and determine that instructional guidelines are being met. Site supervisors have an opportunity to expose interns to the myriad tasks and activities inherent in the library, ideally integrating theory and practice while permitting interns to examine their own perspectives on the art and science of librarianship (Aho, Franklin, Wakefield, & Wakefield, 2006; Callison, 1995; Orchowski, 2005; Stueart, 1989). In an online facilitated internship, the development of skills and understanding of practice within community is dependent upon skilled supervision within the situated learning experience (Batson, 2011).

PRECEDE-PROCEED Model

This study of the site supervisor role is also examined through the lens of the PRECEDE-PROCEED model. The PRECEDE-PROCEED model has been used to plan and evaluate health behavior change programs. The model has two main components, the PRECEDE and the PROCEED (Green & Kreuter, 1999). The PRECEDE component serves well in evaluation of perceptions and was the focus of this study. PRECEDE is the acronym for "Predisposing, Reinforcing, and Enabling Constructs in Educational/Environmental Diagnosis and Evaluation" (Figure 1). Those constructs are factors that influence the behavior change process. Predisposing factors include individuals' knowledge, skills, beliefs, et cetera.

Reinforcing factors are those rewards or incentives that motivate people to continue existing behaviors, such as vicarious reinforcement, peer influence, et cetera. Enabling factors include programs, services, policies, resources, et cetera. Site supervisors' perceptions of their roles, responsibilities, and online facilitated internship programs can be classified into three domains: predisposing, reinforcing, or enabling. These domains have direct and indirect effect on the success of internship programs.

PURPOSE OF THE STUDY

While studies highlight the advantages of an internship and extensive research exists as to the value of an internship within the graduate study program, currently, according to the National Council for Accreditation of Teacher Education (2010), there is not a large research base on what makes clinical preparation effective particularly in online facilitated programs such as the one under examination for this study. More specifically, there is little research drawing upon the perceptions of site supervisors who represent a key component in the internship process, in regard to evaluating the process (Church, Dickinson, Everhart, & Howard, 2012; Shannon, 2008). Acknowledging the significance of site supervision in the process of the internship, the researchers in this study were led to examine the concerns and perceptions of the site supervisor. Current data on the perceptions of the site supervisor in an online facilitated program is

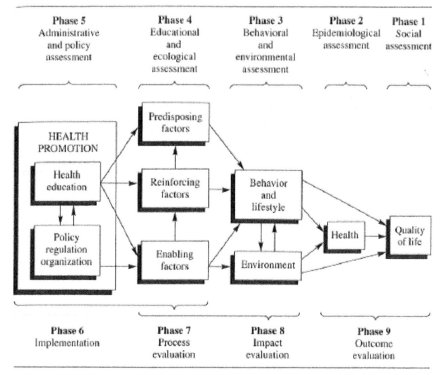

PRECEDE

Phase 5
Administrative
and policy
assessment

Phase 4
Educational
and
ecological
assessment

Phase 3
Behavioral
and
environmental
assessment

Phase 2
Epidemiological
assessment

Phase 1
Social
assessment

HEALTH
PROMOTION

Health
education

Policy
regulation
organization

Predisposing
factors

Reinforcing
factors

Enabling
factors

Behavior
and
lifestyle

Environment

Health

Quality
of life

Phase 6
Implementation

Phase 7
Process
evaluation

Phase 8
Impact
evaluation

Phase 9
Outcome
evaluation

PROCEED

Source: Green and Kreuter (1999). Reprinted with permission from McGraw-Hill Companies.

Figure 1. PRECEDE-PROCEED model.

needed to improve the online facilitated internship and to assist the library science profession in producing the most prepared graduates. As this crucial element was lacking, this study will fill the gap regarding current data addressing the perceptions of site supervisors and will maximize effectiveness and efficiency of online facilitated internship programs.

This research looks specifically at the perceptions of site supervisors regarding the roles and responsibilities of those serving interns in the field. This is an important step toward empowering site supervisors of library and information science interns to meet the educational needs of those they mentor, and to offer avenues for improving and strengthening the library science professional internship at the program under review.

RESEARCH QUESTIONS

Applying a PRECEDE model, the following research questions were examined:

1. What were site supervisors' perceptions regarding predisposing, enabling, and reinforcing domains for the online facilitated internship program?
2. Were there significant relationships between the three domains and the success of the internship program?
3. What did qualitative data clarify for us regarding the site experience?

METHOD

Participants

A total of 72 participated in the study from May 2010 to July 2012. The data were collected over a five-semester time period. One person who was not a certified site supervisor was removed from the study, which leads to 71 valid responses. The participants worked in different settings, with 43.1% at primary settings, 24.6% at intermediate settings, and 32.3% at secondary settings. They held a wide range of leadership positions such as principal, chair, manager, media coordinator, team leader, director, school improvement team member, etc.

According to the literature there is a general conclusion that leadership style and situational differences are strong predictors of association (Edwards, 1994; Hunt & Liebscher, 1973). Findings from Vecchio (1987) indicate that supervisors are likely to react differently based upon individual preferences. Therefore the use of demographic scores for participants of this study was limited.

Design and Procedure

A mixed methods design was implemented to collect both quantitative and qualitative data at the same time. This study used a 19-item web-based survey, "Internship Site Supervisor Perceptions Survey" (ISSPS), which was developed by the author/researcher to gather data. Content validity was used to assess the validity of the instrument and to measure the language and construction of questions. Additionally a pilot study was conducted with a small group of practicing librarians, a convenience sampling of 8 librarians engaged in supervisory positions. The Internship Site Supervisor Perceptions Survey included both open- and closed-ended questions.

Data were collected from a predetermined population including certified librarians nationally, but predominantly from the southeastern United States, because this was the area in which most of the interns served. Individuals who have served as site supervisors for online facilitated internships were invited to participate in the confidential survey. The research population was accessed through the cooperation of fieldwork supervisors affiliated with the graduate school under review. Site supervisors included individuals from public schools, including large, small, rural, and urban. Surveys were sent to site supervisors at the end of each student internship experience. Site supervisors were questioned about their experiences and perceptions during the process of intern supervision in the library science program. The university's institutional board approved the research prior to implementing the study.

Measures

The Internship Site Supervisor Perceptions Survey included 15 closed-ended questions and four open-ended questions in order to collect data on site supervisors' perceptions regarding the online facilitated internship program. Four questions asked participants to report their leadership position, working setting, certified librarian status, and supervisor status.

Ten questions tapping predisposing domain, enabling domain, and reinforcing domain were measured with a 5-point Likert scale (1 = *strongly disagree*, 5 = *strongly agree*), excepting one question which asked the length of the internship and used a dichotomous response option.

Predisposing Domain

Two questions measured supervisors' self-confidence in having the skills necessary to mentor interns in best practices, including appropriate use of resources and technologies, and in feeling comfortable with the internship (Cronbach's alpha = .85). One question reflected the need of additional preparation for site supervision.

Enabling Domain

Five questions explored the length of the internship, the clarity of expectations for an internship supervisor and the role in the assessment of an intern's performance made by the university's department of library science, and the university program supports available when supervisors had questions about an internship (Cronbach's alpha = .80, $n = 5$).

Reinforcing Domain

Two questions assessed the perceived values of the internship for both the intern and the school program or organization, addressing the benefits of hosting an intern and whether they would continue taking interns from the department (Cronbach's alpha = .81, n = 2).

Open-Ended Questions

Four open-ended questions asked participants to list any specific areas on which the graduate internship program should focus for site supervisors' preparation, necessary skills and challenges of being a site supervisor, and any comments about experience with the intern.

Outcome

One question was used to evaluate the success of the internship process based on site supervisors' views.

ANALYSIS

The quantitative data were analyzed using SPSS 20.0. Variables for three domains were regrouped into dichotomous variables (agree versus disagree and neutral). Fisher's exact tests were conducted to examine the relationship between predisposing, enabling, and reinforcing domains and success of the internship.

For the open-ended questions, the texts were read and coded. The notes were made directly on the print out, and key words, sentences, and quotes were highlighted. A two-person coding team, first and second authors, independently coded qualitative data into themes and reviewed the texts again when there were discrepancies. Then the themes were grouped into similar categories based on the PRECEDE model.

RESULTS

A majority reported positive perceptions of all three domains including self-confidence in assuming supervisor responsibilities, preparation and program support from the university, and incentive for continuing the internship. Fisher's exact tests showed that there were significant associations between success of the internship and predisposing domain (except for additional preparation) and reinforcing domain (p's < .05). Clarity of expectation from the university was the only significant factor influencing success of the on-site internship in enabling domain (p < .05) (Table 1).

**Table 1.   Associations Between
PRECEDE Model Domains and Success of Internship**

| PRECEDE Model Components | Success of Internship | | | | P^* |
| | Agree | | Disagree/Neutral | | |
	N	%	n	%	
Predisposing Domain					
Necessary skills					.03
Agree	57	86.4	2	40.0	
Disagree/neutral	9	13.6	3	60.0	
Felt comfortable					.00
Agree	64	97.0	1	20.0	
Disagree/neutral	2	3.0	4	80.0	
Additional preparation					.31
Agree	14	21.2	2	40.0	
Disagree/neutral	52	78.8	3	60.0	
Enabling Domain					
Adequate length of internship					.12
Yes	59	89.4	3	60.0	
No	7	10.6	2	40.0	
Clarity of expectation					.049
Agree	55	83.3	2	40.0	
Disagree/neutral	11	16.7	3	60.0	
Clarity of role					.17
Agree	56	86.2	3	60.0	
Disagree/neutral	9	13.8	2	40.0	
Program supports: contact					.09
Agree	60	90.9	3	60.0	
Disagree/neutral	6	9.1	2	40.0	
Program support: responses					.37
Agree	41	63.1	2	40.0	
Disagree/neutral	24	36.9	3	60.0	
Reinforcing Domain					
Perceived values					.04
Agree	62	95.4	3	60.0	
Disagree/neutral	3	4.6	2	40.0	
Continue taking interns					.01
Agree	59	90.8	2	40.0	
Disagree/neutral	6	9.2	3	60.0	

Note: $^*p$ corresponds to the Fisher's exact test.

Table 2.   Themes Generated from Qualitative Data

Themes	*Quotations*
Predisposing Domain	
Technology skills	"In-depth knowledge of software packages that allow creativity in creation of PR."
Collaboration/communication skills	"Excellent communication skills both written and oral; ability to interact with coworkers and understand the needs."
Enabling Domain	
Direct contact	"I would recommend direct contact with the site supervisor as to role and expectations of the program."
Adequate information	"I would have liked to have had a better understanding of how the hours would be carried out."
Time	"Hours required should have guidelines such as a certain number of hours of consecutive attendance not just an hour here or there for the entire internship."
Reinforcing Domain	
Positive feedback	"This has been a rewarding experience for both intern and Supervisor."

The analyses of open-ended responses yielded six themes grouped in predisposing, enabling, and reinforcing domains: technology skills, collaboration/communication skills, direct contact, adequate information, time, and positive feedback (Table 2). When asked about any specific area the graduate program should focus upon to prepare site supervisors better, respondents focused on two themes: direct contact from the university with the site supervisors sharing adequate information about roles, expectations, internship design; and expectations and guidance regarding the time commitment of interns. For example, one stated, "I would recommend direct contact with the site supervisor as to role and expectations of the program." The response also implied that additional information was needed by the site supervisor. As another participant explained, "information prior to the beginning of the internship would have been helpful: what to expect, how many hours, what types of items was the intern expected to perform within the internship time period."

When asked about any specific challenges as a site supervisor, respondents indicated time was an issue of concern. Additional time would help interns to see and get involved in the full scope of the job within the established schedule. One participant described, "for an opportunity to receive the full benefit of the internship, students should work through longer periods of time during a day." Another pointed out "if an intern is only at the site one day a week for x number of weeks, they never get to see a project from the planning stages through to the end." Even more specifically, another shared, "hours required should have guidelines such as a certain number of hours of consecutive attendance not just an hour here or there for the entire internship." These concerns mirror National Council for Accreditation of Teacher Education's (2010) report on clinical preparation and partnerships of educators regarding the time commitment of interns.

When asked about any specific skills which the graduate program should focus on to prepare students for professional positions, participants indicated two important skills: technology skills and collaboration/communication skills. Respondents mentioned a broad range of technology, such as technology in teaching, in-depth knowledge of software packages, smart boards, and iPads. As they explained, "use of technology, development of collaborative lessons in classroom using technology, more software training, current instructional technology strategies for engaging student learning," and "they will need familiarity with upcoming technologies and currently in use technology such as LCD projectors, DVD burners, mobies, PowerPoint clickers, digital camcorders." Participants also specified that "interpersonal skills and collaborative abilities" were important for job preparation. For example, one participant reported a need for "excellent communication skills both in written and oral, ability to interact with coworker and understand the needs of patrons, in depth knowledge of current and emerging technology." Another stated, "I feel that a clear set of guidelines for students on how to interact with site supervisors would be appropriate and effective."

The last question in the survey asked for any comments the supervisors would like to make. Most who responded to this question gave very positive feedback about their experiences with interns. They appreciated the great jobs that their interns did and emphasized that this valuable experience is beneficial to supervisors, organizations, and interns and they are more likely to continue taking interns from the university. For example, "I enjoyed working with Ms. D [the intern's name], it was a pleasant and learning experience for both of us"; "This has been a rewarding experience for both intern and supervisor'; "I would welcome other interns in the future"; "very enjoyable, a benefit to the school and intern."

DISCUSSION

Through a quantitative lens, it is clear that factors from the predisposing domain such as self-confidence in having necessary skills and feeling comfortable as a site supervisor influenced the success of internship, but the reality is that most school based site supervisors have not had training prior to the assumption of the role as on-site supervisor. They are usually not presented with any standardized mandates to follow because each school is unique and interns are permitted flexibility to a degree, to shape their experience to fit their needs and interests. In this study, participants generally reported confidence in their skills needed for supervision. However, a supervision training seminar prior to the experience could be beneficial and is indicated by the significant factor influencing success of the internship exposed in this study. That factor—"clarity of expectation"—could be addressed with prior training. A more intentional approach in communicating roles and expectations to future site supervisors would be helpful.

Results from qualitative data showed that technology skills and communication skills were listed by site supervisors as the two most important abilities that students should have to be prepared for the future professional positions. This finding also reflects the importance of those same skills for supervisors, highlighting the value of continued professional development for professionals in the field. The field is changing rapidly and those who aspire to serve as site supervisors have a responsibility themselves to continue to develop skills to make optimum use of evolving technology. The findings, regarding technology and communication skills, provide valuable information about what areas the university program should focus on to prepare graduate students for the internship positions and to provide site supervisors for their roles as well.

When the quantitative and qualitative data are integrated, the evidence strongly suggests that the perceived values and benefits of mentoring interns play an important role to reinforce the supervisors to continue taking interns in the future and ensure the success of internships. Participants appraised that this rewarding experience was valuable not only for interns, but for schools and supervisors as well. Site supervisors gained information about areas future school librarians must focus upon as a result of their programs, effectively keeping them abreast of new developments. Site supervisors were able to interact with educators of future librarians, sharing issues they found to be significant. Supervising an intern kept them informed about current trends and best practices as a result of networking with both intern and university supervisor. Further, site supervisors found benefits in being able to add the practice of supervision to their school service and to develop themselves as leaders through the process. These benefits together support career satisfaction as, through their work with interns, participants were able to both support and impact their chosen profession.

Site supervisors indicated that internship programs should focus on directly contacting site supervisors prior to the beginning of the internship. Detailed information about the entire internship, especially the clarity of expectations in all aspects, is very important to enable site supervisors to assume their responsibilities. Although guidelines may have been developed and shared, these guidelines are general, dealing with the professional dispositions, knowledge, skills and competences needed for an effective school librarian. The concerns expressed by some participants as to more information with clearer goals and practical guidelines, defined requirements, roles and expectations of the program, and how the internship hours would be planned, indicates a need for increased structure within the experience.

The findings of this study will lead to the updating of guidelines for on-site supervisors for the program under review. The findings are, however, limited to the study of one university program. A comparison of multiple programs would provide results that could be generalizable to other school library education programs. This study could be implemented at any library science school.

CONCLUSIONS

This study, designed to gather data to strengthen the internship, provided direction toward program improvement. In general, the current study points to the need for development of a site supervisor training program to help prepare future site supervisors for the expectations of the role and to enhance communication between university program and internship site supervisor. To professionalize and support the on-site supervisor more effectively, ongoing professional networking opportunities are strongly recommended. These experiences will help with role preparation, evaluation of the intern, and understanding of the program. A mandatory prerequisite for site supervisor training would assist in the development of a sustainable pool of well prepared, skilled site supervisors. The significance of this essential role should not be overlooked. It is recommended that site supervisor training be developed, implemented and followed by longitudinal research aimed at following and observing site supervision for program improvement. Researchers for this study are responding to results of the study by developing a proposal for a program to provide training for site supervisors based upon data from this study.

This study brings attention to the significance of the dedicated, skilled professionals in the field who will serve as supervisors to preservice librarians and emphasizes the need to support these professionals who are serving online programs with well-designed training to help enhance their skills as supervisors. A series of focus group interviews among site supervisors and university program supervisors to gain more information about issues that may not have been addressed in the current study could bring additional insight and is also recommended for future study. The perspectives of site supervisors must be thoughtfully cultivated, considered, and used for responsive online program improvement. Further research should encompass additional library science programs.

REFERENCES

American Association of School Librarians. (2010). *ALA/AASL standards for initial preparation of school librarians with statements of scope.* Retrieved from http://www.ala.org/aasl/sites/ala.org.aasl/files/content/aasleducation/schoollibrary/2010_standards_with_rubrics_ and_statements_1-31-11.pdf

Aho, M., Franklin, M., Wakefield, S., & Wakefield, S. (2006). Internships are the appetizers of the library world so nibble, nibble, nibble. Retrieved from http://www.libraryjournal.com/article/CA6341364.html

Ball, M. (2008). Practicums and service learning in LIS education. *Journal of Education for Library and Information Science, 49*(1), 70-82.

Batson, T. (2011). Situated learning: A theoretical frame to guide transformational change using electronic portfolio technology. *International Journal of ePortfolio, 1*(1), 107-114.

Berry, J. (2005). The practice prerequisite. *Library Journal, 130*(15), 8.

Brown, J. S., Collins, A., & Duguid, S. (1989). Situated cognition and the culture of learning. *Educational Researcher, 18*(1), 32-42.

Callison, D. (1995). Restructuring pre-service education. In B. J. Morris (Ed.), *School library media annual* (pp. 100-112). Englewood, CO: Libraries Unlimited.

Church, A., Dickinson, G., Everhart, N., & Howard, J. (2012). Competing standards in the education of school librarians. *Journal of Education for Library and Information Science, 53*(1/3). Retrieved from http://jelis.org/featured/competing-standards-in-the-education-of-school-librarians/

Daix, E. C., & Epps, S. K. (2001). The University of Delaware library residency program: Two former residents perspectives. In R. V. Cogell & C. A. Gruwell (Eds.), *Diversity in libraries: Academic residency programs* (pp. 131-141). Westport, CT: Greenwood.

Dixon, M. A., Cunningham, G. B., Sagas, M., Turner, B., & Kent, A. (2005). Challenge is key: An investigation of affective organizational commitment in undergraduate interns. *Journal of Education for Business, 80*(3) 172-181.

Dotson, K. (2010). A paradigm shift in 21st century education: How effective are on-line facilitated graduate internship programs? *International Journal of Instructional Technology and Distance Learning, 7*(7). Retrieved from http://www.itdl.org/Journal/Jul10/article04.htm

Edwards, J. (1994). The study of congruence in organizational-behavior research: Critique and a proposed alternative. *Organizational Behavior and Human Decision Processes, 58*(1), 51-100.

Feldman, M. D., Huang, L., Guglielmo, B. J., Jordan, R., Kahn, J., Creasman, J. M., ... Brown, J. S. (2009). Training the next generation of research mentors: The University of California, San Francisco, Clinical & Translational Science Institute Mentor Development Program. *Clinical and Translational Science, 2*(3), 216-221. doi:10.1111/j.1752-8062.2009.00120.x

Green, L., & Keuter, M. (1999). *Health promotion planning: An educational and ecological approach* (3rd ed). Mountain View, CA: Mayfield.

Guoying, Z., Shunxing, Z., & Jiyue, H. (2005). Designing and teaching practice of online English writing course. *28th Annual Proceedings, Association for Educational Communications and Technology, 2,* 229-233.

Hunt, J., & Liebscher, V. (1973). Leadership preference, leadership behavior, and employee satisfaction. *Organizational Behavior and Human Performance, 9,* 59-70

Jones, J., & Bush, G. (2009). What defines an exemplary school librarian? An exploration of professional dispositions. *Library Media Connection, 27*(6), 10-12.

Jurkowski, O., Antrim, P., & Robins, J. (2005). Building bridges between students and practitioners. *Journal of Education for Library and Information Science, 46*(3), 198-209.

Kelsey, P., & Ramaswamy, M. (2004). Designing a successful library school field experience. *Library Management, 26*(6/7), 311-323.

Kirshner, D., & Whitson, J. (Eds.). (1997). *Situated cognition.* Mahwah, NJ: Erlbaum.

Lave, J., & Wenger, E. (1991). *Situated learning: Legitimate peripheral participation.* Cambridge, England: Cambridge University Press.

National Council for Accreditation of Teacher Education. (2010). *Transforming teacher education through clinical practice: A national strategy to prepare effective teachers.* Washington, DC: Author.

Orchowski, P. (2005, August 29). Internships give students a sense of the workplace. *Community College Week, 18*(28), 3-16.

Shannon, D. (2008). School library media preparation program review: Perspectives of two stakeholder groups. *Journal of Education for Library and Information Science, 49*(1), 23-42.

Stefl-Mabry, J., Dequoy, E., & Stevens, S. (2012). Retrospective reflection: Insight into pre-service school librarians' competencies and skill development as revealed through field notes. *School Library Research, 15.* Retrieved from www.ala.org/aasl/slr/volume15/dequoy-stefl-mabry

Stueart, R. (1998). Preparing information professionals for the next century. *Education for Information, 16*(3), 243-51.

Vecchio, R. (1987). Situational leadership theory: An examination of a prescriptive theory. *Journal of Applied Psychology, 72*(3), 444-451.

Wagner, T. (2008). Rigor redefined. *Educational Leadership, 66*(2), 20-25.

PART IV

LEADING THE DEVELOPMENT AND SUPPORT OF ONLINE FACULTY AND STAFF

CHAPTER 16

EFFECTS OF STAFF TRAINING AND DEVELOPMENT ON PROFESSIONAL ABILITIES OF UNIVERSITY TEACHERS IN DISTANCE LEARNING SYSTEMS

Shahinshah Babar Khan
Pakistan Atomic Energy Commission Model College

Saeed-ul-Hasan Chishti
International Islamic University, Pakistan

Quality education may be termed as the primary way that leads to development of nations and can play an exclusive role in maintaining the standards of education. It is understood that using conventional teaching methods, desired products cannot be achieved; making the need for modern approaches to be evolved for sound qualitative work. The target of quality education can be achieved once the quality of teachers may be enhanced because quality in education is heavily linked with the quality of teachers and their quality of teaching (Zaki, 2006). Competence is a fundamental element for delivering quality education and the teacher is a primary agent

Beyond the Online Course: Leadership Perspectives on e-Learning
pp. 267–279
Copyright © 2016 by Information Age Publishing

for imparting quality education. Higher education can work best only if there is quality in its research work, and there is a direct relationship between the research work at higher education and the product of higher education for the served. Quality in research work of students depends on the teacher's guidance as well as competence. Staff training and development is a tool for generating competence among research supervisors/university teachers—which, in turn, will have an impact on the quality in research work of students/supervisees. By using staff training and development, teachers' teaching methods, concepts, and new knowledge in the fields can be enhanced, which ultimately affects the students' work. Allama Iqbal Open University (AIOU) offers education from certificate level to PhD level through distance education. At MPhil and PhD level, research work is a compulsory component like other conventional and distance education universities globally. AIOU arranges staff development workshops for its teachers regularly. The objectives of the study were: (1) To find the opinion of the faculty members of AIOU about the learning of ICT's in staff training and development programs and its impact on research work and; (2) To find the opinion of the teachers about the effects of staff training and development on their teaching methods, material development and content knowledge. The sample for the study was based on the faculty members of AIOU. A questionnaire was developed for determining the opinion of faculty members about the effects of staff training and development on learning of ICT and its use for research work and on teaching methods, material development and content knowledge.

INTRODUCTION

The role of a teacher in the entire educational setup remains unique. A teacher is considered a change agent who trains individuals for society as well as facilitates development of skills that are necessary for an individual's grooming; and at the same time necessary for the economic development of the nation. A student's thinking style, problem solving approach, and use of knowledge and skills in different situations depends largely on his or her learning and the main source of information and learning for a student is his or her teacher. It is generally inferred that teachers teach the way they learnt in a teacher training program. If teachers merely shift their knowledge to the students without real understanding, students can obtain a degree by reproducing this knowledge, but it cannot be an asset for them. Teachers who have up-to-date knowledge of their field, clear concepts of their subject, and a strong grip on how to shift their knowledge to the students, are considered good teachers in general terms. At present, quality education is needed that is "fit for purpose." Curriculum, activities in the classroom, assessment system, and examination system are some variables that contribute to quality and all these variables depend on the teacher. In an educational system, only quality teachers can guarantee for quality education.

Higher education institutions are responsible for generating productive knowledge that serves the nation. National Education Policy (Government of Pakistan, 2009, p. 55) documented that good quality, merit-oriented, equitable and efficient higher education is the most crucial instrument for translating the dream of a knowledge-based economy into reality. In Pakistan, distance education is a popular mode working parallel to the traditional educational system. Allama Iqbal Open University (AIOU) of Pakistan is a mega-university, imparting higher education through its distance learning system. At the higher education level, major clients of AIOU are those people who completed their master's level education at traditional universities and engaged in their services being unable to attend traditional institutions due to one or the other problems. AIOU provided an alternative to their education at their doorstep with nominal fees as compared to traditional institutions. In the changing scenario, teaching is not as it was 1 or 2 decades ago. In the global age, it is necessary for university teachers to have knowledge of new approaches of teaching, emerging trends in the field, and must add new knowledge their existing knowledge. If a university teacher does not follow the current changes in the field, he or she may help to produce degree holders, but not intellectuals for the society. Information and communication technologies (ICT's) have made tremendous changes in the field of education and make the whole world a global village. Now it is the duty of a university teacher to indulge in opportunities for new knowledge for his or her career as well as for guiding students in the right direction. All over the world, organizations and institutions arrange such programs that enhance knowledge and skills of their staff. Staff training and development serves as a genuine tool to successful implementation of total quality management (Abid, 2008). AIOU arranges training sessions and staff development workshops and seminars for capacity building of the staff. These training sessions and staff development programs affect the teaching styles, content knowledge, and research work of the faculty members, which they utilize in their teaching and which ultimately affects the students' performance.

LITERATURE

The role of the teacher has changed. Two decades ago, a teacher was a person who transferred knowledge to the students and now a teacher is a guide who leads the students to find facts and enables them to understand the mysteries of the world and contribute toward the economic growth of the nation. The role of a teacher in higher education institutions is to prepare students to accept the challenges of the present and future. Higher education institutions are considered to be knowledge-generating agencies that preserve old knowledge and generate knowledge that is useful for all human beings as well as useful for the economic development of the nation. Sutton (1998), with reference to Newman, noted that it was not the prime purpose of universities to advance knowledge or to train graduates for professional specialties but to make their students into enlightened and morally upstanding human beings and leaders of their societies.

Quality Education

National Education Policy (Government of Pakistan, 1998-2010) states that the quality of education is directly related to the quality of instruction in the classrooms ... [teacher's] academic qualification, knowledge of subject matter, competency and skills of teaching and commitment of teacher have effective impact on teaching learning. National Education Policy (2009) documented that improving quality requires action in the areas of teacher quality, curriculum and pedagogy, textbooks, assessment approaches and in learning environment and facilities. Now, it is the responsibility of teachers to update themselves according to the need of the time. Society expects its teachers to care for students, to care about their learning, to be knowledgeable about curriculum content, and to know how to induce learning in others (Jeans, 1993). Robinson (1992, p. 77) defines quality as a product of planning, monitoring, control, and coordination. The British Standards Institution (1999) defines quality as the totality of features and characteristics of a product or service that bear on its ability to satisfy the stated or implied needs. Higher education is considered essential for development of a nation.

Quality Higher Education
and Higher Education Institutions

Higher education prepares young people for an effective role in the society and for meeting the challenges of the future. Boston Report (2002) states that, "higher education has always been an important component of the social agenda; but it has acquired a new importance today." In the emerging knowledge economy nations that fail at creating a decent learning environment will lag behind, and may end up becoming virtual colonies of those that do succeed in this regard. Across the world, universities are responsible for generating new knowledge and for providing new paths to progress. It is considered that universities must produce skilled individuals who may play their role for development of the society. Universities "should produce human resources trained to meet the needs of the economy, to concentrate on practice and on lifelong learning" (Commission of the European Communities, 2005, p. 3). In the global age, quality higher education is necessary for growth and development. Frazer (1992) says that quality higher education is important because universities must be accountable to society, to employers, to students, and to each other.

Staff Training and Development

Staff development is a process of enhancing capabilities of the staff in terms of pedagogical skills and content knowledge. Hassel (1999) defines staff development as the process of improving staff skills and competencies needed to produce outstanding educational results for students. Ladd and Fiske (2008) argue that quality professional development programs reduce teacher attrition and improve the quality of the existing teaching population. About professional development Guskey (2000) notes that one constant finding in the research literature is that notable improvements in education almost never take place in the absence of professional development. Wenglinski (2002) reiterates that effective professional development programs indirectly increase student performance by improving teacher instruction

Quality Education and ICTs in Staff Training and Development

Quality education depends on quality teachers; without quality teachers, quality education cannot be achieved and staff training and development is a step to ensure quality education. ICT's gave a new dimension to distance education. The term "ICT" embraces the many technologies that enable us to receive information and communicate or exchange information with others (Anderson, 2010). The quality assurance in open and distance learning become more complex with additional latest tools of Information and communication technology (Rashid & Iqbal, 2010). Now computers and the Internet are becoming an essential part of an effective education system. Higher learning institutions consider ICT's an integral part of imparting quality higher education. In a distance learning system, ICT's are essential for efficient systems. With the use of ICT's, teachers can guide and monitor students competently. Teachers involved in distance education need some special skills and knowledge for ensuring quality within distance learning systems. Distance may cause some serious problems in research work at higher level learning, where the teacher and the taught are at a distance. In distance learning system, a teacher must have a good grip over the use of ICT's. Iqbal and Ahmad (2010) recommend that teachers in distance learning programs should be given mandatory training and retraining of ICT programs to provide them with practical and functional knowledge of computers, the Internet, and associated areas of ICT.

Staff Training and Development in Distance Education

Distance education is a popular mode around the world. Distance learning programs are a reflection of this new world. They offer education without borders (Levine & Sun, 2002).

Distance education accommodates those people who are unable to attend traditional institutions. The new majority of college students are very different: they are older, attend classes part time, hold jobs, have families, and live off campus. Unlike traditional students, nontraditional students do not consider school to be central to their lives (Levine & Sun, 2002).

About staff training and development in distance education system, Murangi (2009) states,

> Ongoing professional development and training of staff is vital for the success of any dedicated ODL institution. Effective development and delivery of ODL programs require appropriate systems of support for both part-time and full-time staff, and this at policy, materials and learner support levels. (p. 85)

Many changes are occurring in the field of education. A teacher cannot survive without updating his or her knowledge and pedagogical skills. In Pakistan, it is generally a perception that higher education is only possible through the traditional learning system and in this regard distance mode cannot work effectively (Khan & Jumani, 2010).

AIOU's Faculty Development Programs

Professional development includes formal experiences (such as attending workshops and professional meetings, and mentoring) and informal experiences (such as reading professional publications and watching television documentaries related to an academic discipline) (Ganser, 2000). AIOU provides these opportunities to its faculty members with regard to professional development. At its main campus in Islamabad, AIOU arranges educational seminars and conferences. AIOU provides funds to its faculty members to attend international conferences around the world.

AIOU's Vice Chancellor's Report (2007) documented the following steps taken by the university for faculty development:

- For training of staff and faculty, programs were designed to enhance the professional skills.
- For quality input AIOU staff development program was developed and got approved through statutory bodies (p. 69).

Objectives of the Study

The objectives of the study were:

1. To find the opinion of AIOU faculty members about the learning of ICTs in staff training and development programs and its impact on research work.
2. To find the opinion of teachers about the effects of staff training and development on their content knowledge, teaching methods, material development, and research work.

THE STUDY

Sample

Using convenience sampling, 60 faculty members were selected to participate in the study. The faculty members had attended seminars on education, a training program, ICT training, and national and international conferences.

Instrument

A questionnaire was developed on 5-point Likert scale for obtaining the opinion of faculty members about the role of staff training and development in professional growth in terms of content knowledge, teaching methods, material development and use of ICTs and its impact on research work.

Table 1. Effects of Training and Staff Development on Content Knowledge

Item	Statement	SA	A	UNC	DA	SDA	χ^2
1	Staff training and development programs refresh the prior knowledge	23	37	0	0	0	98.2
2	Staff training and development programs introduce new concepts in the field.	12	48	0	0	0	144.0
3	Staff training and development programs help in presenting content knowledge in an effective way.	18	22	10	0	0	35.7
4	Staff training and development programs help in understanding the content in a broader sense.	22	28	7	0	0	55.8
5	Staff training and development programs guide to interrelate the content which improve the quality of learning.	19	41	0	0	0	110.2
	Effects of Staff Training and Development on Teaching Method						
6	Staff training and development programs help in understanding the use of right method for different topics.	15	28	16	1	0	45.5
7	Staff training and development programs guide teachers to overcome deficiencies while teaching in the classrooms.	18	42	0	0	0	114.0
8	Staff training and development programs train the teachers to create learning environment in the class.	19	35	5	1	0	74.3
9	Staff training and development programs affect the teaching method, which ultimately affects the learning of the students.	24	36	0	0	0	96.0
10	Staff training and development programs inculcate new pedagogical skills among the teachers.	11	38	6	5	0	73.5
	Staff Training and Development Programs and Material Development						
11	Staff training and development programs introduce new trends in the field.	17	36	7	0	0	44.5
12	Staff training and development programs enable teachers to add new concepts in the learning material.	21	37	2	0	0	91.2
13	Staff training and development programs enable the teachers to develop material according to the needs of the time.	13	22	11	0	0	88.5

14	Staff training and development programs help in making comparisons with international advancements in the material.	32	24	4	0	0	74.7

ICTs in Staff Training and Development Programs and its Impact on Research Work

15	ICTs reduce the distance between teacher and student.	15	42	3	0	0	106.5
16	ICTs give smartness to distance education.	35	24	1	0	0	90.2
17	Use of ICT is a necessary element in higher education.	15	32	12	1	0	56.2
18	Learning of ICTs in staff training and development programs help in research work.	21	32	7	0	0	66.2
19	ICTs are a tool for guiding students in research work.	12	35	8	5	0	61.5
20	A good grip over the use of ICTs increases the efficiency of research work.	15	38	7	0	0	83.2

Note: $df = 4$. Table value of $\chi^2 = 9.488$.

275

Validation of the Questionnaire

For validation, the questionnaire was sent to five faculty members of AIOU who had completed ICT training and had attended national and international conferences. Some items were rephrased in the light of experts' views. The experts pointed out some irrelevant items, which were deleted.

Final Version of the Questionnaire and Distribution

In the final version of the questionnaire, there are 20 items; 5 items about effects of training and staff development on content knowledge; 5 items were about effects of staff training and development on teaching methods; 4 items were about staff training and development programs and material development; and 6 items were about the ICTs in staff training and development programs and its impact on research work.

The questionnaire was distributed to the faculty members of AIOU by the researchers, and they collected the completed questionnaires. There was a cover letter, describing the purpose of research and the respondents were assured that their provided information would be used only for research purposes.

Data Analysis and Results

After collecting data, each statement was checked by applying the chi-square technique with a significance level of 0.05.

DISCUSSION

The respondents agreed that staff training and development programs refresh prior knowledge and introduce them to new trends in the field. They further concur they learn the content knowledge in a broader sense in interrelationship of the content and learn effective ways of presenting content knowledge to the students. Training helps teachers select the right method according to the demand of the topic. This decreases the shortcomings in the classrooms and teachers are able to provide a good environment for learning. In addition, teachers learn new pedagogical skills in training, which affects the learning of the students.

In distance education, AIOU provides its own published material to the students. The respondents confirm that they were introduced to new concepts in the field; they make comparisons with the international material and inculcate new advancements while updating the material. ICT's give a new smartness to distance education by minimizing the distance between teacher and student. Use of ICT's affects the research being conducted and acts as a tool for guiding students in research work. By using the Internet, the best available knowledge is collected at a desk and this increases the efficiency in research work.

FINDINGS

The principal findings of the study were:

- Staff training and development programs provide opportunity to refresh prior knowledge.
- Staff training and development programs introduce new concepts in the field.
- Staff training and development programs help teachers understand content knowledge in a broader sense and enable them to interrelate the concepts imparted.
- In staff training and development programs, teachers learn new pedagogical skills for effective teaching.
- Staff training and development programs enable teachers to inculcate new and emerging trends in the material.
- Staff training and development programs guide teachers to new methods of updating reading material.
- ICT's give smartness to distance learning.
- ICT's decrease the distance between the teacher and the student.
- ICT's are very beneficial in research work.

REFERENCES

Abid, H. (2008). Total quality concept: Implementation in teacher training Institutes of Pakistan. *Proceedings of the 3rd International Conference on Assessing Quality in Higher Education*. Lahore, Punjab: University of the Punjab.

Allama Iqbal Open University. (2008). *AIOU's Vice Chancellor's report 2007*. Islamabad, Pakistan: Allama Iqbal Open University.

Anderson, J. (2010). *ICT transforming education: A regional guide*. Bangkok, Thailand: UNESCO.

The Boston Group. (2002). *Higher education in Pakistan: Towards a reform agenda*. Northboro, MA: Author.

British Standards Institution. (1999). *Management systems of schools: Guidance notes for the application of ISO 9002 for the management system of schools*. London, England: Author.

Commission of the European Communities. (2005). *Proposal for a recommendation of the European Parliament and of the Council on Key Competencies for Lifelong Learning*. Brussels, Belgium: Author.

Frazer, M. (1992). Quality assurance and higher education. *Proceedings of the International Conference*. Hong Kong: Falmer.

Ganser, T. (2000). An ambitious vision of professional development for teachers. *NASSP Bulletin, 84*(618), 6-12.

Government of Pakistan. (1998). *National education policy.* Islamabad, Pakistan: Ministry of Education.

Government of Pakistan. (2009). *National education policy 1998-2010.* Islamabad, Pakistan: Ministry of Education.

Guskey, T. (2000). *Evaluating professional development.* Thousand Oaks, CA: Corwin.

Hassel, E. (1999). Professional development: Learning from the best. Oak Brook, IL: North Central Regional Educational Laboratory.

Iqbal, J., & Ahmad. M. (2010). Enhancing quality of education through E-learning: The case study of Allama Iqbal Open University. *Turkish Online Journal of Distance Education, 11*(1).

Jeans, B. (1992). School effectiveness and teacher education: Matters of judgment. *Unicorn, 18*(2), 30-37.

Khan, S. B., & Jumani, N. B. (2010). Perceived assurance of educational quality in higher education through distance learning mode in Pakistan. *Proceedings of the 3rd International Conference on Assessing Quality in Higher Education.* Lahore, Pakistan: University of the Punjab.

Ladd, H., & Fiske, E. B. (2008). *Handbook of research in education finance and policy.* London, England: Routledge Taylor and Francis.

Levine, A., & Sun, J. C. (2002). *Barriers to distance education.* Washington DC: American Council on Education Center for Policy Analysis.

Murangi, H., V. (2009). Open schooling in educational transformation: The case of the Namibian College of Open Learning. In D. A. Abrioux & F. Ferreira (Eds.). *Perspectives on distance education: open schooling in the 21st century* (pp. 85-109). Vancouver, British Columbia, Canada: Commonwealth of Learning.

Rashid, M., & Iqbal, J. (2010). Developing the strategy for quality assurance of open and distance learning in Pakistan: The higher education perspective. In *Proceedings of the 3rd International Conference on Assessing Quality in Higher Education* (pp. 338-353). Lahore, Pakistan: University of the Punjab.

Robinson, B. (1993). *Quality relevance and effectiveness in distance education, Unit 11. Course 2, The Development of Distance Education, MA/Diploma in Distance Education.* Cambridge, England: IEC, University of London.

Sutton, F., X. (1998). Higher education: A pathway to development. In J. Talati, C. W. Vellani, P. Herberg, R. A. L. Sutton, A. F. Qureshi, S. Pardhan, & K. Bacchus (Eds.), *Higher education: A pathway to development.* Karachi, Pakistan: The Agha Khan University.

Wenglinsky, W. (2002). How schools matter: The link between teacher classroom practices and student academic performance. *Education Policy Analysis, 10*(12), 1-30.

Zaki, S. (2006). Rethinking quality through components of teaching process in teacher education. In *Proceedings of International Conference on Quality in Education* (pp. 746-755). Karachi, Pakistan: AKU-IED.

Zaki, S., & Rashidi, Z. (2010). Reasserting improved pedagogical practices for enhanced quality instruction at higher education. *Proceedings of the 3rd Inter-*

national Conference on Assessing Quality in Higher Education. Lahore, Pakistan: University of the Punjab.

CHAPTER 17

MAXIMIZING HR PROFESSIONALS' LEADERSHIP ROLE IN E-LEARNING FOR ORGANIZATIONAL EFFECTIVENESS

Jane Waweru
Nova Southeastern University

INTRODUCTION

According to Cornish (2004), technology has become the "great transformation of human life" (p. 9). Our society's increasing dependence on technology has affected all facets of our lives to include the human resource management function. Lockwood (2006) predicted that human resources (HR) leaders will be the personnel who will do most to focus efforts on innovative and creative learning in their organizations. E-learning methods have been proposed as a key means of accomplishing the goal of fostering effective, ongoing learning within these organizations. However, it has been reported that due to a variety of barriers, HR professionals are not taking the lead in promoting the use of e-learning. More information is needed to confirm whether or not this problem exists by assessing current levels of e-learning leadership by HR professionals.

Beyond the Online Course: Leadership Perspectives on e-Learning
pp. 281–293

PERCEPTIONS OF INNOVATION ATTRIBUTES

Rogers (2003) discussed five characteristics that help predict how an innovation is adopted. According to Rogers, the relative advantage, compatibility, complexity, trialability, and observability are characteristics of innovations that can help predict the overall rate and extent of adoption. A study of HR professionals may help show innovative attributes that are desirable for HR professionals. Organizations may be able to use this information to hire HR professionals with competencies that would help enhance e-learning effectiveness. In addition, results from the study will help readers understand why HR professionals adopt or fail to adopt e-learning.

Society for Human Resource Management (2009) said practitioners in the HR industry reported that learning in "organizations not only promotes retention and career development, but also supports the organization's ability to innovate and remain competitive" (Advocating for Education section, para. 4). Researchers and practitioners stated that HR professionals should be cognizant of the need to lead in creating a learning environment to help meet the demands of a knowledge-based economy (Lawler & Mohrman, 2003; Society for Human Resource Management, 2009). Saghafian (2011) said that technology is associated with excellence and advancement; consequently, various stakeholders that include the management expect technology to be implemented in the training programs. Hence, there is an increase in popularity in the use of e-learning (Bell, Lee, Yeung, 2006; Forum Corporation, 2003; Long, DuBuois, & Faley, 2008). The reasons for this increase include reduced costs, the ability to manage the changes in the courseware, increased content in the course, and because employees do not have to miss work when participating in e-learning because they can take the course anywhere and at any time.

Hall (2005) supported the same perspective when he stated that every HR professional needs to know the case for e-learning, which includes cost benefits, an increase in the competitive advantage, adaptability to change, attracting and retaining the workforce, training in a new product, and increased advantage with mergers. Hence, the increased pressure for HR professionals to produce training that meets the demands of the organizations is required by the management (Saghafian, 2011).

Implications of Limited e-Learning

Because HR workers play such a key role in promoting e-learning within organizations, lack of e-learning use by HR professionals may

Table 1.   e-Learning Opportunities for HR Professionals

Human Resource Management Function	e-Learning Opportunities
Recruiting and hiring	HR professionals can utilize e-learning to educate the applicants on the organization's mission, vision, and organizational values being sought.
Benefits administration	e-Learning can be utilized to educate employees on company benefits such as the Flexible Spending Account or the Family Medical Leave, not only as new hires but also on an ongoing basis.
Compensation administration	Educating employees on equal pay and Lilly Ledbetter among other pay acts through e-learning would help save the organization time while ensuring all employees are receiving similar information through e-learning (Phillips & Phillips, 2009).
Compliance and policy development	e-Learning provides an organization with the opportunity to communicate state, local, and federal regulations at the same time.
Employee relations	Managers can utilize e-learning to engage their employees on several organizational fronts, which includes educating the staff on the latest product development.
Organizational and employee development	e-Learning can also be utilized to help build effective teams.
Performance management	Performance management is enhanced by e-learning based on the fact that it enhances (a) collaboration among various stakeholders; (b) communication; (c) knowledge function by having the capability of providing analytical results; and (d) task function, which makes it possible to sieve data from various sources (Hsiao-Ya, Chieh-Chung, & An-Pin, 2008).
Safety and security	E-learning can be utilized to educate employees on a company's safety and security.

result in a failure by organizations to take advantage of the benefits associated with e-learning. The consequences of this failure may be organizations with employees who lack the skills and insights that can contribute to innovations to make the organization more competitive. According to Lawler and Mohrman (2003), "Many companies in the knowledge economy rely on the processing of knowledge by skilled knowledge workers—on its development and utilization of human capital" (p. 4). Thus, e-learning may be a key to whether or not organizations survive in an increasingly competitive economic environment.

Most important is organizations will fail to take advantage of the convenience of learning that can be conducted at anytime and anyplace. Organizations may also fail to take advantage of the reduced costs associated with e-learning and course materials that can be edited and produced instantly. In addition, organizations may fail to take advantage of consistent and reliable data and standardized information among other e-learning advantages, all of which may contribute in the failure of organizations to compete in the global market.

According to the Society for Human Resource Management (2008), e-learning is not only useful for delivering high-quality and timely instruction and assessment of skills in formal courses, better employee performance is also supported in less formal ways by supplying reference tools and job aids and by facilitating ongoing communications among instructors, experts, and colleagues from which they learn. These formal and informal strategies provide valuable information in a number of areas that affect organizational performance, including recruiting and hiring, benefits administration, compensation, compliance, employee relations, organizational and employee development, and safety and security.

Researchers said that the utilization of e-learning can help organizations focus more on the strategic role of HR, thereby increasing the opportunity to grow the organization (Panayotopoulou, Vakola, & Galanaki, 2005). Most importantly, organizations would fail to obtain benefits associated with e-learning as it relates to benefits administration, compensation, compliance, employee relations, and safety and security as issues from these areas of the human resource management may arise on a day to day. Failing to take advantage of such benefits would decrease learning opportunities, thereby affecting the organization's performance and production.

FOCUS GROUP QUALITATIVE DATA

In an effort to establish HR professionals' use or nonuse or e-learning and the barriers as perceived by HR professionals to the adoption of e-learning, qualitative data was collected using a pilot study and three focus groups to help better understand HR professions views and attitudes on e-learning (Gay, Mills, & Airasian, 2009). Gay et al. stated that qualitative data helps in the understanding of a "deep and holistic or complex understanding of a particular phenomenon" (p. 399). According to Fink, qualitative data "collect information on the meanings that people attach to their experiences and on the ways they express themselves" (p. 61).

Targeted HR professionals worked in various industries that included retail, technology, manufacturing, nonprofit, government, health, finance, research, education, marketing, consulting, and international. All industries were expected to be represented. Only willing HR professionals volunteered to participate. A total of 22 HR professionals participated and provided their rationale on why they do or do not participate in e-learning.

Reasons for Use or Nonuse of e-Learning

Common themes for HR participation in e-learning included the following:

1. Professional/personal development. Most HR professionals stated they participated in e-learning for their own professional or personal development. On professional development, participants indicated they utilized e-learning resources to recertify their credentials and take classes online, among others. Participants indicated they utilized e-learning for exploratory learning and for self-knowledge.
2. Convenience. Participants generally perceived that e-learning provides easy access to learning. Consequently, distance from a training site or even time of day was not an obstacle when training was done through e-learning. One participant stated she enjoyed the convenience of being able to be "trained at 2 A.M." Other participants cited the ability to use multiple locations for learning.
3. Compliance. Participants stated they were able to educate employees on mandated courses such as code of ethics and harassment policies among others through e-learning.
4. Facilitate/instruct/intervention. Several participants indicated they had been exposed to e-learning as facilitators or instructors or utilized e-learning as an intervention.
5. Customized training. Participants stated that e-learning provided the ability to provide customized training to employees with special needs. A HR professional stated that "different learners require unique needs which may not be met through e-learning."

Potential Barriers

HR professionals provided their rationale on barriers and challenges that contributed to their nonuse of e-learning. Five of the leading themes cited included the following:

1. Lack of face-to-face interaction. Participants stated that a lack of face-to-face interaction or engagement does create a barrier to e-learning. A participant was of the view that online interaction "can be strange." The participant added by stating, "I do not learn well learning on software, it is not my format." Another participant stated that "in person, one can tell a person story which is lost in e-learning, and would probably not learn very well if instruction was all online" while another stated "some people need motivation for structure to take classes online. There is need for a face-to-face to expand the network. 'You can't fax a handshake'." Another HR professional stated that although one is forced to take some certifications classes online, she preferred face to face because she "belongs to that era."

2. Accessibility and usability. Some participants were of the view that technical challenges can create a barrier to e-learning. Participants stated that, sometimes, e-learning may not be easy to use because of "terrible technology." An HR professional stated that "web-based e-learning the system is sometimes down and you cannot do anything until Information Technology team is ready to resolve the problem." Participants believed there is need for better designed e-learning content.

3. Cost. Participants stated that cost of e-learning can be a barrier to e-learning because finances are needed to support the software, people, developers, and designers of the innovation. Some believed that due to hard economic challenges, compliance issues were on the back burner. Others were of the view that capital was needed to develop and maintain e-learning. Some HR professionals said that financial cost associated with e-learning can be a challenge when trying to promote the innovation to the top management.

4. Effectiveness. Participants believed that the inability to measure the effectiveness of e-learning was a barrier to learning.

5. Lack of time. HR professionals stated they were sometimes busy and may not have had time for e-learning on the job. One participant stated that not having enough time at work made e-learning "a bother at work." Others felt that interruptions on the job presented a barrier to e-learning because they were not able to concentrate.

INTERPRETATION OF THE FOCUS GROUP RESULTS ON THE USE OR NONUSE OF E-LEARNING

Findings of this study showed that focus group members identify mainly advantages of e-learning, rather than disadvantages, thereby confirming that at least some HR professionals were aware of the advantages of e-learning. Taking advantage of professional/personal development through e-learning is a clear indication that HR professionals recognize the advantages of e-learning methods. HR professionals seem to realize that e-learning has conveniences to their professional life and that e-learning can help them assist their organization on compliance issues.

However, because these focus group participants mainly focused only on what they liked about e-learning, it seems likely the group contained only e-learning advocates/leaders. Findings indicated that given the right environment, these particular HR professionals would take charge and lead the e-learning process. However, they may not be characteristic of all HR professionals.

INTERPRETATION OF RESULTS
FOR THE BARRIERS OF E-LEARNING

Previous studies showed that attitudes about innovation attributes contributed to HR decisions on whether or not to adopt, and this study was not an exception (Martin & Reddington, 2009; Vaughan & MacVicar, 2004). As an example, one focus group participant stated that taking into account that HR professionals' style is generally one that prefers face-to-face interaction, many may tend to be resistant to e-learning. This rationale was shared by Martin and Reddington (2009) who stated, "HR staff have been resistant to technology mediation because it conflicts with their view of HR as best carried out through face-to-face relationships with clients" (p. 529). Lack of a face-to-face interaction had the highest number of frequency (22) of comments on barriers to e-learning. Another participant stated that given her generation, she preferred face-to-face learning because it provides interaction. Her comments were supported by another participant who stated that a lot of people prefer face-to-face training. Another participant stated she did not want to sit at the computer all day learning. A need for a human face was cited as critical in the learning process because some employees would like someone to assist them throughout the process.

A few comments cannot be used to reflect the perception of the entire HR population but the examples provide an opportunity to show a possible connection between e-learning barriers and the perceptions of compatibility. HR professionals would like to ensure that e-learning is compatible with their personal and organizational values prior to trying it. Hassan (2007) defined *organizational values* as "beliefs and attitudes that go deep inside and constitute a collective understanding regarding norms and standards of behavior acceptable in the organization" (p. 437).

Hassan reported that organizational values "set the tone" (p. 437) for how members of the organization ought to behave. Consequently, organizational values help employees bond towards a common purpose with the goal of achieving business goals (Hassan, 2007). HR professionals can use e-learning to help educate the applicants and employees of the organization's values by modeling these uses in their own work.

This study confirmed that real problems exist that may be contributing to lack of e-learning leadership by HR professionals. These include difficulties with accessibility and usability of e-learning, the cost of e-learning, challenges in measuring e-learning effectiveness, and the quality of the learning information. This indicates that HR professionals, like any people who choose to adopt a given innovation, need to see the relative advantage of the innovation (in this case, e-learning) prior to adopting it. Most importantly, HR professionals would like to ensure that e-learning is compatible with their personal and organizational values prior to trying it.

IMPLICATIONS FOR PRACTICE

This study's results indicate that much work remains to be done to demonstrate the value of e-learning for HR purposes and ensure that e-learning methods are more adopted. Suggestions for future practice include (a) publication of this research for awareness raising, (b) workshops, (c) technical support, (d) training that focuses on innovative attributes, (e) organizational synergy, and (f) communication within the organization.

Publication of the Research

This study provides updated information on the current state of e-learning leadership on HR Professionals. Publishing this research on e-learning leadership in relevant HR professional publications could help create awareness of the advantages and disadvantages of e-learning.

The publication of the study could help provide an important body of knowledge to HR professionals as it would introduce them to Rogers' (2003) diffusion of innovation theory and illustrate how it applies to their situation. Bauck (2002) stated that "professional development is most effective when it includes theory, demonstration, practice, feedback and coaching" (p. iv).

Offering Workshops

Study findings suggested that e-learning advocates should do more to increase acceptance and use of e-learning. In HR, e-learning advocates could be HR professionals themselves or the management within the organization. If workshops on e-learning benefits were offered in HR-related conferences, they could provide professional development with the assistance of opinion leaders.

Opinion leaders who advocate increased use of e-learning could help educate the HR professionals on its benefits. Consequently, conference-learning workshops could help confront and address the barriers to adoption of e-learning while emphasizing the benefits. The workshop could emphasize the relative advantage and compatibility attributes of e-learning, because HR professionals prefer seeing the advantage of e-learning, and that innovation aligns with their values and that of the organization. Opinion leaders could emphasize that using e-learning is the modern way to do things.

Offering Technical Support

Organizations could do much to encourage e-learning acceptance by providing increased technical support to HR professionals to help minimize challenges that were cited in the focus groups. When possible, the management could designate a technical support person in every department to help address issues related to usability of e-learning. Researchers stated that a support system and adequate support resources are needed to ensure successful diffusion of an innovation (Demuth, 2010).

Most importantly, Dublin (2007) stated that an effective integration of e-learning solutions often requires a shift in roles, responsibilities, and jobs within the organization. This means there is a need for HR professionals to wear a training hat that will enable them to take advantage of every available opportunity to educate employees on any task in the human resource management cycle. As educators, HR professionals will serve the role of being information and resource providers to the employees.

As organizational educators of e-learning, HR professionals will serve the critical role of launching new ideas within the organization and make others within the system aware of it (Rogers, 2003). Rogers (2003) said this can best be achieved if HR professionals understand the diffusion of innovation as a "process by which (1) an innovation (2) is communicated through certain channels (3) over time (4) among the members of a social system" (p. 11). Researchers stated that a trainer's desire to want to learn more and discover knowledge can result in an increase in the trainer's skill level (Boyatzis, 2008). This would eventually help improve the learning outcomes toward a desired state.

Enhancing Organizational Synergy

Researchers stated that the human resource management function is best achieved when evaluated as a whole (Lawler & Mohrman, 2003). The human resource management function is better placed to understand the complex and intricate organizational dynamics and ways that human capital can be used to help achieve the organization's strategic goals. Being able to see an opportunity to educate or train employees in the use of e-learning can help accelerate its use. A coordinated and systematic approach to innovative advances is needed in order to address organizational problems.

Organizational problems can best be addressed with management support. Input received from the focus group participants indicated that managerial, organizational, and technological barriers do contribute to or prevent the adoption of e-learning. According to Hung et al. (2009), "Managerial and organizational variables were all found to have a positive influence on the adoption decision, whereas technological variables were all found to have a negative influence on a hospital's decision to adopt" e-learning (p. 250). Most importantly, managerial support was found to be indispensable in the adoption of e-learning. Consequently, Hung et al. stated that for a successful adoption of e-learning, the top management would need to be educated on the benefits.

The management can help reduce the lack of adoption by providing HR professionals with the resources they need to make e-learning part of the organizational learning culture. In exchange, the management can hold HR professionals accountable, through performance management, to ensure that they provide well-designed training. Most importantly, management can set criteria that metrics be provided to link organizational strategic goals and the effectiveness of e-learning.

Enhancing Communication Within the Organization

The open-ended comments from focus groups in this study represented advantages, disadvantages, barriers, and challenges of e-learning in the workforce. Failure to lead in an e-learning initiative is an area of improvement for HR professionals. They should ensure they actually have had the opportunity to lead an e-learning initiative if it is available to them as an option. This opportunity might arise if HR professionals communicated this concern with the stakeholders and helped them understand the role of HR and the importance of being able to lead e-learning initiatives.

IMPLICATIONS FOR FUTURE RESEARCH

The section recommends possible research studies that could shed more light on e-learning leadership and provide information to build on the results.

Conducting Studies in Specific Companies

Respondents from this study were HR professionals from various industries. Further studies of this research could be conducted in specific companies with the goal of obtaining specific data on e-learning leadership and challenges experienced by HR professionals within such firms. If organizations were to conduct their own exploration of e-learning leadership on the part of HR professionals, they could obtain internal data that could help enhance organizational and employee development. Consequently, the organizations would conduct the study and report them to a larger population. Grgurovic (2010) recommended further studies in a specific organization, as a unit of analysis, in order to build on the diffusion of innovation study on technology-enhanced blended language learning in an English as a second language class. This view was supported by Tyan (2004), who stated that the size of the organization may not be issue; consequently, there is need to obtain data from specific companies in order to understand the challenges that are faced by corporations.

RESEARCH ON SPECIFIC HR MANAGEMENT FUNCTIONS

The focus group in this study focused on barriers and challenges of e-learning as a whole in the organization. There is need for further research to help understand the challenges and barriers faced by HR professionals when advocating e-learning for specific HRM job functions such as recruiting and hiring, benefits administration, compensation, employee relations, performance management, organizational and employee development, and safety and security. Research could be conducted in specific organizations with the goal of obtaining specific data on e-learning leadership on HR responsibilities and challenges that are experienced by HR professionals. Researchers recommended the need to conduct diffusion of innovation research in specific organizations (Grgurovic, 2010; Tyan, 2004). Research in this diffusion of innovation could be done in companies where they could obtain direct feedback on HR on specific area of concerns.

SUMMARY

Although it seems important that HR professionals take a leadership role in helping organizations maximize the advantages of e-learning, there were few studies that indicated how much this was happening. This study helped provide this evidence by exploring e-learning leadership among HR professionals, obstacles to adoption, and possible ways to promote higher rates of adoption.

REFERENCES

Bauck, T. (2002). Diffusion of videoconferencing using the Digital Dakota Network (Doctoral dissertation). Nova Southeastern University, Fort Lauderdale, FL.

Bell, B. S., Lee, S. W., & Yeung, S. K. (2006). The impact of e-HR on professional competences in HRM: Implications for the development of HR professionals. *Human Resource Management, 45*, 295-308. doi:10.1002/hrm.20113

Boyatzis, R. (2008). Competencies in the 21st century. *Journal of Management Development, 27*, 5-12. doi:10.1108/02621710810840730

Cornish, E. (2004). *Futuring: The exploration of the future.* Bethesda, MD: World Future Society.

Demuth, L. (2010). Accepting technology as a solution: A qualitative study investigating the adoption of technology at colleges. (Doctoral dissertation). Capella University, Minneapolis, MN. (UMI No. 3402090)

Dublin, C. (2007). *Success with e-learning.* Alexandria, VA: American Society for Training and Development.

Forum Corporation. (2003). *E-learning: Adoption rates and barriers.* Boston, MA: Forum.

Gay, R. L., Mills, G. E., & Airasian, P. (2009). *Educational research: Competencies for analysis and applications* (9th ed.). Upper Saddle River, NJ: Merrill Prentice Hall.

Grgurovic, M. (2010). *Technology-enhanced blended language learning in an ESL class: A description of a model and an application of the diffusion of innovations theory* (Doctoral dissertation). Retrieved from ProQuest Dissertations and Theses database. (UMI No. 3438697)

Hall, B. (2005). *E-learning: What every HR needs to know.* Alexandria, VA: Society for Human Resource Management.

Hassan, A. (2007). Human resource development and organizational values. *Journal of European Industrial Training, 31*, 435-448. doi:10.1108/03090590710772631

Hsiao-Ya, C., Chieh-Chung, S., & An-Pin, C. (2008). Modeling agent-based performance evaluations for e-learning systems. *The Electronic Library, 26*(3), 345-362.

Hung, S., Chen, C., & Lee, W. (2009). Moving hospitals toward e-learning adoption: An empirical investigation. *Journal of Organizational Change Management*, 22(3), 239-256.

Lawler, E. E., III, & Mohrman, S. A. (2003). HR as a strategic partner: What does it take to make it happen? Retrieved from http://ceo.usc.edu/pdf/G032430.pdf

Lockwood, N. (2006, July). Building learning cultures series Part 1: Human resource management for learning and building talent. Retrieved from http://www.shrmindia.org/building-learning-cultures-series-part-i-human-resource-management-learning-building-talent

Long, L. K., DuBuois, C. Z., & Faley, R. H. (2008). Online training: The value of capturing trainee reactions. *Journal of Workplace Learning*, 20, 21-37. doi:10.1108/13665620810843629

Martin, G., & Reddington, M. (2009). Reconceptualising absorptive capacity to explain the e-enablement of the HR function (e-HR) in organizations. *Employee Relations*, 31(5), 515-537.

Panayotopoulou, L., Vakola, M., & Galanaki, E. (2005). E-HR adoption and the role of HRM: Evidence from Greece. *Personnel Review*, 36, 277-294. doi:10.1108/00483480710726145

Phillips, J. J., & Phillips, P. (2009). Using ROI to demonstrate performance value in the public sector. *Performance Improvement*, 48(4), 22-31.

Rogers, E. M. (2003). *Diffusion of innovations* (5th ed.). New York, NY: Free Press.

Saghafian, M. (2011, March). A critical review of research on technology-based training in business organizations. *Research in Higher Education Journal*, 10. Retrieved from http://www.aabri.com/manuscripts/10632.pdf

Society for Human Resource Management. (2009, October). *Educating for advocacy, advocating for education*. Retrieved from http://www.shrm.org/Research/Articles/Articles/Pages/EducatingforAdvocacy.aspx

Society for Human Resource Management. (2008). *Introduction to the discipline of human resources technology*. Retrieved from http://www.shrm.org/hrdisciplines/employeerelations/Pages/EmpRelIntro.aspx

Tyan, K. (2004). *Diffusion barriers to e-learning in corporate Taiwan: A factor analysis of practitioners' perspectives* (Doctoral dissertation). Retrieved from ProQuest Dissertations and Theses database. (UMI No. 3133982)

Vaughan, K., & MacVicar, A. (2004). Employees' pre-implementation attitudes and perceptions to e-learning: A banking case study analysis. *Journal of European Industrial Training*, 28(5), 400-413.

CHAPTER 18

OFF-SITE FACULTY

Perspectives on Online Experiences

Barbara L. Stewart, Carole Goodson, and Susan L. Miertschin
University of Houston

This report presents a cross case analysis involving faculty teaching online from off-site international and interstate locations. The study yielded enabling factors, benefits, communication systems, and challenges in the areas of administration, curriculum, communications, and faculty characteristics. The benefits included the opportunity to be involved in an online teaching and learning model where both the student and the faculty members were at a distance from the physical campus. Retention of experienced faculty, continued utilization of faculty with critical expertise, expansion of the faculty teaching pool, faculty development, and enhanced program visibility were judged to be additional benefits. The major challenges primarily involved communications.

INTRODUCTION

While increasingly large numbers of students are flocking to online courses (Sloan, 2008), a small but perhaps critically important number of faculty are now teaching online from locations that are at a distance from a phys-

Beyond the Online Course: Leadership Perspectives on e-Learning
pp. 295–302

ical campus. This newer phenomenon was the focus of a study that investigated two purposively selected cases where faculty taught from remote locations. One location was interstate and the other was international.

ABBREVIATED SUMMARY OF REVIEW OF LITERATURE

Previous research regarding faculty members involved in online instruction has focused on various aspects of online teaching including attitudes (Baldwin, 1998; Bonk, 2001, 2009; Institute for Higher Education Policy, 2000; Lee, 2001; Maguire, 2005; National Education Association, 2000; Northrup, 1997; O'Quinn & Corry, 2002; Parisot, 1997), barriers (Berge, 1998; Betts, 1998; Chizmar & Williams, 2001; Dooley & Murphrey, 2000; Jones & Moller, 2002; Maguire, 2005; O'Quinn & Corry, 2002; Parisot, 1997; Rockwell, Schauer, Fritz, & Marx, 1999; Schifter, 2000) and motivators (Betts, 1998; Bonk, 2001; Chizmar & Williams, 2001; Dooley & Murphrey, 2000; Jones & Moller, 2002; Lee, 2001; Parisot, 1997; Rockwell et al., 1999; Schifter, 2000) to faculty participation, decisions regarding online teaching and the creation of quality courses (Green, Alejandro, & Brown, 2009; Institute for Higher Education Policy, 2000; National Education Association, 2000; O'Quinn, 2002; Shea, 2007), and faculty engagement as a contributing factor for student success (McClure, 2007; Shelton & Saltsman, 2005).

These sources, while not specifically focused on the location of the faculty member, were reviewed and considered as related to this investigation. Similarly, literature from business involving managing and developing off-site employees was considered as useful (Dwyer, 2010; Janove, 2004; Javitch, 2007; Nichols, 2010). This investigation of the literature suggested that study was needed to contribute to understanding the emerging issues related to the use of off-site faculty for online instruction.

METHODOLOGY

Case methodology was selected for this study. The work of Yin (1994) informed this choice. Eisenhardt's (1989) guidance regarding theoretical rather than statistical sampling led to the selection of the two cases chosen for investigation. Pettigrew's (1988) recommendation that, when the number of cases is small, case selection should be made so as to extend or develop the emergence of theory was also used. Hence, the experiences of one faculty member teaching internationally and one faculty member teaching interstate were recorded, tabulated, and analyzed. Additionally, data was collected and analyzed from a department chair who had either present or past administrative responsibility for the program areas of these case faculty members. Both faculty members and the administrator are tenured and have been employed by the same university for more than 25 years. The university is a large, urban, public institution with a solid commitment to online delivery of courses.

For both cases, the relocation of a spouse was the primary driver for the desire to teach online from the remote location. For case one, the international experience, the faculty member continues to teach from the off-site location and had done so for approximately 5 years at the time of data collection. For case two, the interstate experience, the faculty member returned to campus after teaching from the remote location for 2 years. In both cases, during the time off-campus, faculty responsibilities, loads, and full-time equivalence were adjusted to compensate for absence from campus. Adjustments were made to match full-time equivalence with teaching load and professional service, while expectations for scholarly productivity remained the same.

Each researcher also assumed the role of participant-as-observer, collecting and recording data over a 12-month period. Within-case analysis (Eisenhardt, 1989) provided preliminary familiarity with the data. Then, cross-case analysis facilitated considerations beyond the initial impressions (Eisenhardt, 1989). Themes began to emerge as data grids were developed (Miles & Huberman, 1984; Pratt, 2009). This enumeration and categorization of the data further facilitated analysis.

FINDINGS

Three critical components emerged as important aspects related to the success of off-site faculty: administration, curriculum and instruction, and faculty characteristics. Greater investigation then revealed that for each of these components four elements played a critical role: enabling factors, benefits, communications, and challenges. For example, with respect to administration, enabling factors, benefits, communications issues, and challenges were found to exist. Similarly, for curriculum and instruction, there were enabling factors, benefits, communications issues, and challenges. Finally, with regard to faculty characteristics there were enabling factors, benefits, communications issues, and challenges. These are described in brief below.

Administration

Enabling Factors. Administrative philosophical support and systems for accomplishing essential tasks were critical.

Benefits. Identified benefits to the university administration included retention of productive faculty members; utilization of personnel with specific expertise; extension of the faculty pool; workload balancing for instruction, curriculum development, or special projects; cross-country or international program exposure; and release of funds back into the instructional budget when partial leaves were involved. Further, faculty could be used who were knowledgeable about the courses and programs; had training, interest, and experience in online course delivery; and had existing productive relationships with on-campus program faculty to facilitate future program development.

Communications. Administrative venues for communication included e-mail, periodic campus visits, instant messaging, Elluminate *Live*! or a similar web conferencing tool, fax, Skype or a comparable voice over Internet protocol application, document scanning, and telephone. Consistent and timely communication among the faculty, staff, and administrators was imperative.

Challenges. Primary administrative challenges were identified as changed contact venues, constraints by upper administration, peer perceptions, and missed opportunities for training and mentoring.

Curriculum and Instruction

Enabling Factors. The personal attributes of faculty including positive philosophy of online education, online teaching experience, content area expertise, and instructional design capability were enabling factors related to curriculum and instruction. Support systems, personnel, and equipment were also deemed important. These factors in combination enabled committed faculty members with extensive experience to continue curriculum development and instruction in a consistent manner. Additionally, funds released into the instructional budget by partial faculty leaves allowed additional course sections to be taught by part-time faculty.

Communications. Communications with students, other faculty members, and staff on curricular issues was facilitated in multiple ways. A learning management system (WebCT in the two cases) together with a faculty developed website used discussion boards, games and simulations, content modules, e-mail, telephone, assignments, and evaluation tools to communicate faculty-to-student and vice-versa regarding course content and processes. E-mail, phone, and campus visits enabled curriculum management communications with other faculty members and staff.

Challenges. Many of the challenges related to curriculum and instruction in these cases were the same as those encountered when converting face-to-face courses to online courses. Additionally, building a classroom community and facilitating teamwork were judged by these faculty members to require a high level of faculty engagement, including frequent instructor-student interactions. In general, student and faculty engagement with each other and with the course was critical. Techniques to foster engagement included asynchronous discussion boards; synchronous discussions, presentations, and question/answer sessions; and increased faculty presence online.

Faculty Characteristics

Enabling Factors. Faculty characteristics that appeared as beneficial for successful off-site instruction included being adaptive, technologically literate, self-disciplined, able to work without social reinforcement, and not a procrastinator; and having an independent work style, good time management skills, a highly developed work ethic, collegial relationships with other faculty, strong grasp of the content area, ability and interest in instructional design, and ability to develop and maintain connections with on-campus personnel. An off-site workstation and environment conducive to online instruction was essential.

Benefits. Retention of employment, flexibility to work independently, increased productivity based on fewer workplace distractions, and intellectual stimulation were found to be benefits to the faculty members in these cases.

Communications. In addition to communicating with students, retaining and developing effective communications with faculty, staff, and administrators was important. Lack of immediacy and facial input inherent in the use of e-mail as the primary communication tool inhibited effective communications.

Challenges. The faculty members in these cases missed the collegiality of peers and the stimulation of interacting in person with students. Informal interactions such as casually sharing an idea were less likely to occur. Establishing new collegial relationships was, similarly, more challenging.

REFLECTION

Reflection on the cross case analysis of these cases involving faculty members teaching off-site from international and interstate locations yielded enabling factors, benefits, communication systems and challenges in the pertinent areas of administration, curriculum, communications, and faculty characteristics. Most notably, the benefits found included the opportunity for both faculty and students to be involved in an online teaching and learning model where both the student and the faculty member were at a distance from the physical campus. Retention of experienced faculty, continued utilization of faculty with critical expertise, expansion of the potential faculty teaching pool, faculty development, and enhanced program visibility in international and interstate settings were judged to be additional benefits. The major challenges identified primarily involved communications.

With continued growth in the popularity and delivery of online instruction, new opportunities and challenges emerge. Among these are issues related to the physical location of instructional faculty. Investigation of these cases yielded a preliminary look at some of the inherent factors that can exist in the use of off-site faculty members. Further investigation, including diverse cases and situations, is likely to be prudent to achieve more complete consideration of this facet of the expanding practice of online education.

REFERENCES

Baldwin, R. G. (1998, Winter). Technology's impact on faculty life and work. *New Directions for Teaching and Learning, 76*, 7-21.

Berge, Z. L. (1998, Summer). Barriers to online teaching in post-secondary institutions: Can policy changes fix it? *Journal of Distance Learning Administration, 1*(2). Retrieved from http://www.westga.edu/~distance//Berge12.html

Betts, D. S. (1998, Fall). An institutional overview: Factors influencing faculty participation in distance education in postsecondary education in the United States: An institutional study. *Journal of Distance Learning Administration, 1*(3). Retrieved from http://www.westga.edu/~
distance //betts13.html

Bonk, C. J. (2001). Online teaching in an online world. *CourseShare.Com.* Retrieved from http://www.publicationshare.com/docs/corp_survey.pdf

Bonk, C. J. (2009, April). Online learning frameworks: Past, present, and future. *Newsletter for Commission for Accelerated Programs #6*. Retrieved from http://cap-network.org/modules.php?op=modload&name=News&file =article&sid=82

Chizmar, J. F., & Williams, D. B. (2001). What do faculty want? *Educause Quarterly, 24*(1), 18-24. Retrieved from http://net.educause.edu/ir/library/pdf/equ0112.pdf

Dooley, K. E., & Murphrey, T. P. (2000). *How the perspectives of administrators, faculty and support units impact the rate of distance education adoption.* Retrieved from http://www.westga.edu/~distance/ojdla/winter34/dooley34.html

Dwyer, K. P. (2010). How to manage employees in remote locations. *BNET.* Retrieved from http://www.bnet.com/2403-13059_23-165147.html

Eisenhardt, K. M. (1989). Building theories from case study research. *Academy of Management Review, 14,* 532-550.

Green, T., Alejandro, J., & Brown, A. H. (2009). The retention of experienced faculty in online distance education programs: Understanding factors that impact their involvement. *International Review of Research in Open and Distance Learning, 10*(3). Retrieved from http://www.irrodl.org/index.php/irrodl/article/view/683/1279

Institute for Higher Education Policy. (2000). *Quality on the line: Benchmarks for success in Internet-based distance education.* Washington, DC: Author.

Janove, J. W. (2004, April 1). Management by remote control. *HR Magazine.* Retrieved from http://www.allbusiness.com/human-resources/workforce-management/136248-1.html

Javitch, D. (2007, February 9). Managing a satellite staff. *Entrepreneur.* Retrieved from http://www.entrepreneur.com/humanresources/employeemanagementcolumnistdavidjavitch/article174342.html

Jones, A. E., & Moller, L. (2002). A comparison of continuing education and resident faculty attitudes towards using distance education in a higher education institution in Pennsylvania. *College and University Media Review, 9*(1), 11-37.

Lee, J. (2001). Instructional support for distance education and faculty motivation, commitment, satisfaction. *British Journal of Educational Technology, 32*(2), 153-160.

Maguire, L. L., (2005, Spring). Literature review: Faculty participation in online distance education: Barriers and motivators. *Online Journal of Distance Learning Administration, 8*(1). Retrieved from http://www.westga.edu/distance/ojdla/spring81/maguire81.htm

McClure, A. (2007, November). *Distant, not absent: Keeping online learners engaged can help them reach the finish line.* Retrieved from http://222.23w5ga.edu/~distance//ojdla/fall33/mckenzie33.html

Miles, M., & Huberman, A. M. (1984). *Qualitative data analysis.* Beverly Hills, CA: SAGE.

National Education Association. (2000). *A survey of traditional and distance learning higher education members.* Washington, DC: Author.

Nichols, S. (2010). Managing remote employees: Off site management in 6 principles. *EzineArticles.* Retrieved from http://ezinearticles.com/?Managing-Remote-Employees---Off-Site-Management-in-6-Principles&id=1881933

Northrup, P. T. (1997). Faculty perceptions of distance education: Factors influencing utilization. *International Journal of Educational Telecommunications, 3*(4), 343-358.

O'Quinn, L., & Corry, M. (2002, Winter). Factors that deter faculty from participating in distance education. *Online Journal of Distance Learning Administration, 3*(3). Retrieved from http://www.westga.edu/~distance//ojdla/fall33/mckenzie33/htm

Parisot, A. H. (1997). Distance education as a catalyst for engaging teaching in the community college: Implications for institutional policy. *New Directions for Community Colleges, 99,* 5-13.

Pettigrew, A. M. (1988). Longitudinal field research on change: Theory and practice. *Organizational Science, 3*(1), 264-292. Retrieved http://www.jstor.org/stable/2635006?cookieSet=1

Pratt, M. G. (2009). From the editors: For the lack of a boilerplate: Tips on writing up (and reviewing) qualitative research. *Academy of Management Journal, 52,* 851-855.

Rockwell, S. K, Schauer, J., Fritz, S. M., & Marx, D. B. (1999, winter). Incentives and obstacles influencing higher education faculty and administrators to teach via distance, *Online Journal of Distance. Learning Administration, 2*(4). Retrieved from http://www.westga.edu/~distance/reckwell24.htm

Schifter, C. C. (2000). Faculty motivators and inhibitors for participation in distance education. *Education Technology, 40*(2), 43-46.

Shea, P. (2007). Bridges and barriers to teaching online college courses: A study of experienced online faculty in thirty-six colleges. *Journal of Asynchronous Learning Networks, 11*(2), 73-128.

Shelton, K., & Saltsman, G. (2005). *An administrator's guide to online education.* Charlotte, NC: Information Age.

Sloan Consortium. (2008). *Online nation: Five years of growth in online learning.* Retrieved from http://www.sloan-c.org/printable/node/1048

Yin, R. K. (1994). *Case study research design and methods.* Thousand Oaks, CA: SAGE.

CHAPTER 19

PRAGMATIC METHODS TO REDUCE DISHONESTY IN WEB-BASED COURSES

Newell Chiesl
Indiana State University

The Internet, coupled with technology, has enabled institutions of higher learning to offer online distance education classes to a worldwide student body at an increasing rate. In the next 5 years it is estimated that nearly 90% of universities will offer online classes. Unfortunately, the news is not all that good. Students are now cheating at an all time rate. The very nature of distance learning appears to actually nurture academic dishonesty on the part of its students. This article will present some practical suggestions to reduce the occurrence of cheating by students enrolled in online higher education classes.

INTRODUCTION

According to the United States Department of Education, the growth of online distance education courses offered by universities in the United States experienced rapid growth in the 1990s (U.S. Department of Education, 2003). Actual enrollment for distance education courses approached 3 million during the 2000-01 academic year (Kiernan, 2003). Continuing

Beyond the Online Course: Leadership Perspectives on e-Learning
pp. 303–315

education and distance learning will grow 10 times faster than on-campus growth over the next 10 years (Burns, 2006).

The reasons for the increased popularity of online distance education courses have been well documented, and include:

- Universities offer a wide range of subject areas online from art to zoology;
- Classes are accessible when students have available time, for example, students are not required to be at a specific class at 8 A.M. (this eliminates the time-bound requirement for students);
- Online learning does not require physical attendance at a specific geographical location (this solves the problem for place-bound students);
- Courses are available 24/7, allowing students to study at home, work, or on the road (World Wide Learning, 2006).
- The final reason for online popularity, "on the road," is best confirmed by the recent emergence of students enrolled in the numerous online MBA degree programs being offered all across the country (Beal, 2003; Fisher, 2003; Gale Group, 2003).

Although positive benefits accrue from students taking e-learning courses, there are some significant drawbacks. The most noted include: some students might be technophobic; students lack the required technologies; and, more importantly, students experience a reduction in social interaction, the suppression of communication mechanisms, and the elimination of peer-to-peer learning (Kruse, 2002). Perhaps the largest drawback to online learning is the possibility of academic dishonesty on the part of the students enrolled in class.

ACADEMIC DISHONESTY

In grade school we heard the axioms, "Honesty is the best policy" and "Cheaters never win, and winners never cheat." But this is today, how many college students have actually cheated on an exam during their undergraduate work? Apparently, the majority of college students cheat. These are the findings presented from the first comprehensive study on cheating by college students. The study concludes, "Academic dishonesty, or cheating, is a ubiquitous phenomenon in higher education" (Bowers, 1964). Thirty years later, the next major comprehensive study reported that 70% of the students surveyed, cheated on a test at least once (McCabe, 1993). Student cheating is definitely a concern on college campuses. Other studies have reported between 30% and 70% of students cheated on at least one examination (Baird, 1980; Collision, 1990; Davis, Grover, Becker, & McGregor, 1992; Innerst, 1998; Kritz & Newman, 1991; Maramark & Maline, 1993; Wellborn, 1980).

Cheating Rationale

On children's soccer fields all across America, parents now shout today's axioms: "Winning is everything," and "Nice guys finish last." Winning and being a success are the battle cry of too many parents; being a good sport and having fun receive less attention. When parents cheat by driving too fast or by going through a yellow light, they are teaching their children to cheat (Cummins, 2000). Children observe their parents' actions. Small behavioral actions, regardless of how trivial they might seem to be, however, have a cumulative lasting effect on a child's life long perception of norms. A mom fibbing about her age, or a father's bravado over exaggerated income tax deductions are examples of how parents teach their children to cheat. As if these parents' initial indiscretions alone were bad enough, the problem becomes more profound with their futile attempts at rationalization. Parents respond with the following inept rationalizations: "Everyone lies about their age, and doesn't everyone cheat on their income tax?" Thus, our children learn to cheat, and the rationalization process begins early in a child's life (Murdock, 1999; Whitley & Keith-Spiegel, 2001).

Many studies have documented the reasons why students cheat, including: fear of failure, desire for a better grade, pressure from parents to do well in school, unclear instructional objectives, and being graded on a curve (Evans & Craig, 1990). Other studies report: Everyone else is doing it; I see others cheating; It helps me get better grades, a good job, or admitted to graduate school; I see no reason not to cheat; There is little or no chance of getting caught. There is little, or no, punishment if I did get caught (Alschuler & Blimling, 1995). Students believe few cheaters are caught, and that punishments for cheating are generally lenient (Bowers, 1964).

And finally, one professor notes: "In one of my interviews, a student wrote that anything worth having is worth cheating for" (Whitley, & Keith-Spiegel, 2001).

Reducing Classroom Dishonesty

There are many methods used to reduce the amount of student cheating. Diligent professors can virtually eliminate cheating using multiple versions of the same test, having additional proctors oversee the classroom, and by giving verbal warnings about cheating. Using tenured or tenure-track faculty tends to reduce cheating. Using only teaching assistants in a classroom will increase the amount of cheating (Kerkvliet & Sigmund, 1999). Additional research has reported colleges having a strict honor code, coupled with solid pressure from their student peers will discourage students from breaking the rules; and parents and teachers communicating early with students of grade school age will reduce the amount of student dishonesty (Anderson & Obenshain, 1994; Bowers, 1964; Gomez, 2001; McCabe, 1993; McCabe & Bowers, 1994; McCabe & Trevino, 1993; Newstead, Franklin-Stokes, & Armstead, 1996; Whitley & Keith-Spiegel, 2001).

Some experts say reducing competition among students will reduce student cheating, because the pressure to succeed clouds the judgment of many students, making cheating easy to justify and hard to resist. Other suggestions for professors to reduce the amount of student cheating include: affirm the importance of academic integrity. Encourage students to ask questions if they don't understand the material in class. Establish an honor code (Fishbein, 1993, 1994; Jendrek, 1989; Lathrop & Foss, 2002).

Reducing Distance Learning Dishonesty

Unfortunately, cheating also occurs by students enrolled in online distance education classes. According to research conducted, 64% of university professors perceive that it would be easier for students to cheat during online exams. Similarly, 57% of students also believe it is easier to cheat on exams offered in online classes (Kennedy, Nowack, Raghuraman, Thomas, & Davis, 2000).

Several suggestions have been offered to reduce academic dishonesty in web-based courses (Christe, 2003; Kelley & Bonner, 2005; Olt, 2002). However, many of these suggestions are simply not practical, too time consuming, require technical expertise, and are somewhat costly for the average professor at a state university. This article presents a more pragmatic approach for the university professor, requiring only a few mouse clicks on a PC.

SUGGESTED PRAGMATIC APPROACHES TO REDUCE ACADEMIC DISHONESTY

Four practical courses of action are suggested for professors to reduce the amount of cheating by online students: (1) disseminate information to distant students; (2) change the process used by students to turn in written assignments; (3) change the process by which exams are administered; and (4) create a nonsequential chapter assortment of questions.

Disseminate Information to Distant Students

This section summarizes the research reviewed earlier in this paper. The following straightforward methods are easy to implement into online higher education classes:

- Inform students by using e-mails, posting announcements, and incorporating into a syllabus that honesty is the best policy.
- Using the same dissemination methods, notify students that cheating will not be tolerated.
- Professors should warn students that there are strict penalties for cheating.
- Provide a link to a student honor code document.
- Inform students of the professor's qualifications, degrees, consulting work, *pro bono publico*, community leadership roles, grants received, and vita accomplishments.
- Post clear cut course learning objectives. From the first day of class, professors need to communicate to the students an exact list of the requirements necessary to obtain a specific grade for the course.
- Reduce the pressure to get grades. One way to reduce the pressure to get a good grade is not to "curve" student grades. Many professors curve their grade distribution so that a certain percentage of students will receive an As, Bs, Cs, Ds, and Fs. If students perceive a class to be too competitive, the propensity of cheating increases. Therefore, in order to limit academic dishonesty, professors could develop a point system of grading. For example an A grade is equaled to 900 points or more.

Change the Process Used by Students to Turn in Written Assignments

The incidence of plagiarism will theoretically be reduced by changing the process used by students to turn in assignments. Instead of handing in printed hard copy assignments, students should be required to hand in their assignments electronically. Professors then submit the electronic versions to a plagiarism recognition software product. Professors using Blackboard have an available tool called Turnitin to identify plagiarized work (Blackboard, 2007). To detect plagiarism, Turnitin software compares an individual student paper with web pages, past student papers, newsworthy articles, and academic publications (Turnitin, 2007).

Change the Process by Which Exams Are Administered

The third course of action a professor could easily incorporate into an online class would be to change how students take the exams. The newest version of Blackboard's website course development system enables a professor to change how students take exams online. A professor teaching an online course has several Blackboard options that predetermine how students will take exams. The first step consists of importing a course cartridge into a Blackboard class website. Course cartridge modules are offered directly from the publishers of most textbooks. The course cartridge developed by the publisher contains the usual material found on their CDs, such as key terms, definitions, study guide, cool web links, and a computerized test bank. It is an effortless task—simply type in the course module code when prompted in the control panel. The course module is then uploaded automatically to a professor's website.

The second step is to create an exam from a "pool" of potential questions from the cartridge. This is easily done using Blackboard by going to the control panel, clicking creating an exam, and selecting the type of questions desired from a pull-down menu. For example, exam 1 may be composed of 40 multiple choice questions selected randomly from a publisher's pool of questions, covering chapters 1 and 2.

The next step configures how the exam will be taken by students. Blackboard's web course development system offers several test options. The suggested options to include are:

1. Select the tightest time frame possible for students to complete each exam. Most professors have suggested to me, depending on the nature of the questions and the difficulty of the subject material, 40 questions in 40 minutes. I disagree. I suggest 40 questions in 30 minutes. (You will need to perform some trial-and-error exam attempts, with last year's students, to determine the least amount of time allotted for the exam.) A tight time frame will discourage students from cheating. Students will barely be able to complete the exam and will not have time to thumb through the text looking for answers.
2. Select the option "show one question at a time to the student." This will discourage students from conducting a "copy and paste" into a document and then printing out the entire exam. Copying

and pasting one question at a time will be very tedious and time consuming task. Plus, students will go beyond the allotted exam time period.

3. Select "no backtracking" on the part of the student. Once a student has selected an answer, do not allow him or her go back and see the prior questions.

4. Select "randomizing" the exam from a pool of questions.

5. Select allow the exam to be taken for an entire week. This reduces the time pressure to cheat.

6. Create a large number of exams to be taken during the semester—for example, 10 exams. Yes, perhaps a student will persuade a sibling or friend to take an exam and cheat for him or her once. But, will the sibling or friend agree to take 10 exams?

7. Set a low point value for each exam; say, 5% of the total semester points for each exam. This will reduce the pressure to cheat on an exam since the exam is not worth a large percentage of their grade.

8. Finally, select "allow multiple attempts" by students to take the exam. Students are allowed to take each exam as many times as they wish during an entire week, but each time they retake the exam, a new set of randomized questions appear. An additional bonus, for students taking the exams as many times as they wish, will be learning.

Create a Nonsequential Chapter Assortment of Questions

The final suggested method to reduce web cheating is based on the sequencing order of questions. The nonsequential exam method is a system of staggering exam questions by chapters in a nonpredictable assortment. This is accomplished by importing more than one course cartridge from the publisher of the text used by the class.

Without the nonsequential exam method, the professor will usually import one course cartridge from a textbook publisher into the website powered by the Blackboard Academic Suite. The learning cartridge contains, among other items, a pool of exam questions developed for each chapter of the textbook. After a successful importation into the Blackboard Learning System, the professor creates an exam by one of several methods. The random block is one potential method used by a professor that desires granting students the ability to take an exam a multiple number of times. The professor selects the chapters to be covered in the exam. For example, exam 3 might contain 60 questions covering chapters 5, 6, and 7. Each time the student repeats exam 3, the exam will randomly generate a new set of questions from the exam pool. The new exam usually has a mix of questions from the previous exam and new questions from the pool. During the exam creation process the professor will request 20 questions from chapter 5, 20 questions from chapter 6, and 20 questions from chapter 7. When the exam is taken, the student will be presented with the same sequential order of questions: 20 questions from chapter 5; 20 questions from chapter 6; and 20 questions from chapter 7. The above-noted procedure, using only one cartridge, will tempt the student to open their textbook and follow along the exam by the sequential chapters.

To reduce academic dishonesty, the professor needs to import multiple course cartridges from the textbook publisher. The procedure is as follows. A professor using the Blackboard Learning System as the software platform to drive the web course will click the control button and request the course cartridge three times. Usually within about a day, the website will be populated with three duplicate exam pools of questions. For the same hypothetical exam 3 containing 60 questions, the professor might select, for example, 5 questions from chapter 6, 7 questions from chapter 5, 6 questions from chapter 7, 4 questions from chapter 5, 6 questions from chapter 7, 9 questions from chapter 6, 8 questions from chapter 7, 9 questions from chapter 5, and 6 questions from chapter 6. It does sound complicated but, in reality, the nonsequential chapter exam method takes only a couple of extra minutes and is as easy as click, click, and click. The nonsequential chapter exam method is perhaps more easily understood by perusing Table 1. Obviously, there are numerous other potential nonsequential exam method variations available that can be used to construct exams.

FEEDBACK

In an effort to determine the merit of the suggested pragmatic methods, a survey of web-based students was implemented. During a 3-year period, 149 students were asked to complete an online survey asking questions concerning their online experience. By using Blackboard's survey feature, their identities were hidden from the professor. Assurances were also given to students guaranteeing their anonymity.

The overall results of the student feedback survey were extremely favorable. For the first question in the survey, 81% of the students reported taking each exam two to four times, whereas 10% indicated that they take each exam more than four times. The next survey question showed, on average, that 70% of students increased their exam scores in a range from 10-20 points (exam = 100 points). Table 2 presents the results

Table 1.   The Nonsequential Chapter Exam Method to Reduce Academic Dishonesty by Web Students

Chapter	Number of Questions Selected	Cumulative Amount or Each Chapter
6	5	5
5	7	7
7	6	6
5	4	11
7	6	12
6	9	14
7	8	20
5	9	20
6	6	20

Exam 3, 60 questions from Chapters 5, 6, and 7.

to the next question, "How important to you, is the ability to take an exam as many times as you wish during the semester?" Students reported: 63% very important, it really helps; 23% important; 8% neutral, it does not help, or hurt; 4% slightly not important; and 2% not important. As seen in Table 2, an overwhelmingly high amount, 86% of the web students, reported a positive observation of being allowed to take each exam multiple times.

Presented in Table 3 are the equally positive results concerning the quality of learning as perceived by the web students. Only 8% of the students reported a less-than-average learning experience, while the majority, 63%, reported a very positive learning experience, as compared to other web classes.

Tables 4 and 5 report the students' perceptions of cheating in a web class that has implemented the pragmatic methods to reduce web course dishonesty, as suggested in this paper. As seen in Table 4, "Cheating in this web class compared to classroom courses," 17% of the students reported that the average student will cheat more in this web class than most classroom courses, while 42% of the students reported that the average student will cheat less than most classroom courses. Table 5 compared cheating in this web class compared to most web courses. The results of Table 5 indicate only 3% of the students reporting cheating more (in this web class) than most web classes, while a great percentage, 70%, reported that the average student can cheat (in this web class) less than in most web courses.

Table 2.   Importance of Taking Multiple Exam Attempts

How important to you, is the ability to take an exam as many times as you wish during the semester?

Very important it really helps	Slightly important	Neutral, it does not help, or hurt	Slightly not important	Not important
63%	23%	8%	4%	2%

Table 3.   Student Learning

Because I am able to take an exam as many times as I wish to improve my score, I receive instant feedback and learn the material. (Compared to other web courses), my learning increased in this class:

Less than most web courses	Slightly less than most web courses	About the same	Slightly more than most web courses	More than most web courses
4%	4%	29%	40%	23%

Table 4.   Cheating in This Web Class Compared to Classroom Courses

As compared to other classroom courses, do you think the average student, in this web course, can cheat:

More than most classroom courses	Slightly more than most classroom courses	About the same	Slightly less than most classroom courses	Less than most classroom courses
2%	15%	41%	10%	32%

Table 5.   Cheating in this Web Class Compared to Other Web Courses

As compared to other web courses, do you think the average student, in this web course, can cheat:

More than most web courses	Slightly more than most web courses	About the same	Slightly less than most web courses	Less than most web courses
1%	2%	27%	17%	53%

SUMMARY AND CONCLUSIONS

The foundation of this article has been to report the increasing enrollments in online distance education courses, document the occurrence of academic dishonesty by college students, offer the rationale given as to why students cheat, and present suggestions to reduce cheating in both classroom and online higher education courses. After the groundwork for this article had been established, an easy-to-use pragmatic method to reduce academic dishonesty was then proposed.

In an effort to evaluate the pragmatic method, feedback was obtained from students through the use of an anonymous online survey. Overall, the results were very constructive. Students were satisfied with the amount of the learning they achieved. Students appreciated the ability to take each exam multiple times. Most importantly, students reported a lesser incidence of online cheating compared to other web classes. The results presented in Tables 4 and 5 reported a lesser perception of cheating in online classes compared to previous research (Kennedy et al., 2000). This tends to confirm the merit of the pragmatic method to reduce online cheating.

Widespread student academic dishonesty is an unfortunate situation faced by university professors. Nonetheless, professors developing online courses might reduce student cheating by following the recommended pragmatic methods suggested in this article.

REFERENCES

Alschuler, A. S., & Blimling, G. S. (1995). Curbing epidemic cheating through systemic change. *Colleges Teaching, 43*(4), 123.

Anderson, R. W., & Obenshain, S. S. (1994). Cheating by students: Findings, reflections, and remedies. *Academic Medicine, 69*, 323-332.

Baird, J. S. (1980). Current trends in college cheating. *Psychology in the Schools, 17*, 515-522.

Beal, E. (2003). Plenty of players in MBA game. *Crain's Cleveland Business, 24*(35), 15-15.

Blackboard. (2006). Retrieved September 7, 2007, from http://www.blackboard.com/products.

Bowers, W. J. (1964). *Student dishonesty and its control in college.* New York, NY: Bureau of Applied Social Research, Columbia University.

Burns, E. (2006). *Continuing education drives distance-learning enrollment.* Retrieved July 17, 2006, from http://www.clickz.com/stats/sectors/education/article.php/3605321

Christe, B. (2003). Designing online courses to discourage dishonesty. *Educause Quarterly, 4*, 54-58.

Collision, M. (1990). Apparent rise of students cheating has college officials worried. *The Chronicle of Higher Education, 36*(18), 33-34.

Cummins, C. (2000). *Are you teaching your children to cheat?* Retrieved July 17, 2006, from http://www.educationreportcard.com/columns/2000

Davis, S. F., Grover, C. A., Becker, A. H., & McGregor, L. N. (1992). Academic dishonesty: Prevalence, determinants, techniques, and punishments. *Teaching of Psychology, 19*, 16-20.

Evans, E. D., & Craig, D. (1990). Adolescent cognitions for academic cheating as a function of grade level and achievement status. *Journal of Adolescent Research, July*, 325-345.

Fishbein, L. (1993). Curbing cheating and restoring academic integrity. *The Chronicle of Higher Education, 40*(15), 52.

Fishbein, L. (1994). We can curb college cheating. *Education Digest, 59*(7), 58-61.

Fisher, A. (2003). Will I end up getting scammed if I pursue an online MBA? *Fortune, 148*(6), 170.

Gale Group, I. (2003). The e-MBA: More MBA students are getting their degrees without ever stepping into the classroom. *Business and Management Practices: Inside Business, 5*(7), 53.

Gomez, D. S. (2001). Putting the shame back in student cheating. *Education Digest, 67*(4), 15.

Innerst, C. (1998). Students are pulling off the big cheat. *Insight on the News, 14*(9), 41.

Jendrek, M. P. (1989). Faculty reactions to academic dishonesty. *Journal of College Student Development, 30*, 401-406.

Kelley, K. B., & Bonner, K. (2005). Distance education and academic dishonesty: Faculty and administrator perceptions and responses. *Journal of Asynchronous Learning Networks, 9*(1), 43-52.

Kennedy, K., Nowak, S., Raghuraman, R., Thomas, J., & Davis, S. F. (2000). Academic dishonesty and distance learning: Student and faculty views. *College Student Journal, 34*(2), 309-314.

Kerkvliet, J. R., & Sigmund, C. (1999). Can we control cheating in the classroom? *Journal of Economic Education, 30*(4), 331-343.

Kiernan, V. (2003). A survey documents growth in distance education in late 1990s. *The Chronicle of Higher Education, 49*(48), 28.

Kritz, F. L., & Newman, R. J. (1991). Campus cheats. *U.S. News and World Report, 11*(24), 71.

Kruse, K. (2002). *The benefits and drawbacks of e-learning.* Retrieved July 17, 2006, from http://www.e-learningguru.com/articles/art1_3.htm

Lathrop, A., & Foss, K. (2002). Student cheating and plagiarism in the Internet era. Englewood, CO: Libraries Unlimited.

Maramark, S., & Maline, M. B. (1993). *Academic dishonesty among college students.* Washington, DC: Division of Higher Education and Adult Learning, Office of Research, U.S. Department of Education.

McCabe, D. L. (1993). Faculty responses to academic dishonesty: The influence of student honor codes. *Research in Higher Education, 34*(5), 647-658.

McCabe, D. L., & Bowers, W. J. (1994). Academic dishonesty among males in college: A thirty year perspective. *Journal of College Student Development, 35*, 3-10.

McCabe, D. L., & Trevino, L. K. (1993). Academic dishonesty: Honor codes and other contextual influences. *Journal of Higher Education, 64*(5), 522-538.

Murdock, T. B. (1999). Discouraging cheating in your classroom. *Mathematics Teacher, 92*(7), 587.

Newstead, S. E., Franklin-Stokes, A., & Armstead, P. (1996). Individual differences in student cheating. *Journal of Educational Psychology, 88*, 229-241.

Olt, M. R. (2002). Ethics and distance education: strategies for minimizing academic dishonesty in online assessment. *Online Journal of Distance Learning Administration, 5*(3).

Turnitin. (2006). Retrieved September 7, 2007, from http://turnitin.com/static/index.html.

U. S. Department of Education (Ed.). (2003). *Distance education at degree-granting post-secondary institutions: 2000-2001.* Washington, DC: Author.

Wellborn, S. N. (1980). Cheating in college becomes an epidemic. *U.S. News and World Report, 89*(20), 39-42.

Whitley, B. E., Jr., & Keith-Speigel, P. (2001). *Academic dishonesty: An educator's guide.* Mahwah, NJ: Erlbaum.

World Wide Learning. (2006). Retrieved July 17, 2006, from www.worldwidelearn.com/elearning /elearning-benefits.htm

CHAPTER 20

ASSESSING ONLINE FACULTY

More Than Student Surveys and Design Rubrics

Anthony A. Piña and Larry Bohn
Sullivan University System

As online education continues to grow, so do the number of online courses being taught by those who did not develop the courses. However, the most popular rubrics for evaluating the quality of online courses tend to focus upon the course's design, not upon the actions of the instructor teaching the course. In this study, 140 distance education faculty and administrators identified student surveys as the most common method for assessing online faculty, followed by institutional methods based largely upon Quality Matters and other instructional design rubrics. To provide additional objective and observable assessment data, the administrators and faculty, along with 114 students enrolled in online course (total $N = 254$) rated 9 in-course actions by faculty to determine indicators of online instructor quality.

INTRODUCTION

Online education is proving to be highly resilient. Even in the face of the highest declines in total higher education student enrollment since the

Beyond the Online Course: Leadership Perspectives on e-Learning
pp. 317–329
Copyright © 2016 by Information Age Publishing
317

1950s (U. S. Census Bureau, 2013), the latest surveys of online education continue to show a rise in the number of students taking online courses (Allen & Seaman, 2013). Although the number of online courses is growing, not all online courses are of equal quality. We have experienced instances of successful courses where a highly engaged and involved instructor has mitigated the effects of a poorly designed course. Conversely, we have also witnessed well-designed courses that have been taught poorly and were ultimately unsuccessful. Clearly, the quality of the individual instructor is crucial to the quality of the course (Piña, Harris, & Ashbaugh, 2013).

At professional conferences, we have heard the concerns of those who oversee distance education programs at colleges and universities that the metrics used for evaluating online instructors, often limited to end-of-course student surveys, do not provide academic deans and chairs with adequate information to make informed decisions about their online faculty, particularly adjunct faculty (Piña & Bohn, 2013). In many cases, the methods that have been used to evaluate face-to-face instructors are less effective when used to evaluate online instructors (Mandernach, Donnelli, Dailey, & Schulte, 2005). Research has shown that colleges and universities tend to not do a very good job at recognizing and rewarding exceptional online teaching, particularly with professional incentives such as promotion, tenure and institutional recognition programs (Piña, 2008). A contributing factor to this situation may be the inability of institutions to adequately measure quality online teaching.

As online programs grow, the paradigm of the faculty member as developer and sole teacher of an online course is changing. Many adjunct instructors teach online courses developed by other faculty members, often in partnership with instructional designers (Cheski & Muller, 2010). At institutions with many sections of the same course, a single "master" course is sometimes used to house the course's instructional content and assessments, which are copied into the various sections and taught by different instructors (Borgemenke, Holt, & Fish, 2013). Colleges and universities are also relying more frequently upon department- or institution-wide templates for their online courses, providing a common look, feel and navigation for students (Ley & Gannon-Cook, 2014).

Online Course Quality

Standards for online course quality have been promoted by accrediting bodies (Commission on Colleges, 2012), statewide agencies (Illinois Online Network, 2012), teachers' unions (American Federation of Teachers, 2000) and independent education organizations (American Council on Education, 2003; Council on Higher Education Accreditation, 2002; Phipps & Merisotis, 2000). Rubrics to evaluate the quality of online courses have been formulated by a diverse group of organizations, such as Quality Matters (Maryland Online, 2008), iNacol (2012), California State University Chico (2012), Towson University (Ashcraft, McMahon, Lesh, & Tabrizi, 2008), Blackboard, Inc. (2014), and the United States Distance Learning Association (2012).

Limitations of Quality Rubrics

While the various online quality rubrics can provide useful direction for *building* online courses and assessing the quality of *course design*, they provide little guidance for *teaching* online courses and assessing the quality of online *instructors*. Quality online education, as measured by the most popular rubrics, tends to be focused upon the instructional design of the course, such as with Quality Matters (Maryland Online, 2008), or upon the resources and services offered by the institution, such as with the Sloan-C Quality Scorecard (Shelton, 2010; 2011).

A weakness of the existing "online teaching rubrics" is that they have been created with the assumption that the instructor who is teaching the course is the same person who developed the course and is, therefore, responsible for the course design (Innovations in Distance Education, 1998). Since an ever-increasing number of institutions are using "master" courses developed by faculty or other subject matter experts with instructional designers, many instructors are teaching online courses that they did not develop themselves. In these cases, it would be unfair to evaluate an instructor based on the how well (or how poorly) the course was designed.

This problem is exemplified by Sonoma State University's Quality Online Learning & Teaching Rubric (Sonoma State University, 2012). The rubric contains 53 evaluation criteria; however, 49 of these criteria relate directly to the course design, while only four relate to actions undertaken by the course instructor. Park University's Online Instructor Evaluation System recognizes the difference between course content and online pedagogy and integrates formative and summative evaluation with mentoring of new online faculty by experienced online instructors (Mandernach et al., 2005); however, it requires multiple faculty with 50% release time to mentor the new instructors throughout the course—a resource that is not available at many institutions.

Class Observation/Indicators of Online Quality

So, how do we assess the quality of instructors teaching courses that they did not design? We must look at the actions performed by the instructors within the course. In face-to-face courses, evaluation of an instructor's teaching quality is often done via a peer or supervisor observation of a live class session. This class observation method results in a "snapshot" view of what occurs during a small portion of the course (Marshall, 2012). In contrast, the online course's learning management system preserves information about student and instructor activity throughout the course, including logged in time, course announcements, course discussions, feedback, and grades. An online class observation would provide a much more complete picture of what the instructor and students have done in the class. However, deans, program chairs, and others without significant online teaching and development experience might not know what to look for when observing an online course. It would be extremely useful to have an evaluation instrument for an online "class observation" of the instructor's actions and teaching—with indicators of online teaching quality that are separate and distinct from those features that are part of the course's instructional design (Piña & Bohn, 2013).

In this study, distance learning administrators and faculty were surveyed to determine measures that are currently being used to evaluate the quality of online faculty at higher education institutions. Additionally, these professionals, along with students enrolled in online courses, were asked to validate nine observable indicators of online instructor quality.

METHOD

Participants

The sample consisted of 254 total respondents, including 140 online learning professionals (evenly split between faculty teaching online courses and administrators with responsibility for online education) and 114 students enrolled in online courses.

Instrumentation

A comprehensive review of distance education literature yielded many different sources for best practices and measures for online faculty evaluation (e.g. Mandernach et al., 2005; Tobin, 2004; Sonoma State University, 2012). In each case, the evaluation measures included items outside the control of the faculty member teaching the course, such as the instructional design of the course and policies for faculty staffing and support. There was no instrument identified that was designed to evaluate faculty apart from the course design.

A survey instrument was developed to include two items on methods that institutions use currently to assess online instructor quality, including an "other" category, where respondents could provide additional information or examples. The instrument also included nine suggested indicators of online instructor quality gathered from the literature review and from distance learning administrators and faculty at professional conferences. Each indicator was accompanied by a 4-point Likert-type scale. Respondents chose the level of importance of each item as an indicator of online instructor quality. Responses to the instrument were coded for analysis as follows: *critical* = 3, *important but not critical* = 2, *minimally important* = 1, and *not important* = 0. Respondents also selected minimum standards of instructor activity for six of the indicators.

A preliminary paper-based draft of the survey instrument was pilot-tested during the 2013 Distance Learning Administration Conference with 23 professionals who were representative of the target audience. The survey items were determined by these professionals to be appropriate for the target audience, with only minor modifications recommended. The survey was distributed online via SurveyMonkey to attendees of the Distance Learning Administration Conference and to members of the Association for Educational Communications and Technology. A shorter form of the survey, excluding the items on methods that institutions use to assess online instructor quality, was distributed to students enrolled in online courses at a medium-sized private university in the Southern United States. Cronbach's alpha for internal consistency was 69.3. Anonymity of the respondents was assured by configuring SurveyMonkey to provide each respondent with a unique identifier that would not allow the researchers to trace respondents' identities (SurveyMonkey, 2014).

Data Analysis

Mean scores and standard deviations were calculated for each of the indicators of online instructional quality. Scores fell between 3.0 (critical) and 0.0 (not important) for the rated importance of each indicator of faculty quality. Analysis of variance was used to test for statistically significant differences and alpha level for significance was set at $P < .05$. Frequencies and percentages were calculated for methods used by institutions to assess online instructor quality and for minimum standards for instructor activity.

RESULTS

Assessment Methods Used by Institutions

Table 1 contains the responses to the question "Which measures does your institution use to assess the quality of online instructors?" Respondents were allowed to select multiple measures, if applicable. Student surveys were, by a significant amount, the most widely used measure for evaluating instructors. Supervisor evaluations were used by slightly more than one third of respondents' institutions, followed by online class observations, metrics from the learning management system, and peer evaluations. Just below eight percent of institutions used no assessment measures at all and less than three percent used other measures, which included enrollment in professional development programs and self-evaluations. The fact that there were so few items in the "other" category indicates that the survey captured the domain of measures used at these institutions. Other comments offered by respondents indicated that metrics from the learning management system included reports of instructor login and discussion forum activity.

Table 2 below contains the responses to the item, "Do you use a rubric to measure online instructor quality?" Responses were almost evenly divided among Quality Matters, In-House Developed, and Do Not Use a Rubric. Twenty-two respondents selected more than one response. Comments for this survey item indicated that this reflected the use of multiple rubrics across different departments. The rubrics identified by the respondents (Quality Matters, CSU Chico ROI, USDLA, and iNacol) were all designed primarily for evaluating the instructional design of online courses, rather than the actions and contributions of the online instructor. The Sloan-C Quality Scorecard was designed to evaluate the administra-

Table 1.   Assessment Measures Used By Institutions

Measure	Frequency	Percent
Student surveys	125	89.3
Supervisor evaluations	47	33.6
Online class observations	46	32.9
Metrics from the learning management system	35	25.0
Peer evaluations	32	22.9
None	11	7.9
Other	4	2.9

Note: $N = 140$.

Table 2.   Assessment Rubrics Used By Institutions

Measure	Frequency	Percent
Quality Matters	47	33.6
In-house developed	46	32.9
None	46	32.9
Sloan-C Quality Scorecard	7	5.0
CSU Chico Rubric for Online Instruction	5	3.6
USDLA	4	2.9
Other	4	2.9
iNacol	3	2.1

Note: $N = 140$.

tion of distance education programs, rather than the quality of online faculty (Piña & Bohn, 2012; Shelton, 2010). Comments offered by 13 of the respondents indicated that their in-house rubrics were based upon Quality Matters, while one respondent indicated that the in-house rubric was based upon a combination of standards from by the Association for Educational Communications and Technology and the International Society for Technology in Education. The four "other" rubrics listed were IDEA Education (2), QOCI-Quality Online Course Initiative (Illinois Online Network, 2012) and the *Best Practices for Electronically Offered Degree and Certificate Programs* (WICHE Cooperative for Educational Telecommunications, 2000).

Importance of Indicators for Assessing Instructor Quality

Table 3 reports the results of respondents' ratings of importance for the indicators of online instructor quality. ANOVA revealed no significant differences between online faculty and distance learning administrators for any of the nine indicators of online teaching quality, so instructors and administrators were grouped together ($n = 140$) and were compared with students ($n = 114$). Administrators and faculty considered responding to student inquiries, providing feedback for assignments, responding in a timely manner, login frequency, and moderating discussion forums to be the most important indicators of online instructor quality. Students judged feedback on assignments, responding to student inquiries, responding in a timely manner, posting class announcements, and login frequency as the most critical indicators. ANOVA revealed significant dif-

Table 3.   Indicators for Assessing Online Instructor Quality

Indicator	Admin/Fac (n = 140)		Students (n = 114)		Total (n = 254)	
	Mean	SD	Mean	SD	Mean	SD
Faculty login frequency	2.71	0.527	2.32	0.672	2.54	0.626
Faculty biography	1.90	0.859	1.96	0.803	1.93	0.833
Posting announcements	2.16	0.833	2.34	0.649	2.24	0.760
Concise announcements	1.61	0.987	1.86	0.986	1.72	0.992
Responding to inquiries	2.94	0.262	2.83	0.496	2.89	0.388
Timeliness of response	2.79	0.429	2.55	0.550	2.68	0.499
Participation in discussions	2.27	0.821	2.07	0.827	2.18	0.829
Moderation of discussions	2.29	0.682	2.04	0.866	2.18	0.778
Feedback on assignments	2.89	0.374	2.90	0.297	2.89	0.341

ferences between administrators/faculty and students for five of the nine indicators. Administrators/faculty rated responding to student inquiries, timeliness of response, login frequency, and moderation of discussions significantly higher than did students, while students rated conciseness of course announcements as significantly higher. Overall, administrators and faculty had higher ratings for faculty involvement in discussion forums, while students had higher ratings for course announcements.

Minimum Standards for Assessing Instructor Quality

Six of the indicators included four possible minimum standards for instructor activity. Each respondent could select a single minimum standard for each indicator. Table 4 reports the response frequency and percentages for administrators/faculty and for students. For frequency of instructor login, no clear picture of student preference emerged, while administrators/faculty indicated that instructors should log in to their online courses either every day or every other day. Having instructors post weekly course announcements was clearly favored by both students and online professionals, with the highest responses of any standard and with a notable minority (particularly students) favoring announcements more than once per week. Nearly half of administrators/faculty preferred to have no word limits on course announcements, while students were undecided. Both groups rated this indicator as lowest overall in importance.

Table 4.   Minimum Standards for Instructor Activity

Indicator	Admin/Faculty (n = 140)		Students (n = 114)	
	Frequency	%	Frequency	%
Frequency of Instructor Login				
Daily	40	28.6	27	23.7
4 times per week	50	35.7	21	18.4
3 times per week	38	27.1	34	29.8
2 times per week	12	8.6	32	28.1
Frequency of Course Announcements				
Multiple times per week	19	13.6	27	23.7
Weekly	98	70.0	73	64.0
Every 2 weeks	6	4.3	10	8.8
Less than every 2 weeks	17	12.1	4	3.5
Conciseness of Course Announcements				
No word limit	69	49.3	31	27.2
300 word limit	22	15.7	21	18.4
200 word limit	22	15.7	31	27.2
100 word limit	27	19.3	31	27.2
Response to Student Inquiries				
1 day	77	55.0	70	61.4
2 days	51	36.4	25	21.9
3 days	10	7.1	15	13.2
4 days	2	1.4	4	3.5
Completeness of Instructor Biography				
Full descriptive bio with vita	10	7.1	24	21.1
Full descriptive bio	29	20.7	34	29.8
Single paragraph brief bio	84	60.0	53	46.5
Contact info only	17	12.1	3	2.6
Minimum Instructor Discussion Posts				
Post more than 4 times	40	28.6	16	14.0
Post 3-4 times	40	28.6	26	22.8
Post 2-3 times	30	21.4	58	50.9
No requirement to post	30	21.4	14	12.3

Responding to student inquiries within one day garnered high percentages—especially with students, followed by responses within two days. Waiting three or four days to respond was acceptable only to a minority of respondents. Students indicated that they wanted instructors to provide more robust information about themselves than merely contact information. While providing a single paragraph brief bio was most popular with both groups, more students showed a preference toward having faculty provide a more fully descriptive biography. Administrators and faculty did not offer a consistent view regarding the involvement of instructors in discussion forums but showed a higher tolerance than students for instructors not having a requirement to post.

CONCLUSION

Overwhelmingly, the institutions in our study rely upon student surveys as the primary method for assessing their online faculty. Student evaluation of teaching is a widely researched area of education and recent meta-analyses have not resulted in clear answers regarding the validity of such assessments for formative and summative evaluation purposes (e.g., Spooren, Brockx, & Mortelmans, 2013). After outlining some of the possible sources of bias in student evaluations of faculty, Baldwin and Blattner (2003) recommended that multiple methods be used to evaluate teaching quality. Several of the institutions surveyed do use additional methods, such as supervisor or peer evaluations and online class observations. These methods, however, appear often to be based upon rubrics and standards formulated to evaluate the quality of the course's instructional design, which assumes that instructor being assessed is also responsible for the design and development of the online course. This is often not the case and may lead to judgments being made based on criteria that are not relevant to the actual role played by instructors in their online courses.

Our desire was to identify a set of criteria that would yield objective data easily examined by supervisors and peers during an online course observation and serve as a balance to the more subjective data gathered from student surveys. This study focused upon quantitative measures of instructor actions and behaviors that could be readily observed in the online course and/or collected using the reporting tools of the learning management system:

- Has the instructor logged in at least an average of every other day?
- Has the instructor posted a biography of at least a paragraph, in addition to contact info?

- Has the instructor posted announcements at least weekly?
- Is there evidence that the instructor answers student inquiries in two days or less?
- Does the instructor participate in discussion forums where appropriate?
- Does the instructor provide feedback on assignments?

Where Do We Go From Here?

We started with what could be considered the "low-hanging fruit" of easily observable and quantifiable instructor actions. More difficult will be to determine the levels of quality within these indicators. For example, what constitutes higher versus lower quality course announcements, instructor bios, feedback on assignments, or instructor discussion forum posts? What are the indicators of an instructor who successfully facilitates online discussions? How do instructors leverage their expertise to add value to an already developed online course? These questions of quality online teaching are fruitful areas for further research.

Most learning management systems are adept at generating reports that can catch student or instructors doing the wrong thing (e.g., not logging in, not posting in discussions, inappropriate communications, taking a long time to respond to inquiries or grade assignments, not providing feedback). However, these systems need to become better at catching people doing the right thing or doing exceptional things (e.g., flagging highly responsive instructors and identifying courses with high levels of interaction).

As the number of online courses continues to increase, our efforts to adequately and accurately assess and develop those who teach these courses also needs to increase. Ultimately, the quality of our student's educational experience will depend upon these efforts.

REFERENCES

Allen. I. E., & Seaman, J. (2013). *Changing course: Ten years of tracking online education in the United States*. Babson Park, MA: Babson Survey Research Group.

American Council on Education. (2003). *Guiding principles for distance learning in a learning society*. Washington, DC: Center for Lifelong Learning, American Council on Education.

American Federation of Teachers (2000). *Distance education: Guidelines for good practice*. Washington, DC: Higher Education Program and Policy Council, American Federation of Teachers AFL-CIO.

Ashcraft, M., McMahon, J, Lesh, S., & Tabrizi, M. (2008). *Rubric: Peer review for online learning* (Towson University). Retrieved from http://pages.towson.edu/mcmahon/peerreview/On-linerubric.pdf.

Baldwin, T., & Blattner, N. (2003). Guarding against potential bias in student evaluations. *College Teaching, 51*(1), 27–31.

Blackboard, Inc. (2014). *Rubric: Exemplary course program.* Retrieved from http://www.blackboard.com/Community/Catalyst-Awards/Exemplary-Course-Program.aspx.

Borgemenke, A. J., Holt, W. C., & Fish, W. W. (2013). Universal course shell template design and implementation to enhance student outcomes in online coursework. *Quarterly Review of Distance Education, 14*(1) 17–23.

California State University Chico. (2012). *Rubric for online instruction.* Retrieved from http://www.csuchico.edu/celt/roi/

Cheski, N., & Muller, P. (2010, August). Aliens, adversaries, or advocates? Working with the experts (SMEs). *Proceedings from the Conference on Distance Teaching & Learning.* Madison WI: University of Wisconsin Extension.

Commission on Colleges. (2012). *Distance and correspondence education policy statement.* Decatur, GA: Southern Association of Colleges and Schools. Retrieved from http://www.sacscoc.org/policies.asp

Council on Higher Education Accreditation. (2002). *Accreditation and assuring quality in distance learning.* Washington, DC: CHEA Institute for Research and Study of Accreditation and Quality Assurance

Illinois Online Network. (2012). *Rubric: Quality online course initiative.* Retrieved from http://www.ion.uillinois.edu/initiatives/qoci/index.asp.

iNACOL. (2011). Version 2: National standards for quality online courses. Vienna, VA: International Association for K–12 Online Learning.

Innovations in Distance Education. (1998). An emerging set of guiding principles and practices for the design and development of distance education. College Park, PA: Pennsylvania State University. Retrieved from http://colfinder.net/materials/Supporting_Distance_Education_Through_Policy_Development/resources/web1/innovation.pdf

Ley, K., & Gannon-Cook, R. (2014). Continuous improvement: The case for adapting online course templates. In A. A. Piña & A. P. Mizell (Eds.) *Real-life distance education: Case studies in practice* (pp. 253–266). Charlotte, NC: Information Age.

Mandernach, B. J., Donnelli, E., Dailey, A., & Schulte, M. (2005). A faculty evaluation model for online instructors: Mentoring and evaluation in the online classroom. *Online Journal of Distance Learning Administration, 8*(3).

Marshall, K. (2012). Fine-tuning teacher evaluation. *Educational Leadership, 70*(3), 50–53.

Maryland Online, Inc. (2008). *Rubric: Quality matters.* Retrieved from http://www.esac.org/fdi/rubric/finalsurvey/demorubric.asp.

Phipps, R., & Merisotis, J. (2000). *Quality on the line: Benchmarks for success in Internet-based distance education.* Washington, DC: The Institute for Higher Education Policy with Blackboard, Inc. and the National Education Association.

Piña, A. A. (2008). How institutionalized is distance learning? A study of institutional role, locale and academic level. *Online Journal of Distance Learning Administration, 11*(1).

Piña, A. A., & Bohn, L. (2012, June). Using Sloan-C's quality scorecard & accreditation standards as administration tools. *Proceedings of Selected Papers from the Distance Learning Administration Conference* (pp. 149–152). Carrollton, GA: University of West Georgia.

Piña, A. A., & Bohn, L. (2013, June). Beyond quality matters: Assessing online instructors, not just the courses. *Proceedings of the Distance Learning Administration 2013 Conference* (pp. 153–157). Carrollton, GA: University of West Georgia.

Piña, A. A., Harris, B. R., & Ashbaugh M. L. (2012, November). *A faculty, instructional designer and administrator dialogue on the continuing evolution of distance education.* Presented at the annual convention of the Association for Educational Communications and Technology, Louisville, KY.

Shelton, K. (2010). A quality scorecard for the administration of online education programs: A delphi study. *Journal of Asynchronous Learning Networks, 14*(4), 36–62.

Shelton, K. (2011). A review of paradigms for evaluating the quality of online education programs. *Online Journal of Distance Learning Administration, 14*(1).

Sonoma State University. (2012). *Rubric: Quality online learning & teaching.* Retrieved from http://enact.sonoma.edu/content.php?pid=218878&sid=2552680

Spooren, P., Brockx, B., & Mortelmans, D. (2013). On the validity of student evaluation of teaching: The state of the art. *Review of Educational Research, 83*(4), 598–642.

SurveyMonkey. (2014). *Web survey creation tool.* Portland, OR: SurveyMonkey.com. Retrieved from http://www.surveymonkey.com/

Tobin, T. J. (2004). Best practices for administrative evaluation of online faculty. *Online Journal of Distance Learning Administration, 7*(2).

U. S. Census Bureau. (2013, September 3). *After a recent upswing, college enrollment declines, census bureau reports.* Retrieved from https://www.census.gov/newsroom/releases/archives/education/cb13-153.html

United States Distance Learning Association. (2012). *Rubric: Best practice in distance learning programming.* Retrieved from http://www.usdla.org/html/events/dlAwards/criteria_online.pdf

WICHE Cooperative for Educational Telecommunications. (2000). *Best practices for electronically offered degree and certificate programs.* Boulder, CO: Western Interstate Commission for Higher Education.

CHAPTER 21

HOW UNIVERSITY FACULTY MEMBERS DEVELOPED THEIR ONLINE TEACHING SKILLS

**Steven W. Schmidt, Elizabeth M. Hodge,
and Christina M. Tschida**
East Carolina University

INTRODUCTION

Online courses in higher education have grown tremendously in scope and volume in the past decade. In fact, the "explosive growth of distance education is transforming postsecondary education" (Moller, Foshay & Huett, 2008, p. 66). Allen and Seaman (2007, 2010) have tracked online enrollment for years and found that online enrollments have actually grown at rates that far exceed total student populations in higher education. In 2006, more than 96% of the largest colleges and universities in the United States offered online courses and nearly 3.2 million students took at least one online course during fall 2005 (Gaytan, 2009). Between fall 2007 and fall 2008 alone, there was a 22% increase in distance education enrollments (Shattuck, Dubins, & Zilberman, 2011).

Technological advancements have certainly influenced this growth, but budgetary crises affecting institutions of higher education across the country have also made online education vital to many institutional fiscal

Beyond the Online Course: Leadership Perspectives on e-Learning
pp. 331–344
Copyright © 2016 by Information Age Publishing

plans. Colleges and universities see distance education as an effective means for sustaining growth (Moller et al., 2008; Young & Lewis, 2008). There is growing evidence of the cost-effectiveness of online learning as courses can be developed, copied, and reused by other instructors. In addition, the replication and standardization of online courses offers, to some extent, quality control in terms of content presented and course design (Wise & Rothman, 2010).

From the standpoint of the student, online programs and courses offer flexibility to learners whose lifestyles or life responsibilities do not match traditional college schedules (Ke, 2010; Larreamendy-Joerns & Leindhardt, 2006; Young & Lewis, 2008). Pontes and Pontes (2012) note that low-income students enrolled in distance education courses are more likely to have fewer enrollment gaps and stay enrolled in their programs, suggesting it is due to the easy accessibility of courses and convenience of completing coursework on their own schedules.

Colleges and universities have embraced online education as a way of increasing enrollment and managing financial difficulties. As a result, faculty has had to change, as well. Faculty used to teaching in traditional face-to-face classrooms now find themselves transitioning to teaching online. In the process, they are learning that teaching online is not as simple as transferring face-to-face courses to the Internet. As Smith (2005) notes, "Teaching online requires a specific set of skills and competencies" (p. 1). Furthermore, "faculty cannot be expected to know intuitively how to design and deliver an effective online course" (Palloff & Pratt, 2001, p. 23). Research says most teachers teach as they were taught. In discussing how professors learn to teach, Kugel (1993) summarizes "Most of what they have learned, they have learned from watching others and, as they start to do it on their own, they usually wish they had paid more attention to what their professors did as they taught" (p. 317). However, distance educators lack a model or benchmark for online teaching, because many of them have not even taken online courses as students. Results of the aforementioned circumstances are understandable. A 2012 study conducted by *Inside Higher Ed* found that 58% of the almost 5,000 faculty members who responded to the study described themselves as more fearful than excited about the growth of online education (Kolowich, 2012).

Have faculty been forgotten in this rush to online learning? Or is it simply assumed that faculty are able to teach in any situation? The problem is that not enough is known about the online instructor in higher education and about the experiences of instructors who move from face-to-face to online teaching. It is within the context of higher education that this research project on the processes by which faculty learn to teach online was conducted. The purpose of this research was to better understand the experiences of these instructors and the processes they went through when learning to teach online. Specifically, the study addressed the following questions:

1. How did university professors begin teaching online? What were the experiences associated with that initial online teaching experience?
2. What have these professors learned about teaching online as a result of their online teaching experiences?
3. How have these professors evolved as online instructors?

REVIEW OF LITERATURE

Given the current environment in higher education, it is easy to see that distance education is here to stay. Therefore, the need for quality online instruction must be a priority for institutions offering distance education programs and courses. However, due to the speed at which distance education has grown, most colleges and universities find themselves behind in understanding what it means to teach online (Orr, Williams & Pennington, 2009) and in offering quality professional development for faculty who are asked to teach online courses (Macdonald & Poniatowska, 2011; Orr et al., 2009; Shattuck et al., 2011). Despite rapid growth in online course offerings, "institutional efforts to improve online teaching [are] generally sporadic and ad-hoc in nature" (Orr et al., 2009, p. 264). In fact, according to Allen and Seaman (2010) "19% of institutions with online offerings report that they have no training or mentoring programs for their online teaching faculty" (p. 3). Further complicating the issue, adjunct instructors are more likely to teach online courses than are full-time faculty, often teaching from home or off-campus; however, "the most common training approaches … are internally run training courses (65%) and informal mentoring (59%)" (Seaman, 2010, as cited in Shattuck et al., 2011). Often professional development efforts are in the form of hands-on workshops and "concentrated on approaches to *using* the tools" versus how the tools might be used appropriately within a specific context of teaching and learning (Macdonald & Poniatowska, 2011, p. 124). Adjunct faculty are less likely than their full-time faculty counterparts to attend such on-campus workshops or engage in informal mentoring and face-to-face discussions about teaching online, missing opportunities for professional development, reflection, and dialogue about their practice.

Developing online courses requires mastery of technologies that many faculty are not familiar with, and that some actually fear. Also required is an understanding of how to plan activities for the online student that are interesting, motivating and self-directed (Orr et al., 2009). In a study conducted by the Educause Center for Applied Research in 2009, fewer than half of students surveyed at 125 institutions in the United States felt that their online instructors used information technology effectively (Macdonald & Poniatowska, 2011). Institutions face the dilemma of providing professional development that not only ensures understanding of how to use technology effectively but how to consider online learners and pedagogies.

As a result of these conditions, faculty involvement and acceptance has been slow. Many faculty members hold perceptions of online education as time-consuming and unable to support student learning (Baran, Correia & Thompson, 2011; Gaytan, 2009). Often, faculty asked to teach online have little or no experience with online course development, teaching, or learning, and they are offered little support from their institutions. They learn quickly that online teaching takes more time than face-to-face teaching (Gaytan, 2009). Faculty are also forced to rethink their assumptions about teaching and learning as well as the roles they play in online courses (Baran et al., 2011).

Some researchers have found interest among online instructors for collaborative approaches to online course design and delivery. Most often, collaborative efforts, or the creation of "instructional teams" including faculty and instructional technology experts or technical support staff have been discussed as ways to improve online teaching (Baran et al., 2011; Fish & Wickersham, 2009; Macdonald & Poniatowska, 2011; Orr et al., 2009; Shattuck et al., 2011). Professional development that is available for online instructors tends to fall into two categories: the collaborative teams model and the workshop model. The Jumpstart Program at Indiana University-Purdue University-Indianapolis (IUPUI) is an example of the collaborative team model. New faculty go through a 4-day workshop during which they learn the basics of online teaching, create a vision for their work, and develop a learning module for their online course with the help of a "developmental support team" (Xu & Morris, 2007). Such collaborative course development models exist at some universities but require strong institutional support. More often professional development for online instructors comes in the form of workshops, training sessions, and one-on-one support (Macdonald & Poniatowska, 2011; Orr et al., 2009). The issue with these models is that they tend to focus on technology tools over pedagogy, leaving faculty to figure out when and where to incorporate such technology into their courses. As a result, faculty learning about online teaching and course development has most often happened in informal ways: through informal mentoring relationships and small communities of practice (Orr et al., 2009).

METHOD

In order to address the research questions, a basic qualitative approach using focus groups was employed. Merriam (1998) notes that a characteristic of basic qualitative research rests on the fact that individuals construct reality through interactions in their social worlds. Basic qualitative research examines "(1) how people interpret their experiences, (2) how they construct their worlds and (3) what meaning they attribute to their experiences" (Merriam, 2009, p. 23). This is an appropriate method to examine the ways in which professors learn to teach online, because these processes involve individuals' perceptions based on reflection and interaction with their environments. The goal of basic qualitative research is to understand something (Merriam, 1998). In this study, it is to understand the perspective and views of the subjects with regard to their professional identity.

Data for this study were collected over the course of one academic year (2011-12). Purposeful sampling was used to identify participants (Patton, 1990). Merriam (2009) noted that a major benefit of purposeful sampling is that researchers can study information-rich cases, and can learn a great deal about the topics in question. The use of focus group sessions was determined to be the best approach for this study, as it allowed the researchers to gather data directly from participants and it allowed participants to hear and discuss each other's responses (Merriam, 2009).

Participants were instructors of online courses from various program areas and levels of experience within the college of education at a large southeastern university. The instructors varied in their professional status and each instructor in the focus group had taught a distance education course a minimum of 1 year. All instructors interviewed had taught both face to face and distance education during their teaching careers. Participants' level of technical literacy varied from novice to expert. Each focus group consisted of a mixture of novice and veteran instructors, a range of experience with online teaching, and members of different program areas to get a strong sample of experience across levels and programs as well as encourage discourse among instructors across departments.

Participants volunteered to attend the focus group sessions and were provided an introductory message regarding the topic of discussion. All signed confidentiality agreements and release forms prior to their focus group sessions. A series of three 90-minute focus groups was conducted and audio taped. Two researchers participated in each focus group with one leading the semistructured discussion and the other taking field notes. Each focus group discussion was transcribed; transcripts were read and coded for themes by individual researchers then compared for reliability. Specific themes were identified and transcripts were reread for additional instances of each.

Findings come from transcripts of the three focus groups, field notes from the focus groups, and notes from researcher discussions following the groups. Researchers distinguished specific themes that arose from the focus group questions. The data were analyzed for specific words, context, consistency, frequency, specificity, and intensity of comments as suggested by Krueger (1994). Utilizing Krueger's systematic approach, the researchers were able to see trends emerge.

FINDINGS

Findings can be categorized according to the research questions. They are presented as follows: initial experiences, learning from early experiences, and the evolution of the online instructor.

Initial Experiences

Many faculty members had abrupt starts to their online teaching careers. Many respondents used phrases like "jumped right in" or "got thrown in" when describing how they started teaching online. One respondent said she knew she would be teaching online at some point in her career, but due to some personal circumstances, the day she started teaching online came sooner than she had expected. Another response was similar: "I knew there were online courses from the beginning, but I didn't know it would be my first teaching assignment." These types of responses came from faculty who had no previous experience teaching online when arriving at the institution. That was not the case with all participants, however. A few participants had had experience teaching online, as adjunct instructors or teaching assistants in graduate school, before they began work at the institution. Whether or not the participant had prior experience teaching online (before the faculty member came to the institution) seemed directly related to the subject matter taught by that faculty member. For example, instructors in the instructional technologies areas came to the institution with prior experience teaching online as adjuncts or graduate assistants. Those in other disciplines typically did not.

When asked about the circumstances under which participants started teaching online, most were either asked, by department administration, to teach online, or told that their courses were online (and inherent in that statement was the fact that they would be teaching online). One respondent was blunt in her assessment about the circumstances: "Administration says no one was made to teach online; however, I was made to teach online." Some participants came into their programs knowing that most courses were taught online, so the expectation was present throughout the interview/hiring process.

Preparing for that first online teaching experience proved challenging to participants. Many described their initial reactions using words like "terrified," "worried," and "apprehensive" at the initial thought. Most felt they were unprepared for the experience, and were overwhelmed at the prospect of having to teach using a method they knew little to nothing about. Overall, the transition to online teaching from traditional face-to-face teaching resulted in a great deal of role ambiguity and confusion for those with no prior online teaching experience. Almost all immediately made comparisons to what they knew, which was teaching in a traditional classroom setting. One participant noted, "I remember the 4 days between orientation and classes starting and having index cards [on] my living room floor. And trying to plan out, if I was doing this face-to-face, then this is how I would do it [online]." These comparisons caused further angst, however, as most could not see how teaching, as they knew it, could "transfer" to teaching online. Planning and scheduling were also factors initially considered by participants. The idea of developing a course website, making sure course materials could be placed online, questions about what content would "transfer" to the online environment and what would not, confusion about what teaching online would actually look like, and uncertainties about whether students would actually participate and learn in the class all caused respondents to feel overwhelmed at the initial prospect of teaching online.

Role ambiguity and confusion was less for those faculty members who had prior experience teaching online or teaching in blended learning situations, and for those who had prior experience as an online student. As noted earlier, many of these faculty members had moved into the online teaching arena gradually and with supervision and guidance, as graduate assistants or as adjuncts. Some started teaching online in blended learning situations, as well, and were able to make the transition to complete online teaching by using what they had learned as instructors in blended learning classrooms. Experience as an online student was very helpful in understanding how to be an online instructor. The ability to look at online teaching from the standpoint of the online learner was beneficial to those who made the transition; however, most did not have this experience from which to draw.

While participants' initial reactions were all fairly similar (as noted above), the paths each participant took after the initial shock or surprise wore off were very different. First, many looked into formal support in the form of courses, tutors, "how to teach online"-type training modules, or other resources that might be available at the institution. However, the consensus among participants was that there was little formal support, nor were processes in place to help faculty members new to online teaching. Those who did find formal support found it to be somewhat archaic. One participant described a series of online training modules available to those who were new to online teaching: "It was more like independent study. It kind of reminded me of the correspondence courses I took a long time ago when I was in college where you would just work independently and submit something to your professor." Several faculty likened early examples of online courses they reviewed to correspondence-type courses. This fact became a motivating factor to these instructors, who were adamant that their online courses would not be like correspondence-type courses they had seen. The experience taught them that their online courses had to be something more in order for the online student to have an experience similar to the face-to-face student.

Those who did have prior experience teaching online used what they had learned in the past, at other institutions or in graduate assistantship experiences, to help them prepare for their initial online teaching experiences at the institution. Some asked for help from colleagues in the department and in the college—often from faculty members in departments related to online teaching and learning, such as the college's instructional technologies department. A few engaged in different types of self-directed learning activities, such as reviewing articles and websites on online teaching. Some called on colleagues at other universities, as well. When they asked for help from colleagues at their own university, some participants were met with a "do what you want"-type of response, which was frustrating to them, as they did not know where to begin. One participant noted that she was told by administration "just take your face-to-face class and put it online." This type of advice frustrated participants, as it was overly simplistic and often offered by people who had no experience teaching online.

Learning From Early Experiences

At some point in this learning process, each participant began to realize that teaching online meant not only teaching, but also designing the online course. They began to make distinctions between course design and development and actual online teaching. The support that faculty found at this stage was mostly related to online course design. As one participant said: "The one piece of support I got from the department was a professor that had been here for 10 years had given me the design of the course, but how to teach online was zero." There was consensus that learning to teach online involved learning how to put appropriate course content on a website, and develop activities, projects, and assignments. But a separate skill was still the actual process of teaching online. Participants struggled with the teaching component of online teaching, and the issue of facilitating learning among online students. One respondent discussed this issue as follows:

> One of the problems with distance learning that makes it difficult is so often, people want to do it by themselves. They want to take the course because it fits into their schedule. The problem is that's not how learning happens. If I want to sit in my bedroom and read a book then I'm just going to continue to think the same thoughts unless I'm out with other people. And I think that's the real difficulty of distance learning. It's got to be adept at helping collaborate and work together. It's really hard to change how people think and to affect them if they're not part of a community.

Before respondents started to teach online, many noted that they had preconceived perceptions of online teachers. Some made comments like, "online instructors were anti-social," or "aliens." However, some noted that they had taken online courses or developed them during their graduate program and understood the online teacher's role. Many participants described their perceptions of online instructors before they, themselves, began to teach online. Some participants noted that they were "skeptical" of teaching online and equated online teaching to "students and instructors being isolated." One participant who prefers face-to-face instruction stated that "I could not understand how someone could teach online, it was so foreign." While others noted that the common perception of teaching online was that it was easier because it didn't require interaction. One respondent in the curriculum and instruction field noted frustration regarding the misconception that online teaching was easy. Many in the group agreed with one respondent who said that "because online education is marketed as you can earn an online degree in your pajamas that it implies that it is easy and relaxed." The respondents note that this is a misconception because in their view online instruction is an investment, is stressful, and is "more time consuming because you feel like you work 24/7."

Participants who had little or no prior experience teaching online were asked to reflect on their preparation for their first online teaching experience. The general consensus on their first online courses was summed up by one participant as follows: "I would be embarrassed to show you what I had done (for that first class). I had no help and basically had to figure it out on my own. It was terrible." Another stated "I knew those (first) courses were poorly designed. I wasn't happy with that but that's the process for improving as you move along." Upon reflection, most participants recognized that their initial attempts at online teaching were less than successful, and there was a motivation to improve that was expressed by many. That motivation was based, in part, on fear of failure. As one participant noted, "Everything that I learned I learned on my own because of that very factor—failure, and I didn't like what I saw." Another stated, "There's nothing like the thought of failing to help motivate you to seek it (help) out." Concern for the student was paramount in these discussions, and there was a great sense that instructors couldn't fail to give their students meaningful learning experiences. They simply did not want to let their students down. When discussing initial online teaching experiences, that motivation derived from the need to provide quality learning experiences to students was present throughout each focus group. Although many focus group members have since gained a good deal of experience teaching online, that motivation was still present, and seemed to serve as an ongoing source of motivation for continuously improving online courses.

There were definite patterns or characteristics of instructors who had successful experiences learning to teach online, and they typically involved smaller steps toward teaching online (as opposed to jumping in, as was the experience of many). One participant who had prior experience teaching online discussed her experience at a different institution. That institution provided an in-depth face-to-face training session that all faculty new to online teaching had to attend before becoming online instructors. Another started out as a graduate assistant in an online course, which allowed her to learn how the instructor taught. One more talked about her experience developing a blended learning course, which was partially online and partially face to face, as a good way of moving gradually into online teaching. These experiences gave participants time to learn and provided them with role models from whom to learn. Participants who had more experience with technology, in general, seemed to have an easier time than those who were not tech savvy. Those who were interested in learning to teach online also had better first-time experiences than those who were not as interested in teaching online.

The Evolution of the Online Instructor

Even the most experienced online instructors in these focus groups did not see themselves as "there" yet, in terms of their online teaching abilities. Most agreed that with experience came more strategies and options they could employ. Reflections on early online teaching experiences were mainly focused on the overall course level: getting a course set up, and teaching a course, for example. As online instructors matured in their experience, they became able to focus more on individual student needs within a course. One participant summed up her feelings about teaching online versus face to face as follows:

> It's like throwing darts at a dart board. You're just trying to find one way to hit a bull's eye with each and every student. It is harder (than teaching in a traditional classroom). Someone who is good at distance ed., (they) are finding different ways (to reach each student) and you are spending so much more time and it is hard.

The idea that online instructors find different ways to connect with students resonated with focus group members. Examples of those different ways were discussed by several focus groups. They included the use of video conferencing in place of face-to-face lectures, having students read course materials posted online and then participating in online discussions rather than face-to-face discussions, and holding Skype sessions to provide students with one-on-one feedback that would have normally taken place after formal face-to-face class sessions. All of these examples illustrate the creative ways online instructors have found to reach students. They also demonstrate the maturation process of online instructors, and the increasing complexity, based on an individual student focus, with which online courses are taught by these experienced instructors.

Focus group participants agreed that the finding of "different ways," along with changes to course content and advances in technology mean that they spend much more time on their online courses than they would have in similar face-to-face courses. One respondent noted that her online courses were continually evolving due to both updates in the field and new content being developed, but also due to new technologies becoming available. In any given semester, one or both of those areas may change. One participant noted that, "If you look at one course from one semester to the next, the course will have the same content, but the way that it arrived will be significantly different."

LIMITATIONS AND RECOMMENDATIONS FOR FUTURE RESEARCH

As this study was focused on faculty in one college of a major southeastern university, more research is needed in order to determine the generalizability of the outcomes across departments, schools, and colleges in the variety of postsecondary institutions offering online courses. The researchers believe their findings are noteworthy and provide good bases for future research on this topic in other settings.

This research addressed the topic of online teaching in a college of education, where the focus of the college is in line with the topic of this research. Research in other, noneducation schools and colleges is advocated, as is research in other types of postsecondary educational venues, including community or junior colleges.

DISCUSSION

The haste to move to online teaching and learning caught many entities off guard. The advent of the online course meant entirely new ways of teaching in higher education. Courses were put online with little thought to the differences between online and face-to-face teaching. There was no consideration given to the different roles of online instructors, nor to the skills or knowledge needed by those new online instructors. There was also very little time for instructors to learn to teach online, as the growth of online learning happened very quickly.

When asked to teach online, instructors looked to their institutions for support and guidance. However, those institutions were able to offer limited support simply because they were in the same situation as the instructors. The concept of online teaching and learning was new to everyone. Institutions could draw from few resources in order to help instructors prepare, simply because there were no resources. There was no history at which to look for guidance, there were no models to follow, and there was a paucity of research on the topic. That seemed to result in a "do what you think is best"-type philosophy with regard to support given to new online instructors, and further resulted in instructors learning through a trial and error-type approach while they were actually teaching. Formal resources at the institutional level only improved after a body of knowledge on online teaching began to be developed.

IMPLICATIONS

With the growing popularity of distance education, institutions must ensure quality online instruction, which includes supporting instructors in transitioning to online teaching via professional development. This study presents specifics on the paths instructors follow when they learn to teach online and their experiences regarding how they improved their online instruction. This study is different because it examined the trial-and-error processes used by novice online instructors as they learned to teach online, and documents the process of skill development in the online instructor. It followed the processes instructors took to develop expertise, as they became experienced online instructors.

It is important to develop a body of knowledge on how instructors learn to teach online so that best practices can be found and used by future online instructors. This research will help to develop that body of knowledge. This research has practical implications, as well. An understanding of how faculty learn to teach online is helpful for those who develop continuing professional development for faculty members. For example, results of this study show that small group learning opportunities and the use of mentors were both helpful in learning to teach online. These types of activities could be implemented as part of continuing education for faculty members learning to teach online. This study also presents information on what these instructors found unhelpful, and what methods and strategies did not work. Unfortunately, many of these methods focus group members found unhelpful are still being used today.

Crawford-Ferre and Weist (2012) note that "Most instructors new to online teaching begin with little to no training or preparation specific to this delivery model" (p. 13). To this point, the practice of learning to teach online has been a haphazard, often trial-and-error process. Will this change for the next generation of online instructors? What will the experiences of new online instructors 10 years from now look like? It is believed that research of this nature will help in the preparation of future online instructors.

REFERENCES

Allen, E., & Seaman, J. (2007). *Online nation: Five years of growth in online learning*. Needham, MA: The Sloan Consortium.

Allen, E., & Seaman, J. (2010). *Learning on demand: Online education in the United States, 2009*. Retrieved from http://www.sloanconsortium.ord/publications/survey/pdf/learningondemand/pdf

Baran, E., Correia, A. P., & Thompson, A. (2011). Transforming online teaching practice: Critical analysis of the literature on the roles and competencies of online teachers. *Distance Education, 32*(3), 421-439.

Crawford-Ferre, H. G., & Weist, L. R. (2012). Effective online instruction in higher education. *Quarterly Review of Distance Education, 13*(1), 11-14.

Fish, W. W., & Wickersham, L. E. (2009). Best practices for online instructors: Reminders. *Quarterly Review of Distance Education, 10*(3), 279-284.

Gaytan, J. (2009). Analyzing online education through the lens of institutional theory and practice: The need for research-based and -validated frameworks for planning, designing, delivering, and assessing online instruction. *The Delta Pi Epsilon Journal, 51*(2), 62-75.

Ke, F. (2010). Examining online teaching, cognitive, and social presence for adult students. *Computers and Education, 55*(2), 808-820.

Kolowich, S. (2012). Conflicted: Faculty and online education, 2012. Retrieved March 20, 2013 from http://www.insidehighered.com/news/survey/conflicted-faculty-and-online-education-2012

Krueger, R. A. (1994). *Focus groups: A practical guide for applied research*. Thousand Oaks, CA: SAGE.

Kugel, P. (1993). How professors develop as teachers. *Studies in Higher Education, 18*(3), 315-329.

Larreamendy-Joerns, J., & Leindhardt, G. (2006). Going the distance with online education. *Review of Educational Research, 76*(4), 567-605.

Macdonald, J., & Poniatowska, B. (2011). Designing the professional development of staff for teaching online: An OU (UK) case study. *Distance Education, 32*(1), 119-134.

Merriam, S. B. (1998). *Qualitative research and case study application in education*. San Francisco, CA: Jossey-Bass.

Moller, L., Foshay, W., & Huett, J. (2008). The evolution of distance education: Implications for instructional design on the potential of the web. *TechTrends, 52*(4), 66-70.

Orr, R., Williams, M. R., & Pennington, K. (2009). Institutional efforts to support faculty in online teaching. *Innovative Higher Education, 34*(4), 257-268.

Palloff, R. M., & Pratt, K. (2001). *Lessons from the cyberspace classroom: The realities of online teaching*. San Francisco, CA: Jossey Bass.

Patton, M. Q. (1990). *Qualitative evaluation and research methods*. Thousand Oaks, CA: SAGE.

Pontes, M. C. & Pontes, N. M. H. (2012). Distance education enrollment is associated with greater academic progress among first generation low-income undergraduate students in the US in 2008. *Online Journal of Distance Learning Administration 15*(1).

Shattuck, J., Dubins, B., & Zilberman, D. (2011). MarylandOnline's inter-institutional project to train higher education adjunct faculty to teach online. *The International Review of Research in Open and Distance Learning, 12*(2), 41-61.

Smith, T. C. (2005). Fifty-one competencies for online instruction. *The Journal of Educators Online, 2*(2), 1-18.

Wise, B., & Rothman, R. (2010). The online learning imperative: A solution to three looming crises in education. *Education Digest, 76*(3), 52-58.

Xu, H., & Morris, L. V. (2007). Collaborative course development for online courses. *Innovative Higher Education, 32*(1), 35-47.

Young, A., & Lewis, C. W. (2008). Teacher education programmes delivered at a distance: An examination of distance student perceptions. *Teaching and Teacher Education, 24*(3), 601-609.

PART V

LEGAL AND ACCREDITATION ISSUES

CHAPTER 22

STANDARDS, ACCREDITATION, BENCHMARKS, AND GUIDELINES IN DISTANCE EDUCATION

Soonhwa Seok
D'youville College

Standards are the results of concerted efforts to improve the quality of education found in distance education. Legal and ethical standards are needed to ensure a positive educational environment. Participants from different cultural, physical, economical, and intellectual backgrounds should have equal access to all the positive aspects of distance education. Standards support the consistent ways to maintain high quality distance education via collaborations among different regional institutions. They ensure the efficiency and usability of learning by reducing the differences between learning experiences of different regions. The standards allow all stakeholders access and adapt learning experiences based on their needs and learning goals.

INTRODUCTION

This article reviews the standards, accreditation, benchmarks, and guidelines in distance education. Technology is changing everything around us at unprecedented speeds. We are currently in a new culture, aptly named the digital age. These massive technological advancements have brought

Beyond the Online Course: Leadership Perspectives on e-Learning
pp. 347–364

about significant evolutions in the mode of instruction. One of benefits from this rapidly evolving approach to education is the increased access to distance education. The needs of modern society have placed new demands on distance education. It is now, more than ever, a necessity in the ever evolving world of education.

Distance education has also produced and promoted favorable learning environments for learners who have limitations of time and space (Ciavarelli, 2003). The same is true for individuals in living remote areas who do not have convenient access to institutions of higher education (Leh, 2002).

Postsecondary institutions of higher education have responded to the instructional opportunities afforded by the World Wide Web and the Internet through the offering of courses and online degree programs (Guri-Rosenblit, 1999). Additionally, there has been a movement to establish new universities that primarily focus on distance education utilizing the Internet as a primary source for the delivery of instruction (Tait, 2003). Leh (2002) stated, "It is estimated that in 2002 about 85% of two- and four-year colleges would offer distance education programs and that by the year 2006 enrollment in distance education learning programs will increase by 1.5 million students" (p. 88).

This growth has been largely due to the ease of accessing instruction offered over the Internet and in combination with other forms of distance education (Belanger & Jordan, 2000). Students who previously were not able to conveniently participate in higher education through traditional campus-based environments are now able to enroll and complete coursework or degree programs without relocating or changing their lifestyles (Rossman, 1992).

The number of postsecondary educational institutions implementing distance education continues to increase. With this increase, concerns regarding the quality of distance education have arisen. A major concern is the need for evaluation strategies which assess the effectiveness of the online courses (Childress, Heaton, & Pauley, 2002).

Program evaluation and processes are needed to ensure high quality instruction given the growth in distance education and the varied circumstances under which online courses and degrees of distance education are offered. Standards, guidelines, and benchmarks are the criteria used to develop distance education programs.

STANDARDS

Marshall (2004) stated that "standards represent a significant investment of resources and are consequently driven by a desire to solve specific problems in particular context that are relevant to those providing the resources" (p. 599). Dean (1990) argued that standards were to play a role as "the performance expectations within the profession" (p. 2). Dean believed that standards were to facilitate the productivity of performance by clarifying and explaining the goals and main accomplishments.

Many educators, educational institutions, and governments have increased their scrutiny regarding distance education standards. Improved standards are the result of the effort to solve the specific problems (Dean, 1990; Marshall, 2004). A way that guarantees the maintenance of the quality of distance education pedagogic approaches is the development of e-learning standards (Oliver & Liber, 2003).

The leading international distance education institutions are developing new standards for distance education because their standards support the need of distance education innovation (Jones, 2002; Marshall, 2004).

Two benefits of standards are summarized through the literature review. First, standards are created, in part, to reduce the costs of content resource discovery and to develop and maintain the quality of content. These standards represent rigid guidance of distance education implementation regarding the quality of instructional content and need. Therefore, the implemented standards yielded quality distance learning experiences. These experiences are so good that some learning resources are reused for several years following their initial implementation. It should be noted that online courses has to be updated within three or four years of their amendments.

For example, resources consistently meeting the prescribed standards have provided a large extent of available online learning material, enough so, that users choose learning resources which meet their instructional needs without having to waste time or incur increased financial expenditure (Center for Educational Technology Interoperability Standards, 2004; Jones, 2002; Marshall, 2004; Olivier & Liber, 2003). Second, standards guarantee greater efficiency through interoperability between systems. Individual distance education resources can be easily accessed from learning system to learning system.

Universal standards also reduce the difference between the learning experiences in varying educational systems. These differences can be minimized so much that different educational bodies can collaborate their distance education material in order to create a higher quality program while reducing the time and money required in developing and maintaining distance education resources (Dobbs, 2000; Jones; Olivier & Liber).

ACCREDITATION

With increasing attention on distance education, the six U.S. accrediting bodies have completed a set of recommendations that evaluate and develop distance education programs in America (Carnevale, 2001; McDonald, 2002). Lezberg (1998) defines accreditation as "a status granted to educational institutions found to meet or exceed stated criteria of institutional quality" (p. 27).

Regional commissions have defined their distance education standards through a series of guidelines, recommendations, and sets of commitments.

Because online education is a relatively new approach, most regional commissions emphasize standards that are broad and flexible in order to learn and adapt to the unforeseeable conditions and expectations placed on this form of distance education. Each regional institution also has different online learning experiences, needs, instructional traditions, and values and principles.

However, accreditation brings consistency and stability along with improved learning conditions through collaboration among commissions; "commitment to cooperation among the eight regional commissions directed toward a consistent approach to the evaluation of distance education informed through collaboration with others and commitment to supporting good practice among institutions" (Council of Regional Accrediting Commissions, 2000, p. 1).

Although the standards or commitments are different among regional organizations based on their distance education experiences, each commission grants accreditation to an institution when the institution has (a) distinctly stated postsecondary educational goals, (b) collective and systematic learning resources to implement distance education experience, and (c) the quality distance learning to gain the expected learning outcomes (Lezberg, 1998).

Lezberg noted that the regional accrediting associations were private and not seeking profits. The federal government also identified these associations as reliable and professional judges of quality learning institutions. Lezberg also stated that the regional accrediting agencies' main responsibility was to control the quality of education. In order to fulfill this responsibility, the regional accrediting agencies created three general requirements for distance education. Distance education:

- is assumed to be a part of the educational system curriculum;
- pursues the institution's academic responsibilities and has been standardized based on the general accreditation standards already in place; and
- is to be evaluated for accreditation in the same manner as all other components of the learning experience.

The seven regional accrediting commissions are:

1. Commission on Higher Education, Middle States Association of Colleges and Schools;

2. Commission on Institutions of Higher Education, New England Association of Schools and Colleges;

3. Commission on Institutions of Higher Education, North Central Association of Colleges and Schools;

4. Commission on Colleges, The Northwest Association of Schools and Colleges;

5. Commission on Colleges, Southern Association of Colleges and Schools;

6. Accrediting Commission for Community and Junior Colleges, Western Association of Schools and Colleges; and

7. Accrediting Commission for Senior Colleges, Western Association of Schools and Colleges.

The standards of the regional accrediting associations are to be comprehensive. Similar standards of quality are to be fulfilled throughout the different regions, although the specific comments of the regional standards happen to be dissimilar (Council of Regional Accrediting Commissions, 2000).

BENCHMARKS AND GUIDELINES

In response to attention to the quality of distance education, higher education organizations developed guidelines for distance education. Most are related across and alike in terms of facilitating the best practice, performance, and implementations as well as designing instructional strategies in order to ensure the quality. Therefore, the guideline represents integral comments on what is thought highly of as prevalent best learning practice. The guidelines are intended to provide online learning institutions with a whole source to guide their distance education plans and instructional experiences. Therefore, the guidelines play a role as the self-assessment framework for distance education programs. Quite a few researchers reported that technology was productive and had gains in distance education experiences. Distance education administrators and faculties believe that a systematic device should be developed in order to facilitate the effective distance education.

A significant amount of research focuses on integrating new experimental and pedagogical models. The researchers studied how to (a) build the effective collaborative learning community, (b) evaluate the learning programs, (c) develop distance learning curriculum as well as instructional delivery methods, and (d) define distance learning participants' roles. In response to those efforts to yield the productive pedagogical gains and regional accrediting commissions require their accredited institutions to develop their own practical guideline as the framework. The guidelines should be developed based on their own distance education experiences and needs. They are the promulgations of their instructional implementations to ensure the quality distance learning because they are the written list of carrying out the instructional procedures.

The guidelines are also meant to assess and evaluate their own distance education experiences (Dasher-Alston & Patton, 1998; Lezberg, 1998; Western Cooperative for Educational Telecommunications, 2000). Accrediting commissions argue that through the guidelines the accredited institutions should clearly show their sincere intentions:

- To develop the institutions' academic processes of implementing effective distance learning. There should be clearly defined institution's educational mission, learning goals, and objectives. Curriculum development including instructional tools, learning resources, and the appropriate use of technology. The instructional delivery medium should be demonstrated to achieve the expected end results through the learning experience.

- To professionally assist the learner and faculty with easy access to learning resources. The resources are meant to stimulate learners' intellectual curiosity and support the instructor.

- To provide staff development opportunities through which the faculty will be efficient in managing the instructional technology.

- To assess the learner outcomes and evaluate the effectiveness of the online learning products and courses.

Some higher educational institutions developed guidelines for distance education practices. The guidelines are the outcome of the need of implementing the best learning experience and adapting effective instructional methods in order to ensure the quality of distance education. Therefore, they are similar across the accredited organizations in different regions (Dasher-Alston & Patton, 1998). The Western Cooperative for Educational Telecommunications (WCET) published, *Best Practices for Electronically Offered Degree and Certificate Programs*, or *Guidelines for the Evaluation of Electronically Offered Degree and Certificate Programs in 2000* (Carnevale, 2001). The eight regional accreditation commissions developed them.

The best practices are regarded as the essentials that are the mirror of the pedagogical quality considered worthwhile in the contemporary, digital age considering the region's educational experience. They are to be increased by the regional commissions' member accredited institutions. Therefore, they are considered a product moving in improvement. The goals of best practices are to assist the accredited institutions—as the criteria—in developing the online learning curriculum including instructional strategies, learning materials, and selecting the appropriate learning resources and technologies. In addition, best practices plays a major role as the framework for the evaluation of the accredited institutions' distance education programs (WCET, 2000). Therefore, best practice stands for the primary pedagogical value across the regional commissions. WCET said that the values were:

- The collaborative learning community; the best educational experiences are to be yielded when the instructional activities are built through the qualified educators cooperative involvements in designing, deploying and facilitating the learning activities.
- The learning experience filled with active interactions.
- The systematically organized, integral instructional programs as the outcome of coherent curricula; the program should specify the learning outcomes.
- The capability to provide the learning resources as well as students' academic needs in pursuing learners' achievement.
- Self-assessments and evaluations of their own programs with the specific learning emphases.

WECT (2000) also argued that best practices had five dimensions, each of which was a particular and comprehensive element of distance education. They are institutional context and comment, curriculum and instruction, faculty support, student support, and evaluation and assessment:

- Institutional Context and Commitment: Electronically offered programs both support and extend the roles of educational institutions. Increasingly they are integral to academic organization, with growing implications for institutional infrastructure (p. 2).
- Curriculum and Instruction: Methods change, but standards of quality endure. The important issues are not technical but curriculum-driven and pedagogical. The big decisions are made by qualified faculty and focus on learning outcomes for an increasingly diverse student population (p. 4).
- Faculty Support: Faculty roles are becoming increasingly diverse and reorganized. For example, the same person may not perform both the tasks of course development and direct instruction to stu-

dents. Regardless of who performs which of these tasks, important issues are involved (p. 8).

- Student Support: College and universities have learned that the twenty-first century student is different, both demographically and geographically, from students of previous generations. These differences affect everything from admissions policy to library services. Reaching these students, and serving them appropriately, are major challenges to today's institutions (p. 9).

- Evaluation and Assessment: Both the assessment of student achievement and evaluation of the overall program take on added importance as new techniques evolve. For example, in asynchronous programs the element of seat time is essentially removed from the equation. For these reasons, the institution conducts sustained, evidence-based and participatory inquiry as to whether distance learning programs are achieving objectives. He results of such inquiry are used to guide curriculum design and delivery, pedagogy, and educational processes, and may affect future policy and budgets perhaps have implications for the institutions' roles and mission (p. 12).

The National Education Association (NEA) and Blackboard Inc. validated the current benchmarks to examine whether they are essential and necessary to maintain the quality online through the case study. The 24 benchmarks are regarded as the essential within seven categories. They are (a) institutional support benchmarks, (b) course development benchmarks, (c) teaching/learning benchmarks, (d) course structure benchmarks, (e) student support benchmarks, (f) faculty support benchmarks, and (g) evaluation and assessment benchmarks.

Appendix A contains the 24 benchmarks. The first category, institutional support benchmarks deals with technology as the medium of delivery, infrastructure and its security matters. The second category, course development benchmarks, deals with (a) course development, (b) instruction delivery and the technology appropriate to learning outcomes, (c) instructional materials, (d) student involvement as the self-director regarding analysis, and (e) synthesis and evaluation. The third category, teaching/learning benchmarks, deals with students' interaction, feedback, and the appropriateness of resources. The fourth category, course structure benchmarks, deals with (a) advice on self-motivation, (b) access to the minimal technology, (c) the outlines of course objectives, (d) concepts, (e) ideas, (f) library resources, (g) the expected times for student assignment completion, and (h) faculty response. The fifth category, student support benchmarks, dealt with information about programs and hands-on training assistance in learning resources. The sixth category, faculty support

benchmarks deals with assistance in technology and transition from traditional instruction to online teaching. The seventh category, evaluation
and assessment benchmarks, deals with the evaluation of learning outcomes and program effectiveness (The Institute for Higher Education
Policy, 2000). The *Seven Principles of Good Practice* were developed by
Chickering and Zelda, and first published in 1987 (Chickerign & Ehrmann, 1997). The seven principles include:

- Good practice encourages contacts between students and faculty.
- Good practice develops reciprocity and cooperation among stu-
  dents.
- Good practice uses active learning techniques.
- Good practice gives prompt feedback.
- Good practice emphasizes time on task.
- Good practice communicates high expectations.
- Good practice respects diverse talents and ways of learning.

Guiding Principles for Distance Learning and Teaching was published in
1999 by American Distance Education Consortium (ADEC, 1999) and
they were revised to four categories with 24 principles (American Distance
Education Consortium, 2002). ADEC argues that online learning has the
quality of (a) facilitating constructive communications, (b) learner centered, (c) directed learning systems, (d) interchanged learning and teaching experience, (e) collaborative knowledge building community, and (f)
authentic learning (American Distance Education Consortium, 1999).
ADEC believes the principles are the most effective strategies in order to
ensure the quality of online learning experiences. ADEC guiding principles for distance learning are contained in Appendix B and C. The outlines are:

- The learning experience must have a clear purpose with tightly
  focused outcomes and objectives.
- The learner is actively engaged.
- The learning environment makes appropriate use of a variety of
  media.
- Learning environments must include problem-based as well as
  knowledge-based learning.
- Learning experiences should support interaction and the development of communities of interest.
- The practice of distance learning contributes to the larger social
  mission of education and training in a democratic society (pp. 1-2).

The four categories included (a) design for active and effective learning, (b) support the needs of learners, (c) develop and maintain the technological and human infrastructure, and (d) sustain administrative and organizational commitment" (American Distance Education Consortium, 2002, p. 1).

Based on the published guidelines before 1999, the University of Illinois faculty seminar team from sixteen different affiliations suggested six questions assumed to be critical to evaluate online education. They included:

- Is the teaching style innovative?
- Is learning competence equal or superior to that of a traditional classroom?
- Are students engaged in the material?
- Is there interaction between professors and their students, and between the students themselves?
- Is access to technical support readily available? and
- For online programs that are more extensive, such as entire degree programs, are the signs of academic maturity present? (The University of Illinois faculty seminar team, 1999, p. 39).

Ragan (2000) said that an emerging set of guiding principles and practices reflected the assembled thoughts of faculty from Penn State, Lincoln, and Cheyney universities. The set is meant to evaluate the technology integration into the learning practice and the instructional methodologies. The set includes three main and two supplementary categories, which represent that the most important goal is to enhance quality learning. Ragan believed technology and learner support categories were supportive of the goal of quality learning and the major components of the educational events were "learning goals and content presentation, interactions, and assessment and measurement" (p. 4). Five categories addressed as:

- "Category I: Learning Goals and Content Presentation"
- "Category II: Interactions"
- "Category III: Assessment and Measurement"
- "Category IV: Instructional Media and Tools"
- "Category V: Learner Support Systems and Services" (pp. 4-6)

The authors, the publishing dates, the names, and the URLs of the guidelines are listed in Table 1.

Table 1.   The Authors, the Publishing Dates, the Names, and the URLs of the Guidelines

Authors, Date	Name	URL
WCET, 2000	Best practices for electronically offered degree and certificate programs	http://www.wcet.info/resources/accreditation/Accrediting%20-%20Best%20Practices.pdf
NEA & Blackboard Inc., 2000	Quality On the Line: Benchmarks for Success in Internet-Based Distance Education	http://www.ihep.org/Pubs/PDF/Quality.pdf
Chickerign & Ehrmann, 1996	The seven principles of good practice	http://www.tltgroup.org/programs/seven.html
ADEC, 1997	Guiding principles for distance learning and teaching	http://www.adec.edu/admin/papers/distance-learning_principles.html
Penn State University, 1999	An emerging set of guiding principles and practices	http://www.outreach.psu.edu/DE/ide/guiding_principles/

CONCLUSION

Part I of the *Research in Distance Education Series* reviewed research examining and analyzing the research topics, methodologies, and quality in distance education. The researchers said that to enhance the quality of distance learning program evaluations should be implemented. Standards, guidelines, and benchmarks are the criteria to evaluate the program.

Part II of the series outlined the definitions, benefits, practices of standards, guidelines, and benchmarks. They are "performance expectations within the profession" of pedagogy and curriculum, instructional strategies, supports for learners' and faculty's need, administration and technology. They are to enhance accessibility, adaptability, and clarity of communication in distance education, examining the quality of learning, learning community, digital resources and inclusion. The various stakeholders developed standards, guidelines, and benchmarks based on their experience and their needs at institutional or regional level to maximize their best practice.

This literature review indicates three problems regarding the existing standards. First, they do not include the matters of inclusion of cultural, physical, economical and intellectual differences and learners' learning preferences. Flexibility and contextual accommodation is the biggest benefit of distance education. Therefore, the standard on digital inclusion should be strengthened. Second, as mentioned earlier, standards, benchmarks, and guidelines were developed at the regional or institutional level. We assume that if everyone can share information via the Internet, then the standards exerting an ethical or legal effect on distance education, should also be considered. Third, stakeholders and technology in distance education build an intellectual partnership. Who teaches? Who is the stakeholder? Who delivers distance education? Will there be developed standards which protect the human's intellectual property?

We, stakeholders of distance education hope that standards will be developed at the national and international level to enhance accessibility, adaptability, clarity of communication, and humanization.

REFERENCES

American Distance Education Consortium. (1999). *ADEC guiding principles for distance learning and teaching.* Retrieved August 21, 2005, from http://www.adec.edu/admin/papers/distance-teaching_principles.html

American Distance Education Consortium. (2002). *ADEC guiding principles for distance learning.* Retrieved September 22, 2005, from http://www.adec.edu/admin/papers/distance-learning_principles.html

Belanger, F., & Jordan, D. (2000). *Evaluating and implementation of distance learning: Technologies, tools, and techniques.* Hershey, PA: Idea Group.

Carnevale, D. (2001). Accrediting groups issue recommendations for distance-education programs. *The Chronicle of Higher Education, March.* Retrieved September 18, 2005, from http://chronicle.com/free/2001/03/2001032301u.htm

Center for Educational Technology Interoperability Standards. (2004). *Learning technology standards: An overview.* Retrieved September 9, 2005, from http://www.cetis.ac.uk/statics/standards.html

Chickering, W. A., & Ehrmann, C. S. (1997, October). Implementing the seven principles: Technology as lever. *AAHE Bulletin,* 3-6. Retrieved September 30, 2005, from http://www.clt.astate.edu/clthome/Implementing%20the%20Seven%20Principles,%20Ehrmann%20and%20Chickering.pdf

Childress, R., Heaton, L. A., & Pauley, R. (2002). Quality control for online graduate course delivery: A case study. *Computers in the School, 19*(3/4), 103-114.

Ciavarelli, A. (2003). *Assessing the quality of online instruction: Integrating instructional quality and web usability assessments* (Report No. CG032657). (ERIC Document Reproduction Service No. ED480084)

Council of Regional Accrediting Commissions. (2000). *Draft: Statement of the regional accrediting commissions on the evaluation of electronically offered degree and certificate programs and guidelines for the evaluation of electronically offered degree an certificate programs.* Retrieved September15, 2005, from http://www.wcet.info/resources/publications/Guidelines.PDF

Dasher-Alston, M. R., & Patton, W. G. (1988). Evaluation criteria for distance learning. *Planning for Higher Education, 27*(1), 11-17.

Dean, J. P. (1990). Using standards to improve performance. *Australian Journal of Educational Technology, 6*(2), 75-91.

Dobbs, K. (2000). The state of online learning—what the online world needs now: quality. *Training Magazine, 37,* 84-94.

Guri-Rosenblit, S. (1999). *Distance and campus universities: Tensions and interactions.* New York: Pergamon.

Institute for Higher Education Policy. (2000). *Quality on the line: Benchmarks for success in Internet-based distance education.* Washington, DC: Higher Education Policy.

Jonassen, D., Davidson, M., Collins, M., Campbell, J., & Hagg, B. B. (1995). Constructivism and computer-mediated communication. *The American Journal of Distance Education, 9*(2), 7-26.

Jones, R. E. (2002). *Implications of SCORM and emerging e-learning standards on engineering education.* Retrieved September 30, 2005, from http://falcon .tamucc.edu/~ejones/papers/ASEE02.pdf

Leh, A. S. (2002). Striving for quality control in distance education. *Computers in the Schools, 19*(3), 87-102.

Lezberg, K. A. (1998). Quality control in distance education: The role of regional accreditation. *American Journal of Distance Education, 12*(2), 26-35.

Marshall, S. (2004). E-learning standards: Open enablers of learning or compliance strait jackets? In R. Atkinson, C. McBeath, D. Jonas-Swyer, & R. Phillips (Eds.), *Beyond the comfort zone: Proceedings of the 21st ASCILITE Conference* (pp. 596-605). Perth, West Australia. Retrieved August 30, 2005, from http:// www.ascilite.org.au/conferences/perth04/procs/marshall.html

McDonald, J. (2002). Is "as good as face-to-face" as good as it gets? *Journal of Asynchronous Learning Networks, 6*(2), 10-23.

Olivier, B., & Liber, O. (2003). Learning technology interoperability standards. In A. Littlejohn (Ed.), *Reusing online resources: A sustainable approach to e-Learning* (pp. 146-155). London: Kogan Page.

Ragan, C. L. (2000). Good teaching is good teaching: The relationship between guiding principles for distance and general education. *The Journal of General Education, 49*(1), 10-22.

Rossman, P. (1992). *The emerging worldwide electronic university: Information age global higher education.* Westport, CT: Greenwood.

Tait, A. (2003). Rethinking learner support in the Open University UK: A case study. In A. Tai & R. Mills. (Eds.), *Rethinking learner support in distance education* (pp. 185-197). New York: Routledge Falmer.

University of Illinois Faculty Seminar Team. (1999). *Teaching at an Internet distance: The pedagogy of online teaching and learning: The report of a 1998-1999 University of Illinois Faculty Seminar.* Retrieved September 23, 2005, from http:// www.vpaa.uillinois.edu/reports_retreats/tid_final-12-5.doc

Western Cooperative for Educational Telecommunications. (2000). *Best practices for electronically offered degree and certificate programs.* Retrieved September 20, 2005, from http://www.wcet.info/resources/accreditation/Accrediting%20- %Best%20Practices.pdf

APPENDIX A

Quality on the Line

Benchmarks for success in Internet-based distance education prepared by the Institute for Higher Education Policy (2000).

Institutional Support Benchmarks

- A documented technology plan that includes electronic security measures (i.e., password protection, encryption, backup systems) is in place and operational to ensure both quality standards and the integrity and validity of information.
- The reliability of the technology delivery system is as failsafe as possible.
- A centralized system provides support for building and maintaining the distance education infrastructure.

Course Development Benchmarks

- Guidelines regarding minimum standards are used for course development, design, and delivery, while learning outcomes—not the availability of existing technology—determine the technology being used to deliver course content.
- Instructional materials are reviewed periodically to ensure they meet program standards.
- Courses are designed to require students to engage themselves in analysis, synthesis, and evaluation as part of their course and program requirements.

Teaching/Learning Benchmarks

- Student interaction with faculty and other students is an essential characteristic and is facilitated through a variety of ways, including voice-mail and/or e-mail.
- Feedback to student assignments and questions is constructive and provided in a timely manner.
- Students are instructed in the proper methods of effective research, including assessment of the validity of resources.

Course Structure Benchmarks

- Before starting an online program, students are advised about the program to determine (1) if they possess the self-motivation and commitment to learn at a distance and (2) if they have access to the minimal technology required by the course design.

- Students are provided with supplemental course information that outlines course objectives, concepts, and ideas, and learning outcomes for each course are summarized in a clearly written, straightforward statement.
- Students have access to sufficient library resources that may include a "virtual library" accessible through the World Wide Web.
- Faculty and students agree on expectations regarding times for student assignment completion and faculty response.

Student Support Benchmarks

- Students receive information about programs, including admission requirements, tuition and fees, books and supplies, technical and proctoring requirements, and student support services.
- Students are provided with hands-on training and information to aid them in securing material through electronic databases, interlibrary loans, government archives, new services, and other sources.
- Throughout the duration of the course/program, students have access to technical assistance, including detailed instructions regarding the electronic media used, practice sessions prior to the beginning of the course, and convenient access to technical support staff.
- Questions directed to student service personnel are answered accurately and quickly, with a structured system in place to address student complaints.

Faculty Support Benchmarks

- Technical assistance in course development is available to faculty, who are encouraged to use it.
- Faculty members are assisted in the transition from classroom teaching to online instruction and are assessed during the process.
- Instructor training and assistance, including peer mentoring, continues through the progression of the online course.
- Faculty members are provided with written resources to deal with issues arising from student use of electronically accessed data.

Evaluation and Assessment Benchmarks

- The program's educational effectiveness and teaching/learning process is assessed through an evaluation process that uses several methods and applies specific standards.
- Data on enrollment, costs, and successful/innovative uses of technology are used to evaluate program effectiveness.
- Intended learning outcomes are reviewed regularly to ensure clarity, utility, and appropriateness.

APPENDIX B

ADEC Guiding Principles for Distance Teaching and Learning

Retrieved May 1, 2005, from http://www
.adec.edu/admin/papers/distance-teaching_
principles.html

- The learning experience must have a clear purpose with tightly focused outcomes and objectives.

    Web-based learning designs must consider the nature of content, specific context, desired learning outcomes and characteristics of the learner. Learner-centered strategies include modular, stand-alone units that are compatible with short bursts of learning. Learning modules may also be open, flexible and self-directing.

- The learner is actively engaged.

    Active, hands-on, concrete experiences are highly effective. Learning by doing, analogy, and assimilation are increasingly important pedagogical forms. Where possible, learning outcomes should relate to real-life experiences through simulation and application.

- The learning environment makes appropriate use of a variety of media.

    Various learning styles are best engaged by using a variety of media to achieve learning outcomes. Selection of media may also depend on nature of content, learning goals, access to technology, and the local learning environment.

- Learning environments must include problem-based as well as knowledge-based learning.

Problem-based learning involves higher order thinking skills such as analysis, synthesis, and evaluation while knowledge-based learning involves recall, comprehension, and application.

- Learning experiences should support interaction and the development of communities of interest.

  Learning is social and sensitive to context. Learning experiences based on interaction and collaboration support learning communities while building a support network to enhance learning outcomes. Multiple interactions, group collaboration and cooperative learning may provide increased levels of interaction and simulation.

- The practice of distance learning contributes to the larger social mission of education and training in a democratic society.

  Changing mental models and constructing new knowledge empowers learners and encourages critical thinking. "Knowledge becomes a function of how the individual creates meaning from his or her experiences; it is not a function of what someone else says is true" (Jonassen, 1995).

APPENDIX C

ADEC Guiding Principles for Distance Learning updated, July 24, 2002

Retrieved October 1, 2005, from http://www
.adec.edu/admin/papers/distance-teaching_
principles.html

Design for active and effective learning
Principle: Distance learning designs consider

- specific context;
- needs, learning goals, and other characteristics of the learners;
- nature of the content;
- appropriate instructional strategies and technologies;
- desired learning outcomes; and
- local learning environment.

Support the needs of learners

Principle: Distance learning opportunities are effectively and flexibly supported, including

- initial disclosure of information on the learning opportunities;
- orientation to the process of learning at a distance, including use of technologies for learning;
- site and tutorial support;
- student advising and counseling;
- provision of technical support and library and information services; and
- problem-solving assistance.

Develop and maintain the technological and human infrastructure

Principle: The provider of distance learning opportunities has both a technology plan and a human infrastructure to ensure that

- appropriate technical requirements are established;
- compatibility needs are met;
- technology at origination and receive sites are maintained to ensure technical quality;
- learners and learning facilitators are supported in their use of these technologies; and
- partnering and collaboration are explored as appropriate.

Sustain administrative and organizational commitment.

Principle: Distance education initiatives are sustained by an administrative commitment to quality distance education, as indicated by

- integration of distance education into the mission of the organization;
- financial commitment to accommodate diverse distance learning needs;
- faculty development and reward structures;
- training to support learners, site facilitators, and technicians;
- marketing and management structures to promote and sustain distance education;
- cost-effectiveness reflected through best use of fiscal, technical, and human resources; and
- ongoing evaluation and research.

CHAPTER 23

WHO OWNS ONLINE COURSE INTELLECTUAL PROPERTY?

Douglas A. Kranch
North Central State College

Faculty develop intellectual property needed for online courses while employed by an academic institution. That institution has a claim on the copyright because the instructional materials developed by the faculty members could be seen as "works for hire." On the other hand, both tradition and case law have seen faculty as the copyright possessors of any instructional materials they develop. The interests of both the administration and faculty may be best served with a negotiated agreement that gives the institution ownership rights while allowing use and distribution rights to remain with the authoring faculty.

INTRODUCTION

The controversy over who owns academic coursework materials has intensified with the proliferation of online courses. Many faculty believe the intellectual property they produce for coursework belongs entirely to them. Harvard Law School's Arthur Miller demonstrated the profit that can be made from freelance academic work when he produced a video series on (ironically) civil procedure and intellectual property for a course offered at a different online institution. Miller saw this as no different

Beyond the Online Course: Leadership Perspectives on e-Learning
pp. 365–376
Copyright © 2016 by Information Age Publishing
All rights of reproduction in any form reserved.

from book publishing deals he had been negotiating for many years (Alger, 2000). At the same time, college and university administrations believe the intellectual property rights of course materials developed by the faculty they employ belong to them. Both faculty and administration believe they have strong arguments in their favor. Intellectual property ownership is especially important in the context of computer-based distance education. This article discusses the merits of the arguments faculty and administration for retaining online intellectual property rights and proposes a compromise that can serve the interests of both the administration and the faculty.

OWNERSHIP AND CONTROL IN THE DISTANCE LEARNING AGE

Distance education is growing in importance as well as in numbers in the United States. In the 2000-01 academic year, the National Center for Education Statistics (NCES) reported that 2,320 two- and 4-year degree-granting institutions in the United States, or 56%, offered distance education courses, an increase of 12% over the 1997-1998 academic year (Tabs, 2003). While distance education has the altruistic benefit of taking "the tools of success to those who have the least access to resources" (Nemire, 2007, p. 27), there is a more pecuniary reason for the recent growth in distance learning courses.

After the passage of the Bayh-Dole Act (Public Law 96-517) in 1980, universities and other small entities (included "as an afterthought" (Nelsen, 1998, ¶3)) were able to own the patent rights to inventions they discovered while conducting research sponsored with federal funds. Rhoades (2001) noted that this provision was intended to help spur the growth of small technology businesses. While universities were required by law to use any profits derived from royalties for further research, it may also have begun the slow turn of academic institutions from nonprofit organizations toward the "commodification" ("Academic Commodities," ¶ 2) of academic products. At the same time, the rise of personal computers and the Internet have produced a resurgence of distance education and have allowed faculty to improve both their instructional methods and products (Rhodes, 2001).

While opportunities for revenue enhancement from technology appeared, Rhoades (2001) also highlighted revenue pressures from decreasing state support for public colleges and universities. The Association of American Universities (AAU) (1999) indeed hoped distance learning over the Internet would stimulate "a new form of 'academic free agency'" that would allow universities to reach "large numbers of students and other audiences" ("Boundary Problems and Likely Contested Zones

Involving Intellectual Property in the New Digital Media," ¶16). Whether it is faculty selling their instructional talents and intellectual property to private companies or universities acquiring a more business-like model toward the fruits of academic labor, contention for the intellectual property rights of faculty is rising rapidly (Rhoades, 2001).

COPYRIGHT LAW AND INTELLECTUAL PROPERTY RIGHTS

The concept of intellectual property is intimately related to copyright. American Association of University Professors (n.d.) defined copyright as "that bundle of rights that protect original works of authorship fixed in any tangible medium of expression, now known or later developed, from which they can be perceived, reproduced, or otherwise communicated, either directly or with the aid of a machine or device." Included in "works of authorship" were the outputs of virtually any intellectual endeavor as preserved in an open-ended list of media formats ("What is Intellectual Property?" ¶2). The intent was to give faculty the right to control what they have produced. The United States Copyright Law is intended to provide that control to U.S. citizens; however, its relationship to faculty-produced work has been murky. The 1909 Copyright Law, for example, gave copyright privileges to employers for works made for hire, although it made no attempt to define either *works for hire* or *employer*. The courts filled in the definitions through case law, and the consensus was that an employer was one who exercised control of the production of the finished work, no matter the actual relationship between producer and supervisor (Bunker, 2001).

Little case law was developed regarding the relationship between faculty and the products of their teaching. Bunker (2001) related one significant case that was tried before the California Supreme Court regarding a professor Williams, who took notes and course materials he had developed at UCLA with him to use at his next post. A publisher published Williams' notes without his permission and Williams sued. The publisher defended itself by asserting that Williams' notes were works for hire so that UCLA held the rights to the notes, giving Williams no basis for his suit. The court, however, found for Williams as owner of the copyright based on two arguments: First, that if UCLA owned the copyright, it could prevent Williams from using the notes he created at his next post and, by extension, would similarly block all faculty from using their instructional materials at any but the institutions at which they created them; and second, that UCLA had exerted little supervisory control over Williams. The court also noted how little value the notes would be to UCLA (Bunker, 2001). This implicit ownership faculty had of their course materials became the teacher exception to works for hire and effectively barred educational institutions from owning the intellectual products of their faculties (Quigley, 2001, "Opposing Points of View," ¶2).

With the passage of the Copyright Act of 1976, the works for hire provision remained, expressly provided in section 101 Definitions, where a "work made for hire" is:

1. a work prepared by an employee within the scope of his or her employment; or
2. a work specially ordered or commissioned for use as a contribution to a collective work (U.S. Copyright Office, 2003, p. 7).

Whether the teacher exception transferred to the new act is unclear and remains untested. Bunker (2001) noted that the Supreme Court attempted to provide a definitive ruling on works for hire in *Community for Creative Non-Violence v. Reid.* In a unanimous decision, the Supreme Court ruled that the assignment of copyright should be based on many factors, namely:

> the skill required; the source of the instrumentalities and tools; location of the work; the duration of the relationship between the parties; whether the hiring party has the right to assign additional projects to the hired party; the extent of the hired party's discretion over when and how long to work; the method of payment; the hired party's role in hiring and paying assistants; whether the work is part of the regular business of the hiring party; whether the hiring party is in business; the provision of employee benefits; and the tax treatment of the hired party. (*Community for Creative Non-Violence v. Reid,* 1989)

The problem with this ruling is that the court explicitly noted that no single factor should have precedence over any other in making the determination of who owns the copyright. Thus, applying this ruling to faculty, they are provided salary and benefits and their taxes are paid through the college or university; on the other hand, the extent of the institution's control over when and how long faculty work is minimal. While there would be little doubt that institutions would retain the copyright of institutional documents such as brochures and prospectuses, the decision concerning teaching materials is not so clear cut (Farrington, 2001). Faculty regularly relinquish copyright to the publishing houses that publish their articles, which universities allow (Nemire, 2007), thus appearing to soften the claims of universities on faculty-produced work. At the same time, patents and software are contested by both faculty and institutions (Rhoades, 2001). A look at the arguments made by higher education administrators and by faculty for ownership of intellectual property rights may help identify which of the Supreme Court's criteria support their cases.

THE ADMINISTRATION VIEW

Massive amounts of intellectual property support higher education courses, and these courses may come into being for several reasons. They may be commissioned by the educational institution, developed by faculty in concert with the administration, or produced for the institution with the help of an outside agency (Rhoades, 2001). Bolstering the case of ownership by colleges and universities is their often significant resource investment in distance education courses. For example, a joint project by Oxford, Stanford, and Yale Universities produced 50 courses ranging in cost of between $10,000 and $150,000 each (Klein, 2005). These institutions, and any others that provide resources to bring a creative distance education idea to fruition, can rightfully expect to receive compensation (Farrington, 2001), one aspect of which could be seen as the ownership of the resulting course. Klein (2005) adds that such ownership can also prevent faculty from providing the same courses for competing institutions. The Association of American Universities (1999) bluntly stated that "the university should own the intellectual property that is created at the university by faculty, research staff, and scientists and with substantial aid of its facilities or its financial support" ("Elements in a Policy for Research Universities on Intellectual Property and New Media Technologies," ¶1). AAU, however, added that, since the content is created by collaboration, any revenue generated from the content should be shared by all who participated in its creation.

Farrington (2001) seemed to agree with AAU to a point, especially "where staff are hired specifically to produce materials for, or in support of, teaching and learning" (p. 80). This, he noted, would view a faculty member's transporting a similar or identical course to another institution as a copyright infringement, a conclusion that is not universally accepted. In support of faculty ownership, Farrington cites the question of academic freedom and the more important issues of the creativity of faculty members in bringing courses to life and the relative lack of supervisory oversight (cf. Bunker, 2001). Additional considerations favorable to faculty include just compensation for contributions made to course development that may be beyond that called for in faculty contracts, as well as the longstanding practice of faculty's retaining the copyright of works they produce and of taking those works with them as they move between institutions. Often, writes Klein (2005), faculty seek to generate revenue for themselves from their courses, believing that the amount of labor required to create and teach an online course earns them ownership. It should be noted, however, that the amount of effort expended on projects is not equated to ownership in most other fields, professional or otherwise.

THE FACULTY VIEW

The American Association of University Professors (n.d.) comes firmly down on the side of the faculty and states unequivocally: "Intellectual property created, made, or originated by a faculty member shall be the sole and exclusive property of the faculty, author, or inventor, except as he or she may voluntarily choose to transfer such property, in full, or in part" ("Who Owns Intellectual Property?" ¶2). AAUP sees as the overriding principle that "academic freedom, free inquiry, and freedom of expression within the academic community may be limited to no greater extent in electronic format than they are in print" (American Association of University Professors, 2005, ¶3). As for the claim by universities and colleges that they should have a return on their investment in distance learning courses, AAUP counters that "a work should NOT be treated as 'made for hire' merely because it is created with the use of university resources, facilities, or materials of the sort traditionally and commonly made available to faculty members" (American Association of University Professors, n.d., "Who Owns Intellectual Property?" ¶3, emphasis in the original). Note the reference to "resources, facilities, or materials of the sort traditionally and commonly made available to faculty members." Presumably, since face-to-face and distance education courses use the same resources to produce syllabi, handouts, and digital media information, these should be the property of the faculty members when they develop online courses.

AAUP does give three conditions under which the college or university can claim copyright ownership. The first two are the faculty's being directed by the university to produce the work or signing over copyright to the institution. The third condition seems to apply especially to distance education courses:

> The institution can exercise joint ownership under this clause when it has contributed specialized services and facilities to the production of the work that goes beyond what is traditionally provided to faculty members generally in the preparation of their course materials (American Association of University Professors, n.d., "Who Owns Intellectual Property?" ¶ 4).

Distance education courses typically require twice the development time as traditional courses, with adequate training correlated with distance education participation (Lee & Busch, 2005). Hence, with as much as 80% of course development needing to be completed before the coursework is offered, higher education institution typically provide staff to assist instructors in fulfilling "the additional roles of instructional designer, technology specialist, and administrative advisor" (Restauri, 2004, p. 32). Therefore, it seems that distance education courses generally involve the provision of specialized services and facilities that go beyond what are required for face-to-face education. By AAUP's provision above, jointly produced distance education course materials should involve at least joint ownership by both the faculty and the institution. The American Educational Research Association (2000) lends support to this view when it states: "Individuals or groups who fund or otherwise provide resources for the development of intellectual products are entitled to assert claims to a fair share of the royalties or other profits from the sale or disposition" (p. 7). While some may see using the production means to determine intellectual rights ownership (rather than the source of creative input) a sign that the academy is following a corporate model (Rhoades, 2001), faculty often depend on the additional creative input of institutional staff when producing a distance education course. Finally, Reid (2004), while noting the continued strong support in the institutional policies he examined for academics retaining the intellectual property rights of the materials they produce, adds that this notion is fixed only in traditional policy. In common law and statute, the employer is the presumed owner of the academic's intellectual production. It is therefore the position of the writer that, in agreement with Farrington (2001), "all copyright material, in whatever form, generated by staff in the course of their employment belongs to the employer" (p. 83).

COPYRIGHT OWNERSHIP OR RIGHTS AND REMUNERATION

Care must be taken to provide incentives for all parties to continue the development of distance education materials (Nemire, 2007). While acknowledging that colleges and universities retain the intellectual property rights of materials produced by its faculty will be a severe adjustment for some faculty members (Bunker, 2001), it will replace a patchwork system of negotiated and nonnegotiated rules caused by the ambiguity of the current Copyright Law (Klein, 2005) that may or may not serve the interests of faculty or the institution.

The American Association of University Professors urges faculty to negotiate contracts that supersede the Copyright Law of 1976 and return to them institution by institution the teacher exception they enjoyed under judicial case law based on the 1909 Copyright Law (Quigley, 2001). However, such contracts do not serve the best interests of faculty in general. The first reason is that, despite the provisions of any contract, individual faculty can negotiate their way to exceptions (Rhoades, 2001), which may be unfair to the rest of the faculty. As a second reason, as Klein (2005) notes, many current agreements award property rights based on the degree to which the institution financed the development of the course materials, the same argument put forward above for granting the ownership of distance education materials to the sponsoring institution.

A third reason is that, when the argument of intellectual property ownership is based on the control of faculty time, it is done so with great inconsistency across institutions. Rhoades (2001) observes that unionized institutions tend to see the faculty members' time as their own, while non-unionized institutions claim the time faculty use to create their course and research materials. Even with unionized contracts' bias toward faculty ownership, Rhoades (2001) admits that "some contracts differentiate between routine and significant uses of institutional resources" ("Ownership Issues," ¶10) and would call the latter a work for hire.

Finally, even with a contract that allots copyright to the faculty who produce a course, it may not be at all certain that those faculty also have the rights to *develop* that course or *transport* it to another institution. Quigley (2001) reminds readers that contracts have awarded faculty copyright while granting the institution "exclusive, lifetime rights to develop the faculty member's content into a multimedia course, often with credit but with no remuneration" ("Know Your Copyrights," ¶1). This is analogous to owning the title to a parcel of land while ceding the mineral rights and their plundering to outside investors.

A NEGOTIATED ALTERNATIVE

With these reasons arguing against leaving the question of intellectual property ownership to individual contract negotiations, until either case law or statute establishes a firm national policy, the proposal that intellectual property rights should be vested in the institutions employing the faculty forms a firm foundation upon which to decide how the various parties involved in the creation of the materials should be compensated with either remuneration or rights. For example, AAUP recommends that agreements "allow for institutions to use works created by faculty members without charge for educational and administrative purposes within the institution" and that institutions "be permitted to use such material for internal instructional, educational, and administrative purposes" ("Who May Use the Intellectual Property?" ¶ 1). These recommendations are met if the faculty who had a significant role in developing courses were permitted by institution/faculty intellectual property agreement to use the materials developed for those courses without royalty payment at any future institution by which those faculty may be employed.

To codify the assignment of permissions and rights, each institution should create a facultywide "formal written policy" that stipulates the ownership of intellectual property and the rights of both the institution and the developing faculty. A committee should be formed to help manage the implementation of institutional policy (AAU, 1999). Both AAUP and AAU see this committee as involved in formulating or recommending policy, keeping the campus alert concerning legislative and technological developments, and resolving disputes (AAU, 1999; AAUP, n.d.).

As part of the policy governing the use of institutional intellectual property, AAU (1999) recommends that faculty be restricted from producing commercial distance education products for other institutions or companies without the permission of the faculty's home institution. As most faculty contract have within them a clause that gives the institutions first use of a faculty member's time and requires faculty to notify the institution of any other employment they may undertake, this provision seems unremarkable. AAU also concludes that intellectual property produced by faculty with their own resources and not for coursework at the institution belongs solely to the faculty member. Thus, AUU recognizes that faculty can produce materials on their own time. Interestingly, even when intellectual property is owned by the institution, AAU advises honoring the long-standing tradition of allowing faculty to continue receiving royalties from their written works.

Zhang and Carr-Chellman (2006) note two possible models of faculty/institutional ownership and rights. Pennsylvania State University faculty agreed to grant copyright ownership to the university's new World Campus for all materials developed by faculty at the request of the university and for which they are compensated. Penn State also claims the right to use royalty-free any materials faculty may produce on their own. Faculty are prohibited from producing course materials for Penn State competitors. The University of Wisconsin System claims university ownership for courses developed as work for hire, assigned duty, or with substantial use of institutional resources. Course materials developed by the faculty on their own with minimal use of university resources (including the use of university labs and equipment) are considered the property of the faculty. As authors of the material, respect for academic freedom is such that the faculty are consulted when the courses are to be distributed externally, or when they are to be altered or revised. This second model seems more in keeping with the goals of both AAU and AAUP.

Should disputes arise (as they inevitably will), both AAU and AAUP recommend a committee be used to settle the question. Klein (2005) recommends a three-step process that gradually increases the scope of those involved. The first step would be an attempt to solve the dispute between the parties claiming copyright ownership or rights to a product. The second step would bring in the standing committee to help bring the dispute to a close. The final step would be formal arbitration.

CONCLUSION

The ownership of the rights to distance education courses is important because of the value of the intellectual property to both the faculty members and the institution, and the resources that both have invested in its creation. Strong arguments can be made for granting intellectual property rights for distance education course materials to either the academics who produce them or the institution that employs the academics. Arguing for academics retaining the rights are long-standing tradition regarding print and video materials, the personal investment academics make in course materials, the threat to academic freedom perceived in the loss of ownership and the control it represents, and the need to preserve the ability to transport the course materials with the authoring academics as they move to new locations. Arguing for institutional ownership of these intellectual property rights are the "work for hire" provision of copyright law, the resources that the institution provides over and above those used for producing resources for face-to-face courses, the generally uncertain nature of individually negotiated faculty/institution property rights agreements, and the need to protect the name of the institution associated with the course material. Granting intellectual property rights of distance education materials to the sponsoring institution best preserves the institution's investment of staff, resources, and name. Including in this ownership the provision that authoring faculty retain the perpetual right of use, augmentation, and remuneration best preserves the faculty member's investment of creativity. With these two principles as the foundation, the interests of both administration and faculty can be served, with the details concerning the use of distance education property decided by a negotiated committee decision at the local institution.

REFERENCES

Alger, J. R. (2000). Legal watch: A. Miller's tale: Free-agent faculty [Electronic version]. *Academe, 86*(3). Retrieved May 4, 2008, from http://www.aaup.org/AAUP/pubsres/academe/2000/MJ/Cols/lw.htm

American Association of University Professors. (n.d.). *Sample intellectual property policy & contract language*. Retrieved May 4, 2008, from http://www.aaup.org/AAUP/issues/DE/sampleIP.htm

American Association of University Professors. (2005). Academic freedom and electronic communications [Electronic version]. *Academe, 91*(1). Retrieved May 4, 2008, from http://www.aaup.org/AAUP/pubsres/policydocs/contents/electcomm-stmt.htm

American Educational Research Association. (2000). *Ethical standards of the American Educational Research Association*. Retrieved May 4, 2008, from http://www.blackburn.edu/IROffice/Office_Links/AIR_Model.pdf

Association of American Universities. (1999). *AAU intellectual property and new media technologies: A framework for policy development at AAU institutions*. A report to the AAU Digital and Intellectual Property Management Committee by the Intellectual Property Task Force. Retrieved May 4, 2008, from http://www.aau.edu/reports/IPReport.html

Bunker, M. D. (2001). Intellectuals' property: Universities, professors, and the problem of copyright in the Internet age. *Journalism and Mass Communication Quarterly, 78*(4), 675-687.

Community for Non-Violence v. Reid, 490 U.S. 730. (1989). Retrieved May 5, 2008, from http://supreme.justia.com/us/490/730/case.html

Farrington, D. J. (2001). Borderless higher education: Challenges to regulation, accreditation and intellectual property rights. *Minerva: A Review of Science, Learning & Policy, 39*(1), 63-84.

Klein, M. W. (2005). "Sovereignty of reason": An approach to sovereign immunity and copyright ownership of distance-education courses at public colleges and universities. *Journal of Law & Education, 34*(2), 199-254.

Lee, J. A., & Busch, P. E. (2005). Factors related to instructors' willingness to participate in distance education. *The Journal of Educational Research, 99*(2), 109-115.

Nelsen, L. (1998). The rise of intellectual property protection in the American university. *Science, 279*(5356), 1460-1461.

Nemire, R. (2007). Intellectual property development and use for distance education courses: A review of law, organizations, and resources for faculty. *College Teaching, 55*(1), 26-30.

Quigley, A. (2001). Share and share alike: Division of ownership rights may resolve academic intellectual property disputes. *eLearn, 9*(1). Retrieved May 10, 2007, from http://elearnmag.org/subpage.cfm?section=articles&article=23-1

Reid, T. (2004). Academics and intellectual property: Treading the tightrope. *Deakin Law Review, 9*(2), 759-774.

Restauri, S. L. (2004). Creating an effective online distance education program using targeted support factors. *TechTrends, 48*(6), 32-39.

Rhoades, G. (2001). Whose property is it? Negotiating with the university [Electronic version]. *Academe, 87*(5), 39-43. Retrieved May 4, 2008, from http://www.aaup.org/publications/Academe/2001/01SO/so01rho.htm

Tabs, E. D. (2003). *Distance education at degree-granting post-secondary institutions: 2000-2001*. Washington, DC: National Center for Education Statistics. Retrieved May 4, 2008, from http://nces.ed.gov/pubs2003/2003017.pdf

U.S. Copyright Office. (2003). *Copyright law of the United States of America and related laws contained in Title 17 of the United States Code.* Washington, DC: Author. Retrieved May 28, 2007, from http://www.copyright.gov/title17/circ92.pdf

Zhang, K., & Carr-Chellman, A. A. (2006). Courseware copyright: Whose rights are right? *Journal of Educational Computing Research, 34*(2), 173-186.

CHAPTER 24

INTELLECTUAL PROPERTY AND ONLINE COURSES

Policies at Major Research Universities

Kathryn Ann Loggie
Marathon (Florida) High School

**Ann E. Barron, Elizabeth Gulitz,
Tina N. Hohlfeld, and Jeffrey D. Kromrey**
University of South Florida

Phyllis Sweeney
Nova Southeastern University

This study describes an investigation of the intellectual property policies of a stratified random sample of public and private Carnegie Doctoral Research-Extensive Universities. University policies were examined to determine whether or not they included provisions for distance education materials or courseware, what provisions were made for ownership, and what exceptions, if any were applicable. Using a framework based on earlier work, policy differences between public and private universities and changes across time were analyzed. Results were interpreted in terms of the need for explicit policies to support online course development and delivery.

Beyond the Online Course: Leadership Perspectives on e-Learning
pp. 377–400
Copyright © 2016 by Information Age Publishing

OVERVIEW AND INTRODUCTION

The purpose of this study was to investigate current intellectual property policies of doctoral research universities with respect to copyright ownership of online course materials. As the proliferation of distance-learning opportunities continues in this era of educational accountability, educators, administrators, and institutions need to ensure that institutional policies protect and support an environment that fosters creativity, productivity, and academic freedom. This study provides a foundation upon which to analyze, critique, and further develop coherent and comprehensive copyright and ownership policies at academic institutions.

This research is intended to build on the findings of Lape (1992) and Packard (2002) by analyzing current copyright policies and specifically focusing on faculty intellectual property ownership issues related to courseware and other educational digital media. Online courses are flourishing at institutions of higher learning. The National Center for Education Statistics reported: "In 2000–2001, 90 percent of public 2-year and 89 percent of public 4-year institutions offered distance education courses" (Waits & Lewis, 2003, p. iii). In addition, *Growing by Degrees: Online Education in the United States, 2005,* reported: "The overall percent of schools identifying online education as a critical long-term strategy grew from 49% in 2003 to 56% in 2005" (Allen & Seaman, 2005, p. 2). The trend toward online courses raises questions about the ownership of course materials and can increase tensions between faculty members and their universities regarding rights and responsibilities associated with intellectual property. These questions and tensions are especially important issues for digital resources because of the portability of such courses. As Twigg (2000) pointed out, "there has never been much need to figure out if one party owned a course as a commodity that could be sold elsewhere. But information technology and the Internet appear to have changed the status quo" (p. 1).

BACKGROUND

Previous research suggests university policies are in a state of flux. For example, Lape (1992) investigated 70 research universities and found that 11 had no written policy and 5 had only draft policies. Less than 10 years later, Packard (2002) studied the same sample of universities and found that all but one had adopted a policy. In both studies, all of the policies that were analyzed asserted the university's claim to ownership of at least some faculty works. The typical justification for such ownership was that faculty works were created with university resources.

Of note is that Lape (1992) found 16 policies that disclaimed owner-ship of "traditional" scholarly works and Packard (2002) found 49 policies with such disclaimers. However, only 12 universities in the latter study evidenced policies giving explicit control of educational materials to faculty. The American Association of University Professors (AAUP) takes the position that the traditional practice of faculty copyright ownership of academic work should extend to courseware that is used in distance education, but does admit that there are situations in which a college or university could claim copyright ownership (AAUP, 2006).

With the implementation of distance learning through digital delivery tools such as courseware, electronic mail, and other Internet technologies, care must be taken to ensure that both faculty and institutional rights are provided for. In fact, the AAUP's Statement on Copyright recommends that ownership, control, and use rights be negotiated in advance and contained in a written agreement (AAUP, 2006). The statement further articulates that except in unusual circumstances, academic work is not "work made for hire," and that while faculty should retain copyright ownership, the institution should be reimbursed for

> unusual financial or technical support. That reimbursement might take the form of future royalties or a nonexclusive, royalty-free license to use the work for internal educational and administrative purposes. Conversely, where the institution holds all or part of the copyright, the faculty member should, at a minimum, retain the right to take credit for creative contributions, to reproduce the work for his or her instructional purposes, and to incorporate the work in future scholarly works authored by that faculty member. In the context of distance-education courseware, the faculty member should also be given rights in connection with its future uses, not only through compensation but also through the right of "first refusal" in making new versions or at least the right to be consulted in good faith on reuse and revisions. (AAUP, 2006, p. 216)

While the Association of American Universities (AAU) generally concurs with the AAUP's statement regarding traditional copyright ownership for textbooks, journal articles, and other scholarly works regardless of medium, the AAU sets forth the following policy guidelines on Intellectual Property and New Media Technologies (AAU, 1999):

- The university should own the intellectual property when substantial use of facilities or financial support is provided.
- Works are inherently collaborative in nature, so returns should be shared among scholars, scientists, schools, departments and the larger university.
- Any generated revenue should be reinvested in new initiatives.

- The works should protect the university's name and reputation when that work is presented as sponsored by the institution.
- The institution should provide its community with a formal written policy
- Until revenue approaches a stated threshold, the faculty member or researcher should be able to receive the entire returns.

COPYRIGHT LAW

Article I, § 8 of the U.S. Constitution provides Congress with the power "to promote the Progress of Science and useful Arts, by securing for limited Times to Authors and Inventors the exclusive Right to their respective Writings and Discoveries." The first Copyright Act was passed in 1790, and there have been a number of subsequent revisions.

Copyright is an author's independent and original expression recorded in a fixed and tangible form. As soon as the copyrighted material is recorded in a tangible format, such as a manuscript or an electronic file, it automatically becomes protected; however, registration with the U.S. Copyright Office provides additional protections in case of infringement and is often in the best interest of the author if infringement becomes an issue. A copyrighted work can be reproduced, adapted to create derivative works, distributed, displayed, or performed in public by the author. The author can also transfer rights to others. If copyrighted material is reproduced without the permission of the owner, the violator can be liable for copyright infringement. Some examples of copyrightable works are poems, software, and multimedia materials. In the context of copyrightable works in an academic setting, with which this paper is primarily concerned, examples consist of books, scholarly publications, syllabi, PowerPoint files, Web-based course content, and lecture notes.

Work Made for Hire

A revision to the Copyright Act in 1909 specified that the "author" of a copyrightable work "shall include an employer in the case of works made for hire" (Copyright Act of 1909, §26), however "work made for hire" was not defined. In the 1976 revision to the Copyright Act, work made for hire has two definitions, the first of which is "a work prepared by an employee within the scope of his or her employment" (Copyright Act of 1976, 17 U.S.C § 101). In 1989, the U.S. Supreme Court concluded that an individual is an "employee" for the purpose of the work made for hire provision when the copyrighted work is created in a traditional employer-employee relationship, characterized by factors such as a long-term employment relationship with salary and benefits for the employee, the employer provides the work resources and space to produce the copyrightable material, and the employer assigns the work schedule and projects (*Committee for Creative Non-Violence v. Reid*, 1989). The second definition is

> a work specially ordered or commissioned for use as a contribution to a collective work, as a part of a motion picture or other audiovisual work, as a translation, as a supplementary work, as a compilation, as an instructional text, as a test, as answer material for a test, or as an atlas, if the parties expressly agree in a written instrument signed by them that the work shall be considered a work made for hire. For the purpose of the foregoing sentence, a "supplementary work" is a work prepared for a publication as a secondary adjunct to a work by another author for the purpose of introducing, concluding, illustrating, explaining, revising, commenting upon, or assisting in the use of the other work, such as forewords, afterwords, pictorial illustrations, maps, charts, tables, editorial notes, musical arrangements, answer material for tests, bibliographies, appendixes, and indexes; and an "instructional text" is a literary, pictorial, or graphic work prepared for publication and with the purpose of use in systematic instructional activities. (17 U.S.C. § 101)

Faculty Exception

Faculty have traditionally benefited from an exception to the work for hire doctrine even though they may enjoy a long-term employment relationship, with benefits covered by academic institutions, are assigned a teaching and research load by the employer, and use university resources to produce their work. This exception was established by case law subsequent to the 1909 revision of the Copyright Act (see, for example, *Williams v. Weisser*, 1969).

The exception reserved to faculty work was often explained by academic institutions' policy, custom, and effort to promote academic creativity and freedom of thought and expression. Traditionally, faculty members have been free to select their research agenda, course materials, and presentation materials.

But when the Copyright Act was amended in 1976, no faculty exception to the work for hire doctrine was incorporated therein. While some concluded that this omission meant that the faculty exception had been eliminated, others took the view that a specific provision was not necessary inasmuch as the faculty exception was so widely acknowledged to exist (Townsend, 2003). Townsend (2003) supports this theory by comparing two cases, *Weinstein* and *Hays*, both of which influence current court decisions. In *Weinstein v. University of Illinois (1987)*, the court found that an article written by a professor did not fall within the categories specified by the university's copyright policy for university ownership and, therefore, the copyright belonged to the professor. In so holding, the court recognized the existence of a historical academic exception, while noting that the revisions to the Copyright Act did not incorporate any such wording. Likewise, in *Hays v. Sony Corporation of America (1988)*, the court did not reach a decision based on the existence of an academic exception, but it strongly suggested that the exception still exists.

Lape (1992) asserted that "the 1976 Act did not disturb the professors' exception from the work-made-for-hire doctrine; to the extent that such an exception ever existed, it continues to exist" (p. 246). Nevertheless, since the statute is silent on the faculty exception and there has been no definitive case law subsequent to the 1976 Copyright Act revision, ownership rights to faculty materials should be clarified in writing.

PREVIOUS RESEARCH ON INTELLECTUAL PROPERTY POLICY

Stretching over a decade, two previous studies sought to document the rights of university professors as they related to the creation of intellectual work. Lape (1992) and Packard (2002) reviewed the policies related to intellectual property rights policies of 70 Research I universities. They found that a primary reason for a university to claim a faculty member's work is the use of a substantial amount of university resources in the work's creation. There are many variations to the definition of "substantial" across the universities, but Lape (1992) found that 42 of the 70 universities studied included this type of claim. Packard found that this number increased to 52 universities in 2002.

In cases of disagreements about claims of ownership, some policies delineate arbitration processes to be followed to resolve such disputes. In the policies that address arbitration, most rely on a committee of some sort within the university system to make judgments and clarifications. The Lape study does not provide numbers, but Packard notes that 33 of the reviewed institutions require this type of in-house arbitration. It is also interesting to note here that both studies found that many policies contained conflicting information, and were poorly worded with confusing language and undefined terms.

There was a shift in addressing "academic freedom" across the two studies. Lape (1992) found that 26% of the university policies recognized academic freedom for professors, while Packard (2002) found that 42% of the university policies recognized academic freedom almost 10 years later. This corresponds to a change in protection of what a university policy defines as traditional scholarly work. In 1992, 23% of the universities studied protected this work. This figure rose to 71% in 2002.

The "work made for hire" concept is used by many universities to define what faculty work can be owned by the university. The number of universities using this justification jumped from 25 to 37 from Lape in 1992 to Packard in 2002. It is important not to look at just these numbers in comparison, but also at how the university defines work made for hire. Some define this work as it relates to the first definition of "work made for hire" under the Copyright Act while others have created their own unique definitions within their policies and may even require faculty member signatures before they begin such work.

Packard found that 34 universities include software in some way in their policies. Almost ten years earlier, Lape found that 19 policies listed computer programs in their policies. Intellectual property issues associated with software and other electronic materials are more complex with the growing number of online courses and programs at universities, and the increasing use of technology by faculty members to administer their courses. The advent of digital formats may affect how universities define traditional scholarly work in future policies. It is also not clear how well university policies hold up under the scrutiny of the courts. The outcome of future cases will likely mean changes in how these policies are written and enforced.

DIGITAL COURSE MATERIALS

In the context of distance education, some institutions and faculty tend to face an impasse when no policy is present to dictate who owns produced materials. One of the reasons advanced for university ownership is that digital course content development often consumes a significant amount of institutional resources such as instructional design and multimedia time, server space, management and maintenance, specialized software, and other infrastructure-related expenditures. Conversely, faculty members devote considerable time and effort, and wish to be recognized accordingly to help fund and develop their future research and publications.

One element that complicates matters is that materials developed by faculty with institutional resources can easily be transferred through digital media, and can rapidly reach large audiences. Therefore, the need to have a clear understanding of who owns the digital materials becomes extremely important to ensure creators are compensated appropriately, institutions are awarded a return on their infrastructure and other investments, and both conflicts and frustration are minimized for everyone.

METHOD

A stratified random sample of 42 Carnegie Doctoral Research-Extensive universities was drawn, consisting of 28 public universities and 14 private universities. A sample of 42 policies provides statistical power of .80 for tests of differences in proportions, if the effect size is at least medium (Cohen, 1988) and provides 95% confidence intervals that are no larger than ±13%. Although some of the universities are the same as those studied by Lape (1992) and Packard (2002), many are different because Carnegie classifications have changed over the years. However, the sample for each study represents the top classification of research universities at the time. This research design represents a *cohort study* (a separate sample selected from the population of top research universities at each time point) rather than a *panel study* (the same sample of institutions followed across time.

Copyright and intellectual property policy documents were obtained from university Web sites (Appendix A). In some cases, more than one Web document was located for a single university. Common locations for the policies included faculty rules, administration rules, faculty manuals or handbooks and, in some cases, a stand-alone Intellectual Property policy.

A preliminary framework for content analysis was developed based on the work of Lape (1992) and Packard (2002). The preliminary framework resulted in 36 categories, including copyright, compensation, use, portability, third-party licensing, and exclusions/limitations. Additional themes (focusing on distance education) were then incorporated into the framework. The final worksheet used to code the universities' policies contained 40 categories. It is attached as Appendix B. Coding was limited to yes, no, or not mentioned.

Eight researchers worked on coding the university policies using the 40-item framework. After extensive discussion and agreement on terms by the entire research team, each university's policy was independently coded by two individuals who then resolved any differences in item ratings. Inter-rater agreement for these data was 87%.

RESULTS

The results of this study are presented in three sections: an analysis of differences between public and private research universities in the 2005 sample, an analysis of policy changes across the three samples, and a description of the typical research university policy in 2005.

Public Versus Private Research Universities

The initial analysis of the universities' policies investigated differences between public and private institutions. The framework percentages by type of university are displayed in Table 1. Differences in sample percentages were tested using a chi-square test of independence for each item in the framework.

Of the 40 items in the framework, only three items evidenced statistically significant differences between public and private universities: claiming works created with substantial resources, explicit statement of commitment to academic freedom, and citation of the works made for hire aspect of the Copyright Act (Figure 1).

Although a majority of both types of institutions claimed works created with substantial resources, a significantly larger percentage of private universities (93%) asserted such claims than did public universities (64%). Similarly, 79% of the private universities in the sample claimed works made for hire pursuant to the Copyright Act or within the scope of employment in their copyright policies, while only 46% of the public universities did so. In contrast to these aspects of the universities' policies, 100% of the private universities' policies stated a commitment to academic freedom, but only 64% of the public universities included such a statement.

Policy Changes Across Time

The framework percentages by year are displayed in Table 2. Differences in sample percentages were tested using logistic regression for each item in the framework (logistic regression was used instead of the usual Pearson chi-square because the former allows the overall test of significance to be disaggregated into specific contrasts between pairs of years). Although the analysis of public versus private universities suggested few differences, the analysis of policy changes across time indicated that statistically significant differences were obtained on 26 of the 40 items in the framework.

**Table 1.   Intellectual Property Policy Characteristics
of Public and Private Research Universities**

Policy Characteristic	Institution Type	
	Private	*Public*
Online policy	100%	100%
U claims some faculty works	100%	93%
U claims works created with any university resources	36%	36%
U claims works created with substantial resources*	93%	64%
U defines substantial resources	71%	50%
U disclaims ownership of traditional scholarly works	93%	93%
U lists exceptions to (J)	79%	68%
U includes courseware or DL materials in definition of scholarly works	36%	43%
U cedes control of syllabi, tests, notes, etc. to professors	50%	50%
U includes materials posted on the Web in (M)	36%	29%
U says it is committed to academic freedom or free dissemination of ideas*	100%	64%
U claims ownership using academic freedom as basis	14%	4%
U distinguishes computer programs from other works	79%	61%
U has separate policy dealing with software	29%	25%
U treats computer programs under patent policy	36%	29%
U has separate policy or section for distance learning courses or courseware	21%	21%
U claims ownership of courseware or distance learning materials	50%	29%
U claims works produced due to specific, direct, or written job assignment/duties	64%	82%
U claims works produced by persons hired to produce such works	86%	71%
U claims commissioned works	57%	71%
U claims works for hire pursuant to Copyright Act or within scope of employment*	79%	46%
U considers work made for hire to be extra work assigned to professor	14%	32%
U requires work made for hire agreement to be signed before work begins	21%	25%
U claims joint ownership	21%	29%
U claims royalty-free license	64%	43%
U offers to share a percentage of royalties	93%	96%
Provisions for allowing professors to control use of a work within university	21%	25%
Policy allows professors to revise their works	14%	32%
Policy grants authors right to continued use for nonprofit academic purposes	29%	21%
Policy grants authors the right to make derivative works	14%	21%
Policy gives professors unilateral control of work licensed for use outside university	7%	14%

(Table continues on next page)

Table 1.   (Continued)

	Institution Type	
Policy Characteristic	Private	Public
Copyright ownership transfer to professor if commercialization or publication does not take place within period of time	43%	50%
Even if ownership transfers to professor, university retains license or right to derivative work	43%	21%
Committee decides ownership	57%	54%
Binding arbitration	21%	4%
Administration settles disputes	71%	61%
Agreement signed by professor	29%	46%
Agreement signed by university	14%	25%
Policy provides provisions for enforcement	43%	29%
Policy contains undefined terms, inconsistencies or vague language	36%	39%

* $p < .05$

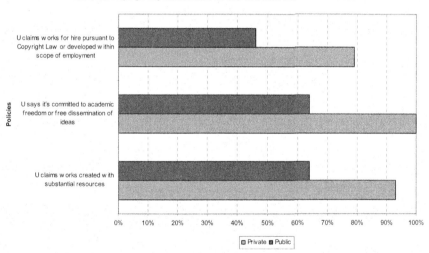

Intellectual Property Policy Characteristics of Public and Private Research Universities

Figure 1.   Significant differences between public and private universities.

The percentage of universities with adopted policies increased from 77% in 1992 to 100% in 2002 and remained at 100% in 2005. Further, policies that claim at least some faculty works increased from 77% in 1992 to 100% in 2002, then dropped slightly to 95% in the 2005 sample (with both the 2002 and 2005 sample percentages being significantly larger

**Table 2. Changes in Intellectual Property
Policy Characteristics Between 1992 and 2005**

	Year		
Policy Characteristic	1992	2002	2005
Adopted Copyright Policy*	77%	100%	100%
U claims some faculty works*	77%	100%	95%
U claims works created with any university resources	—	—	36%
U claims works created with substantial resources*	60%	83%	74%
U defines substantial resources*	23%	29%	57%
U disclaims ownership of traditional scholarly works*	23%	71%	93%
U lists exceptions to (above)*	3%	1%	71%
U includes courseware or DL materials in definition of scholarly works	—	—	40%
U cedes control of syllabi, tests, notes, etc. to professors*	—	17%	50%
U includes materials posted on the web in (above)	—	—	31%
U says it is committed to academic freedom or free dissemination of ideas*	26%	42%	74%
U claims ownership using academic freedom as basis	—	—	7%
U distinguishes computer programs from other works*	27%	28%	67%
U has separate policy dealing with software*	7%	7%	26%
U treats computer programs under patent policy*	6%	3%	31%
U has separate policy or section for distance education courses or courseware	—	—	21%
U claims ownership of courseware or distance education materials	—	—	36%
U claims works produced due to specific, direct, or written job assignment or duties*	36%	54%	76%
U claims works produced by persons hired to produce such works*	13%	17%	76%
U claims commissioned works*	14%	33%	67%
U claims work made for hire pursuant to Copyright Act or within scope of employment*	9%	26%	57%
U considers work made for hire to be extra work assigned to professor	—	—	26%
U requires work made for hire agreement to be signed before work begins	—	—	24%
U claims joint ownership*	26%	7%	26%
U claims royalty-free license*	14%	23%	50%
U offers to share a percentage of royalties*	66%	72%	95%

(Table continues on next page)

Table 2.   (Continued)

Policy Characteristic	Year		
	1992	2002	2005
Provisions for allowing profs to control use of a work within university*	7%	10%	24%
Policy allows professors to revise their works	10%	14%	26%
Policy grants authors right to continued use of work for nonprofit academic purposes	—	—	24%
Policy grants authors the right to make derivative works*	1%	9%	19%
Policy gives professors unilateral control of work licensed for use outside university*	—	—	12%
Copyright ownership transfer to professor if commercialization does not take place*	9%	23%	48%
Even if ownership transfers to professor, U retains license or right to derivative work	—	—	29%
Committee decides ownership	—	48%	55%
Binding arbitration	—	4%	10%
Administration settles disputes*	—	43%	64%
Agreement signed by professor6	9%	12%	40%
Agreement signed by university*	9%	—	21%
Policy provides provisions for enforcement*	—	12%	33%
Policy contains undefined terms, inconsistencies or vague language	—	—	38%

*$p < .05$ from logistic regression.

than the 1992 sample). Policies that claim works produced with "substantial resources" increased significantly from 60% to 83%, then reduced to 74% in 2005 (a decrease that was not statistically significant). Conversely, the 2005 sample evidenced a significantly larger percentage of policies that explicitly defined substantial resources (57%, vs. 23% and 29% for 1992 and 2002, respectively).

Policies that disclaimed ownership of traditional scholarly works increased from 23% to 71%, and further increased to 93% in the 2005 sample. A similar pattern of significant increases across each of the 3 years was evident for the percentage of policies that contain explicit statements of commitment to academic freedom (26%, 42%, and 74% for 1992, 2002, and 2005, respectively).

The percentage of policies addressing software and computer programs showed no change between 1992 and 2002, but increased significantly in 2005. Specifically, policies that distinguished computer programs from other works increased from 27% and 28%, to 67%; and separate policies dealing with software increased from 7% (in both 1992 and 2002) to 26% in 2005. Finally, the treatment of computer programs under the patent policy increased from 6% and 3%, to 31% in 2005.

The 2005 data evidenced significant increases in the percentage of policies that asserted university claims to works produced as a result of specific, direct, or written job assignments or duties (76% vs. 36% and 54% for the earlier years). Similarly, policy statements claiming works produced by persons hired to produce such works increased from 13% and 17%, to 76%; and the claiming of commissioned works increased from 14% and 33%, to 67% in 2005. Finally, the inclusion of works made for hire claims increased from 9% in 1992, to 26% in 2002, and to 57% in 2005.

Twenty-six percent of the universities claimed joint ownership of some works in 1992, a percentage that dropped significantly to 7% in 2002, but returned to 26% in the 2005 sample. Conversely, increases were evident in the percentage of universities that claimed royalty-free license (14%, 23%, and 50% in 1992, 2002, and 2005, respectively), the percentage that offered to share royalties (67%, 72%, and 95%), and the percentage that transferred copyright ownership to the work's creator if commercialization did not occur in a specified time period (9%, 23%, and 48%). Further, increases were seen in the percentage of universities that allowed the author to control the use of the works (7%, 10%, and 24%), and the percentage that granted authors the right to make derivative works (1%, 9%, and 19%), although both aspects were present in only a minority of universities' policies.

An increase was evident in the percentage of universities' policies that asserted settlement of disputes by the university administration (64% in 2005 vs. 43% in 2002), and the percentage that required written agreements signed by the professor (9%, 12%, and 40%) and signed by university officials (9% in 1992 and 21% in 2005). Finally, the proportion of universities with policies that provided a provision for policy enforcement increased from 12% in 2002 to 33% in 2005.

Typical Policy at a Research University in 2005

An examination of the percentages of universities in the 2005 sample that include specific characteristics in their policies can suggest a profile of the intellectual property policy at a "typical" research university. The following characteristics were identified in more than 50% of the universities, indicating that they are likely to appear in university policies related to intellectual property (see Table 2):

- University has adopted an online policy for intellectual property;
- University claims some faculty works;
- University claims works created with substantial resources;
- University defines substantial resources;
- University disclaims ownership of traditional scholarly works;
- University lists exceptions to traditional scholarly works;
- University cedes control of syllabi, tests, notes, etc., to professors;
- University says it is committed to academic freedom or free dissemination of ideas;
- University distinguishes computer programs from other works;
- University claims ownership of courseware or distance education materials;
- University claims works produced due to specific, direct, or written job assignment/duties;
- University claims works produced by persons hired to produce such works;
- University claims commissioned works;
- University claims works made for hire pursuant to Copyright Act or within scope of employment;
- University claims royalty-free license;
- University offers to share a percentage of royalties;
- Committee decides ownership; and
- Administration settles disputes.

All of the universities selected for this study had an online policy related to intellectual property—in fact some had more than one! The policies were located via Web searches (such as Google) as well as targeted searches on university Web sites. In many cases, the policy was a part of the faculty handbook; in others, it was located in the "Research" area of a Web site. Some of the policies were very concise—a paragraph or two; others were extremely comprehensive. At some universities, two or more, sometimes contradictory, policies were located. For example, the Oregon University Systems' *Policies relating to Inventions, License Agreements, Educational and Professional Materials Development, Patents, and Copyrights* specify that "Educational and professional materials, whether or not registered for copyright, that result from the instructional, research or public service activities of the institutions" (Section 580-043-0011) be assigned to the Oregon Board of Higher Education. In contrast, the *Internal Management Directives of Oregon State University* stipulate:

the ownership rights to all forms of educational and professional materials in the form of books, musical, or dramatic composition, architectural designs, paintings, sculptures, or other works of comparable type developed by institution and Board employees, either in conjunction with or aside from their employment, shall accrue to the author, unless the material is prepared in compliance with contractual provision or as a specific work assignment, or significant institutional and Board resources were utilized. (Section 6.215)

All of the universities claimed they were committed to academic freedom and almost all (93%) disclaimed ownership of traditional scholarly works. For example, the policy at Notre Dame states: "In keeping with the University's general policy of not claiming ownership in the scholarly works of its creators, educational materials produced in the normal course of our educational mission will, generally speaking, be owned by the creators of the material" (University of Notre Dame, Faculty Handbook, p. 133). However, most of the universities claimed at least some of the faculty works, generally those that were commissioned or that were created with "substantial" university resources. The definition of "substantial" varied slightly from university to university, but was generally interpreted to mean the use of equipment and resources beyond the professor's office computer and university library. For example, Virginia Commonwealth University policy states, "customary and normal usage of University facilities, telecommunications systems (telephone and Internet access), web and file servers, course management software (e.g. Blackboard), library resources, secretarial help, office equipment, or other support services do not constitute a significant use" (Virginia Commonwealth University, p. 6).

The "typical" university policy has a separate section or separate policy related specifically to computer programs. In many cases, computer programs are covered in a specific section of the copyright or intellectual property policy; in other cases, they are included with the policies related to patents. It is also interesting to note that materials related to distance education would not appear in a separate section of a "typical" policy, since only 21% of the universities specifically addressed distance education materials.

If the "typical" university obtains royalties from works that are created by its employees, the university will share a percentage of the royalties with the creator(s). For example, at the University of Illinois, "the creator (or creator's heirs, successors, and assigns) normally shall receive forty percent (40%) of net revenue" (Intellectual Property Policy, Section 8). However, if the creator retains ownership, the university may claim a royalty-free license. The Marquette University policy states, "Authors of teaching and classroom materials, such as class notes, syllabi, curriculum guides, or laboratory notebooks, shall grant the University a non-exclusive, Royalty-free, perpetual license to use, display, copy, distribute, and prepare derivative works for internal University use" (Marquette University Intellectual Property Policy, Section 4.A.1).

Typical policies related to intellectual property would also include verbiage related to the settlement of disputes. Although most universities have committees (consisting of faculty members and administrators) to decide ownership, the final decision (in the case of a dispute) often rests with the administration. For example, the University of Kansas policy states, "Final decisions on disputed matters will be made by the Chancellor or designee and shall constitute final University action" (Section D, The University of Kansas Intellectual Property Policy).

DISCUSSION AND CONCLUSIONS

The interpretation of the results of this research must be tempered with recognition of its limitations. First, the university policies analyzed in this project represent only a sample of policies rather than the complete corpus. Although the stratified random sampling design employed provides a representative sample of policies, the potential impact of sampling error must not be neglected. In addition, the policies obtained from the sample universities were those provided online as part of the universities' Web site. The currency and accuracy of these policies were assumed but were not verified with university administration. The potential exists that some of the policy documents may not be the most recent employed at the studied institutions.

In light of these limitations, the following interpretations and conclusions are suggested. Although few differences were evident between public and private institutions, substantial changes are clear in the comparison of policies in 1992, 2002, and 2005. Lape (1992) found that most of the universities' copyright policies tried to protect some of the interests of professors. She concluded that university copyright policy must be written into the employment contract and signed by both the university and the professor in order to protect and maintain the copyright ownership of the professor. Nearly 10 years later, Packard (2002) found that although universities were disclaiming some faculty works in their policies, they were claiming others. Many of the universities in her study did protect faculty rights to their traditional scholarly works; however, in order to enforce these policies and assure the rights of faculty to control these works, contracts had to be signed by both the professor and the university. In our study, this continues to be an area of concern, since 40% of the intellectual property policies require faculty to sign agreements, but only 21% also require the university to sign.

By 2005, all of the universities in our study had published their intellectual property rights policy on the Internet. Our investigation found that most universities are writing intellectual property rights policies to delineate the rights of faculty to their works. Although 93% of these policies designated that professors should have control of their traditional scholarly works; 71% of these universities specifically listed exemptions to this policy. Most universities (95%) claimed some faculty works, especially if the works required substantial use of university resources (83%). On a positive note, when the university did claim rights to the intellectual property of a faculty member, 95% offered to share a percentage of the royalties.

Our research also revealed some areas of concern. Although half of the universities gave control of syllabi, tests, and notes to faculty, only 31% of these institutions also included materials posted to the Web, and 36% of the universities claimed ownership of courseware and distance learning materials. A substantial majority of universities claim the intellectual property rights for materials that faculty are given specific assignments to produce (76%), are specifically hired to produce (76%), or are commissioned to produce (67%). Another area of concern is the increase in the number of universities that make some claims in their policies to works developed within the scope of employment or according to the Copyright Act for works made for hire (currently 57%). The last trend of concern is the significant increase in having administration settle copyright disputes with the faculty (64%).

From a budget and finance perspective, as the trend of digitizing course content to meet the needs of learners continues to expand and provide significant sources of income for universities, the need increases for comprehensive and coherent policies that will not only ensure the quality of products delivered with the university's stamp, but also ensure future sources of income in an era of decreasing state funding. Conversely, from a scholarly perspective, as the demand for distance learning and digital courseware increases, we expect that universities will be pressed by both their boards of trustees as well as their faculty senates and unions to protect the abilities of both the university and the faculty to retain control over their creative educational endeavors. Unless universities and their faculty are willing to allow outside private enterprises to capitalize on their efforts without recompense, they must assure the rights of the professor by writing specific intellectual property rights policies that are signed by both the faculty member and the university. Without the support of the institution in protecting the rights of its faculty to their creative products, faculty may be unwilling to publish to the Internet and the universities will be hard-pressed to meet the demand of their students for distance education courses. Ultimately, faculty and universities must work together in order to specify and protect ownership of their scholarly work.

This work was supported, in part, by the University of South Florida and the Fund for the Improvement of Postsecondary Education, under Grant No. P339Z000006. $2,774,950 in federal funds were provided for the project, representing 50% of the total project costs. The remaining 50% of the project costs ($2,774,950) were financed by nonfederal sources. The opinions expressed are those of the authors and do not reflect the views of the United States Department of Education or the University of South Florida.

REFERENCES

Allen, I., & Seaman, J. (2005). *Growing by degrees: Online education in the United States, 2005*. Retrieved November 1, 2006, from http://www.sloan-c.org/publications/survey/pdf/growing_by_degrees.pdf

American Association of University Professors. (2006). *Policy documents and reports.* Baltimore: Johns Hopkins University Press.

Association of American Universities. (1999) *Intellectual property and new media technologies: A framework for policy development at AAU Institutions.* Retrieved May 31, 2005, from http://www.aau.edu/reports/IPReport.html

Cohen, J. (1988). *Statistical power analysis for the behavioral sciences* (2nd ed.). Hillsdale, NJ: Erlbaum.

Committee for Creative Non-Violence v. Reid, 490 U.S. 730 (1989).

The Constitution of the U.S., Article 1, § 8.

Copyright Act of 1909, ch. 320, § 62, 35 Stat. 1075, 1087-88.

Copyright Act of 1976, 17 U.S.C. § 101.

Hays v. Sony Corporation of America, 847 F.2d 412 (7th Cir. 1988).

Lape, L. G. (1992). Ownership of copyrightable works of university professors: The interplay between the copyright act and university copyright policies. *Villanova Law Review, 37*(2), 223-271.

Marquette University. (1999). *Marquette University intellectual property policy.* Retrieved November 1, 2006, from http://www.marquette.edu/orsp/policies/ippolicy.pdf

Oregon State University. (2005a). *Internal management directives, copyright center: Printing and mailing services.* Retrieved October 26, 2006, from http://printmail.oregonstate.edu//copyright /imds6.html

Oregon State University. (2005b). *Policies relating to inventions, license agreements, educational and professional materials development, patents, and copyrights.* Retrieved November 1, 2006, from http://oregonstate.edu/research/technology/policies/higher_education.htm

Packard, A. (2002). Copyright or copy wrong: An analysis of university claims to faculty work. *Communication Law and Policy, 7*, 275–316.

Townsend, E. (2003). *Legal and policy responses to the disappearing "teacher exception," or copyright ownership in the 21st century university.* 4 Minn. Intell. Prop. Rev. 209. Retrieved May 1, 2005, from http://mipr.umn.edu/archive/v4n2/townsend.pdf

Twigg, C. A. (2000). *Who owns online courses and course materials? Intellectual property policies for a new learning environment.* Troy, NY: Center for Academic Transformation.

University of Illinois. (2004). Intellectual *property policy, policies: The general rules concerning university organization and procedure.* Retrieved November 1, 2006, from http://www.uillinois.edu/trustees/trusteesfromold/rules.html

University of Kansas. (1995). *The University of Kansas intellectual property policy.* Retrieved November 1, 2006, from http://www.provost.ku.edu/policy/intellectual_property_policy/

University of Notre Dame. (2005). Faculty handbook. Retrieved April 6, 2006, from http://www.nd.edu/~provost/pdf/Faculty_HB_04.pdf

Virginia Commonwealth University. (2005). *Intellectual properties policy.* Virginia Commonwealth University, Office of Research. Retrieved November 1, 2006, from http://www.pubinfo.vcu.edu/wss/ipp/ipp.pdf

Waits, T., & Lewis, L. (2003). *Distance education at degree-granting postsecondary institutions: 2000-2001 (NCES 2003-017).* U.S. Department of Education. National Center for Education Statistics. Washington, DC: U.S. Government Printing Office. Retrieved November 3, 2006 from http://nces.ed.gov/pubsearch/pubsinfo.asp?pubid=2003017

Weinstein v. University of Illinois, 811 F.2d 1091 (7th Cir. 1987).

Williams v. Weisser, 273 Cal.App. 2d 726 (1969).

APPENDIX A:
WEB SOURCES FOR INTELLECTUAL PROPERTY POLICIES

University	URL
Brown University	http://www.brown.edu/Faculty/Faculty_Governance/rules.html
Colorado State University	http://facultycouncil.colostate.edu/files/manual/sectionj.htm
Duke University	http://www.provost.duke.edu/fhb.pdf
Emory University	http://www.ott.emory.edu/share/policies/intellectual_property.pdf
Georgetown University	http://otl.georgetown.edu/GU_Patent_Policy_12.01.03.pdf
Loyola University Chicago	http://www.research.luc.edu/informationpolicies/procedures/copyrightpolicya
Marquette University	http://www.marquette.edu/orsp/policies/ippolicy.pdf
Oklahoma State University	http://home.okstate.edu/policy.nsf/483c0b76d56e01c2862562b100059b03/37f5475bbb9a4e5f862562d800604ad9!OpenDocument
Oregon State University	http://oregonstate.edu/admin/printing/copyright/imds6.htm and http://arcweb.sos.state.or.us/rules/OARS_500/OAR_580/580_043.html
Pennsylvania State University – University Park	http://guru.psu.edu/policies/RA11.html and http://guru.psu.edu/policies/RA17.html and http://grants.psu.edu/PSU/res/ip.htm
Purdue University	http://www.purdue.edu/oop/policies/pages/teach_res_outreach/b_10_print.html
Rice University	http://professor.rice.edu/professor/Patent_and_Software_Policies.asp and http://fachandbook.rice.edu/emplibrary/fac_handbook.pdf
Stanford University	http://www.stanford.edu/dept/DoR/rph/Chpt5.html
SUNY – Stony Brook	http://www.rfsuny.org/tto/cpyrgt.htm and http://www.rfsuny.org/tto/softsuny.htm and http://www.suny.edu/Board_of_Trustees/index.cfm
Tufts University	http://www.tufts.edu/tccs/p-intellectual.html
University of Alabama	http://facultysenate.ua.edu/handbook/Append-h.html and http://facultysenate.ua.edu/handbook/append-g.html
University of Arizona	http://vpr2.admin.arizona.edu/Interim_IPP/IP-UA-interim.pdf
University of California – Berkeley	http://otl.berkeley.edu/inventor/uccopyright.php

University of California – Santa Barbara	http://ucsbuxa.ucsb.edu/policies/vcas/business-serv/5210_copyrights.html
University of Connecticut	http://www.policy.uconn.edu/
University of Denver	http://www.du.edu/intellectualproperty/
University of Florida	http://rgp.ufl.edu/pdf/otl/ipp.pdf
University of Georgia	http://www.ovpr.uga.edu/rpph/rph_chp2.html
University of Hawaii - Manoa	http://www.svpa.hawaii.edu/svpa/ar/arch3.pdf
University of Idaho	http://www.webs.uidaho.edu/fsh/5300.html
University of Illinois - Urbana-Champaign	http://www.uillinois.edu/trustees/rules.html
University of Iowa	http://www.uiowa.edu/~our/opmanual/v/30.htm
University of Kansas	http://www.ku.edu/~vcinfo/Copyright/KBOR%20IP%20Policy.htm and http://www.provost.ku.edu/policy/intellectual_property_policy/
University of Louisville	http://thinker.louisville.edu/ippolicy.htm
University of Maryland – College Park	http://www.umd.edu/
University of Missouri-Columbia	http://www.umsystem.edu/ums/departments/gc/rules/business/100/030.shtml
University of New Mexico	http://www.unm.edu/~handbook/E70.html
University of Notre Dame	http://www.nd.edu/
University of Pennsylvania	http://www.upenn.edu/assoc-provost/handbook/v_e.html and http://www.upenn.edu/almanac/volumes/v51/n22/pdf_n22/patent_policy.pdf
University of Rhode Island	http://www.uri.edu/facsen/Appendix_H.html and http://www.uri.edu/facsen/CHAPTER_1004.html and http://www.uri.edu/facsen/CHAPTER_504.html
University of Rochester	http://www.rochester.edu/provost/Faculty_Handbook_Master_for_Printing_082404.pdf and http://www.rochester.edu/ott/policies/#general
University of Southern Mississippi	http://www.usm.edu/pubs/fachbook/Faculty_Handbook_9_2_04.pdf
University of Utah	http://www.admin.utah.edu/ppmanual/6/6-7.html
Utah State University	http://www.usu.edu/hr/policies/327.htm
Virginia Commonwealth University	http://www.pubinfo.vcu.edu/wss/ipp/ipp.pdf
Virginia Polytechnic Institute and State University	http://www.policies.vt.edu/13000.html
Washington University	http://www.wustl.edu/policies/intelprop.html and http://www.wustl.edu/policies/intelpropfaq.html

APPENDIX B: POLICY CODING FRAMEWORK

University

URL

Date Accessed

Name of document

1. On-line policy
2. U claims some faculty works
3. U claims works created with any university resources
4. U claims works created with substantial resources
5. U defines substantial resources
6. U disclaims ownership of traditional scholarly works
7. U lists exceptions to (6.)
8. U includes courseware or distance learning materials in definition of scholarly works
9. U cedes control of syllabi, tests, notes, etc. to profs
10. U includes materials posted on the Web in (9.)
11. U says it's committed to academic freedom or free dissemination of ideas
12. U claims ownership using academic freedom as basis
13. U distinguishes computer programs from other works
14. U has separate policy dealing with software
15. U treats computer programs under patent policy
16. U has separate policy or section for distance learning courses or courseware
17. U claims ownership of courseware or distance learning materials
18. U claims works produced due to specific, direct, or written job assignment or duties
19. U claims works produced by persons hired to produce such works
20. U claims commissioned works
21. U claims works for hire pursuant to Copyright Act or developed within scope of employment
22. U considers work-for-hire to be extra work assigned to prof
23. U requires work-for-hire agreement to be signed before work begins
24. U claims joint ownership
25. U claims royalty-free license
26. U offers to share a percentage of royalties
27. Provisions for allowing profs to control use of a work within U
28. Policy allows profs to revise their works
29. Policy grants authors right to continued use of work for nonprofit academic purposes
30. Policy grants authors the right to make derivative works

31. Policy gives profs unilateral control of work licensed for use outside univ
32. Copyright ownership transfer to prof if commercialization or publication does not take place w/i period of time
33. Even if ownership transfers to prof pursuant to (32.), U retains license or right to derivative work
34. Committee decides ownership
35. Binding arbitration
36. Administration settles disputes
37. Agreement signed by prof
38. Agreement signed by univ
39. Policy provides provisions for enforcement
40. Policy contains undefined terms, inconsistencies or vague language

Note. Items are coded yes, no, or not mentioned

CHAPTER 25

THE LEGAL ENVIRONMENT OF ACCESSIBLE POSTSECONDARY ONLINE LEARNING

Kevin L. Crow
Harper College

Recent innovations in technology have made it possible for many individuals to receive education and training at a distance through the use of the Internet. There is little doubt that ability to utilize the Internet as a delivery modality for postsecondary education offers enormous practical value for many individuals. For individuals who have disabilities, however, this technology also offers the potential to create barriers that violate their rights under U.S. law. This article has been written in order to help postsecondary educators and administrators better understand the current legal environment of online postsecondary learning in the United States. In order to achieve this goal this article provides a basic overview of 5 pieces of U.S. legislation; it then discusses practical implications of these laws as they relate to the administration of accessible online postsecondary education. This article is not intended to offer or infer any specific legal advice.

Beyond the Online Course: Leadership Perspectives on e-Learning
pp. 401–416
Copyright © 2016 by Information Age Publishing

OVERVIEW: FEDERAL DISABILITY LEGISLATION
AND ONLINE POSTSECONDARY LEARNING

Postsecondary educational institutions are not expressly mandated by any single piece of federal legislation to provide or maintain accessible websites. Postsecondary educational institutions are, however, required by the Americans with Disabilities Act of 1990 (ADA) and by Section 504 of the Vocational Rehabilitation Act of 1973 (Section 504) to provide equal access to the communication and information that is contained on their websites (or other delivery systems) to their students who have disabilities (Edmonds, 2004; Johnson, Brown, Amtmann, & Thompson, 2003). These two pieces of legislation, combined with Section 508 of the Vocational Rehabilitation Act (Section 508) and Telecommunications Act of 1996 (Telecommunications Act), effectively weave a safety net that is designed to ensure that all qualified people have equal access to all of the products and services that are offered by U.S. postsecondary institutions.

Section 504 of the Vocational Rehabilitation Act of 1973

Section 504 of the Vocational Rehabilitation Act of 1973 prohibits any federal agency or any entity that receives federal funding from discriminating in any way against individuals with disabilities. Specifically, Section 504 states the following regarding the rights of individuals who have disabilities:

> No otherwise qualified individual with a disability in the United States as defined in section 7(20) shall, solely by reason of her or his disability, be excluded from the participation in, or be denied the benefits of, or be subjected to discrimination under any program or activity receiving federal financial assistance or under any program or activity conducted by any Executive agency or by the United States Post Office. (Rehabilitation Act of 1973, § 504, 1973, ¶ a)

Section 504 clearly asserts that it applies to any entity that receives or distributes federal funding, including: state and local governments, departments, agencies and special purpose districts; colleges, universities, or other postsecondary institutions; public systems of higher education; local educational agencies; and vocational education and other school systems. Section 504 also applies to private organizations including sole proprietorships, partnerships, and corporations that are principally engaged in the business of providing education, health care, housing, parks, recreation, or social services (Rehabilitation Act of 1973, 1973).

Section 504 and Postsecondary Online Learning

Paragraphs 2A and 2B of Section 504 explicitly state that Section 504 has authority over public postsecondary institutions that receive any type of federal funding. Paragraph 3A expressly notes that Section 504 has authority over nonpublic entities which receive federal funding if a given entity is "principally engaged in the business of providing education" (Rehabilitation Act of 1973, 1973).

Section 504 provisions are broad-sweeping and apply to nearly every aspect of postsecondary education. Consequently, most US postsecondary institutions refer to Section 504 when creating or addressing institutional-wide accessibility policies and procedures. Section 504 does not make specific reference to online learning; nor does it specifically mandate postsecondary institutions to make their web content accessible. Nonetheless, Section 504 provisions do apply to all instructional delivery modalities, including online learning.

The intent of Section 504 legislation is both simple and clear. Any entity that receives federal funding is prohibited from discriminating in any way against any individual on account of his or her disability. Determining and implementing a defensible strategy to comply with Section 504 remains the responsibility of the individual institution.

The Americans With Disabilities Act

The Americans with Disabilities Act of 1990 was adopted by Congress and signed into law by President George H. W. Bush on July 26, 1990. Provisions of the law became (or will become) effective at various times ranging from 30 days to 30 years from the date that it was signed into law (Department of Labor, 2006).

The ADA was established in order to accomplish four broad purposes. First, the ADA establishes a clear and complete national mandate for the elimination of discrimination against individuals with disabilities. Second, the ADA provides unambiguous and enforceable standards that address discrimination against individuals with disabilities. Third, the ADA authorizes the federal government to play a key role in the enforcement of the standards established in the ADA on behalf of individuals with disabilities. Fourth, the ADA has the ability to summon congressional authority including the power to enforce the Fourteenth Amendment of the United States Constitution, and to regulate commerce in order to address the major areas of discrimination faced day-to-day by people with disabilities (Americans with Disabilities Act, 1990).

ADA Titles

The ADA consists of five primary sections that are referred to as "titles." Each title pertains to a specific aspect of disabilities rights. Title I requires employers who have 15 or more employees to provide all qualified individuals with disabilities equal employment opportunities. Title II (Part One) requires all public entities to ensure that individuals with disabilities have an equal opportunity to benefit from all programs, services, and activities that are offered by the public entity. These services include, but are not limited to, courts, public education, employment, health care, recreation, transportation, voting, and town meetings. Title II (Part Two) requires public transportation services to provide services to individuals with disabilities. Title III requires all business and nonprofit organizations such as theaters, hotels, retail stores, and private schools to provide accommodations to individuals with disabilities. Title III also requires all course and examinations that lead to professional, educational, and vocational-related applications, licensing, certification, or credentialing to be administered in a place and manner that is accessible to people with disabilities. Title IV requires telecommunication carriers to provide access to individuals with speech and hearing disabilities. Title IV also requires closed-captioning of all federally funded service announcements (Americans with Disabilities Act, 1990).

The ADA and Postsecondary Online Learning

Titles II and III of the ADA expressly require colleges and universities to provide communications to people with disabilities that are equivalent to communications that are provided to those who are nondisabled. It also requires colleges and universities to provide individuals with disabilities equal access to all of the institution's products and services.

The United States Department of Justice (USDJ) (2004) claims that Title II of the ADA applies to public education. Additionally the USDJ claims that Title II generally requires state and local governments to provide qualified individuals with disabilities equal access to their programs, services, or activities, unless doing so would fundamentally alter the nature of their programs, services, or activities or would impose an undue burden (Department of Justice, 2005).

The United States Department of Justice notes that nonpublic (private) postsecondary institutions qualify under the ADA as public accommodations; therefore, under Title III of the ADA these institutions are required to comply with basic nondiscrimination ADA requirements that prohibit exclusion, segregation, and unequal treatment of individuals who have disabilities. Moreover, nonpublic postsecondary institutions are required by the ADA to provide effective communication with people who have special accessibility requirements including hearing, vision, speech, or other disabilities (Department of Justice, 2004).

Auxiliary Aids and Services

The U.S. Department of Education, Office of Civil Rights (OCR), interprets the ADA as requiring postsecondary educational institutions to provide auxiliary aids and services to qualifying students. The ADA defines auxiliary aids and services as follows:

> The term "auxiliary aids and services" includes (A) qualified interpreters or other effective methods of making aurally delivered materials available to individuals with hearing impairments; (B) qualified readers, taped texts, or other effective methods of making visually delivered materials available to individuals with visual impairments; (C) acquisition or modification of equipment or devices; and (D) other similar services and actions. (Americans with Disabilities Act, 1990, § 3, ¶ 1)

In order to qualify for an auxiliary aid or service, a student must formally identify himself or herself to the institution as an individual with a disability, be able to verify his or her specific disability, and request a specific auxiliary aid or service. Once these conditions are met, the institution is generally charged by Section 504 and the ADA to provide the qualifying student an appropriate auxiliary aid or service in a timely fashion in order to assure the student's effective participation in the programs, goods, and services that are offered by the educational institution; providing that the auxiliary aid or service does not cause undue hardship on the institution. The OCR notes that institutions do not have to provide the latest or most sophisticated auxiliary aid or service to students who have disabilities; rather, institutions have the flexibility to choose the specific aid or service as long as the selected aid or service is effective (Department of Education, 1998).

Johnson et al. (2003) note that whether or not postsecondary institutions are legally required to provide assistive technologies as auxiliary aids to distance learners with disabilities is currently debatable. Johnson et al. also assert that postsecondary institutions that require all distance learners (disabled and nondisabled) to have compatible computer hardware, software, and network access as a condition for online learning may not be required to provide assistive technologies to disabled students. Under these circumstances, disabled students would most likely be responsible for the acquisition of any needed assistive technology. What is certain, however, is that the OCR recognizes that providers of distance education courses and courseware are responsible for making certain that any information and/or communication that is stored on and facilitated by distance education courseware must be readily accessible to individuals who have disabilities (Waddell, 1998).

U.S. Department of Education, Office of Civil Rights

The OCR has issued several official documents asserting that institutions of higher education are considered by the U.S. Department of Education as being covered by the ADA and Section 504. These documents help clarify several of the OCR's positions regarding the implementation of federal legislation pertaining to the rights of US postsecondary students who have disabilities.

One example of these documents is titled "In RE: Docket No. 09-99-2041." In this 1999 letter to the President of California State University, Long Beach, the OCR affirms that the OCR has responsibility for enforcing Section 504 and the ADA matters that occur in higher education, that California State University Long Beach is subject to Section 504 and ADA regulation, and that Title II of the ADA ensures that communications with disabled persons are to be as effective as communications with nondisabled persons. The OCR also points out that the three essential components that construct the term "as effective as" are "timeliness of delivery," "accuracy of the translation," and "provision in a manner and medium appropriate to the significance of the message and the abilities of the individual with the disabilities" (Scott, 1999, ¶ 9). The OCR letter notes that *Tyler v. City of Manhattan*, 857 F. Supp. 800 (D.Kan.1994) establishes that public entities violate their obligations under the ADA by only providing accommodations on an ad hoc basis. The OCR letter also notes that when determining what type of communications auxiliary aid to offer an individual with a disability, California State University must give primary consideration to the requests of an individual.

Three Additional Acts

Three other pieces of federal legislation affect distance and/or online learning in the United States. They are Section 508 of the Vocational Rehabilitation Act of 1973, the Telecommunications Act of 1966 (Telecommunications Act), and the Assistive Technology Act of 1998 (Tech Act). Compared to Section 504 and the ADA, these three pieces of legislation play diminutive roles regarding accessible online postsecondary learning. Nonetheless, these acts are currently active and do contribute to the overall legal environment of online postsecondary learning; therefore, they merit a brief mention.

Section 508

On August 7, 1998, President Bill Clinton signed the Workforce Invest-ment Act of 1998 (which included Section 508) into federal law. Section 508 requires that when federal agencies develop, procure, maintain, or use electronic and information technology, these technologies must pro-vide federal employees with disabilities access to and use of information and data that are comparable to the access by federal employees who are not disabled. Additionally, Section 508 guarantees the rights of members of the general public with disabilities who are seeking information or ser-vices from a federal agency to have access to and use of information that is comparable to that provided to individuals who are not disabled, unless doing so would create an undue burden on a given agency (Workforce Reinvestment Act of 1998, 1998). Section 508 includes provisions for lim-ited exemptions pertaining to national security systems as detailed in the Clinger-Cohen Act of 1996. These exemptions apply to specific military command, weaponry, intelligence and crypto-logical systems and activi-ties (Access Board, 2005).

Section 508 applies only to electronic and information technology that was procured on or after June 25, 2001. Electronic and information tech-nology that was procured prior to June 25, 2001, does not require retrofit-ting under Section 508; however, qualified individuals may request a reasonable accommodation according to provisions put forth in Section 504 or ADA law (Baquis, 2003).

Section 508, subpart "b" contains a broad set of technical rules pertain-ing to the accessibility of electronic communications. Located within this subpart are 16 accessibility rules for web-based, intranet, and Internet information and applications. This subsection is commonly referred as "Section 508 Standards." Appendix A lists these 16 web-accessibility rules.

Federally owned educational institutions are directly affected by Sec-tion 508 provisions. Consequently, Section 508 permits individuals to file a complaint against any federally owned educational institution that does not offer accessible electronic or information technology. Section 508 also permits individuals to file a civil action against a qualified agency in order to seek injunctive relief and to recover attorney fees (Baquis, 2003).

State- and privately-owned postsecondary institutions are not directly affected by Section 508; however, compliance with Section 508 can yield these entities an ancillary benefit. When faced with disability-related liti-gation, all postsecondary institutions need to demonstrate that they are making a good-faith effort to have their electronic information and com-munication comply with all applicable federal laws. Many disabilities-law experts believe that compliance with Section 508 Standards or with the World Wide Web Consortium's (W3C) Web Content Accessibility Initiative (WAI) guidelines demonstrates that an institution is making a good-faith effort to meet Section 504 and ADA requirements. This, in turn, can help establish a strong legal defense to disability-related litigation.

The Telecommunications Act of 1966

The Telecommunications Act of 1966 is an amendment of Section 255 and Section 251(a) of the Communications Act of 1934. The Telecommunications Act of 1966 requires makers of telecommunication equipment and providers of telecommunication services to provide services and/or equipment that are accessible to individuals who have disabilities. Examples of equipment and services that are covered by the Telecommunications Act of 1966 include (but are not limited to) telephones, cell phones, pagers, call-waiting, and operator services. The Telecommunications Act directly affects the delivery of distance education via telecourses, in that it requires all educational telecourses to contain closed-captioning for individuals who are hearing impaired. Section 255 is enforced by the Federal Communications Commission (FCC) (Communications Act, 1934; DOJ, 2004).

Assistive Technology Act of 1998

The Assistive Technology Act provides federal grant funding to individual states in order to build awareness about and to address the assistive technology needs of individuals with disabilities (Assistive Technology Act, 1998).

Specifically, the Tech Act provides financial assistance to individual states in order to help each state create, maintain, and strengthen a permanent comprehensive statewide program of technology-related assistance for individuals with disabilities; identifies federal policies that facilitate payment for assistive technology devices and assistive technology services; identifies federal policies that impede payment for assistive technology devices and assistive technology services; and eliminates inappropriate barriers to payment for assistive technology devices and assistive technology services (Assistive Technology Act, 1998).

The Tech Act also provides individual states with financial assistance that promotes public information and awareness, encourages improved interagency and public- and private-sector coordination, provides technical assistance and training, and funds national and regional initiatives that help promote the understanding of assistive technology devices and assistive technology (Assistive Technology Act, 1998).

Currently, all 50 states receive federal grants through the Tech Act. Additionally, American Samoa, the District of Columbia, Guam, the Northern Mariana Islands, Puerto Rico, and the U.S. Virgin Islands receive Tech Act funding (ATAP, 2006, ¶ 1).

Why Be Concerned?

Over the past decade there has been a proliferation in the utilization of the Internet and computers as delivery modalities for distance education. The U.S. Department of Education reports that 95% of the 2,320 two- and 4-year institutions that offered distance education courses during the 2000-2001 academic year reported that they had used websites for their distance education courses (Waits & Lewis, 2003, p. 15). Allen and Seaman (2006) report that 3,180,050 U.S. students took at least one online postsecondary course during the fall of 2005.

The U.S. Department of Education reports that 45% of all 2- and 4-year colleges and universities that offered distance courses between the years of 1997 through 2000 received requests to provide accommodations for distance education students (Waits & Lewis, 2003, p. vi). Moreover, a study by the U.S. Department of Education has revealed that up to 8.5% of Americans may have at least one disability that can have a negative effect on their ability to use a computer or to access the Internet (DOC, 2002, p.1). These figures suggest that the need for accessible online postsecondary education is very real. Moreover, when considered in the context of the legal environment of postsecondary online education, these figures strongly suggest that it would be beneficial for postsecondary educators to take proactive steps that would insure that their institutions' online resources, goods, and services are accessible to individuals who have disabilities.

First Steps Toward Accessible Online Content

Accessibility experts note that there are at least two key actions that postsecondary educators can take in order to provide constant, long-term accessible online education. First, each college and university that offers online education should establish and implement official high-level policies pertaining to the accessibility of its electronic and information technologies. Second, colleges and universities should utilize universal design processes when creating electronic information (Crow, 2006).

Policies

Colleges and universities need to establish, implement, and enforce accessibility policies that apply to all electronic and information technology that is procured, developed, and disseminated by the college or university. These accessibility policies need to be officially sanctioned by the institution's governing agencies and utilized systemically throughout the institution.

In general, accessibility policies tend to generate different results depending on the level of formal recognition they receive from the institution. Consequently, in order for an accessibility policy to be effective it must be officially sanctioned by top-level administration and institutional governance bodies. One accessibility expert believes that an institution's accessibility policies should be at a level that is equivalent to the institution's sexual harassment policy. This needs to occur because the more formal the policy is within the institution, the more that it is likely to be accepted, embraced, and enforced by the institution's administration, faculty, and staff (Crow, 2006).

In order to make a meaningful impact, an institution's accessibility policies need to apply to every component of the institution's electronic and information technologies, including web pages, electronic documents, multimedia, text messaging, AJAX-based documents, or any other vehicle that is used to deliver electronic information to students. Additionally, accessibility policies need to apply to every occurrence of institutional electronic and informational technology, including online application, class registration, financial transactions, access to library holdings, campus health services, and any other electronic information that pertains to the college or university experience.

Institutions should also have policies in place that define the university's positions regarding the identification of individuals who have disabilities, auxiliary aids and services, and the granting of accommodations for online students. Finally, institutions need to establish and implement policies that ensure that purchased electronic and information technologies meet the institution's accessibility requirements. Examples of such services include course management systems, learning management systems, research databases, publisher-produced study software, and any commercially produced course-related software.

Universal Design

Universal design refers to the designing of products so that they can be used by the greatest number of people without the need for assistive technologies. Universal design also commonly refers to the designing of products so that they are compatible with available assistive technologies.

Generally, three elements need to be present in order to implement universal design principles in postsecondary online learning. First, designers and developers of online materials need to be aware of the accessibility requirements that may be encountered by online learners. Second, designers and developers of online learning materials must have the means to develop accessible online materials. Third, designers and developers must be willing to utilize the universal design process in order to develop online materials that can be accessed without the use of auxiliary aids or accommodations by the greatest number of individuals as is reasonably possible.

Many accessibility experts note that it is wise for postsecondary institutions to adopt an official institutionalwide accessibility standard regarding the (universal) design of online materials. Typically, it is recommended that a postsecondary institution adopt the Section 508 Standards, one of the W3C Web Accessibility Initiative Guidelines, or a proprietary set of web-accessibility standards. Postsecondary institutions are advised to adopt/create and implement a set of accessibility standards for two reasons. First, in a case of disability-related litigation the adoption and implementation of a set of web-accessibility standards may help demonstrate that the institution is proactively making a good-faith effort to ensure that the institution is attempting to provide accessible content and services to disabled students. Second, the adoption and implementation of a set of web-accessibility standards will, in fact, help make the institution's electronic and web-based materials more accessible to individuals who have disabilities.

SUMMARY

Several federal laws work together in harmony in order to establish and guarantee the rights of individuals who have disabilities to enjoy full and equal participation in and benefit from the products and services that are offered by postsecondary institutions. This legislation affect nearly every aspect of postsecondary education; both on-campus and online. Currently, there are two key pieces of U.S. legislation that shape the delivery of online postsecondary education. Each federal piece of legislation contributes to the legal environment in a unique way. First, Section 504 prohibits any federal agency or any entity that receives federal funding from discriminating in any way against any individual on account of his or her disability. Second, the ADA require colleges, universities, and other entities to provide products, services, and communications to individuals with disabilities that are equivalent to those that are provided to individuals who are nondisabled. Three other pieces of federal legislation affect distance and/or online learning in the United States. They are Section 508 of the Rehabilitation Act of 1973, the Telecommunications Communications Act of 1966, and the Assistive Technology Act of 1998.

There are at least two key actions that postsecondary educators can take in order to ensure that they are providing the delivery of accessible online education. First, each college and university needs to establish and implement official high-level policies pertaining to the accessibility of its electronic and information technologies. Second, colleges and universities should adopt and implement official universal design standards for the design and implementation of all institutionally-related electronic information.

FURTHER READING AND ADDITIONAL RESOURCES

This article has been written in order to help postsecondary educators and administrators better understand the issues and elements of federal legislation that governs the accessibility of online postsecondary learning in the United States. Admittedly, this article is far from exhaustive. Consequently, the author has provided in Appendix B a list of resources pertaining to the topic of accessible online postsecondary education. This list is also far from exhaustive; however, Appendix B along with this article's references offer the reader many excellent additional resources regarding the trends and issues relating to accessible postsecondary online learning.

REFERENCES

Access Board. (2005). *Questions and answers about section 508 of the rehabilitation act amendments of 1998.* Retrieved December 29, 2005 from http://www.access-board.gov/sec508/FAQ.htm

Allen, I. E., & Seaman, J. (2006). *Making the grade: Online education in the United States.* Needham, MA: Sloan Consortium.

Americans with Disabilities Act of 1990, 42 U.S.C. 12101 et seq. (1990).

Assistive Technology Act of 1998, 29 U.S.C. 2432 et seq. (1998).

Association of Assistive Technology Act Programs. (2006). Retrieved January 23, 2006, from http://www.ataporg.org/stateatprojects.asp

Baquis, D. (2003). *Federal standard for electronic and information technology. Information Technology and Disabilities.* Retrieved December 01, 2005, from http://www.rit.edu/~easi/itd/itdv09n2/baquis.htm

Communications Act of 1934, 47 U.S.C. 151. 255 et seq. (1996).

Crow, K. L. (2006). *Accommodating online postsecondary students who have disabilities.* ProQuest Digital Dissertations. (UMI No. 3251012)

Department of Commerce. (2002). *A nation online: How Americans are expanding their use of the Internet.* Retrieved January 28, 2006, from http://www.ntia.doc.gov/ntiahome/dn/html/anationonline2.htm

Department of Education. (1998). *Higher education's obligation under Section 504 and title ii of the ADA.* Retrieved December 30, 2005, from http://www.ed.gov/print/about/offices/list/ocr/docs/auxaids.html

Department of Justice. (2004). *A guide to disability right laws.* Retrieved December 20, 2005, from http://www.usdoj.gov/crt/ada/cguide.htm

Department of Justice. (2005). *Accessibility of state and local government Websites to people with disabilities.* Retrieved January 30, 2005, from http://www.usdoj.gov/crt/ada/Websites2.htm

Depart of Labor. (2006). *The American with Disabilities Act public law 101-336.* Retrieved January 24, 2006, from http://www.dol.gov/odep/pubs/fact/ada92fs.htm

Edmonds, C. D. (2004). Providing access to students with disabilities in online distance education: Legal and technical concerns for higher education. *American Journal of Distance Education, 18*(1), 51-62.

Johnson, K. L., Brown, S. E., Amtmann, D., & Thompson, T. (2003). Web accessibility in post-secondary education: Legal and policy considerations. *Information Technology and Disabilities.* Retrieved December 1, 2005, from http://www.rit.edu/~easi/itd/itdv09n2/johnson.htm

Rehabilitation act of 1973, 29 U.S.C. 791 st seq. (1973).

Scott, R. E. (1999). *California State University, docket number 09-99-2041.* Retrieved January 02, 2006, from http://www.rit.edu/~easi/law/lbeach.htm

Section 508 Standards, 29 U.S.C. 1194.1 et seq. (1998). [Aka: Rehabilitation Act of 1973, Section 508 Standards, 29 U.S.C. 1194 et seq. 508 (1998)].

Waddell, C. D. (1998). *Applying the ADA to the Internet: A web accessibility standard.* Retrieved November 26, 2005, from http://www.icdri.org//CynthiaW/applying_the_ada_to_the_internet.htm

Waits, T., & Lewis, L. (2003). *Distance education at degree-granting post secondary institutions: 2000-2001.* Washington: U.S. Department of Education, National Center for Education Statistics.

Workforce Investment Act of 1998, PL 105-220, 1998 HR 1385 PL 105-220, enacted on August 7, 1998, 112 Stat 936 codified as: Section 504 of the Rehabilitation Act, 29 U.S.C. § 794d

APPENDIX A

Section 508 Standards: 16 Accessibility Rules For Web-Based, Intranet, And Internet Information And Applications

§ 1194.22 Web-based intranet and Internet information and applications.

(a) A text equivalent for every nontext element shall be provided (e.g., via "alt", "longdesc", or in element content).

(b) Equivalent alternatives for any multimedia presentation shall be synchronized with the presentation.

(c) Web pages shall be designed so that all information conveyed with color is also available without color, for example from context or markup.

(d) Documents shall be organized so they are readable without requiring an associated style sheet.

(e) Redundant text links shall be provided for each active region of a server-side image map.

(f) Client-side image maps shall be provided instead of server-side image maps except where the regions cannot be defined with an available geometric shape.

(g) Row and column headers shall be identified for data tables.

(h) Markup shall be used to associate data cells and header cells for data tables that have two or more logical levels of row or column headers.

(i) Frames shall be titled with text that facilitates frame identification and navigation.

(j) Pages shall be designed to avoid causing the screen to flicker with a frequency greater than 2 Hz and lower than 55 Hz.

(k) A text-only page, with equivalent information or functionality, shall be provided to make a web site comply with the provisions of this part, when compliance cannot be accomplished in any other way. The content of the text-only page shall be updated whenever the primary page changes.

(l) When pages utilize scripting languages to display content, or to create interface elements, the information provided by the script shall be identified with functional text that can be read by assistive technology.

(m) When a web page requires that an applet, plug-in or other application be present on the client system to interpret page content, the page must provide a link to a plug-in or applet that complies with §1194.21(a) through (l).

(n) When electronic forms are designed to be completed on-line, the form shall allow people using assistive technology to access the information, field elements, and functionality required for completion and submission of the form, including all directions and cues.

(o) A method shall be provided that permits users to skip repetitive navigation links.

(p) When a timed response is required, the user shall be alerted and given sufficient time to indicate more time is required.

http://www.section508.gov/index
.cfm?FuseAction=Content&ID=12#Web

APPENDIX B: ADDITIONAL RESOURCES

Introduction to Web Accessibility:

DO-IT: University of Washington: Disabilities, Opportunities, Internet-working, and Technology, http://www.washington.edu/doit/

EASI: Equal Access to Software and Information, http://www.rit.edu/~easi/

National Center on Disability and Access to Education, http://www.ncdae.org/

The University of Wisconsin Trace Center, http://trace.wisc.edu/

Webaim.org, http://www.webaim.org/intro/

World-Wide Web Consortium (W3C), http://www.w3.org/WAI/intro/accessibility.php

Disabilities Law:

Section 508 Government Web site, http://www.section508.gov/

Section 508 Standards - Section 508,
http://www.section508.gov/index.cfm?FuseAction=Content&ID=12#Web

Section 504 (US Department of Education), http://www.ed.gov/about/offices/list/ocr/504faq.html

The Americans With Disabilities Act (ADA Home Page), http://www.usdoj.gov/crt/ada/

A Guide to Disabilities Rights Law (US Department of Justice), http://www.usdoj.gov/crt/ada/cguide.htm

Cynthia Waddell JD., http://www.icdri.org/CynthiaW/cynthia_waddell.htm.
   Ms. Waddel is an attorney and a leading expert in the area of disability legislation; especially as it pertains to online learning.

Universal Design:

Accessify.com, http://www.accessify.com/default.php

Building Accessible Websites, http://joeclark.org/book/sashay/serialization/
   An excerpt of a book by *Joe Clark*
Center for Applied Special Technology (CAST), http://www.cast.org/

The *HTML Writers Guild* (HWG.org),
http://www.hwg.org/resources/accessibility/sixprinciples.html
    Six Principles of Accessible Web Design

The *CPB/WGBH National Center for Accessible Media* (NCAM), http://
ncam.wgbh.org/
    Software and Web Accessibility Guidelines, http://ncam.wgbh.org/
    cdrom/guideline/

W3C's Web Content Accessibility Guidelines (WCAG), http://www.w3.org/
WAI/intro/wcag.php

ABOUT THE EDITORS

Anthony A. Piña is associate provost for online learning at Sullivan University. Tony is coeditor of the book *Real Life Distance Education: Case Studies in Practice* (Information Age Publishing) and author of the book *Distance Learning and the Institution: Foundations, Importance and Implementation*. He is president of the Division of Distance Learning of the Association for Educational Communications & Technology.

Jason B. Huett is associate dean of online development and USG Core at the University of West Georgia. Jason is coeditor of the books *The Next Generation of Distance Education: Unconstrained Learning* and *Learning and Instructional Technologies for the 21 Century: Visions of the Future*. He is past-president of the Division of Distance Learning of the Association for Educational Communications & Technology.

ORIGINAL PUBLICATIONS

The original publication of each chapter is noted below:

PART I: LEADING INNOVATION AND CHANGE

1. Piña, A. A. (2008). Factors influencing the institutionalization of distance learning in higher education. *Quarterly Review of Distance Education, 9*(4).

2. Neben, J. (2014). Attributes and barriers impacting diffusion of online education at the institutional level: Considering faculty perceptions. *Distance Learning, 11*(1).

3. Chen, B. (2009). Barriers to adoption of technology-mediated distance education in higher-education institutions. *Quarterly Review of Distance Education, 10*(4).

4. Gutman, D. (2012). Six barriers causing educators to resist teaching online, and how institutions can break them. *Distance Learning, 9*(3).

5. Wickersham, L. E., & McElhany, J. A. (2010). Bridging the divide: Reconciling administrator and faculty concerns regarding online learning. *Quarterly Review of Distance Education, 11*(1).

PART II: LEADING COURSE AND PROGRAM DESIGN

6. Ashbaugh, M. (2013). Expert instructional designer voices: Leadership competencies critical to global practice and quality online learning designs. *Quarterly Review of Distance Education, 14*(2).

7. Hirumi, A. (2013). Three levels of planned e-learning interactions: A framework for grounding research and the design of e-learning programs. *Quarterly Review of Distance Education, 14*(1).

8. Paul, J. A., & Cochran, J. D. (2013). Key interactions for online programs between faculty, students, technologies, and universities: A holistic framework. *Quarterly Review of Distance Education, 14*(1).

9. Borgemenke, A. J., Holt, W. C., & Fish, W. W. (2013). Universal course shell template design and implementation to enhance student outcomes in online coursework. *Quarterly Review of Distance Education, 14*(1).

10. Engstrom, M. E., Santo, S. A., & Yost, R. M. (2008). Knowledge building in an online cohort. *Quarterly Review of Distance Education, 9*(2).

11. Tau, O. S. (2008). Converting a conventional university to a dual mode institution: The case of the University of Botswana. *Quarterly Review of Distance Education, 9*(2).

PART III: LEADING THE DEVELOPMENT AND SUPPORT OF ONLINE STUDENTS

12. Huett, J., Moller, L., Young, J., Bray, M., & Huett, K. (2008). Supporting the distant student: The effect of ARCS-based strategies on confidence and performance. *Quarterly Review of Distance Education, 9*(2).

13. Walker C. E., & Kelly, E. (2007). Online instruction: Student satisfaction, kudos, and pet peeves. *Quarterly Review of Distance Education, 8*(4).

14. Cobb, A. (2011). Assistive technology: Enhancing the life skills of students with learning disabilities. *Distance Learning, 8*(4).

15. Dotson, K. & Bian, H. (2013). Supervision on site: A critical factor in the online facilitated internship. *Quarterly Review of Distance Education, 14*(2).

PART IV: LEADING THE DEVELOPMENT AND SUPPORT OF ONLINE FACULTY AND STAFF

16. Khan, S. B., & Chishti, S. (2012). Effects of staff training and development on teachers in a distance learning program. *Quarterly Review of Distance Education, 13*(2).

17. Waweru, J. (2013). Maximizing HR professionals' leadership role in e-learning for organizational effectiveness. *Distance Learning, 10*(4).

18. Stewart, B. L., Goodson, C., & Miertschin, S. L. (2010). Off-site faculty: Perspectives on online experiences. *Quarterly Review of Distance Education, 11*(3).

19. Chiesl, N. (2007). Pragmatic methods to reduce dishonesty in web-based courses. *Quarterly Review of Distance Education, 8*(3).

20. Piña, A. A., & Bohn, L. (2014). Assessing online faculty: More than student surveys and design rubrics. *Quarterly Review of Distance Education, 15*(3).

21. Schmidt, S., Hodge, E., & Tschida, C. (2013). How university faculty members develop their online teaching skills. *Quarterly Review of Distance Education, 14*(3).

PART V: LEGAL AND ACCREDITATION ISSUES

22. Seok, S. (2007). Standards, accreditation, benchmarks, and guidelines in distance education. *Quarterly Review of Distance Education, 8*(4).

23. Kranch, D. A. (2008). Who owns online course intellectual property? *Quarterly Review of Distance Education, 9*(4).

24. Loggie, K., Barron, A., Gulitz, E., Hohlfeld, T., Kromrey, J., Venable, M., & Sweeney, P. (2007). Intellectual property and online courses: Policies at major research universities. *Quarterly Review of Distance Education 8*(2).

25. Crow, K. L. (2008). The legal environment of accessible postsecondary online learning. *Quarterly Review of Distance Education 9*(2).

CPSIA information can be obtained
at www.ICGtesting.com
Printed in the USA
BVOW08s0156140717
489296BV00013B/140/P